REVISITING MODERN INDIAN THOUGHT

This book presents a comprehensive account of the socio-political thought of prominent modern Indian thinkers. It offers a clear understanding of the basic concepts and their contributions on contemporary issues.

Key features:

- Explores the nature, scope, relevance, context, and theoretical approaches of modern Indian thought and overviews its development through an in-depth study of the lives and ideas of major thinkers.
- Examines critical themes such as nationalism, swaraj, democracy and state, liberalism, revolution, socialism, constitutionalism, secularism, satyāgraha, swadeshi, nation-building, humanism, ethics in politics, democratic decentralisation, religion and politics, social transformation and emancipation, and social and gender justice under sections on liberal-reformist, moderate-Gandhian, and leftist-socialist thought.
- Brings together insightful essays on Raja Ram Mohan Roy, Ishwar Chandra Vidyasagar, Dayānanda Saraswati, Ramakrishna Paramhansa, Pandita Ramabai, Periyar E. V. Ramasamy, Jyotirao Govindrao Phule, Babasaheb Ambedkar, Dadabhai Naoroji, Gopal Krishna Gokhale, Mahatma Gandhi, Jawaharlal Nehru, Subhas Chandra Bose, Ram Manohar Lohia, Babu Jagjivan Ram, Vinoba Bhave, Acharya Narendra Deva, Manabendra Nath Roy, and Jayaprakash Narayan.
- Traces different perspectives on the way India's composite cultures, traditions, and conditions influenced the evolution of their thought and legacy.

With its accessible style, this book will be useful to teachers, students, and scholars of political science, modern Indian political thought, modern Indian history, and political philosophy. It will also interest those associated with exclusion studies, political sociology, sociology, and South Asian studies.

Suratha Kumar Malik is Assistant Professor in the Department of Political Science, Vidyasagar University, West Bengal, India.

Ankit Tomar is Assistant Professor in the Department of Political Science, Lakshmibai College, University of Delhi, India.

"A well organised textbook on Indian Political Thought, written by reputed writers. It would be of immense help for students and civil services aspirants".

Prakash Chandra Sarangi, *Former Vice-Chancellor, Ravenshaw University & Former Professor of Political Science, University of Hyderabad, India*

"A long-awaited, timely and useful contribution for a very wide variety of audience".

Upendra Choudhury, *Professor, Department of Political Science, Aligarh Muslim University, Aligarh & Former Member Secretary and Director, Indian Council of Social Science Research, New Delhi, India*

"Revisiting Modern Indian Thought is an important contribution to the field of Indian Political Thought. It attempts to cover major thinkers of modern India. The work of Suratha Kumar Malik and Ankit Tomar will be immensely helpful to students, researchers and teachers as it has widely covered the revised curricula (syllabi) of different Indian universities".

Shri Prakash Singh, *Professor, Department of Political Science, University of Delhi, New Delhi, India*

"Malik and Tomar have accomplished a truly academically rewarding endeavour by bringing together these brilliantly written essays about the political ideas of some of the greatest thinkers of modern India. A must-read for all those who may be interested in making sense of the idea of India".

Ashutosh Kumar, *Lala Lajpat Rai Chair Professor of Political Science, Panjab University, Chandigarh, India*

"This edited volume is a commendable attempt to bring out a compendium not only to providing an overview of the major political thinkers of modern India but also proclaiming to revisit the liberal-reformist, Gandhian and socialist traditions of modern Indian thought. It is undoubtedly a readable and appreciable book of its kind".

Sanjeev Kumar Sharma, *Vice-Chancellor, Mahatma Gandhi Central University, Motihari (Bihar) & General Secretary and Treasurer, Indian Political Science Association (IPSA), India*

REVISITING MODERN INDIAN THOUGHT

Themes and Perspectives

Edited by Suratha Kumar Malik and Ankit Tomar

NEW YORK AND LONDON

First published 2022
by Routledge
2 Park Square, Milton Park, Abingdon, Oxon OX14 4RN

and by Routledge
605 Third Avenue, New York, NY 10158

Routledge is an imprint of the Taylor & Francis Group, an informa business

© 2022 selection and editorial matter, Suratha Kumar Malik and Ankit Tomar; individual chapters, the contributors

The right of Suratha Kumar Malik and Ankit Tomar to be identified as the authors of the editorial material, and of the authors for their individual chapters, has been asserted in accordance with sections 77 and 78 of the Copyright, Designs and Patents Act 1988.

Disclaimer: The views and opinions expressed in this book are solely those of the authors and do not necessarily reflect those of the publisher. The analyses based on research material are intended here to serve general educational and informational purposes and not obligatory upon any party. The editors have made every effort to ensure that the information presented in the book was correct at the time of press, but the editors and the publisher do not assume and hereby disclaim any liability with respect to the accuracy, completeness, reliability, suitability, selection and inclusion of the contents of this book and any implied warranties or guarantees. The editors and publisher make no representations or warranties of any kind to any person, product or entity for any loss, including, but not limited to special, incidental or consequential damage, or disruption alleged to have been caused, directly or indirectly, by omissions or any other related cause.

All rights reserved. No part of this book may be reprinted or reproduced or utilised in any form or by any electronic, mechanical, or other means, now known or hereafter invented, including photocopying and recording, or in any information storage or retrieval system, without permission in writing from the publishers.

Trademark notice: Product or corporate names may be trademarks or registered trademarks, and are used only for identification and explanation without intent to infringe.

British Library Cataloguing-in-Publication Data
A catalogue record for this book is available from the British Library

Library of Congress Cataloging-in-Publication Data
A catalog record for this book has been requested

ISBN: 978-0-367-53654-1 (hbk)
ISBN: 978-0-367-63316-5 (pbk)
ISBN: 978-1-003-11877-0 (ebk)

Typeset in Bembo
by Apex CoVantage, LLC

This work is dedicated to our teachers

CONTENTS

List of contributors   *x*
Foreword   *xvii*
   Sudha Pai
Preface and acknowledgements   *xxii*
   Suratha Kumar Malik and Ankit Tomar

Introduction   1
Sanjukta Banerji Bhattacharya

PART I
Liberal-reformist thought   21

1. Ram Mohan Roy   23
   Anuranjita Wadhwa

2. Ishwar Chandra Vidyasagar   36
   Sibaji Pratim Basu

3. Dayānanda Saraswati   47
   Ankit Tomar

4. Jyotirao Govindrao Phule   57
   Basanta Kumar Mallik

5. Ramakrishna Paramhansa   73
   Praveen Kumar

6 Pandita Ramabai 81
   Avneet Kaur

7 Periyar E. V. Ramasamy 96
   Debi Chatterjee

8 Bhimrao Ramji Ambedkar 110
   Narender Kumar

9 Jagjivan Ram 127
   Meena Charanda

PART II
Moderate-Gandhian thought **137**

10 Dadabhai Naoroji 139
   Radha Kumari

11 Gopal Krishna Gokhale 152
   Abha Chauhan Khimta

12 Mohandas Karamchand Gandhi 161
   Ambarish Mukhopadhyay

13 Vinoba Bhave 182
   Suratha Kumar Malik

PART III
Leftist-socialist thought **201**

14 Manabendra Nath Roy 203
   Aritra Majumdar

15 Narendra Deva 219
   Satrajit Banerjee

16 Jawaharlal Nehru 234
   Surya Narayan Misra

17 Subhas Chandra Bose 249
   Sumit Mukerji

18 Jayaprakash Narayan *Anand Kumar and Sipra Sagarika*	266
19 Ram Manohar Lohia *Dev Nath Pathak and Divyendu Jha*	279
Index	*298*

CONTRIBUTORS

Satrajit Banerjee is Assistant Professor in the Department of Political Science, Bankura University, West Bengal, India. He has contributed articles in journals such as *Socialist Perspective* and others. He has also contributed chapters in edited books. He has organised an International Seminar on 'Rethinking Democracy: Indian Context' and has presented papers in seminars and conferences.

Sibaji Pratim Basu is Professor and former Head in the Department of Political Science, Vidyasagar University, Midnapore, West Bengal, India. He is the Dean, Faculty of Arts and Commerce of the same university. He has authored many books and contributed articles and chapters in journals and edited volumes. Among his writings, most notables are *Forced Migration and Media Mirrors*, 2014, (Editor); *Politics in Hunger-Regime: Essays on the Right to Food in West Bengal*, 2011, (Co-Editor); *The Poet and the Mahatma: Engagement with Nationalism and Internationalism*, 2009, (Author); *The Fleeing People of South Asia: Selections from Refugee Watch*, 2009, (Editor); 'The Chronicle of a Forgotten Movement: West Bengal – 1959 Revisited' in Samir Kumar Das (ed.), 2015, *Understanding Democracy and Violence in India*; 'Globalisation and Right to Information', in Sabyasachi Basu Ray Chaudhury and Ishita Dey (ed.), 2011, *Sustainability of Rights after Globalisation*; and 'State: In Europe and in the Third World' in Satyabrata Chakraborty (ed.), 2005, *Political Sociology*. He is a regular contributor to the Bangla newspaper *Anandabazar Patrika* and to the TV news channel *Chabis Ghonta* (24 Hours). His areas of interest include Indian thought, political theory, Western thought, and cultural politics.

Sanjukta Banerji Bhattacharya is former Professor of International Relations, Jadavpur University, Kolkata, India. She has had a long academic career of over 35 years spanning Jadavpur University, Delhi University, Gargi College, and an entry-level position at Jawaharlal Nehru University. She received the prestigious Fulbright Award twice and did post-doctoral work in the United States. She has published four books and over 50 articles/chapters in journals and edited volumes. Her academic interests include U.S. politics, Third World studies, India's history and foreign policy, West Asia, Africa, terrorism, refugee and migration studies, and religion and politics. She currently serves in various boards of studies, doctoral committees, and academic councils of prestigious universities in and around Kolkata, West Bengal.

Meena Charanda is Assistant Professor in the Department of Political Science at Kalindi College, University of Delhi, India. She holds a Ph.D. in Political Science from the University of Delhi. She has published three books and many articles in reputed journals. She is also associated with the quarterly journal *Apeksha*.

Debi Chatterjee is former Professor of International Relations at Jadavpur University, Kolkata, India. She was also a coordinator of PG Diploma Course in Human Rights and Duties Education, Department of International Relations, Jadavpur University. She was invited as a visiting professor in the Department of Political Science and Department of Human Rights and Human Developments at Rabindra Bharti University. She is also a founding editor of the bi-annual journal *Contemporary Voice of Dalit*. She has published six books and various articles in journals. Her areas of interest include *Dalit* studies, Indian society and social problems, human rights, gender issues, and public administration.

Divyendu Jha is a Ph.D. Scholar in the Department of Political Science, University of Delhi, India. He is also an Assistant Professor (Guest) and teaches Political Science at Kirori Mal College, University of Delhi. His research interests are in the areas of political theory, political thought and philosophy, and he has contributed chapters in edited volumes and articles in journals.

Avneet Kaur is Assistant Professor in Amity Institute of Public Policy, Amity University, Noida, India. She wrote a book on *Empowering Women through Electronic Governance* (2016) and conference proceedings on *Gender Perspective in Electronic Initiative in India: Use of ICT for Women Empowerment* in 2016. She has also qualified for UGC-NET and the Junior Research Fellowship in Political Science. Her areas of interest are public administration, political theory, and Indian political thought.

Abha Chauhan Khimta is Associate Professor of Political Science at Himachal Pradesh University, India. She is a gold medalist in M.Phil. and was awarded a Ph.D. from Himachal Pradesh University. She has participated in conferences, and her research articles are published in various journals. She has a keen interest in political thought and international relations.

Anand Kumar is former Professor of Sociology, Jawaharlal Nehru University, India. He received his M.A. in Sociology from Banaras Hindu University (BHU), Varanasi; an M.Phil. in Sociology from Jawaharlal Nehru University,

New Delhi; and a Ph.D. in Sociology from the University of Chicago in 1986. He was a lecturer in Sociology at BHU, an Associate Professor of Sociology at JNU, and Professor of Sociology at JNU. He also taught as India Chair professor in Germany (Albert Ludwig University, Freiburg), GSP Scholar at Humboldt University (Berlin, Germany) and was a Fulbright Visiting Scholar at Tufts University. He was an International Faculty at Innsbruck University (Austria), GSP faculty at FLACSO (Buenos Aires, Argentina), and visiting professor at NEHU (Shillong) and Kashmir University (Srinagar). He has been a fellow to the Indian Institute of Advance Studies, Shimla, and presently he is a senior fellow at Nehru Memorial Museum and Library. Prof. Kumar has been extensively writing for the cause of student politics, globalisation, chronic poverty, global studies, and the India–Tibet relationship at several national and international forums. He was an active member of the Jayaprakash Narayan Movement and has been working for the cause of Gandhian philosophy as well. He has several publications in journals and many books. He was a student leader during his JNU days and has been President of JNUTA (Jawaharlal Nehru University Teacher's Association). He has also held the prestigious position of President of the Indian Sociological Society.

Narender Kumar is Professor in the Centre for Political Studies at Jawaharlal Nehru University, New Delhi, India. He has 18 years of experience in teaching and researching in various central universities, including University of Delhi, Jamia Millia Islamia, and Babasaheb Bhimrao Ambedkar University (Lucknow). He has six books to his credit, which include: Jaffrelot, Christophe and Narender Kumar (eds.), *Dr. Ambedkar and Democracy* (2018); Thorat, Sukhadeo and Narender Kumar (eds.), *B. R. Ambedkar: Perspective on Social Exclusion and Inclusive Policies* (2009); Thorat, Sukhadeo and Narender Kumar (eds.), *In Search of Inclusive Policy: Addressing Graded Inequality* (2008); Kumar, Narender and Manor Rai, *Dalit Leadership in Panchayats: A Comparative Study of Four States* (2006); Kumar, Narender, *Dalit Policies, Politics and Parliament* (2004); and Kumar, Narender, *Scheduled Castes and Panchayat Elections in Haryana* (2001). He has also been working on family/dynasty politics in Haryana under a collaborative international project, where academic institutions like King's College London; London School of Economics from Britain; and CERI-Sciences Po, Paris from France were partners. He was awarded the Indo-French Social Scientist Fellowship in 2011 and studied the problems of Roma, a minority and Gypsy community in France. He has also completed two major research projects awarded by the University Grants Commission and the Indian Council for Social Science Research. His areas of interest include political institutions, political process, and public policy, with special reference to marginalised groups.

Praveen Kumar is Associate Professor at the Centre for Political Studies, School of Social Sciences and Policy, Central University of South Bihar, Gaya, India. Formerly, he was Associate Professor at the Department of Geopolitics and

International Relations, Manipal University, Manipal, Karnataka. He has professional experience in teaching, data-driven inter-disciplinary research and analysis, project management, institution-building, and administrative responsibilities of over 14 years with institutions of repute. He completed his higher studies, including a Ph.D. from Jawaharlal Nehru University. His publications include an authored book, book chapters, and research papers/articles in journals such as *Economic and Political Weekly*, *Faultline*, *Strategic Analysis*, *Asian Affairs*, *World Focus*, *Indian Journal of Society and Politics*, and research portals. He has participated and organised seminars, conferences, round tables, and workshops. He has also been invited as a resource person to deliver lectures in institutions of repute.

Radha Kumari is Assistant Professor in the Department of Political Science, Mata Sundri College, University of Delhi, India. She has also served as an Assistant Professor in the Department of Political Science & Non-Violence and Peace, Jain Vishva Bharti University, Ladnun. She completed her Ph.D. on Gandhian peace movements.

Aritra Majumdar is Assistant Professor in the Department of History at Sivanath Sastri College, West Bengal, India. Previously, he served in a similar position in the Government General Degree College in Tehatta in the Nadia district of West Bengal. He undertook his Bachelor of Arts in History from Presidency College, Kolkata (then under University of Calcutta) before completing his Master of Arts in History from the University of Calcutta. Thereafter, he completed his Master of Philosophy on the topic 'Intellectual Foundations of Economic Planning in Modern India'. He is currently pursuing his Ph.D. from Presidency University in Kolkata. His publications include 'Planning, Economic Development and the Constituent Assembly of India' in *Akademos*, a journal published by Kamala Nehru College, University of Delhi, New Delhi.

Suratha Kumar Malik teaches at the Department of Political Science, Vidyasagar University, West Bengal, India and also the Teacher in Charge of the said department. He holds an M.A. and M.Phil. in Political Science from the Centre for Political Studies, Jawaharlal Nehru University, New Delhi. He obtained his Ph.D. from Vidyasagar University. He has published 3 books (authored and co-edited) from renowned global publishers and 20 research articles and chapters in books and journals. He has been invited as resource person, guest of honour, and chief guest to colleges and universities and has also presented papers in more than 35 conferences/seminars, including Imperial College London, UK; Linton University, Kuala Lumpur, Malaysia; and Dubai. He has organised five seminar/conferences in the capacity of convener, organising secretary, sponsored by UGC, New Delhi and NHRC, New Delhi. His areas of interest include Indian political thought and philosophy, political theory, tribal politics and issues, *Dalit* identity, politics and issues. Under his supervision 13 M.Phil. scholars have been awarded their degrees. He has completed UGC Major Research projects on *Land*

Alienation and Politics of Tribal Exploitation: A Study of Koraput District of Odisha and has been awarded the Nirman Foundation Fellowship (Lord Bhikhu Parekh endowment) during his M.A., the UGC Junior Research Fellowship during his M.Phil., and the 'Vivekananda Excellence Award' (presented by Seva Youth Guild, Kolkata affiliate to NYKS, Ministry of Sports and Youth Affairs Department, Government of India) in 2019. In the last three years, Dr Malik has been associated with the National Service Scheme as the Programme Officer of Unit VII, Vidyasagar University and was conferred the 'Best NSS Programme Officer Award'.

Basanta Kumar Mallik is Professor and Head at the P.G. Department of History, Utkal University, Bhubaneswar, Odisha, India. He completed his M.A., M.Phil., and Ph.D. at the Centre for Historical Studies, Jawaharlal Nehru University, New Delhi. He is the Editor of *Utkal Historical Research Journal*, the Chairman of Subject Research Committee in History, and Director and Member (UGC Nominee) of the Centre for Ambedkar Studies, Utkal University. He is the director of the Centre for Study of Social Exclusion and Inclusive Policy, Utkal University. His specialisation and research interests include social movements in Indian history, the *Dalit* movement in colonial and post-colonial India, Ambedkar studies, and human rights issues. He has published the books *Medieval Orissa: Literature, Society, Economy*, 1996; *Paradigms of Dissent and Protest: Social Movements in Eastern India (circa 1400–1700 AD)*, 2004; (ed.) *Eastern India: Essays in History, Society and Culture*, 2004. (ed.) *Dominance and Resistance in Indian History*, 2007. He has also published more than 40 research articles in scholarly journals and conference proceedings. He has attended and organised seminars and conferences and has presented papers. He visited Kiel University, Heidelberg University, and Free University of Berlin, Germany, in 2002 on academic assignment. He presented a paper titled 'Construction of Oriya Identity: Saral Mahabharata as a Marker in Time', in an International Seminar on 'Identities in Time' in 2002 at Salzau, Germany. He also delivered a lecture titled 'Dalit Movement in India: A Historical Analysis' in the Department of Ethnology, Free University of Berlin on May 30, 2002.

Surya Narayan Misra is former Professor, Department of Political Science, Utkal University, Odisha, India. He has a long teaching experience spanning more than four decades. He was a fellow of Charles Wallace (UK), CIDA (Canada), Travel fellowship. He was visiting professor at Rajiv Gandhi University, Arunachal Pradesh and PDPU (Gandhinagar). He has written and edited many books, notable among which are *Party Politics and Electoral Choices in an Indian State* (1990); *India: The Cold War Years* (1994); and *Constitution and Constitutionalism in India* (2000). He has written 4 monographs and published more than 100 papers in journals. He was the former Head of the Department of Political Science, Utkal University, former deputy Registrar, and former Dean of Students' Welfare, Utkal University, Odisha. He was also the coordinator of CDI (Ford Project).

Sumit Mukerji is Professor in the Department of Political Science, University of Kalyani, West Bengal, India. He is also the director of the Centre for Studies on Bengali Diaspora in the same university. He was the former Dean, Faculty of Arts and Commerce, University of Kalyani. Prof. Mukerji was also a recipient of the Fulbright Nehru Award. He has more than 33 years of teaching experience at the undergraduate and post-graduate level. He has published 5 books (authored and edited) and more than 50 research articles in journals. He has also participated in seminars, conferences, workshops, and training programmes. His areas of interest include Subhas Chandra Bose studies and the Indian freedom movement, conflict resolution and peace studies, diaspora studies, and political thought.

Ambarish Mukhopadhyay is Professor in the Department of Political Science, Vidyasagar University, India. He completed his M.A. and Ph.D. from the University of Calcutta. He has more than three decades of teaching experience. He was the former Head, Department of Political Science, Vidyasagar University. He was the former coordinator of the 'Certificate Course on Human Rights' and is presently the coordinator of the M.Phil. Programme, Department of Political Science, Vidyasagar University. He has published articles and papers in journals and in edited books. He has been invited to and has chaired many seminars and conferences, and he has been associated with the Gandhian Studies Centre, Vidyasagar University since its inception.

Dev Nath Pathak is Senior Assistant Professor and teaches Sociology at South Asian University, New Delhi, India. He has a doctorate in Sociology from Jawaharlal Nehru University, New Delhi. His research interests consist broadly of cultural performances, art, music, and popular cinema in the region of South Asia. He has taught at the Department of Sociology, Jamia Millia Islamia, New Delhi; Hindu College and Kamala Nehru College of University of Delhi; and at the Centre for Culture, Media and Governance. He has contributed articles to journals and chapters in edited books. Some of his recent publications include *Culture and Politics in South Asia: Performative Communication* (2017); *Another South Asia!* (2017); and *Intersections of Art, Sociology and Art History* (2016). He is also a review editor with the journal *Society and Culture in South Asia*. The thematic range of his writings include sociology in South Asia, youth subjectivities, anomalies of education, politics of cinema, performance, and visual arts. He was a Charles Fellow at Queen's University, Belfast, United Kingdom, in 2015.

Sipra Sagarika is Assistant Professor in the Department of Sociology at Fakir Mohan University, Balasore, Odisha, India. She completed her M.A., M.Phil., and Ph.D. from the Centre for Study of Social Systems, Jawaharlal Nehru University, New Delhi. She was the former faculty in the Department of Sociology, Panjab University, Chandigarh. She was a Gold medalist of Sociology at Ravenshaw University. Presently, she is a visiting faculty to the Indian Institute of

Management, Indore. She has visited University of Ottawa, Canada (2017); University of Guelph Humberg, Toronto, Canada (2018); and University of Adam Miziwick, Poland (2019) in different capacities to represent the voices of indigenous communities at international forums. She works in political sociology, social anthropology, sociology of minority rights, sociology of mental health and wellness, sociology of leisure, sociology of culture, and media and disability studies. She has contributed more than 30 chapters in edited books and has more than 10 research articles published in journals. She has presented papers across varied areas in more than 50 seminars. She has been working for the cause of indigenous communities; women rights; poverty and unemployment; trafficking of women; and the promotion of Indian classical dance forms, such as Odissi, and folk culture.

Ankit Tomar teaches Political Science at Lakshmibai College, University of Delhi, India. He holds an M.A. in Political Science from University of Delhi and an M.Phil. in International Politics from School of International Studies, Jawaharlal Nehru University, New Delhi. He is on the verge of submitting his Ph.D. to the Centre for International Politics, Organization and Disarmament, Jawaharlal Nehru University. He has contributed chapters and articles to several institutions, including the Institute of Lifelong Learning, University of Delhi. He has also participated in seminars, conferences, workshops, and training programmes. His areas of interest include Indian and Western political philosophy, theories of international relations, and global political economy.

Anuranjita Wadhwa is Assistant Professor in the Department of Political Science, Bharati College, University of Delhi, India. Having graduated from Jesus and Mary College, Delhi University, she went on to complete her post-graduation in the same subject from Hindu College, University of Delhi. She completed her M.Phil. from the same university. She was awarded her Ph.D. degree in 'Political Participation of Migrants in Delhi: A Case Study', from the Department of Political Science, University of Delhi. Her research area is political demography. Her other research interests are Indian political thought, Western political thought, and Indian politics.

FOREWORD

Modern Indian thought and its impact on ideas and thinking in post-independence India has attracted the attention of social scientists in recent years. Traditionally, in most universities, Western political thought beginning from the Greeks to present-day thinkers was a part of the syllabus of political science. It shaped the ideas and political thinking of earlier generations of political scientists and was reflected in their research on Indian politics. While Western political thought remains important in a globalising world, today questions are being raised about its adequacy and usefulness for understanding and interpreting political developments and the functioning of political processes and institutions in post-independent India. Much has changed, and India has moved away from Western models in many ways, particularly the Westminster form, leading to a demand for more indigenous theorising based on the study of India's past and empirical study of the functioning of present-day Indian society, economy, and its democratic polity. Equally important, the recent rise of right-wing forces in India, and their feeling that Hindu culture and tradition and social and political ideas based on it were ignored in the first few decades of independence, requires attention. Hence, a renewed analysis of the process of modernisation and nation-building is needed. As Milton Singer argued in his well-known treatise *When a Great Tradition Modernizes*, there is a need to re-examine our past and its continuing relevance to the present (Singer 1972).

In this context, the volume edited by Suratha Kumar Malik and Ankit Tomar, a comprehensive study of political thought as it evolved during the National Movement, is both timely and needed. It is refreshing that attention is now being paid to political ideas, values, and norms during the Indian National Movement, which has played a seminal role in determining the new nation-State formed in post-colonial India. Here, it is noteworthy that the struggle against imperialism is not limited to the South Asian continent; large parts of Africa also underwent strong anti-colonial movements. However, there are major differences with consequences for the present. In most African countries, national movements arose much later than in India. They were short, and before they could spread and impact the masses, after the Second World War, most colonial powers withdrew rather suddenly, leaving African countries unprepared for self-governance. In contrast, as the essays in this volume illustrate, in India, the National Movement was paralleled by social and identity-based movements that debated the ideas of equality, caste, social justice, representation, federalism and governance, upon which the type of government that should be formed in post-colonial India was based. This enabled the new independent nation which emerged from colonialism, despite partition, to deal with political and social problems much more effectively. The political leadership, having participated in the National Movement and having shaped its underlying ideas, was able to govern a large and diverse nation.

This volume has an introductory essay on ancient and medieval sources of political thought, which provides an excellent backdrop to the study of modern political thought. Pointing to the distinction between political theory and thought, it argues that the roots of political thinking in India are scattered, diverse and often conflicting in their claims regarding the values and norms on which our tradition is based. In fact, political thought and ideas and institutions of governance in the ancient period have not been fully explored, and many scholars argue that it can provide a source for understanding present-day political processes. Historian Ainslie T. Embree, in a significant treatise on political development of the Indian sub-continent, has pointed to three major sources that underlie the post-independence State we are attempting to create, which is different from the notion of the State in Greco-Roman thinking: *Brāhminical*, Islamic, and Western (mainly British). Hence, a contextualisation is needed without which it is not possible to understand modern Indian political thought (Embree 1985).

The medieval period brought Islamic influence, which led to new ideas mingling with the old and brought in different ideas regarding the State, kingship, economy, and relationship to religion in daily life, inclusiveness, and governance, creating a more composite political and social culture. The Mughal period has several valuable written sources from which the ideas of the period and their impact can be understood. These brought change to the way the relationship between the ruler and the governed was viewed. British colonialism introduced Western notions of utilitarianism, modern education, equality, and federalism but also maintained many aspects of Indian tradition, which enabled them to consolidate their hold over the empire. The clash between the old and the new in both periods provided fertile ground for the emergence of ideas and movements during the National Movement.

It is against this backdrop that the contributors to the volume have written on 19 political thinkers who have been brought together under diverse aspects of political thinking during the National Movement. The impact of Western thinking led to an early period of social reformist thinking and action and to the later emergence of many rich and diverse strands of thought and movements, such as moderate-Gandhian, liberal-reformist and leftist-socialist thinking, which have shaped the new nation in the making. Both the ideas of secularism and socialism integral to political thought and action in post-independence India also arose during this period, as did many movements, such as the language movement and the non-*Brāhmin* and depressed classes' movement against the caste hierarchy.

What is significant about this period is the clash between the old and the new leading to a renaissance in terms of thinking, ensuing in social reform and anti-colonial action. The leaders of the anti-colonial movement fulfilled a dual task: on the one hand, they fought against colonialism, and on the other, they were able to form a bridge between modernity and tradition, interpreting older ideas in newer conditions. As Rudolph and Rudolph have argued, India experienced the *Modernity of Tradition* visible in many areas of social and political life (Rudolph and Rudolph 1967). The essays in this volume cover a wide spectrum of thinking in each category; many leaders who contributed to both thought and action have been covered. These ideas and movements arose during the National Movement but are still relevant in post-independence India; this being particularly true of movements against gender inequality and caste-based oppression and untouchability. There has been the re-discovery of important leaders, such as Dr Bhim Rao Ambedkar, Periyar, and Pandita Ramabai, among others whose ideas and thoughts are widely read. In the economic field, the ideologies of socialism and leftist groups are still debated and discussed. The existence of centuries of knowledge and tradition and the impact of Western ideas helped the leaders of the National Movement to fight both an anti-colonial battle and simultaneously establish a secure base to the new nation they were building, a central concept being that of *swaraj*, which attempted to define our nationhood. Thus, a rich tapestry of ideas and values arose during the National Movement which still forms the core of our political discussion and debate today.

The legacy of modern Indian thought has been manifold, but certain concepts have been key to the processes of nation-building: nation, nationalism, and national identity. All three concepts are problematic, as many different versions of the nation in the making arose. Here, the concepts of region, regional identity, and regionalism are useful in understanding the trajectory of nation-building. As Anil Seal has argued in his seminal *Study of Nationalism*, it was not an idea that arose at any one time, nor was it disseminated from a single centre to the various regions. Rather, the feeling of nationalism arose in different regions at different points in time, and its meaning for each region was different. The process was faster in some regions and slower in others, such as Assam and Northeast India. The regions lying in the Hindi heartland standing in the open Gangetic plains did not develop regional identities, but language and culture were unifiers (Seal 1971).

As a result, unlike in Europe, the Indian sub-continent throughout history has developed a civilisational State in which regional and national cultures existing side by side provide the two realities of Indian civilisation (Embree 1985: 19). Pan-Indian and regional forces have existed historically, and the clashes between them have created historical, linguistic, cultural, and structural regions. At the same time, the larger cultural regions, such as Punjab, Andhra, Bengal, or Tamil, had a continuous existence through history and came to have a strong sense of identity during the colonial period due to revival of languages, identities, and movements around them. In post-independence India, many of these have developed sub-regions that are demanding separate political existence within the federation. Consequently, a construction of regional identities and a constant re-definition of their relationship with an emerging national identity is a process that began in the colonial period and is still shaping the modern-day State and democratic politics. The European experience by contrast has been one of "stateness", the result of a narrowing of sovereignty into ethnically defined areas that form the present-day modern States (Rudolph and Rudolph 1985: 40–60). These historical processes shaped the manner in which the Indian National Congress arose and developed, first on regional platforms and regional idioms, which later became part of a larger national organisation (Johnson 1975). These factors underlay the demand for division of States along linguistic lines at independence, which provided every region political and cultural recognition and a place within the federal structure.

Hence, the period of the nationalist movement out of which modern Indian thought has emerged can be understood as having provided fertile ground for many ideas; in fact many visions of the new nation-State emerged, some of which contradicted each other and led to strong differences of opinion and conflicts in the post-independence period. The peripheral areas of India which often felt left out from mainstream thinking and which threw up their own ideas, such as the Deep South and particularly the Northeast, have thrown up ideas of separatism and secessionism. However, despite these differences, the idea of India has survived, and the country has not faced balkanisation at independence, as predicted by Selig Harrison (Harrison 1960).

The volume shows that the formation of modern Indian thought was a long-drawn process and unique in the history of ideas. Post-independence India has been able to draw on this rich source of an amalgam of ideas based both on Western and indigenous traditions. Modern India has been able to create a composite culture which has been able to bring together different conceptions of the new nation, which remains a task in the making. The volume will be of great use to students and researchers and will provide a platform for further research into the process of nation-building in our country.

Sudha Pai
Former Professor and Rector,
Jawaharlal Nehru University, New Delhi, India

References

Embree, Ainslie T. (1985). "Indian Civilization and Regional Cultures: The Two Realities", in Paul Wallace (Ed.) *Region and Nation in India*. New Delhi: Oxford and IBH.

Johnson, Gordon (1975). *Provincial Politics and Indian Nationalism: Bombay and the Indian National Congress, 1880–1915*. Cambridge: Cambridge University Press.

Harrison, Selig S. (1960). *India: The Most Dangerous Decades*. Princeton: Princeton University Press.

Rudolph, I. Llyod and Rudolph, Susanne Hoeber (1967). *The Modernity of Tradition: Political Development in India*. New Delhi: Sage.

Rudolph, I. Llyod & Rudolph, Susanne Hoeber (1985). "The Sub-Continental Empire and the Regional Kingdom in India", in Paul Wallace (Ed.) *Region and Nation in India*. New Delhi: Oxford and IBH.

Seal, Anil (1971). *The Emergence of Nationalism: Competition and Collaboration in the Nineteenth Century*. London: Cambridge University Press.

Singer, Milton (1972). *When a Great Tradition Modernizes: Anthropological Approach to Indian Civilization*. New York: Praeger.

PREFACE AND ACKNOWLEDGEMENTS

To characterise modern Indian thought is a Herculean task and is not an easy exercise as there is no single body of thought that we call "Indian" nor is there a continuity of concerns across time, say, between the early nineteenth century and the late nineteenth century. Taking a synoptic view therefore necessarily reduces the complexities and does not do full justice to minority or subordinate voices, relegating them further to the margins. Modern Indian thought is necessarily an outcome of colonial encounter. It was within this universe that most of our thinkers, hailing from different communities and social groups, embarked on their intellectual-political journey. The great intellectual question most nineteenth century thinkers had before themselves was: how did a huge country like India become subjugated? If that was the question for most of the nineteenth century, the question for those writing in the late nineteenth and early twentieth century was about freedom: how can we become free of colonial rule? So, for each set of thinkers, the "we" in the previous question differed, and we could also call this a "search for the self'".

We can broadly divide modern Indian thought into two phases. The first phase was that of what has often been referred to as the phase of social reform. Thinkers of this phase were more concerned with the internal regeneration of indigenous society, and its first effervescence occurred in Bengal; this phase is better known as the 'Bengal renaissance'. Nationalist historians, of course, even started referring to it as the Indian renaissance, but this is an inaccurate description for several reasons. The second phase, more complex and textured in many ways, we can designate the nationalist phase. The concerns in this phase shift more decisively to questions of politics and power and of freedom from colonial rule. It is important to remember that what we are calling the nationalist phase is merely a shorthand expression because there are many more tendencies and currents that cannot simply be subsumed under the rubric of nationalism. At the very least, there are important currents like the Muslims and *Dalits* that mark the intellectual and political search for the self in this period.

Before we go into the specific features of the thinkers of the two broad periods, it is necessary to make a few clarifications. Though most scholars have tended to see these as two distinct phases or periods, this way of looking at the history of modern Indian thought can be quite problematic. These periodisations can only be very broad and tentative ones, made for the purpose of convenience of study. In fact, we can more productively see them as two broad currents which do not necessarily follow one after the other. As we shall see, there are many social reform concerns that take on a different form and continue into the nationalist phase. In fact, the nationalist phase itself reveals two distinct tendencies in this respect. On the one hand, there is the dominant or hegemonic nationalism, represented by the Indian National Congress (I.N.C.), where the social reform agenda is abandoned in a significant way; on the other, there are other contending narratives that insist on privileging the reform agenda much to the discomfort of the nationalists. In this respect, Gandhi remains almost the lone figure within this hegemonic nationalism, and he keeps trying to bring the reform agenda into the nationalist movement.

There was a veritable explosion of intellectual activity throughout the nineteenth century, particularly in Bengal and Western India. Thinkers and social reformers like Raja Ram Mohan Roy, Ishwar Chandra Vidyasagar, Jyotirao Govindrao Phule, Ramakrishna and Swami Dayānanda Saraswati and such other luminaries directly addressed the question of internal regeneration of Indian society. They launched the most vigorous critique of their own society, with the aim of bringing it out of its backwardness. As Ram Mohan Roy put it, it was the "thick clouds of superstition" that "hung all over the land". As a consequence, he believed, polygamy and infanticide were rampant, and the position of the Bengali woman was "a tissue of ceaseless oppressions and miseries". Idolatry and priest craft were often held responsible for the destruction of the yearning for knowledge. Dayānanda Saraswati believed it was institutions such as these that had made Hindus fatalist and inert. The issues that dominated the concerns of the social reformers were primarily related to the status of women in Indian society. *Sati*, widow remarriage and the education of women were central issues raised by the reformers. To this end, they re-interpreted tradition, often offered ruthless critiques of traditional practices and even lobbied support with the colonial government for enacting suitable legislations for banning some of the more obnoxious practices, like *sati*.

While the position of women was a matter of central concern, there was another equally important question – that of caste divisions and untouchability which became the focus of critique of many of these reformers. However, their approach to caste was different from those of reformers like Jyotiba Phule, Periyar Ramasamy and Dr B. R. Ambedkar. Unlike the latter, they did not seek the emancipation of the lower castes but, rather, their assimilation into the mainstream of Hindu society. Most of the reformers held not only that Hindu society had become degenerate, insulated, and deeply divided into hundreds of different communities and castes, but it had also become thereby incapable of forging any kind of common will. Hindu society therefore had to be reconstituted and reorganised into a single community.

There are two distinct moves made by the reformers. First, their critiques drew very explicitly from the Western liberal ideas. To many of them, British power was the living proof of the validity and invincibility of those ideas. They were therefore open admirers of British rule. It should be remembered that the first generation of reformist thinkers began their intellectual journey in the face of a dual challenge. On the one hand, there was the overwhelming presence of colonial rule that did not simply represent to them a foreign power but also a modern and advanced society that had made breathtaking advances in the field of ideas – of science and philosophy. To them, it embodied the exhilarating developments of science and modern ways of thinking that a country like India should adopt, if it wanted to emerge as a free and powerful country in the modern era. On the other hand, there were continuous challenges thrown before the emerging indigenous intelligentsia by Christian missionaries, who mounted a powerful critique of Hinduism and some of its most inhuman practices, like *sati*, female infanticide and caste oppression – particularly the abominable practice of untouchability. Questions of widow remarriage and the education of women were also major issues of debate and contention.

These formidable challenges required two simultaneous intellectual moves: 1) an acknowledgement of the rot that had set in Hindu society and a thorough critique of it. For this purpose, they welcomed modern liberal ideas and philosophy with open arms. 2) They were also equally anxious to retain a sense of their own self. Complete self-negation could not make people great. So, most of the reformers, drawing on contemporary Orientalist scholarship, claimed a great and ancient past. Even a convinced Anglophile like Ram Mohan Roy, for instance, had the occasion to reply to a missionary critic that "the world is indebted to our ancestors for the first dawn of knowledge which sprang up in the East" and that India had nothing to learn from the British "with respect to science, literature and religion". This awe of Western knowledge and achievements and a simultaneous valorisation of a hoary Indian past were common features of the reformers of all shades – even though the specific emphasis on different aspects varied from thinker to thinker.

There are reasons to believe that the early responses to British rule and the so-called renaissance were a distinctly Hindu phenomenon. It was within Hindu society that the first critical engagement with colonial modernity began. Other responses from communities like the Muslims had their own distinct specificities and history. One immediate reason for the Hindu response was, of course, the fact that it was precisely certain practices within Hindu society that colonial rule sought to address. A second reason was that, for specific historical reasons, it was the Hindu elite that had access to English education and exposure to the radical ideas of the enlightenment.

The tendency to see the division between the reformers and their opponents as one between progressives and traditionalists was an oversimplification of the story of the renaissance where they noted the deeply contradictory nature of the break with the past.

Bhikhu Parekh has suggested that the arguments of these Hindu reformers relied on one or more of the following four modes of arguments derived from tradition but deployed with a distinct newness to meet the demands of changing times. First, they appealed to scriptures that seemed to them to be more hospitable to their concerns. Vidyasagar, for instance, relied on the *Parasharasmṛiti*, while Ram Mohan Roy invoked the *Upaniṣhads*. Second, they invoked what they called *sadharan dhārma*, which they interpreted to mean the universal principles of morality. Third, they appealed to the idea of a *yuga dhārma*, or the principles that accord with the needs of the prevailing *yuga*, or epoch. Fourthly, they invoked the idea of *loksangraha* and argued that the practice in question had such grave consequences that unless eradicated, it would destroy the cohesion and viability of the Hindu social order. As instances, he mentions that Vidyasagar argued that unmarried widows were turning to prostitution or corrupting their families; Keshab Chandra Sen contended that child marriages were endangering the survival of the Hindus; Dayānanda Saraswati believed image worship was leading to internal sectarian quarrels.

V. R. Mehta has suggested that there are at least two important theoretical issues involved in these intellectual initiatives of the reformers. First, they worked strenuously to change the attitude towards fate and other-worldliness and assert the importance of action in this world. Secondly, the main focus of their enquiry remained not the individual but society, community and humanity as a whole. There is a third feature he also mentions in relation to later social reform thought; the concern with the welfare of the people and the attraction of ideas such as socialism and equality. The concern with nation and a rejection of everything British and colonial was strikingly absent among them.

Nationalism could be said to have made its appearance in the last part of the nineteenth century. In this phase, the concerns and approach of the thinkers change in a significant way. Here, there is a strong concern with the freedom of the nation and an almost irreconcilable hostility towards colonial rule. Unlike the social reformers before them, they placed no trust on the institutions of the colonial State for affecting any reform. On the contrary, they displayed a positive opposition to what they now considered interference by the colonial State in the internal matters of the nation. Alongside this, there is a parallel move towards the privileging of the political struggle over social reforms.

However, with the entry of Gandhi into the political scene, we can see a shift from this framework to some extent. Although Gandhi himself resorted to the use of Hindu symbols, he was acutely aware of the unfinished agenda of social reform. Here, it is interesting that while he located himself squarely within the framework of nationalism as defined by his predecessors and held on to the idea of sovereignty in the inner sphere, he nevertheless made an important departure in terms of his insistence on the question of the social reform. Unlike other nationalists, he was not prepared to abandon it altogether and would repeatedly insist upon the need for Hindu society to redeem itself by exorcising untouchability from within itself through self-purification. It is also interesting that while he, himself, used the idea of *Ram rajya* as a utopia of nationhood, he made untiring efforts to draw the Muslims into the mainstream of the nationalist struggle. It is the proclaimed anti-modernist and *sanatani* Hindu Gandhi who stood steadfastly for Hindu–Muslim unity as the pre-condition of India's freedom. It was Gandhi who made the Khilafat non-cooperation movement collaboration of Hindus and Muslims possible. It is true that Gandhi's insistence on a Hindu *sanatani* identity could not eventually convince either the Muslims or the *Dalits*/lower-caste leaders about his sincerity in safeguarding their interests.

Following Gandhi, Vinobha Bhave articulated this location as a leading exponent of *sarvodaya* ideology. Vinobha visualised a total revolution transforming all features of life. The goal for him was to mould a new man, to change human life and create a new world. The departure of the British had not brought Indian society any closer to *sarvodaya*, the main obstacle to which was the centralised government. *Sarvodaya*, for Vinoba, does not mean good government or majority rule, it means freedom from government and decentralisation of power. Central to Vinoba's conceptualisation of politics and power is his distinction between *rajnīti* (the politics of power) and *loknīti* (the ethics of democracy). Subsequently, Jayaprakash Narayan accepted the Gandhian *sarvodaya* conception of politics.

An important point which needs to be registered here in relation to the work and thought of lower-caste leaders like Jyotirao Phule, Periyar Ramasamy and B. R. Ambedkar is that they differed from the trends identified in the case of both Hindu and Muslim thought in two crucial ways. Firstly, at no point, did these thinkers give up the social reform agenda, and in fact their consistent critique of nationalism remained linked to this question. Secondly, they did not suffer from the deep ambivalence regarding the West that marked the thought of reformers and nationalists alike in the case of the Hindu and Muslim thinkers. It is important to note that for most leaders of the lower castes, particularly for the *Dalits*, the notion of a putative Hindu community simply did not carry any positive significance. To them, the memories of past and continuing humiliation and degradation through practices like untouchability constituted their over-riding experience that framed their responses. In their perception, there was something insincere in the efforts of even the reformers who merely wanted the assimilation of lower castes into mainstream Hindu society without disturbing the power structure in any way. Phule's main concern, therefore, is with an all-out attack on Hinduism and caste – where he sees caste as central to the existence of the former. In fact, to most of the radical lower-caste thinkers, Hinduism is merely another name for *Brāhminism*, and they prefer to refer it by that name. Both Phule and Periyar seek to unite all the non-*Brāhmins* or *Śūdra-Atiśūdra* against the power of the *Brāhmins*.

It is also necessary to note that in this struggle, almost all the radical lower-caste leaders give special importance to the question of women's education and emancipation. In this context, Pandita Ramabai's effort is praiseworthy. Phule also established the first school for *Śūdra-Atiśūdra* girls in 1848 with great risk. To them, colonial rule, if anything, appeared as their biggest benefactor. It is precisely for this reason that they saw the continuation of the social reform agenda as being of critical significance for the emancipation of the *Dalits/Śūdras*. It is not as if they had great faith in the social reform of the upper caste, *bhadralok* reformers of the nineteenth century, but the abandoning of even that limited agenda by nationalism was something Ambedkar had occasion to recall bitterly in his writings and speeches. It is significant that even when the focus of *Dalit* and lower-caste thinkers shifted to the explicitly political terrain – for instance, in the work of Periyar and Ambedkar, their central preoccupations remained with the structure of power within the emergent nation: who would wield power within an independent India? What would be the position of the *Dalits* in the new dispensation? Fundamental to Ambedkar's approach for the uplifting of the untouchables was their education. He was always firm on the question of untouchables leading themselves, that is, producing their own leaders. Further, for ensuring that the downtrodden castes got their due, he insisted the government to take responsibility for the welfare of its entire people and create special rights for those who had been denied education and occupational opportunities. To this end, he visualised a strong central government with a clear-cut commitment for the welfare of its entire people.

The growth of socialist thought took lay in India mainly in the twentieth century, unlike in the West where it had flourished in the nineteenth century. Socialism as a philosophy of social and economic reconstruction in India urbanised because of the impact of Western thought. The growth of socialist thought took lay at a time when colonial use had reached intolerable proportions. The land structure was marked by the attendance of innumerable intermediaries, mainly landlords who were woven into a hierarchical structure. The leaders of the Indian national movement were not only against the continuation of British rule; they also wanted to reconstruct the social, political, and economic structure of India after the attainment of independence. The socialist thoughts constituted a significant characteristic of this proposed reconstruction. Although the systematic development of socialist thoughts took lay in India from the 1920s, even before then, some leaders had strongly desired the socio-economic reconstruction of Indian civilisation on radical rows. Jawaharlal Nehru, Subhash Chandra Bose, Acharya Narendra Deva, Jayaprakash Narayan, M. N. Roy, and Ram Manohar Lohia were some of the most significant thinkers of the socialist stream in India. The socialists were influenced by the Russian revolution, but they had serious differences with the Communists on the application of Marxism in its original shape in India. M. N. Roy criticised the bourgeois power of the Congress throughout 1921–1923. This was mainly because he was interested in the establishment of communism in India. Jayaprakash Narayan as a national leader remained primarily concerned with the abuse of political power in India and therefore established himself perpetually in opposition to the Congress. He, too, was a strong advocate of the decentralisation of power and expanded and propagated the concept of 'party-less democracy'.

With the previous discussion on different themes and perspectives of modern Indian thought, it can be said that the present volume, *Revisiting Modern Indian Thought*, is a lucid and comprehensive account of the thread of socio-political thought of major thinkers of modern India which includes liberal-reformist thought, moderate-Gandhian thought, and leftist-socialist thought. It is an outcome of a sustained conversation, continuous dialogue and discussions between its editors regarding the pedagogy of modern Indian thought which have prompted the writing of this book. The book constitutes significant elements of the syllabus of major Indian universities and colleges across disciplines, including political science, sociology, history, and philosophy. Keeping the diversity of its implications, the topics were contributed by faculties across the country as per their specialisation and subject expertise.

Divided into 19 chapters under 3 sections, the text offers a panoramic view and highlights different aspects of modern Indian thought in light of India's peculiar conditions that influenced the evolution of such thoughts. The book begins with a detailed discussion on the development and articulation of Indian thought and traditions that evolved in modern India. It then goes on to provide comprehensive coverage and analyses the ideas and thought of various thinkers of modern India. The chapters on such thinkers not only talk about their lives and the eras in which they lived but also discuss and examine the contributions of those thinkers to the contemporary period. Intended primarily as a comprehensive and well-organised text-cum-reference book on modern Indian thought for the undergraduate as well as post-graduate students of political science, this compact volume will also be of great value for academics at large, especially to aspirants of UGC-NET, Civil Services Examinations and all those who are interested in gaining an in-depth knowledge of political and social thought of modern Indian thinkers. We hope the book will best serve the interests of the students and other teaching communities who are interested in knowing about modern Indian thought.

Acknowledging the contributions of different persons, first, we are immensely grateful to Routledge, especially to Ms Antara Ray Chaudhury and the entire team for helping us at various stages of developing this volume and completing it on time. We are also thankful to the anonymous reviewers for providing their valuable suggestions and comments, which we have strived to incorporate to the best of our abilities. We are pleased to record our gratitude to Professor Sudha Pai (former Professor and Rector, Jawaharlal Nehru University, New Delhi) for writing the foreword for the book. We are highly indebted to Professor Sanjukta Banerji Bhattacharya (former Professor, Jadavpur University, Kolkata) for writing the introductory chapter of the book. We would like to extend our appreciation to Professor Prakash C. Sarangi (former Professor, University of Hyderabad and former Vice-Chancellor, Ravenshaw University, Odisha), Professor Ashutosh Kumar (Lala Lajpat Rai Chair Professor, Punjab University, Chandigarh), Professor Upendra Choudhury (Professor, Aligarh Muslim University and former Member Secretary and Director, ICSSR, New Delhi), Professor Shri Prakash Singh (Professor, University of Delhi), and Professor Sanjeev Kumar Sharma (Vice-Chancellor, Mahatma Gandhi Central University, Motihari, Bihar and General Secretary, Indian Political Science Association) for writing the endorsements for the book. We are indebted to the valuable contributors of the volume and especially to the senior professors, Professor Anand Kumar (former Professor, Jawaharlal Nehru University), Professor Debi Chatterjee (former Professor, Jadavpur University and the editor of *Contemporary Voice of Dalit*), Professor Surya Narayan Misra (former Professor, Utkal University), Professor Narender Kumar (Professor, Jawaharlal Nehru University), Professor Ambarish Mukhopadhyay (Professor, Vidyasagar University), Professor Basanta Kumar Mallik (Professor, Utkal University and Director, Centre for Ambedkar Studies), Professor Sumit Mukerji (Professor, Kalyani University and Director, Centre for Studies on Bengali Diaspora), and other contributors for their support, without which bringing this volume was almost impossible. Last but not least, we are thankful to Professor Sibaji Pratim Basu, Professor of Political Science and Dean, Faculty of Arts and Commerce, Vidyasagar University, for his contribution and valuable suggestions at different stages of preparing the manuscript. We thank our family members and our students for their constant love and support during this strenuous venture.

While this volume has attempted to cover most of the important thinkers of modern India, from Raja Ram Mohan Roy to Ram Manohar Lohia, we have been constrained by the scope and size of the work, leaving out many other important thinkers, such as Rabindranath Tagore, Swami Vivekananda, Bal Gangadhar Tilak, Lala Lajpat Rai, Aurobindo Ghose, Maulana Abul Kalam Azad, and others, who have significant contributions as far as modern Indian thought is concerned. We wish to clarify that the present work is not exhaustive; in fact, it is a continuation of another book on modern Indian thought entitled *Reappraising Modern Indian Thought: Themes and Thinkers* edited by Ankit Tomar and Suratha Kumar Malik which includes other thinkers of modern India. The continuation volume is going to be publish by Palgrave Macmillan (part of Springer Nature) global edition in 2021. The introductory chapter discusses in detail the obvious limitations of, and insights behind such a project and includes some of the ideas from other thinkers with relevance to contemporary times. We have tried our best to serve our readers, and if it fulfils the purpose even to an extent, we will achieve what we are looking for.

Suratha Kumar Malik and Ankit Tomar

INTRODUCTION

Sanjukta Banerji Bhattacharya

1 Introduction: Theoretical background and sources of political thought in India

Political thought and theory are sometimes used synonymously, particularly by students of disciplines other than political science, but it is important to state at the beginning that they are not the same thing: while political theory, very broadly, includes political philosophy, a scientific criterion for the analysis of political ideas and a systematic development of generalisations of political behaviour (Gould and Kolb 1964), political thought, again broadly speaking, comprises all thought, theories, and values of a person or group of persons on the State or issues related to the State. Political thought may or may not comprise a theory, depending on whether it is or is not a systematically developed logical hypothesis to explain political phenomena, political rule, governance, etc. Therefore political thought always pertains to the thought or ideas of a person or group of persons, while political theory is a self-contained explanation/speculation/theory attempting to answer questions of political behaviour or predict future political events based on theoretical analysis. However, the speculative-analytical thinking of a particular political thinker can result in political theory, which is sometimes presented in a single book, an example being John Rawls' *A Theory of Justice*, where Rawls sets out his theory of distributive justice.

Modern political thought cannot and should not be studied in isolation without an understanding of what went before since streams of thought are engrained into the minds of thinkers, and however situational the cause for new thinking may be, older traditions in thought are bound to have an impact on the new. While the sources of Western political thought can be traced back to Greek political philosophy epitomised in Plato's *Republic*, followed by Aristotle's *Politics*, the sources of Indian political ideas, philosophy and thought are scattered and must be culled from various sources: the *Vedās* (which contain information on kings, kingship, institutions like *sabhas* and *samitis*, etc.), the *Mahābhārata* (which is an epic on the art of politics) and the *Rāmāyaṇa* (which details ideal kingship), Kauṭilya's *Arthaśāstra* (which concerns governance and its machinery apart from being a treatise on both economics and war), the *Smṛitis* (which advocated that kings were supposed to serve the subjects and that it was not wrong to kill a tyrant), stone and copper inscriptions that highlight administrative measures and governance and many other sources, like the *Brihaspati Sutra*, Somadeva's *Neeti Vakya Niritha*, the *Rajaneeti Ratnakara*, the *Rajaneeti Mayuka* (the *Nītiśāstras* being treatises on policy, the best known of which is the *Śukranīti*), etc. Ancient Indian political thought must be understood in the context of religious beliefs. Although the art of governance was the theme of *Arthaśāstric* literature, the *Dharmaśāstras* and the *Dharmasūtras*, as their names signify, focus on *dhārma*. However, the very fact that there are many *Dharmasūtras* and *Dharmaśāstras* means that there were conflicting claims on the sources, meaning and significance of *dhārma*, and although many of the *Sūtras* and *Śhāstras* have disappeared over time, the names of many thinkers, like Gautama, Vasistha, *Yājñavalkya*, *Nārada*, and Manu, are well known and studied. The *Dharmaśāstras* are particularly important in the modern Indian context because they were used as the basis for the personal law of the land for all non-Muslims (Hindus, Jains, Sikhs, Buddhists), first by the East India Company and later by the British colonial government, the Muslim personal law being based on the *Sharīʿah*.

The old Sanskritic discourses on religion and the art of governance, kingship, etc. that could be derived from such treatises appears to have faded away well before the Islamic conquests, although commentaries (*bhasyas*) and digests (*nibandhyas*) on the treatises continued well into medieval times. There is a wealth of material on political thought to be gathered from the varied writings regarding the role of the king (who is seen more as a guardian of the law, rather than its maker); mechanism of government; organisation of power (Kauṭilya, *Śukranītishara*, etc.); *dhārma*, or basic law of the State; popular assemblies like the *sabha* and the *samiti*; kingdoms, empires, and tribal republics, or *ganas*, and much more, with political theories and institutions remaining grounded in classical concepts and practices. However, in the earliest literatures, political thought is represented by occasional passages in philosophical or religious writings rather than in organised writing, unlike the Greek and Roman political thinkers. Although Indian political speculations begin as early as the second millennium B.C., if not earlier, ancient Indian political thought cannot be isolated from the main body of Hindu philosophy. In fact, this concept appears to have continued into modern times. To quote M. K. Gandhi, "I claim that human mind or human society is not divided into water-tight compartments called social, political and religious. All act and react upon each other" (Gandhi 1922).

The advent of the Turko-Afghans and, later, the Mughals marked the drying up of the creative phase of classical Indian political thought on the one hand but led to the adaptation of Islamic thought to Indian conditions on the other hand, creating new strands in Islamic ideas on kingship, administration, the relation between the State and religion (or, rather, the ruler and the *Ulema*), the treatment of non-Muslims, etc. Medieval Indian political thought, like its earlier Indian counterpart, had a theological basis, but in the case of Islam, it was derived from fixed texts, the *Qur'ān*, the *Hadis*, and the *Sharīʿah*, and theoretically therefore (not practically), there was not much scope for change (Ahmad 1962: 121–130). However, Islamic political thought is unique in the sense that reasoning and theoretical justifications came, in many cases, after a deed had been done or an action implemented or polity had been adapted to circumstances, and Islamic political thought in India, while keeping to the basics, was no exception. While classical Islamic political theory does not distinguish between the State and religion, with rulers ruling in the name of the Caliph, who was situated in Baghdad when Islamic rule began in India (the seat later shifted to Turkey when the Turkish Sultan assumed the Caliphate in the early sixteenth century), Muslim rulers in India, from a very early time, followed their own path, with the investiture from the Caliph being abandoned at the time of the Tughlaqs (except for Firoz Shah Tughlaq) and never revived by the Mughals, who declared the Mughal emperor as the imam (or head of religion) of the Mughal empire. Emperors like Akbar framed their own set of beliefs, which included *sulh-i-kul* (universal tolerance); he even issued something called the Infallibility Decree in 1579 whereby the *Ulema* had to recognise him as the supreme authority in religious matters, which contravened the orthodox view that the *Sharīʿah* was supreme because it was Allah's law. The *Ulema* also had to declare him to be the *imam-i-adil*, a just ruler. Some of the important works that are the sources of political thought in the medieval period are Ziauddin Barani's *Fatwa-i Jahandari*, Amir Khusru's *Tughlaqnama*, the *Fiqh-i Firuzshahi* and Abul Fazl's *Ain-i-Akbari*, although there are many more works from which political ideas and trends can be culled. Medieval Muslim political thought left behind, broadly, a twofold normative legacy: the primacy of Islam on the one hand, and the primacy of the human ruler, who was variously called *Zil-ullah* (shadow of God: the context here is Balban) and *Nur Parwarda-i Izdi* (Divine Light, in the context of Akbar) on the other hand; however, justice and the consent of the ruled were important considerations, with Abul Fazl insisting that the true king must understand the *miraj-i-zamana*, or spirit of the age (Maloni 2010; Bevir 2010: 694–695).

Modern Indian thought, as mentioned, cannot be viewed in isolation, as is sometimes done, without an understanding of early Indian political ideas and concepts (which, as also noted, overlapped and cannot be compartmentalised), as well as Indian society and history – the modern Indian mind is deeply connected with what has gone before, what has been thought before and what practices were followed before. Therefore, a contextualisation is necessary without which a proper understanding of modern Indian thought is not possible. In fact, Amartya Sen, the Nobel Prize–winning Indian economist has argued in his book *The Argumentative Indian* that democracy was not a Western gift to India like many seem to assume, and neither is there anything unique in Indian history that makes India singularly suited to democracy; the truth is much more complex and lies somewhere between the two. He also talks of Akbar and Ashoka and contends that secularism and inclusiveness were not Western imports, with these two rulers serving as the best examples of India's heterodoxy and inclusiveness (Sen 2005: 18).

Having offered a bird's-eye view of the early sources and nature of Indian political thought, I will next briefly contextualise the impact of the British colonial conquest on Indian intellectuals leading to a fresh flow of political, social, and economic ideas and then go on to broadly categorise the thinking of the intellectuals forming groups based on similarities and dissimilarities in their political outlooks.

II British conquest: Indian renaissance

Colonial intervention in India led to the introduction of new ideas on polity that were unique in that they were rationally and scientifically stated, with some ideas amounting to political theory while others could be categorised as various kinds of thought. In fact, colonialism itself was driven by mercantilism, a theory of trade and accumulation of power through trade, which had been prevalent in European intellectual circles since about 1500, with analytical writings by Sir Thomas Smith, Thomas Mun, Josiah Child, Jean-Baptiste Colbert, and many others all over Europe promoting the idea of power through trade, which served as a rationale for colonialism from the sixteenth to the eighteenth century. Unlike the New World, colonialism in India meant the taking over of existing polity and not the imposition of total Western ideas, concepts, and institutions. The British, in fact, selectively appropriated political ideas and traditions in India that were considered appropriate to the organisation and consolidation of power, for instance, *Brāhminical* ideas of Hindu law, elitist Muslim thought on autocratic rule, etc. However, the British also introduced concepts of rule of law, public good, rights, and colonial authority, and these were introduced as practical dictates of governance rather than as principles governing political authority. It must be remembered that however much the colonial government spoke of rights and public good (inspired by eighteenth-century European liberal thought), the *raison d'etre* of colonialism was power. Therefore, the churning created in intellectual thought following the entry of the British into India was informed on the one hand by the contradictions and possibilities inherent in European colonial thought and on the other by a critique that was partly grounded in past traditions (Bevir 2010: 695). This dual axis of the contradictions of the thought, currents of modernity and the challenges posed by socio-cultural-religious traditions modelled modern Indian thought.

Thus, the moral and political awareness of India's approximately 2,500 years of knowledge traditions helped India's leaders in building the concept of an Indian nation and nation-State – through the idea of *swaraj*, that is, the perception of India's self-hood, which was a pre-requisite for *swa* (self) *raj* (rule/State) – as they faced colonial rule. According to a political analyst, the epistemological crisis where traditional epistemologies fail to acquire the knowledge necessary to understand and explain the world at present, was resolved in the Indian context by modern Indian thinkers, intellectuals and activists like M. K. Gandhi, Aurobindo Ghose and Rabindranath Tagore by engaging with classical texts and concepts, thereby reorienting an indigenous political tradition and rejuvenating it, thereby making an epistemological break (Vajpeyi 2012: 57). While this idea has been modified and debated by others (Nath 2014: 271–304), it may be said that while Gandhi drew on classical non-political concepts like *ahiṃsā* (non-violence) and *dhārma* (variously interpreted as religion, duty, etc.) to draw up a political theory of non-violent direct action, others, like V. D. Savarkar and Golwalkar, were informed by the ideas of a Hindu *rashtra*, or nation, and Muslim thinkers like Muhammad Iqbal (who is also called the *Mufakkir-i-Pakistan*, or the Thinker of Pakistan), drew on Islamic culture and heritage to defy what many Muslims considered the false secularism of the Indian National Congress to demand a separate Muslim State that would embrace an Islamic self-hood. Yet others, like Muhammad Ali Jinnah and Jawaharlal Nehru, were influenced by Western political ideas and adopted Western political terms and concepts, but the subterranean influence of the tradition also informed their thought. Here, one may also mention Georgio Borsa's theory of modernisation in this context, according to which the phenomenon of re-working the key aspects of European liberal thought was part of a wider, complex process of transformation of the Indian society that the Indian intelligentsia undertook to challenge the hegemony of the British *raj*. Indians accepted some Western ideologies and political theories that they regarded as essential elements of modernity. But the exogenous principles and values had to be combined with indigenous ones to be legitimised (Borsa 1977).

So, what were the main Western political ideas that entered India to create an epistemological crisis where traditional ideas apparently faced insurmountable challenges to adapting to new circumstances? What is important here is that values get articulated in a particular context – Western ideas did not totally subsume the traditional, nor were modern political ideas entirely copies of Western thought; ideas were indigenised and shaped in the context of British colonialism and articulated in the perspective of Indian nationalism. What is also important is the recognition that British colonialism, which brought in administrative, economic, and jural changes and introduced an education system that was open to all and differed vastly from the education that had so far been offered in *Brāhminical* schools or Islamic *madrassas*, disturbed the age-old social rigidities of the Indian social order and exposed the Indian mind to Western rationalistic thinking. Not only did it lead to new thinking among the already higher-caste literates but it also aroused deprived sections into logically examining their caste position and demanding change, as is so potently visible in the ideas of B. R. Ambedkar and J. Phule. The first impact of European ideas on Indian minds led to what has been called the Indian renaissance or, rather, the Bengal renaissance: a questioning of old obscurantist ideas that had crept into religion and from thence into society, which accepted them blindly as conventional socio-religious norms and values and viewed religion through the prism of rationalism, humanism, and liberalism, which meant a return to and re-evaluation of original religious texts, which, in turn, led to the discovery that many rituals were not actually grounded in religion but socially reprehensible acts that had been cunningly superimposed on religion by those in power over the weak and intellectually deprived as gospel truths to strengthen their position in society. The first phase of the intellectual rising was therefore reformist, socio-religious, and cultural, with little political content. In contrast, the second phase of the renaissance saw a conscious attempt to converge ideas of anti-colonialism arising from a dissonance between Western political thought with its ideas of liberalism, secularism, democracy, and colonial authoritarian practices that belied these ideas, as well as the social quest for modernity. In fact, what was happening was a process of churning: transformation, destruction, and restructuring in the Indian context, and that was the background for the emergence of modern Indian thought. The inadvertent entrance of new ideologies through Western education, missionaries, and colonial rule, like liberalism, capitalism, nationalism, and democracy, in the face of colonial authoritarianism, which espoused these ideas in their own context but had little wish to share the output of such ideas with the colonised, also produced counter-ideological forces like revivalism, traditionalism, and communalism.

It needs to be pointed out that while the impact of Western thought led to the renaissance (a Western word and therefore a Western interpretation of what was happening in India), the nature of this renaissance was not the same as that of the Western one, which was a kind of revival of that which had gone before (ancient Greek) but had been sort of lost under the burden of medieval Church diktat and orthodoxy, against which the thinkers of the Western renaissance protested, leading to a renewal as well as a new thinking based on not only the past but past rationality as well. In India, the renaissance did not mean abandoning the medieval tradition and returning to the ancient one, but rather, strengthening older traditions by looking at them through the prism of rationality; it was a cultural and intellectual re-discovery rather than a restoration of the past. Western impact did involve a new awakening and expression, but this awakening was in the Indian context, and the Indian historical context contained much that was similar in terms of ideas (but not expressed in Western terminology), something that made it easier for Indian thinkers to accept Western concepts; to give an example, the idea of secularism and tolerance could be found in both ancient and medieval times in *Upaniṣhadic* texts, which spoke of *vasudhaiva kutumbakam* (the world is one family), and Akbar's *sulh-i-kul*. So, the idea of secularism in modern Indian thought was not revolutionary; similarly, the idea of a just ruler, justice and even the notion that a bad ruler could be overthrown were not foreign to ancient or medieval political thought in India.

However, it was the British, in the initial years of the East India Company, who initiated economic and social reform (the latter under indirect pressure from some Indian thinkers) in land that they controlled, which laid the foundations for far-reaching social change and egalitarianism, group consciousness, and, ultimately, nationalism and the growth of the idea of a modern nation-State. Twentieth-century political leaders and thinkers focused on the idea of the Indian State and what form it should take, and the works of Western political thinkers like John Locke, David Hume, Jean Jacques Rousseau, Edmund Burke, John Stuart Mill, Immanuel Kant, Karl Marx, etc., as well as the activities of European patriots active in creating nation-States, such as Cavour, Garibaldi, and Bismarck, influenced and informed their ideas. In fact, the impact of these ideas took practical root among the thinkers, activists, and thinker-activists, as can be seen from the growing demands on the colonial government for incremental doses of self-rule culminating in the demand for independence. These demands for self-rule laid the ground for representative and, later, some degree of responsible government, that is, the basis for the parliamentary system we have today.

III A perspective on the characteristics of modern Indian thought

Having noted the context, in terms of both time and space, of modern Indian thought, which helps to explain the continuity in ideas as well as the emergence of new concepts and further assists in elucidating the difference with Western thought from which it drew by way of concepts, terminology and expression, it is also necessary here to briefly examine its varied features. This is not an easy task because the very word "varied" implies many voices, some prominent and mainstream and others subordinate, minority or of the margins. The thinkers came from vastly different backgrounds, both in terms of community and social group, and they expressed what they culled out of their own lived experiences. Trying to find a common strand of thought apart from the later wish for freedom from British rule is therefore difficult. Historians, therefore, speak of mainstream and parallel movements, the first being the dominant strand which was presided over by leaders like Ranade, Gokhale, Naoroji, Gandhi, Nehru, Patel, Azad, and the like, the latter being peasant, workers', tribal, communist, etc. movements that threw up their own thinkers and activists. But besides these, there were strands of communalism, both Hindu and Muslim, both thinking in terms of exclusivity in terms of religion and seeing the future State as either a Muslim nation or a Hindu *rashtra*. And further beyond this, were those who began to rise as a result of the social reforms, which included universal education as well as the work of socio-political reformers like M. K. Gandhi – variously called the *achhyut* (untouchables), *Harijans* (people of God), or *Dalits* (oppressed), whom the British tried to divide from mainstream Hindu society by giving them separate electorates (in which they failed) – who had their own experience of life in India and wanted no more of it; they, too, began to formulate their own ideas on politics and political life which helped to shape modern India. Additionally, the characteristics of political thinking tended to change focus in the 150 years or so of modern Indian thinking that has been covered in this volume. While in the early and mid-nineteenth century the focus was on reform with little challenge to the colonial government, by the early twentieth century this had changed with the ideas of *swaraj* throwing up different solutions from the political to the economic and administrative. Moreover, the same thinker, in the Indian political context of colonial rule, social exclusiveness, communal divisions, etc., sometimes changed emphasis, a good example being Sir Syed Ahmed Khan, who questioned the authority of the *Ulema* and tried to modernise/reform Muslim society, but who later back-pedalled when faced with the reality of the comparative backwardness of the Muslim community vis-à-vis the Hindu community in the socio-economic sphere. The founding of the Indian National Congress gave Syed Ahmed the opportunity to dissociate with the founders, who were largely Hindus, and the Congress' political ideas, which were initially moderate, but began to become more extreme within a few years. Ultimately, this proved to be the beginning of the communal divide; therefore, any attempt to categorise modern Indian thinkers based on characteristics is bound to create overlaps and sometimes raise uncomfortable questions. Modern Indian thought is therefore deeply related to the contextual milieu covering both time and space, and this is true not only of groups of thinkers but of individual thinkers as well. Given the fluidity of the socio-political context, there is also a fluidity in thought processes. If we grasp this, then it is much easier to understand the contradictions and complexities of modern Indian thought.

However, if we can think of any three concepts that characterise Indian political thought, it has to be nation, nationalism, and national identity (Chakrabarty and Pandey 2009: xxiii). Conversely, the question that arises in this context is: whose nation? The concept of a national identity, given that the nation was not a given, would depend on the particular perception of a nation regarding who they were, and their vision of the State would be informed by this identity. This is true of religious communities; it is also true of caste members who identify with their group or even members of linguistic groups who do not want to be submerged under a dominant sectional or linguistic group. Nationalism itself is problematic, although it is perhaps the most potent mobilising force against a perceived threat or enemy, which in India's case was British colonialism. Nationalism leads to various ideologies depending on how strategies and outcomes are viewed, and in the case of India there were many; however, the two main streams were 1) the non-violent nationalism of Gandhi and the Indian National Congress and 2) the revolutionary nationalism of individuals and later groups, like the Hindustan Socialist Republican Army (the 'socialist' in the name reflecting the ideological bent of the group). The closer independence came, the more complex the concepts of nation, nationalism, and national identity became, as thinker-activists spelt out their different visions of the nation-State they wanted.

In this context, while leaders adopted the ideas of nationalism, nation, and national identity from their essentially Western origin, the mainstream leaders contextualised these to the Indian historico-social context of heterogeneity and diversity and memories that were not shared by all because of social and communal divides. That is perhaps why the mainstream political leader-thinkers speak of pluralism, secularism, and essentially Indian features, like *swadeshi*, as opposed to the foreign. Further, the thinkers also sought to draw up a national identity through drawing on the spiritual strength of India's past. But in doing this, there was a dichotomy: although lip service was paid to the twin conceptualisation of *Ram* and *Rahim* as part of India's tradition, a bifurcation was bound to occur in hypothesising the nation in this context.

Therefore, while nation, nationalism, and national identity form the core and foundation of most Indian political thought in this period, contextualising these in terms of traditions and contemporary politics also leads to the variety that we see in the same. Here, it may be interesting to mention Sudipta Kaviraj's argument that modern colonial education produced two exclusive spheres of English and vernacular discourse, with the former being more concerned with individual liberty and the latter being more concerned with collective freedom from British rule than individual freedom (which is typically akin to Western modernity), thus giving an Indian twist to the idea of nationalism and modernity. He believes the impact of liberal ideas produced nationalistic ideas rather than ideas of equality and individual liberty as in the West. As such, a leader like Gandhi could justify *varṇaāśhrama dhārma* while seeking independence from British rule. Kaviraj also contends that Indian nationalists developed two powerful but entirely opposed arguments in the twentieth century – one, that successful emulation of the European model of the nation-State meant copying all elements of the Western experience, including a homogenous body politic with a single language and a dominant religion. This had its takers, especially from the 1940s, when a nation-State was demanded based on a minority religion, asserting that the Hindus and Muslims formed two different nations and should have two separate States, and further, Hindi (claiming a linguistic majority of Hindi speakers) was called for as the national language. This mono-culture argument was rejected by most Indian nationalists, who offered what Kaviraj calls the argument of improvisation, with Gandhi and Tagore asserting that "proper functioning of modern institutions depended on their chiming with traditional social understandings", and Nehru espousing the idea of unity within diversity, distrusting both a homogenising form of the Western nation-State and a homogenising form of Indian nationalism and claiming that a diverse culture produced richer resources (Kaviraj 2000: 137–162; Kaviraj 2010: 210–233).

The stream of nationalism that led to the creation of Pakistan also cannot be ignored in any analysis of the characteristics of modern Indian political thought because there was the corollary growth of a kind of Hindu nationalism, which acted and reacted on each other as well as developed independently. According to historian Ayesha Jalal, the concept of both Hindu and Muslim nationalism owed their origin to British social engineering, which began as a project after the 1857 revolt when the British conducted a census with the focus on a person's religious inclination. The outcome was a stratification of communities and Syed Ahmed could grasp the implications of this: that the Hindus were in a better position while the Muslims, who had been rulers, were getting left behind (Paracha 2016; Jalal 2001). Although Syed Ahmed initially claimed that modern ideas based on rationality and humanism were not incompatible with Islam, he later backed down and was responsible for stunting the growth of national (pan-Indian) political consciousness among the Muslims and making it uni-directional and exclusivist. Thus, some scholars are of the opinion that he was the intellectual pioneer of Muslim nationalism in India. However, British social engineering was not the only reason for the development of communal thought. The primacy of Islam and the idea of a *Dar-ul-Islam* (land of Islam), where the rule of the *Sharī'ah* could be installed, were intrinsic to Islamic thought, and thinkers like Maulana Abu'l Ala Maududi contextualised it to colonialism and British India. Other politically inclined Muslim leaders were able to use Islamic political thought conveniently to their purpose, but it must be remembered that even though the words *qaum* (nation) and *watan* (territorial homeland) exist in Urdu lexicon, Islam is essentially transnational, seeking a pan-national *umma* (community) rather than a national identity. Yet, in the context of British colonialism and the prospect of a future State where Hindus would be dominant led to the creation of a peculiar sub-continental brand of Muslim nationalism, which had the idea of a future Hindu State as the primary opponent, rather than British colonialism, and sought a distinct State, separate from the dominant Hindu one, as their *watan*.

The corollary of this is so-called Hindu nationalism (Golwalkar 1939), which got an organisational form in response to the rise of the exclusivist Indian Muslim League but the undercurrents of which lay in the idea of a national identity that gave priority to Hindu texts, culture, philosophy, etc., however inadvertently, over other identities. In fact, the early social reformer-thinkers were all Hindus, and the reforms that were undertaken concerned Hindus. It was the Hindu texts that were studied with the purpose of going back to pristine roots, through which the accumulation of centuries of superstition and superstitious practices could be reformed. It is not surprising, therefore, that the group from which the early nationalist thinkers came were Hindus, and early Hindu traditions and texts interacted with their new learning to produce thought which derived much from these traditions and texts. The term '*Hindutva*' was introduced by V. D. Savarkar much later, in 1923 (Savarkar n.d.), but it must be remembered that early political thought in India was informed by much that was derived from Hinduism.

IV An introduction to the thinkers selected for this book

There are many ways a book on modern Indian thought can be arranged. In the previous section, it was mentioned that what all thinkers had in common were the ideas of nationalism, nation and national identity, and the perception of these concepts was not only contextualised to the Indian scenario, but it varied widely given the diversity of India, politically, culturally, socially, and economically.

Therefore, instead of a kind of uni-dimensional concept of the nation, we get many ideas of the nation, and, accordingly, the idea of nationalism and national identity were also wide-ranging. It is easy to characterise modern Indian thought chronologically, even in the modern phase, placing the early reformers together, then going on to the later nineteenth century and following through with Gandhian thought and so on. However, this is simplistic and does not tell the reader of the bent of the thinker's mind and is theoretically restrained. On the other hand, the thinkers can be grouped together based on broad political doctrines, with those with a specific bent of mind being placed under a broad category signifying a political doctrine, for instance, liberalism, irrespective of chronology. This makes it easier for the student to identify the general direction of thought any particular thinker takes. However, it must be remembered that there are overlaps, and sometimes undercurrents of other political doctrines, in the thinking of any specific leader, given the volatile nature of the context of colonialism and independence, and, as has been mentioned, changes in ideology may be detected within the same thinker, again in the context of the political milieu of the time concerned.

It is important to realise that the Indian Constitution formulated post-independence, as well as many of the subsequent amendments and additions, had its roots and precursors in the liberal-moderate-socialist thinking of these early thinker-activists. The idea of a future nation was being imagined by these men (in the context of a colonised State with a long historical background of fragmented autocratic monarchical rule where the idea of a nation or nationalism was non-existent), and each contributed their own conception of their imagined India, making India a democratic, secular, socialist (the latter two being added to the Preamble much later, in 1976) country that was egalitarian, believing in fundamental rights for all while also having the mandate to build a welfare State under the Directive Principles of State Policy, which somewhat limited certain rights of some sections to accommodate remunerative justice for certain deprived sections, and endorsing liberty of thought, expression, worship, equality of status, and opportunity. These concepts cannot be compartmentalised, although some thinkers focused on individual ideas while others had a more holistic view of a future nation. While the liberal-reformist group contributed to social reform which is still a project in progress, the moderate-Gandhians debated not only tactics of how to quit India of the British but contributed to the rights debate in the process, claiming the right to self-determination and independence, which expanded to include the fundamental rights of all. Gandhi also had a blueprint for India's economic development, which, even if denied now, can see its fruition (if in a different contextual format) of the modern-day concept of *atma-nirbhar Bharat* (self-sufficient India). Social justice, a pillar that has helped millions of Indians to get education, livelihood, and equality, could not have been possible without the ideas of the leftists and socialists who helped to implement not only the 'Directive Principles of State Policy' but also to build an industrialised India through planned state policy, simultaneously keeping India's agricultural status in mind, keeping full-blown capitalism at bay but never curbing it. Therefore, the political vision of the early Indian thinkers is crucial to gaining a holistic view of what India is today.

The present book is an intensive study which includes 19 thinkers categorised under 3 sections: liberal-reformist, moderate-Gandhian, and leftist-socialist. This covers the most important thinkers of this era, from Ram Mohan Roy to Acharya Narendra Deva. What is important is the inclusion of some thinkers who normally are not represented in a text of this kind, for instance, Jagjivan Ram, Sri Ramakrishna Paramhansa, and Ishwar Chandra Vidyasagar. While I have discussed the broad parameters of these categories and the reason for their evolution in the Indian context in the earlier sections, it may be pertinent to add a few lines here about the thinkers in the framework of the categories into which they have been placed.

There are nine thinkers identified under liberal-reformist thought: Ram Mohan Roy, Ishwar Chandra Vidyasagar, Dayānanda Saraswati, Ramakrishna Paramhansa, Pandita Ramabai, Periyar E. V. Ramasamy, Jyotirao Govindrao Phule, B. R. Ambedkar, and Jagjivan Ram. While Ram Mohan Roy is one of the earliest reformer-thinkers, Jagjivan Ram belongs to the early and mid-twentieth century, and their thoughts diverge widely, given the major changes that had occurred in Indian polity within the span of more than a hundred years. The earliest sparks of nationalism are to be found in the works of Ram Mohan Roy and Ishwar Chandra Vidyasagar, along with Ramakrishna Paramhansa, belonging to the period of the Bengal renaissance. While Roy's thought reflects his quest for a pristine form of Hinduism and an eclectic selection of what he considered to be the best from every religion, which he rationally organised into a systemic liberal vision, which indirectly was his vision of the Indian nation; Vidyasagar focused on the Bengali nation and tried to introduce reform of customs among the higher caste from which he himself came in order to shape a nation through inclusiveness of learning, which he tried to spread to all castes and women. Ramakrishna Paramhansa did not have any political thought nor was he a social activist, and normally in textbooks on Indian political thought, he is seen through the eyes of Swami Vivekananda, whose initiation to socio-religious activism and indirect contribution to political thought came through Ramakrishna. However, his importance in political thought lies in the fact that he simplified and popularised Hinduism, removing it from the clutches of *Brāhminism*, which, in the long run, would help in the formation of the idea of the nation. Dictums like "*joto mot, toto poth*" (there are many paths to the same goal), showed the essence of toleration in Hinduism – and emphasised its inclusiveness. Dayānanda Saraswati's contribution, on the other hand, promoted the idea of the comprehensiveness of *Vedic* learning, and while introducing religio-reformist ideas, he also believed in the promotion of education in the vernacular. He and Roy both built institutions that reflected their visions of essentially Hindu society, which exist to this day. Pandita Ramabai was a liberal social reformer but is singular in this group because she is a woman, and although Roy, Vidyasagar, Phule, and Saraswati had all advocated women's education and some had gone even further in promoting upper-caste widow remarriage and prohibiting child marriage, Ramabai is the only woman to not only advocate but promote women's education and emancipation. In her book *The High Caste Hindu Woman*, she wrote of the darkest aspects of the life of Hindu women and claimed in an address to Lord Ripon's Education Commission (1882) that 99 percent of educated Indian males were opposed to women's education. Ambedkar, Phule, Periyar and Jagjivan Ram can be classified together, though there is immense difference in their political ideas. They, however, took up the caste issue and advocated emancipation of the lower castes and depressed classes and, hence, are viewed as liberal reformers. Each of them founded organisations for reform of caste, with Periyar and Ambedkar both founding political parties, thus carrying social reform into the realm of the political. What characterises all the thinkers in this group is that, though they are highly varied in the contexts of time and focus of their thought, they were all social reformers, each with his own liberal agenda and focus group, which diverged widely from gender to caste, linguistic group to territory.

The second part of the book is on moderate-Gandhian thought, which includes four thinkers and contains two precursors of Gandhi, Dadabhai Naoroji and Gopal Krishna Gokhale, apart from Gandhi himself and Vinoba Bhave, a strong Gandhian follower. On Gandhi, so much has been said and written that little needs to be said here because his ideas constituted an entire political philosophy and a political theory recognised as the political theory of non-violent direct action, which became a viable tactic for movements against oppression in other parts of the world, both developed and developing. His views on *satyāgraha* and the rationale behind non-violent direct action are well known, and these ideas were carried forward by Vinoba Bhave. Vinoba Bhave's unique contribution is the *bhoodan* or land gift movement, which succeeded in collecting over 4 million acres of land, 1.3 million of which were distributed among the landless poor. He has not only expanded the Gandhian concepts of non-violence, *sarvodaya*, *satyāgraha*, and trusteeship but also added his own ideas of *loknīti*, *shanti sena*, *gramdan*, and *sampatti dan*. However, it needs to be pointed out that Naoroji and Gokhale cannot be called Gandhian because they preceded Gandhi and were his mentors, but they were definitely moderate in their thought and action. Both were nationalists with visions of what a nation-State meant; Dadabhai Naoroji, in fact, with his economic analysis that British rule was draining India of its wealth, gave a plausible argument to extremists during the *swadeshi* movement to ask for *swaraj*. And it was Gokhale's repeated requests that brought Gandhi back from South Africa to spearhead the freedom movement in India. Gokhale is, in a way, Gandhi's political *guru* because he not only familiarised him with the nuances of India's political struggle and gave funds for his one-year trip around the country to get to know the real India, but he himself believed in the promotion of non-violence and reform (although within the system).

The last section is on leftist-socialist thought and discusses six thinkers. This includes a motley of leaders, some of whom were political visionaries of the left or centre-left, and some of whom were activists and leaders whose political thought can be culled from their political actions: Jawaharlal Nehru, Subhas Chandra Bose, M. N. Roy, Ram Manohar Lohia, Jayaprakash Narayan, and Narendra Deva. All these thinker-leaders were leftist or left of centre, but their visions of the nation and nationalism diverged widely. It must also be understood that the socialist movement in India was a form of left nationalism that grew, ideologically and politically, as part of the national movement, and therefore the political thought of the leftists and socialists must be viewed in the context of imperialism, colonialism, and the national movement. They were disappointed with the constitutional drift of the mainstream national movement and wished to incorporate ideas of a socio-economic transformation of India into the nationalist discourse. While M. N. Roy was a communist and founding member of the Communist Party of India (CPI), he broke with the mainstream and promoted a kind of radical humanism called new humanism (Chandra 1992: 152–168; Narisetti 2004). Narendra Deva was a socialist and a founding member of the Congress Socialist Party (CSP), which was responsible for the inclusion of worker's issues into the manifestos of the Indian National Congress. Jayaprakash Narayan, too, was a member and leader of this party, who believed in democratic socialism and after independence, disillusioned with the Congress, led the CSP out of the Congress and formed the Socialist Party. Lohia's importance in political thought consists of the fact that he tried to give a doctrinaire foundation to Indian socialism – his ideas were strongly different from Marxism or other brands of socialism in that he believed the socialist project in India should gain autonomy, both in theory and practice (Tolpadi 2010: 71–77). Jawaharlal Nehru and Subhas Chandra Bose are two vastly different leftists: both were visionaries of what the future India should be, but their political ideas framed different visions. Nehru's ideas of socialism never contained the Marxian concept of class struggle; instead, he believed socialism was not a rigid but a dynamic conception, something that should fit the country's needs. On the other hand, Subhas Chandra Bose, leaving aside his views on the political struggle, did not espouse doctrinaire Marxism and announced at the Haripura Congress (1938) that the State should adopt a comprehensive scheme for socialising both agriculture and industry; to him, liberty signified political, economic, and social freedom.

Each of the thinkers discussed in this book have been critiqued by writers, political scientists, and increasingly, politicians, not only for their ideas and thoughts but also for their actions, since many of the thinkers covered here were thinker-activists, some of them even being activists more than thinkers, their thought and vision having to be culled out of their actions rather than finding them in their writings on political philosophy. In fact, Gokhale, Gandhi, Subhas Bose, Nehru, Jayaprakash Narayan, among others, were all freedom fighters and activists whose ideas developed in their struggle for freedom and in the context of the volatile changing character of the freedom movement and were not thought out in the comfort of homes and study tables where one may have the luxury of having time to read and speculate and form broad theories. Therefore, any critique should factor in the time, situational aspects, India's history at the given space-time, as well as the social and cultural background of the thinker concerned, for a true understanding of his political ideas, his idea of a future India and his actions. The authors of individual chapters have succinctly given the standard critiques of the political thinker that he/she has written on; so, it will just be a duplication to critique them here individually. However, certain points may be raised here of a general nature for speculation, especially in the context of the rapid economic, political, and social changes India is currently undergoing, which raises questions yet again about India as a nation, about what nationalism is, and about issues of nationality. The thinkers discussed in the book were the founding fathers of independent India and its many-hued polity. How relevant are they in the present context?

The simple answer here is that without their contribution to a particular Indian thinking, however multifarious this may have been – a synthesisation of the modern with the traditional, a combination of exogenous ideas with indigenous reality, to envision what would serve the purpose of building an idea of a nation where none had existed in the modern sense earlier – India, as we see it today, however diverse, however muddled, would not have existed. Some authors attempt to categorise Indian thought of this period into three categories: 1) imitative reproduction of the west, 2) revival of classical tradition, and 3) creative blending of both paradigms (Panda and Pujari 2011: 9–17), placing Ram Mohan Roy, Gokhale, Naoroji, and S. N. Banerjee in the first group; Dayānanda Saraswati, Aurobindo, and Vivekananda in the second group; and Ranade, Tilak, Gandhi, and Nehru in the third. This is an oversimplification because all the thinkers mentioned here, as well as those who are not, were products of the indigenisation of liberal ideas that entered India through British education and the creation of modern institutions that were set up to ease colonialism rather than serve the people, which was the purpose of these institutions in Western countries. For instance, Gokhale combined elements of Mazzini's libertarianism with traditional Indian multiculturalism and social reformism of an Indian variety (Valdameri 2015), and his thought was certainly not an imitative repetition of Western ideas. Similarly, Aurobindo and Vivekananda cannot be placed under revival of the classical tradition; Aurobindo's thoughts changed exponentially over time and space, while Vivekananda believed in *karma-yog*, in activism, just like Tilak, Gandhi, and even Subhas Bose, and was far from a revivalist, being a reformer of Hinduism in the line of Ramakrishna, but going beyond in thinking about political, physical as well as spiritual strength.

Even though all the thinkers mentioned here have been critiqued (which is well explained in most of the essays), it may be pertinent to point out that in recent decades the political ideas of our two most important nation-builders have been incrementally critiqued both academically and non-academically: Gandhi and Nehru. While Gandhi has been buffeted around by Marxist, leftist (Desai and Vahed 2015; Anderson 2013), feminist (see Gudavarthy 2008: 83–90) and critics of the far right (cited in Slater 2019; Mantena 2019), Nehru's views and nation-building projects have been the butt of criticism from his politically ideological rivals (Kundu 2019). Gandhi was critiqued in his lifetime by leftists like M. N. Roy, who said "he fed a hungry people 'spiritual moonshine', and the 'cult of nonviolence' was the clever stratagem of the upper class to head off a revolutionary convulsion, without which nationalism will never come into its own" (Roy 1989: 153, 156). Later, Marxist historian Perry Anderson charged that Gandhi's "intellectual development" was "arrested by intense religious belief" (Anderson 2013). Western feminist scholars like Carol Gilligan have likened Gandhi to a "biblical Abraham" (Gilligan 1982: 104–105), while Erik Erikson claims Gandhi subjected the women of Sabarmati Ashram, including his wife, to a kind of psychological violence (Erikson 1969: 230–231), although many Indian women writers acknowledge his contribution in drawing women into the fold of the Indian nationalist movement (Chattopadhyay 1986: 147). Criticisms can be on the basis of one's ideological bent, but the fine print of action must be read along with speeches and writings and contextualised in view of time and social realities when one assesses the political thought of modern Indian thinkers, particularly activists like Gandhi, who had to think not only abstract politico-philosophical thoughts to justify actions but also of strategies on the most effective methods that would be acceptable not only to a populace that was somnolently emerging from millennia of religious dogmatism and patriarchy but also to a liberal British audience who could be prodded into demanding that the moral thing be done by colonial subjects. Violence reacts with violence, and not much is gained except bloodshed. Gandhi's ideas of non-violence, *achhyut-uddhar*, and a future India where the emerging slaves of colonialism would not become slaves of capitalism were churned out in the context of the times in which he lived and require a deeper reading even today. According to Rajmohan Gandhi, the Mahatma's grandson, a "fragment of Gandhi" is being used today to destroy the "core of Gandhi", the "core" being "equality and especially minority rights" (cited in Slater 2019). Today, the Gandhi symbol is being used mainly for the *Swachh Bharat* campaign; while Gandhi did speak of cleanliness, it was certainly not his central message, as is well borne out in his almost 100 volumes of collected works, the central message being a well-thought-out and articulated politics of non-violent dissent.

As far as Nehru is concerned, his contribution to the idea of India has been critiqued passively and actively as a well-designed Nehruvian consensus that depended on uninterrupted Congress rule. Some have called it a carbon copy of the West and his views on secularism as pseudo-secularism, with Nehru skirting the real civilisational-cultural issues of Indian identity under a false garb of secularism. Here, one may ask the critics to remember what Nehru told French intellectual Andre Malraux in 1958 when the latter asked him to identify the greatest challenges he had faced during his 11 years of premiership until then. Nehru replied without hesitation, "creating a just State by just means", and added after a brief pause, "perhaps too creating a secular State in a religious country" (Madan 1997: 245).

V Conclusion

The introductory chapter in no way is meant to be a comprehensive analysis of the political ideas and thought of the 19 modern Indian thinkers included in this study. What I have tried to do is draw the reader's attention to the fact that while some of these political thinkers spilled over into independent India, most of them developed their ideas – even those who became thinker-activists in the post-independence period – within the framework of British colonialism, imperialism and the struggle for, first, an unspecified *swaraj*, which later developed into the full-fledged idea of Indian independence. Since the concept of India as a territorial and politically united entity (let alone a nation) did not exist earlier (at least in the modern form), the discourse that developed centred around the idea of building a nation, but here, given the diversity of India's history, culture and tradition, the question of whose imagined community came to the fore (Chatterjee 1993: 3–13). That is, the idea of the nation as an imagined community varied according to the caste/class background, the religious background, and the educational background of the thinker. It also differed in terms of time and region. The more inclusive the idea of the nation was, the more concrete the concept of nationalism became. Its opposite is also true: the more exclusive the nation, the more exclusive the idea of nationalism and national identity.

The legacy of these 19 thinkers and others who are not examined in these books but who nevertheless helped to shape India as a nation (Pandey 2015; Kumar 1991) can be viewed in context of the fact that India has survived as a democracy to date, unlike most post-colonial States that emerged in South Asia, Southeast Asia, Africa, Latin America and the Middle East, which did not undergo full-fledged colonialism but pseudo-colonialism and authoritarian rule and which succumbed to dictatorships, military rule, theocratic Statehood and one-party dictatorships periodically and for long periods of time. Some of these States were also declared as failed States from time to time. The grounding of the visions that shaped India as a nation was Indian realities combining its past civilisational philosophies with modern Indo-Western ideas to create a strong pluralistic base for a modern State. The fact that the debate on the idea of India continues today only means that the notions and conceptions of these early thinkers were volatile and open-ended, leaving room for further growth and development. Here, one can cite two books that bring the debate to the fore: Sunil Khilnani's *Idea of India* (Khilnani 2017) and Harsh Madhusudan and Rajiv Mantri's *Individual Rights in a Civilizational State: A New Idea of India* (Madhusudan and Mantri 2020). There is no intention here to critique these books since this would take an entire chapter, but it needs to be mentioned that while the first book has been appreciated by many critics of the centre and centre-left, the latter has been applauded by those on the right. In the current political context, while the legacy of many of the early thinker-activist-politicians have not been ignored, they are largely in the limelight for many of the wrong reasons, with some of their ideas and words being appropriated to support certain political biases, while the rest are relegated to the dustbin of history. But what should not be forgotten is that the modern Indian State is built on the edifices of the ideas of these thinkers and ignoring them is akin to throwing the baby out with the bathwater. India is certainly a civilisational State, and all the thinkers discussed in this book were inspired by the very fact of India's long and glorious civilisation, but India's civilisation was a synthesis of all that had gone before; it was syncretic and not exclusive, inclusive of waves of civilisation, not dead, sticking to only one type of thinking. That is what made the majoritarian religion, Hinduism, so volatile – because it was so adaptable; there is no exclusive form of Hinduism. And that is what brings me to my point – there is no exclusive idea of India, there never was, and hopefully there never will be. Each of the thinkers discussed in this book had his/her own vision of India, although there was considerable overlap, as there should be because ancient and medieval Indian political philosophy was also multi-hued and varied, and the legacy of syncretic thinking was passed on to the political thinkers discussed here. Additionally, because their ideas are so varied, we have the capacity and space to continue their debates, that is, their legacy.

The Indian experience of the emergence and consolidation of modern Indian thought was a unique one in that India had a long history of social-political thought, ideas on governance and administration as well as political traditions that were deep rooted: hence, there was much to draw from in addition to the influx of new ideas on liberalism, capitalism, communism, etc. that informed past traditions. The result was not an emulation of Western thought or a rejection of the old. Instead, what developed was an exceptional synthesis of Western thought with Indian thought, rich and varied, with different conceptions of what the independent State should be – and, given the diversity of India, typically Indian in its range and variety.

References

Ahmad, A. (1962). "Trends in the Political Thought of Medieval Muslim India." *Studia Islamica*, No. 17. https://doi.org/10.2307/1595004.
Anderson, P. (2013). *The Indian Ideology*. London: Verso.
Bevir, M. (Ed.). (2010). *Encyclopedia of Political Theory: A to E*. Los Angeles: Sage Publications.
Borsa, G. (1977). *Le originidelnazionalismo in Asia Orientale* (edited by G. C. Calza). Pavia: Università di Pavia, 1965, in Giorgio Borsa, *La nascita del mondomoderno in Asia Orientale. La penetrazione Europea e la crisidellesocietàtradizionali in India, Cina e Giappone*. Milano: Rizzoli, 1977, as cited in Elena Valdameri, "The Influence of Liberalism in the Definition of the Idea of the Nation", vol. 8, 2015: Entre la Révolution et l'Empire: une nouvelle politique dans l'océan Indien, *La Revolution Francaise*, available at https://journals.openedition.org/lrf/1333, accessed on September 18, 2018.
Chakrabarty, B., and Pandey, R. K. (2009). *Modern Indian Political Thought: Text and Context*. New Delhi: Sage.
Chandra, P. (1992). *Political Philosophy of M. N. Roy*. New Delhi: Sarup & Sons.

Chatterjee, P. (1993). "Whose Imagined Community?" In P. Chatterjee (ed.), *The Nation and Its Fragments: Colonial and Postcolonial Histories*. Princeton, NJ: Princeton University Press.

Chattopadhyay, K. (1986). *Inner Recesses, Outer Spaces*. New Delhi: Navrang.

Desai, A., and Vahed, G. H. (2015). *The South African Gandhi: The Stretcher-Bearer of Empire*. Redwood City, CA: Stanford University Press.

Erikson, E. H. (1969). *Gandhi's Truth: On the Origins of Militant Non-violence*. New York: W.W. Norton.

Gandhi, M. K. (1922). *Young India*, Vol. 2, No. 3, cited in M. Ram Murty, *Indian Philosophy: An Introduction*. Peterborough, Canada: Broadview Press, 2012.

Gilligan, C. (1982). *In a Different Voice: Psychological Theory and Women's Development*. Cambridge, MA: Harvard University Press.

Golwalkar, M. S. (1939). *We or Our Nationhood Defined*. Nagpur: Bharat Publications, available at sanjeev.sabhlokcity.com/Misc/We-or-Our-Nationhood-Defined-Shri-M-S-Golwalkar.pdf, accessed on October 3, 2018.

Gould, J., and Kolb, W. L. (1964). *A Dictionary of the Social Sciences*. London: Tavistock Publications.

Gudavarthy, A. (2008). "Gandhi, Dalits and Feminists: Recovering the Convergence." *Economic and Political Weekly*. Mumbai. Vol. 43, No. 22. May 31–June 6.

Jalal, A. (2001). "Nationalism in South Asia." In A. J. Motyl (ed.), *Encyclopedia of Nationalism*. San Diego, CA: Academic Press.

Kaviraj, S. (2000). "Modernity and Politics in India." In *Daedalus*. Cambridge, MA: The MIT Press. Vol. 129, No. 1. Winter.

Kaviraj, S. (2010). *The Imaginary Institutions of India: Politics and Ideas*. New York: Columbia University Press.

Khilnani, S. (2017). *The Idea of India*. New York: Farrar, Straus and Giroux, Anniversary Edition.

Kumar, R. (Ed.). (1991). *Life and Work of Sardar Vallabhbhai Patel*. New Delhi: Atlantic Publishers.

Kundu, S. (2019). "Nehru-bashing: A Full Time Preoccupation for BJP." *Deccan Herald*. Bengaluru. November 14. DH Web Desk, November 14 2019, 17:53 ISTUPDATED: November 15 2019, 19:01 IST, available at www.deccanherald.com/national/national-politics/nehru-bashing-a-full-time-preoccupation-for-bjp-776231.html, accessed on October 10, 2020.

Madan, T. (1997). *Modern Myths, Locked Minds*. Delhi: Oxford University Press.

Madhusudan, H. G., and Mantri, R. (2020). *Individual Rights in a Civilizational State: A New Idea of India*. Chennai: Westland.

Maloni, R. (2010). "Propaganda and Legitimacy of Regime: Akbar and AbulFazl." *Journal of History and Social Sciences*. Allahabad. Vol. 1, No. 1, July–December, available at http://jhss.org/archivearticleview.php?artid=91, accessed on September 18, 2018.

Mantena, K. (2019). "Gandhi and Modern Political Thought." *Hindustan Times*. New Delhi, October 1, available at www.Hindustantimes.com/analysis/gandhi-and-modern-political-thought/story-NhdW8jiYZ3ybPHnPfJfR0J.html, accessed on October 12, 2020.

Narisetti, I. (Compiled) (2004). *M. N. Roy: Radical Humanist, Selected Writings*. New York: Prometheus Books.

Nath, S. (2014). "Changing Trajectories of Indian Political Thought." *Südasien-Chronik - South Asia Chronicle*. Berlin. Vol. 4, available at https://edoc.hu-berlin.de/bitstream/handle/18452/9137/24.pdf?sequence=1, accessed on September 12, 2018.

Panda, S., and Pujari, M. R. (2011). "Themes and Trends in Indian Political Thought." *The Indian Journal of Political Science*. Vol. 72, No. 1, available at JSTOR, www.jstor.org/stable/42761803, accessed November 9, 2020.

Pandey, V. (2015). *Pandit Madan Mohan Malaviya and the Formative Years of Indian Nationalism*. New Delhi: LG Publishers.

Paracha, N. F. (2016). "The Forgotten Future: Sir Syed and the Birth of Muslim Nationalism in South Asia." *Dawn*, August 15, 2016, available at www.dawn.com/news/1277341, accessed on September 18, 2018.

Roy, M. N. (1989). "The Cult of Non-violence: It's Socio-Economical Background." In M. N. Roy (ed.), *Selected Writings*. Vol. II. Delhi: Oxford University Press.

Savarkar, V. D. (n.d.). *Essentials of Hindutva*, available at http://savarkar.org/en/encyc/2017/5/23/2_12_12_04_essentials_of_Hindutva.v001.pdf_1.pdf, accessed on October 3, 2018.

Sen, A. (2005). *The Argumentative Indian: Writings on Indian History, Culture and Identity*. London: Allen Lane.

Slater, J. (2019). "A Hero to the World, Gandhi Is Increasingly Controversial in India." *Washington Post*. Washington, DC, October 2, available at www.washingtonpost.com/world/asia_pacific/a-hero-to-the-world-gandhi-is-increasingly-controversial-in-india/2019/10/02/556be3ee-e3a7-11e9-b0a6-3d03721b85ef_story.html, accessed on October 12, 2010.

Tolpadi, R. (2010). "Context, Discourse and Vision of Lohia's Socialism." *Economic and Political Weekly*, October 2, Vol. XLV, No. 40, pp. 71–77.

Vajpeyi, A. (2012). *Righteous Republic: The Political Foundations of Modern India*. Cambridge, MA: Harvard University Press.

Valdameri, E. (2015). "The Influence of Liberalism in the Definition of the Idea of the Nation in India." *La Révolution française* [Online]. Vol. 8. https://doi.org/10.4000/lrf. 1333, Online since June 24, 2015, available at http://journals.openedition.org/lrf/1333, accessed on November 12, 2020.

PART I
Liberal-reformist thought

1

RAM MOHAN ROY

Anuranjita Wadhwa

> *The present system of Hindus is not well calculated to promote their Political Interests. It is necessary that some change should take place in their religion at least for the sake of Political advantage and Social comfort.*
> – Raja Ram Mohan Roy (cited in Majumdar 1967: 24)

I Introduction

Raja Ram Mohan Roy is hailed as the inaugurator of the Modern Age in India. He surged ahead with his tools despite several obstacles; his view to achieve his earmarked goals undoubtedly earned him the appreciation and quality of an Indian patriot. He initiated social reform in the prevalent Hindu social structure. His contribution to the uplifting of Indian society from decadence of socio-religious backwardness signifies a kind of break with the traditions inherited by his generation. Ram Mohan's originality and greatness lay in his attempt to synthesise Hindu, Islamic, and Western traditions. This implied discrimination and systematic choice, directed by the strands of reason and social comfort. Ram Mohan was a precursor to the awakening of Indian consciousness from the slumbers of socio-religious backwardness in a society ridden with discrimination. His questioning mind led him to assess the worthiness of an idea or an action. His quest for truth in the society of his times continued throughout his life. Tolerance became the key word of his mission to bring out the best in human beings. This quality transcended all narrow frontiers to a vision of a universal man, 'Raja Ram Mohan Roy', who truly appears to illuminate the depths of darkness fully entrenched in nineteenth-century India. Susobhan Sarkar wrote:

> The central characteristics in the life and thoughts of Ram Mohan Roy were his keen consciousness of the stagnant, degraded and corrupt State

into which our society had fallen, his deep love of the people which sought their all-round regeneration, his critical appreciation of the value of modern Western culture and the ancient wisdom of the East alike, and his many untiring efforts in fighting for improving conditions around him.

(cited in Barua 1988: 79)

His holistic approach towards life blossomed into a multifaceted personality with numerous social concerns. His socio-religious ideas, advocacy of the rights of man, particularly freedom of press, indicates a total view of man and society. The wide spectrum of his activities coincided with the range of his interests and concerns.

II Life sketch

Raja Ram Mohan Roy was born on 14 August 1774 to Ramakanta Roy and Tarini Devi in Radhanagar village of Hoogly district, Bengal Presidency. His father was a wealthy *Brāhmin* and orthodox individual and strictly followed religious duties. He was a revenue official and dependent land holder under the *maharani* of Burdwan. At the age of 14, Ram Mohan expressed his desire to become a monk, but his mother vehemently opposed the idea and he dropped it. Following the traditions of the time, Ram Mohan had a child marriage at the age of nine, but his first wife died soon after the marriage. He was married for a second time at ten and had two sons from the marriage. After the death of his second wife in 1826, he married for a third time, and his third wife outlived him.

Though his father was very orthodox, he wanted his son to pursue higher education. Ram Mohan got Bengali and Sanskrit education from the village school. After that, he was sent to Patna to study Persian and Arabic in a *madrasa*. Persian and Arabic were in high demand at that time, as it was still the court language of the Mughal emperors. He studied the *Qur'ān* and other Islamic scriptures. After he completed his studies in Patna, Ram Mohan went to Benaras (Kashi) to learn Sanskrit. He mastered the language in no time and began studying scriptures, including the *Vedās* and *Upaniṣhads*. He learnt English at the age of 22. He read the works of philosophers, like Euclid and Aristotle, which helped shape his spiritual and religious conscience.

In 1803, Ram Mohan went to Murshidabad after the death of his father. In 1809, he entered the services of the East India Company as a clerk. He worked in the Collectorate of Rangpur, under Mr John Digby. He was eventually promoted to be a *dewan*, a post that referred to a native officer entrusted with the role of collecting revenues. But in 1814, he gave up his service under the East India Company and went to Calcutta. In 1816, he started the *Atmiya Sabha* – "spiritual society". In 1818, Ram Mohan began his celebrated crusade for the abolition of *sati*, and in 1829 Lord William Bentick, the Governor General of India, declared *sati* illegal by Regulation XVII. Ram Mohan's crusade to free

Indian women from the ill practices prevalent at that time certainly won immortal recognition (Varma 1974: 16–17).

III Liberalism and Indian renaissance

In the backdrop of British domination over India, a new middle class grew in Bengal. Western education had created revolutionary thinkers imbibed with the characteristics of Western education, such as rationalism, intellectualism, individualism, a critical attitude towards scriptures, and a synthetic approach to religion, secularism, cosmopolitanism, and humanism. The spread of Western education led to the inauguration of new awakening in India heralded by Ram Mohan. The liberal and revivalist thoughts of nineteenth-century India were greatly influenced by the liberal thoughts of the West, which stemmed from the renaissance in Europe in the fifteenth century. The European renaissance was a reassertion of classical rationalism. It was with a sharp gesture of impatience that Europe turned away from the vast literature of scholastic commentaries which the pendants of the Middle Ages had created (Tagore 1975: 1). The flowering of Indian renaissance in the nineteenth century had two fundamental concepts not found in fifteenth-century Europe. Ram Mohan had not failed to notice plural religions on the Indian soil and the lack of amity amongst them. Thus, the synthesis of the religions and unqualified support to democratic struggles for freedom of oppressed people around the world were important ideals towards which Ram Mohan strived, and he had to choose his own path.

As the "Father of Modern India", Raja Ram Mohan Roy is regarded as the pioneer of all religious, social, and educational reforms in the Hindu community in the nineteenth century. As a father of modern Hindu reform, Ram Mohan identified a break with tradition. To restore the moral and rational basis of Hinduism, Ram Mohan championed a version of monotheism. To resuscitate classical Hinduism, Ram Mohan upheld that true realisation of man is his inner consciousness. His rationalistic mental makeup is clearly implicit in his writing *Tuhfat-ul-Muwahhidin*, written in Persian. Through this writing, Ram Mohan points out the general unity of thought among all human beings regarding belief in the existence of one Supreme Being (Tagore 1975: 7–9). He noted that "by giving peculiar attributes to that Being and . . . by holding different creeds consisting of the doctrines of religion and precepts of *haram* (the forbidden) and *halal* (the legal)" (Bishop 1982: 35), people develop discord amongst themselves. Thus, Ram Mohan concluded that the reformation of religion is a prerequisite for social reform and modernisation. Accordingly, he founded the *Atmiya Sabha* in 1815, the Calcutta Unitarian Association in 1821 and the *Brahmo Sabha*, or the Congregation of the Absolute, in 1828.

The *Brahmo Samaj* was founded to promote the vision of Hindu monotheism. Ram Mohan worked to deliver to the world the idea that the crux of all religion is the dichotomy between religion and morality. The belief in one ultimate being who is regulating the collective universe was the teaching of *Brahmo Samaj*, and the realisation of this power could be made through compassion and benevolence towards our fellow beings. *Brahmo Samaj*, popularly called the "society of worshippers", met for the first time in Calcutta on 20 August 1828. Without any organisation or membership, the gathering were encouraged to feel the presence of Supreme God, which Ram Mohan referred to after his reading of *Upaniṣhads*, called *Vedānta*. The year 1830 was marked by a new level of organisation and accomplishment with the publication of the *Brahmo Trust Deed*. With this document, Ram Mohan's desire to create a public form of worship of the ultimate Being irrespective of creed is translated to inculcate the spirit of service to mankind.

Ram Mohan's idea of a unitarian God was directed in eradicating idolatry and polytheism. He believed monotheism paved the way for a universal moral order based on reason. The significance of this was recognised by Bentham when he wrote, "Ram Mohan Roy had cast off thirty three million of Gods and had learnt from us to embrace reason in all the important aspect of religion" (cited in Hatcher 2006: 57–80).[1]

IV Social and religious reforms

The reform movement spearheaded under Ram Mohan's leadership challenged the religious ideas and practices of orthodox Hindu religion. Of all the abominations associated with the faith of the Hindus, which had become the object of derision of the people of an enlightened world, perhaps the greatest was the custom of *sati*, or woman burning. Ram Mohan from an early period came to abhor the custom of blood and murder connected with religious belief and practices. But moral pressure as well as other difficulties had their effect. This provided an apt canvass for Ram Mohan and his liberal group to launch their campaign against the inhuman custom, not only by counter-petitioning government but by publishing tracts to show that the practice was not approved by the Hindu *Śhāstras*, as had been asserted by its votaries. The appearance of Ram Mohan's first tract on *sati* was an innovation for the philanthropist, humanist, and administrator alike. The *Calcutta Gazette* remarked:

> The question itself is of the highest importance, and the true interpretation of the religious law which has stained the domestic history of India for so many ages with blood will no doubt diminish, if not extinguish the desire for self-immolation. The safest way of coming to a right understanding on a point so interesting to humanity, is a rigid investigation of the rules of conduct laid down in the books which are considered sacred by the Hindus.
> *(Sarkar 1975: 114)*

The government could not act against the barbarous act and continued to follow the policy of religious tolerance. They were reluctant to authorise a general prohibition and satisfied themselves by giving a wide discretion to the local authorities regarding the prevention of the custom. The assumption of the office of Governor-General by Lord Bentinck in 1828 gave a new aspect to the agitation. He was one of those who strongly felt that time had come for the heinous practice to be prohibited by legislation with safety. It was largely the efforts of Ram Mohan that yielded to the adoption of the bold and forward measure for the prohibition of the detestable practice in 1829.

The emancipation of women from centuries-old traditions did not stop with the abolition of *sati*; Ram Mohan also advocated other progressive social reforms, such as the prevention of *Koolinism* and the sale of girls, the introduction of widow remarriage, female education, and women's right to property (Majumdar 1941: xxviii–xxxix). Ram Mohan tried to prove the unjustifiability of the caste by holding that "God makes no distinction of caste and that our division into castes . . . has the source of want of unity among us" (Bishop 1982: 21).

V Political ideas

Social and religious reform movements were considered a precursor to India's political advancement. Ram Mohan considered the prevalent social and religious aberrations as causes responsible for India's falling prey to foreign conquest and social degeneration. He stated his convictions on political advancement in the following words:

> I regret to say that the present system of religion adhered to by the Hindus is not well calculated to promote their political interest. The distinction of castes, introducing innumerable divisions and sub-divisions among them, has entirely deprived them of political feeling, and the multitude of religious rites and ceremonies. . . . I think, necessary changes should take place in their religion at least for the sake of political advantage and social comfort.
>
> *(cited in Chandra 1989: 76)*

Ram Mohan idealised Indian society on the lines of democratic values propagated in the West and desired to amalgamate Western liberal learning and Western ethics in the Indian social structure. He believed the Western system was conducive to the enjoyment of extensive civil and political rights. Ram Mohan thus appreciated the liberal aspects of British rule, and his political thought incorporated these aspects. After a thorough study of the English Constitution, Ram Mohan strongly made a demand for individual liberty as enjoyed by the masses in the West. He had a passionate love for liberty of thought. The universal appeal of liberty transformed along political lines with nationalism making ground on the Indian soil.

Ram Mohan, though appreciative of the British rule, was equally vociferous in condemning unjust measures. His protest of the Press Ordinance of 1823 and the Jury Act of 1827 demonstrates the point. These acts paved the way for constitutional agitation for reforms within the existing framework through a major part of nineteenth-century India. He firmly believed the association of India with modern culture would enable the traditional society to modernise and establish a democratic institution. Fully aware of the political machinery ruling over India, Ram Mohan submitted his considered views in the form of his "Communications to the Board of Control" during his visit to England. In these, Ram Mohan suggested the appointment of Indian judicial accessories: joint judges, well-defined codes of civil and criminal laws, separation of the executive from the judiciary, reduction of government expenditure, and the abolition of the standing army and its replacement by a people's militia.

Freedom of press

Ram Mohan passionately advocated freedom of thought. Freedom of press was another important agenda in his programme of political reform. The freedom of press facilitated social, educational, economic, political, and religious reforms. Ram Mohan outlined the necessity of free press as a foremost condition necessary to secure laws beneficial to India. He fought for the freedom of press not because this was an ancient birthright but because he considered a free press essential for the social and economic progress of the community, for the diffusion of knowledge and for an efficient and just government. Restrictions of the press, he believed, would preclude the natives from communicating "frankly and honestly" to their gracious sovereign in England and his council, the real condition of his Majesty's faithful subjects in "this distant part of his dominions" and the treatment they experienced from the local government. The free press, on the other hand, would exercise restraint on the local executive which had absolute power over all the citizens. It would also act as a mirror of public opinion and acquaint the local government with the feelings of its subjects on various government policies. He credited the free press in Bengal with encouraging free discussion, which had "served greatly to improve their [Bengalis] minds and ameliorate their condition" (Nag and Burman 1945: 6–9).

He advanced four arguments in this context: 1) That the freedom of the press would make laws corresponding to public opinion. 2) It would obviate the danger of revolution that might be caused due to underrepresented and un-redressed grievances of the people. 3) It would enable the people of India to appeal to the honour and justice of the British nation against any possible oppressive and tyrannical act of Indian government. 4) The Court of Directors would be able to ascertain correctly whether the systems introduced in their possession proved so beneficial to the natives of the country, as their authors might fondly suppose or would have others believe whether rules and regulations, which may appear excellent in their eyes, are strictly put into practice (Das and Mahapatra 1996: 119–120).

Ram Mohan was fully aware of the stir created by press in European countries and for the onerous task of enlightening his fellow being. Ram Mohan very popularly availed himself of the means that the art of printing had provided. He took to publishing not only books and tracts but newspapers as well, as it, more than anything else, tended to the promotion of good government to the progress of knowledge and information to the enforcement of morality and correction of immorality (Majumdar 1941: iv). Freedom of press, according to Ram Mohan, signified rule of law instead of rule of persons.

Judicial reforms

The judicial system prevalent during the days of the East India Company was in a state of transition. Marred by various shortcomings, Ram Mohan advocated closer association of the people with the institutions of justice. The difficulty in comprehending the problems of the people by the company judges in the languages of the people led to improper readdress of their complaints. Ram Mohan therefore advocated share of Indians in administration who had knowledge of practices and habits of the culture.

Ram Mohan was a prominent figure in the agitations that followed after the British Parliament gave its assent to the Indian Jury Bill (notes) on May 5, 1826.[2] Under this act, both Indo-Britons and Indians were authorised to sit on juries in criminal cases before the Supreme Courts, but a discrimination was made on the rights and privileges of the two communities. While Indo-Britons enjoyed full rights to sit on both grand and petty juries, as well the trials of both Christians and natives, the Indians were given limited rights, as they were allowed to sit on petty juries and in the trials of the natives (Tagore 1975: 79–81).

The government's move to stir up animosity amongst the people of various communities was met with a storm of protest. A petition against the Act was written on August 17, 1829, and signed by Hindus and Muslims. Ram Mohan forwarded the petition to Mr J. Crawford, the agent of the inhabitants of Calcutta in England. Ram Mohan wrote:

> In this famous Jury Bill, Mr Wynn, the late President of the Board of Control, has by introducing religious distinctions into the judicial system of this country, not only just grounds for dissatisfaction among the natives in general, but has excited much alarm in the breast of everyone conversant with political principles. Any natives, either Hindu or Mohammedan, are rendered by this Bill subject to judicial trial by Christians, either European or Native, while Christians including native converts, are exempted from the degradation of being tried either by a Hindu or Mussulman juris, however high he may stand in the estimation of the society. This Bill also denies both to Hindus and Mussalmans the honour of a seat in the Grand Jury even in the trial of fellow – Hindus or Mussalmans. This is the sum total of Mr Wynn's late Jury Bill, of which we bitterly complain.
>
> *(quoted in Ram Mohan Birth Centenary Commemoration)*

Ram Mohan, in a letter to Mr Crawford, had expressed his concern on the advantages flowing from establishing bonds between India and the British Empire. The petition to the British Parliament was presented to the House of Commons on 5 June 1829. The petition created fulminations in the European Press over the decisive role Ram Mohan played in the agitation, demanding rectification of a move to divide people based on their religious beliefs.

VI Plea for modern education

To get rid of the evils keeping Indian society from progress and happiness, Ram Mohan rightly felt the necessity and urgency of the general enlightenment of his countrymen. However, India at no stage of her history been totally illiterate, as every village may be said to have a school to impart education to the boys so they could earn a livelihood. The knowledge gained at these institutions was not calculated to enlighten their minds or to improve their moral feelings. Ram Mohan first came to realise that the time had arrived when something must be done so that India could take her proper place in the world amongst the enlightened countries.

The efforts of the East India authorities for the proper provision of education of its subject had been meager and sporadic. Wherever the institutions were established, they were intended more for the purpose of producing natives able to help the European judges in the judicial administration of the country either as *muftis* or *pandits* than for anything else. While the government was thus engaged in pursuing a policy calculated to encourage orientalism alone, Ram Mohan believed in Occidentalism, thus pursuing a different course. After prolonged deliberations with the English authorities, it was agreed that a college, or *Maha-Vidyalaya*, would be started in 1816. The institution was the first seminary in India and played a most glorious part not only in the matter of education of the native youths but whose alumni in their turn also established English schools in the various parts of the country and were also profitably engaged as teachers in several other institutions (Majumdar 1941: xii).

In 1816–1817, Ram Mohan founded the first English school in Calcutta financed completely by Indians. Ram Mohan's enlightened mind did not rest satisfied with what he could do for the promotion of education of boys alone, he also advocated the education of girls. For the propagation and defense of Hindu Unitarianism, Ram Mohan established the Vedanta College in 1825. Ram Mohan's educational policy was helping India to break from the medieval age of scholasticism and head down the road of modernisation (Tagore 1975: 250).

VII Constitutionalism

Ram Mohan was an ardent supporter of the impersonal authority of law and opposed all kinds of arbitrary and despotic power. He firmly believed in the existence of constitutional government as the best guarantee of human freedom.

He insisted on the use of constitutional means, as when required to safeguard the rights. Drawing heavily on the ideas of Montesquieu and Blackstone, Ram Mohan favoured the separation of powers. Separation of executive and lawmaking functions of the government would not stifle human freedom and dignity. In the wake of debate regarding the future of the Company's administration, Ram Mohan preferred that the legislative authority should vest with the King and the Parliament as the highest sovereign bodies. The distrust in vesting the Government of India with the power to make laws would withhold or put undue restrictions on individual liberty (Majumdar 1967: 26). Ram Mohan was especially concerned in ensuring the autonomy of the peoples' institution by imposing suitable restraints on the powers of the executive.

Liberty was crucial in bringing socio-religious reform in the Indian social fabric. Although Ram Mohan saw the continuance of British rule as beneficial to India in bringing social and religious reforms, he was among the first to speak of political freedom. His agitation against idolatry, the practice of *Sati*, the denial of property rights to women, distrust in the absolute power of the executive, freedom of press, separation of powers, codification of laws, and the necessity of the provision of education were his expression for the uplifting and development of human personality. Ram Mohan's concept of individual freedom thus implied a class society consisting of enlightened free owners. All men are equal in the eyes of God and endowed with the innate quality to free themselves from "the useless restraints of religion" and make "boundless improvement" in intellectual, moral, and social fields.

To Ram Mohan, faith in one God (who is beyond reason) was inseparably connected with his faith in individual freedom. Man must be free to pursue his "worldly affairs" without any "useless religious restraints" and with faith in the omnipresent God. The religious reforms of Ram Mohan aimed at freeing individuals from restraints imposed upon them by religion. These restraints, he believed, denied the Indians "social comfort" and disqualified them from entering difficult economic enterprises. Thus, the freedom of the individual was not an end in itself; rather, it was a means to encourage economic prosperity. To Ram Mohan, as to the English liberal philosophers, freedom (or, as he often called it, "independence of character") was inseparably related to reason and wealth. Man is free as long as he is rational and the owner of his person and capacities.

Ram Mohan was equally a champion of women's rights in India. He laid the foundations of the women's liberation movement in this country. He revolted against the subjection of women and pleaded for the restoration of their rights. He was quick to envision women's independence from the deeply entrenched patriarchal system and help restore the rights of women. According to Ram Mohan, the root cause of the all-around deterioration of Hindu women was the complete denial of their property rights. The Hindu girl was not given the traditional right to share with her brothers the property of her deceased father. The married Hindu woman was refused the right to share with her sons the property left by her deceased husband. In 1822, Ram Mohan, in his book *Brief Remarks*

Regarding Modern Encroachments on the Ancient Right of Females, he pointed out that the ancient Hindu lawgivers gave the mother the right to have an equal share with her sons in the property left by her husband and the daughter to have part of the portion which a son could inherit in the property left by the father. With the passage of time, these rights were gradually taken away by modern lawgivers. The utter helplessness and humiliation of the Hindu widow was a major reason behind the inhuman practice of *Sati*. Women completely robbed of their property rights became economically dependent on male counterparts. Ram Mohan vehemently opposed patriarchal practices and strived for restoring and giving to women their due share.

VIII Humanist vision

In inculcating liberal ideals in a hitherto orthodox, highly conservative, and patriarchal society, Roy saw an opportunity in reforming and humanising the British colony. He saw the advantages accruing from the economic integration of India under the East India Company; at the same time, he spearheaded protest and demanded the reform of discriminatory laws and practices. Both the colonised and colonising societies, he said, must be reformed in their religions, cultures, politics, and economy. The norms and rules were universal and not the monopoly of any civilisation. Being a champion of freedom, Ram Mohan desired to remove all obstacles in the path of the creation of a society premised on tolerance, sympathy, and reason. He believed in tolerance, cooperation, and fellowship. As an exponent of cosmopolitanism, he strived for brotherhood and liberation. A humanist culture needs to be synthesised in respective culture. The synthesis of rationality, deistic strands of Islamic thought, liberal and scientific attitudes of the West and spiritual and communitarian values of the Asian culture needed to be amalgamated in the then emerging world (Pantham 1986: 50).

The fulfilment of the species-wide "social instincts in man" necessitated the removal of barriers imposed by the government of the day. Ram Mohan saw religion as one such barrier and therefore formulated the scheme of fundamental spiritual synthesis, stressing the unity of religious experience based on the worship of a monotheistic God. He wrote, "May God render religion destructive of differences and dislike between man and man and conducive to the peace and union of mankind" (Scott 2016: 85). Ram Mohan also maintained that national sovereignty had to be transcended in solving the problems of the people. He was not giving a blueprint for any organisational or re-structured world; rather, it was the convergence of boundaries to create a humanist and rational world order. Thus, as noted by Brajendranath Seal:

> He paved the way for 'a synthesis between Eastern and Western values and postulates against the common background of humanity'. In other words, he pointed the 'way' to the solution of the larger problem of international

culture and civilisation in human history, and became a precursor . . . a prophet of the coming Humanity.

(cited in Pantham 1986: 50–51)

IX Conclusion

Ram Mohan played a prominent part in popularising liberal ideas in India. His firm conviction in liberal values and consequent demand for the people of India is the most significant political legacy inherited by the coming generation. The line of agitation in the form of petition, pleas, and protest prepared the ground for a national movement to make ground and further the cause of liberation of the masses from inhuman, unjust practices and laws. Backed by a robust intellect and a high degree of rational view, the dynamic personality of Ram Mohan Roy, as Tagore puts it, "vitalised our national being with the urgency of creative endeavour and launched it into the arduous adventure of self-realisation. He is the great path-maker of this country, who has removed ponderous obstacles that impeded our progress at every step" (Das and Mahapatra 1996: 61). "Ram Mohan stands forth as the tribute of new Bengal" (Collet and Sarkar 1914: 155).

Ram Mohan was a patriot who felt concerned at the subordinate and degrading position of Indians in different spheres and desired to uplift them through various reforms pertaining to social and religious matters. The charismatic personality of Ram Mohan, who by virtue of his mission proclaims a religious doctrine or divine commandment, led to the initial success of *Brahmoism*.

However, the vision of charisma did not occur after Ram Mohan's departure to England in 1830 nor after his death there in 1833. The energy and activities of *Brahmo Samaj* were severely weakened. J. N. Farquhar remarked that "The death of the founder was almost fatal to the infant society" (Farquhar 1915: 63). With the dwindling of weekly meetings, it seemed that Ram Mohan's vision would soon fade into memory. However, the concerted efforts of Ramchandra Vidyavagisa were instrumental to keeping the spirit of *Brahmo Samaj* alive. He continued with the weekly meetings, as directed by Ram Mohan, continuing to preach the *Upaniṣhadic* theology. The sustained efforts of Ramchandra could not be sustained for long, as the *Samaj* started facing competition from various religious, social, and political ideologies. The *Samaj* faced numerous challenges on at least three fronts: from English-educated Hindu youth, from Christian missionaries, and from advocates of existing forms of Hindu orthodoxy, leaving new spaces for new beliefs to open up. In a pluralistic world of competitive claims and social groups, the *Samaj* started losing its ground. As Amiya Kumar Sen has noted, "many members of the *Samaj* at this time simply accepted its principles intellectually and did not follow them in their daily lives and activities" (Sen 1979: 65–66). Ram Mohan adopted the path of reform within technique, revealing his eclecticism – his desire to do all things to all people. His later writings and activities left a permanent legacy in the shape of *Brahmo Samaj*. "In the encircling gloom, Roy's sense of hope, faith and optimism backed by action made a move for change" (Barua 1988: 92).

Ram Mohan's attitude towards British rule was considered deliverance from Muslim tyranny, even though he did focus on moderate constitutionalist agitation, such as the Indianisation of services, trial by jury, separation of powers, freedom of the press, and others. In the *Bengal Herald*, he announced its objective, an opposition "equally to anarchy as to despotism".

To conclude, Ram Mohan's achievement as a moderniser was limited and ambivalent. We can appreciate the man and his work with a degree of sensitivity if we view him against the background of the times in which he lived. The limitations were basically those of his time, which marked the beginning of a transition from a pre-capitalist society, not in the direction of full-blooded bourgeois modernity but of a weak and distorted caricature of the same which the colonial subjection permitted. However, much of the criticism directed against him is motivated by a desire to validate a defence of the socio-religious status quo (Sarkar 1975: 44–46).

Ram Mohan's questioning mind led him to adopt a rational approach, which is a source of solace to a man seeking peace and harmony within and for himself. Tolerance is the child of rationalism. Ram Mohan concluded that tolerance brings forth the inner nature of man, underlines basic humanity and is the source of building blocks amongst men, giving life to the Indian social structure embedded by the gloom and darkness of medieval times. Ram Mohan did pioneering work in promoting rationalism through his ideals and activities.

However strong the inclination of the British might have been to uplift Indians from the slough of despondency, another condition was to be fulfilled and that was for the real and patriotic sons of the soil to come forward with bold and enlightened hearts to grasp the new ideas and ideals, as well as to avail themselves of the opportunities and possibilities that were present by the changed circumstances. This happened as never before with the advent of Ram Mohan on the public arena as a pioneer amongst the people of his country.

Notes

1 Bentham admired Ram Mohan's universalism and humanitarianism. In a letter to Ram Mohan, Bentham addresses him as "Intensely admired and dearly beloved collaborator in the Service of Mankind". See Ghosh, Jogendra Chandra. (1901). *The English works of Raja Ram Mohan Roy*. Calcutta: Srikanto Roy.
2 The Indian Jury Bill 1836, also known as the Wynn Act. William Wynn, the President of the Board of Control, was persuaded to introduce the Indian Jury Bill and had it passed by the British Parliament on 5 May 1826.

References

Barua, B. P. (Ed.). (1988). *Raja Ram Mohan Roy and the New Learning*. Calcutta: Orient Longman.

Bishop, D. H. (Eds.). (1982). *Thinkers of the Indian Renaissance*. New Delhi: Wiley Eastern.
Chandra, B. (1989). *India's Struggle for Freedom 1857–1947*. New Delhi: Penguin Books.
Collet, S. D., and Sarkar, H. C. (Eds.). (1914). *The Life and Letters of Raja Rammohun Roy*. Whitefish, MT: Kessinger Publishing.
Das, H. H., and Mahapatra, S. (Eds.). (1996). *The Indian Renaissance and Raja Ram Mohan Roy*. Jaipur: Pointer Publisher.
Farquhar, J. N. (1915). *Modern Religious Movements in India*. New York: The Macmillan.
Ghosh, J. C. (Ed.). (1901). *The English Works of Raja Ram Mohan Roy*, Vol. I. Calcutta: Srikanta Roy.
Hatcher, B. A. (2006). Remembering Ram Mohan: An Essay on the (re)-Emergence of Modern Hinduism. *History of Religions*, August, Vol. 46(1), pp. 50–80.
Majumdar, B. (1967). *History of Indian Social and Political Ideas (From Rammohan to Dayananda)*. Calcutta: Bookland.
Majumdar, J. K. (1941). *Raja Ram Mohan Roy and Progressive Movements in India*. Calcutta: Art Press.
Nag, K., and Burman, D. (Eds.). (1945). *The English Works of Raja Rammohan Roy* (6 Vols.). Calcutta: Sadharan Brahmo Samaj.
Pantham, T. (1986). The Socio-Religious and Political Thought of Ram Mohan Roy. In T. Pantham and K. L. Deutsch (Eds.), *Political Thought in Modern India*. New Delhi: Sage Publications.
Sarkar, S. (1975). Ram Mohan Roy and the Break with the Past. In V. C. Joshi (Ed.), *Ram Mohan Roy and the Process of Modernization in India*. New Delhi: Vikas Publishing House.
Scott, J. B. (2016). *Spiritual Despots: Modern Hinduism and the Genealogies of Self-Rule*. Chicago: The University of Chicago Press.
Sen, A. K. (1979). *Tattwabodhini Patrika and the Bengal Renaissance*. Calcutta: Sadharan Brahmo Samaj.
Tagore, S. (1975). *Ram Mohan Roy: His Role in Indian Renaissance*. Calcutta: The Asiatic Society.
The Father of Modern India, Ram Mohan Birth Centenary Commemoration Volume. Calcutta, 1935.
Varma, V. P. (1974). *Modern Indian Political Thought*. Agra: Lakshmi Narain Agarwal Educational Publishers.

2
ISHWAR CHANDRA VIDYASAGAR

Sibaji Pratim Basu

> *Unfortunately bound by the constraints of customs of shastras, we are forever suffering from the endless misery and irredeemable predicament of child marriage.*
> – Pandit Ishwar Chandra Vidyasagar (Sen 1977: 53)

I Introduction

Pandit Ishwar Chandra Vidyasagar, born as Ishwar Chandra Bandyopadhyay (1820–1891), was one of the key figures of India's renaissance in the nineteenth century. A polymath in the true sense of the term, he was an educationist, a social reformer, and above all, a philanthropist extraordinaire. It was due to his vast erudition that the title of Vidyasagar – the sea of knowledge – was conferred on him. He dedicated his life to women's empowerment and prosperity through education and social reforms. For all his passionate zeal for the uplifting of women and downtrodden and distressed people, he was also adoringly called "*dayar sagar*" in Bengali, which literally means "ocean of kindness". He was also the father of the modern Bengali school system, textbooks, and press. Although deeply influenced by modern Western knowledge, rationalism, and strength of character based on the ideals of the renaissance and enlightenment, he always stood upright with his native identity (like dress and language) and dared to challenge the colonisers when the need arose. But to analyse and critically appreciate his contributions to modern Indian social and political thought, one must put this great man in his historical context.

By the beginning of the nineteenth century, the control of the British East India Company, especially over the Bengal Presidency, was supreme and ubiquitous. With the restructuring of the revenue system, judiciary system and administration, along with new/modern educational systems and social reforms from Warren Hastings (1773–1785) to William Bentinck (1828–1835) through Lord

Cornwallis (1786–1793), the British created a new Bengal, which later became the foundation of the British Empire in India.

The new institutions of learning and initiatives of social reforms inspired the early generations of Indians and especially the Bengalis, who witnessed an intellectual awakening similar to the renaissance in Europe during the sixteenth century. This movement, popularly known as the Bengal renaissance, questioned existing orthodoxies, particularly with respect to women, marriage, the dowry system, the caste system, and religion. Although there is controversy over the term "Bengal renaissance" (Sarkar 1970), this movement was influenced by the values of the European enlightenment of the late eighteenth century and the concept of modernity borne out of it. Some of such values were the belief in and ideas of progress, universal rationalism, secular and scientific education, etc. Thus, the question of imparting modern education to native Indians also occupied a crucial space in the early years of the Bengal renaissance.

The first institution for imparting modern and secular education to the native boys came up in the second decade of the nineteenth century in the form of Hindu College (1917). The college, modelled on the English system of education, had English as the medium of instruction. Soon Hindu College became the centre for modern learning for Indian boys. In 1926, a young man joined the institution at the age of 17 as a teacher of English literature and history. His name was Henry Louis Vivian Derozio (18 April 1809–26 December 1831). His intense zeal for teaching and his interactions with students created a sensation at Hindu College. His students, known as Derozians, participated in debates that Derozio organised in which ideas and social norms were freely discussed. The unorthodox (legendarily free) views on society, culture, and religion, soon took the form of a movement known as the Young Bengal. However, the Bengali Hindu society of that time did not approve of the views and reckless life of Derozio's followers.

Almost at this time, the socio-religious movement *Brahmo Samaj* was founded by Raja Ram Mohan Roy (1772–1883) in the name of *Brahmo Sabha* in 1828. Although it traced its intellectual roots to the *Upaniṣhads*, the *Brahmo* version of Hinduism was actually a critique of contemporary Hinduism and social practices, like *sati* and polygamy, associated with Hinduism of that period. Moreover, it was ultimately a rigid, impersonal, monotheistic faith, which actually was quite distinct from the pluralistic and multifaceted nature of the way the Hindu religion was practiced.

In such a socio-religious context, when the modern educated section of the Indian society bore a profound contempt for everything associated with native Indian (from language to literature to the school system to religion), Pandit Ishwar Chandra Vidyasagar treaded a unique path for reforms of education and society in Bengal and India. Amalesh Tripathy (1974: 1) calls him 'the traditional moderniser' since although he understood the value of modern and rational education but never followed the path of the Derozians (whose activities he witnessed as a young student in Sanskrit College). Instead, he used Sanskrit to develop Bengali as a modern language, wrote popular textbooks (many of which were based on Western knowledge) and founded many modern vernacular schools (in place of traditional *Tola/Chatushpathi* or *Madrasa/Maqtab*), including schools for girls. In this way, he helped the common Bengali native society to imbibe modern and rational values without attending English schools. Secondly, despite being a rational person (almost an atheist), he never joined the *Brahmo* movement (fashionable for the educated people of his time) and sought to initiate social reforms (like widow remarriage or the prevention of polygamy) based on arguments citing the references of age-old codes and laws accepted by the traditional Hindu society. But before we go further, let us take a quick look at his legendary life.

II Life sketch

Let us begin with the famous words of Acharya Ramendra Sundar Tribedi (1864–1919), author, educator, and popular science writer, who commented on Pandit Ishwar Chandra Vidyasagar two decades after his demise and summed up his tribute as follows: "There is a machine called a microscope which shows smaller things as bigger. . . . But [an attempt towards writing] a biography of Vidyasagar is like a machine to turn the bigger [i.e. Vidyasagar] into smaller" (Tribedi 1958). Likewise, we can only get a few glimpses of the life of one of the greatest stalwarts of modern India.

Ishwar Chandra Bandyopadhyay was born into a poor *Brāhmin* family on 26 September 1820 in Birsingha village. The village belonged to the Ghatal subdivision of Hooghly district of British Bengal, which later became a part of Midnapore district and is now West Midnapore district of West Bengal. His father, Thakurdas Bandyopadhyay, was known for his honesty in the locality, and his mother, Bhagavati Devi, was so compassionate towards the poor and distressed that it made an indelible imprint on Vidyasagar's heart since childhood.

Vidyasagar had his early education in the village *pathshala*. In 1829, at the age of nine, he joined Sanskrit College, Calcutta (now Kolkata). His quest for knowledge was so intense that he used to study under a streetlamp, as it was not possible for him to afford a gas lamp at home. He passed out of the college in 1841, qualifying in Sanskrit grammar, literature, dialectics [*alankara śhāstra*], *Vedānta*, *Smṛiti*, and astronomy, and earned the title 'Vidyasagar' for his outstanding knowledge in every field of his studies.

Before 1839, Vidyasagar also successfully cleared his law examination. In 1841, at the age of 21, he joined Fort William College (an institution to train the British civil servants in oriental/Indian culture and language) as the head of the Sanskrit department. After five years, in 1846, Vidyasagar left Fort William College and joined Sanskrit College as an assistant secretary. In his first year of service, Vidyasagar recommended several changes to the existing education system. This report resulted in a serious altercation between Vidyasagar and College Secretary Rasomoy Dutta (Vidyasagar 2016: 18). In 1849, Vidyasagar, against the advice of Rasomoy Dutta, resigned from Sanskrit College and re-joined Fort William College as the head clerk. Vidyasagar came back to Sanskrit College on the request of a higher authority there and redesigned and improved the old college system. Within two years, he progressed to the post of principal in Sanskrit College and then to inspector of schools in 1855.

Vidyasagar always raised his voice about the oppression that the miserable society inflicted on women and uplifted the status of women in India and in his native Bengal. He was close to his mother, who directed him to do some reforms to palliate the helpless situation of Hindu widows. His mother was a woman of great character, and her advice was helpful for Vidyasagar to raise his voice against barbarism and brutality. There was no social justice for women, and they were treated as a burden. Vidyasagar made it his mission to improve the situation and quality of life for helpless poor widows. He claimed that the remarriage of widows is sanctioned by *Vedic* scriptures. He challenged the *Brāhminical* society and then faced opposition from orthodox societies. He took his authentic arguments about widow's remarriage to the British authorities. His pleas were heard, and his arguments were accepted when the Hindu Widow Remarriage Act of 1856 was decreed on 26 July.

Vidyasagar reconstructed, modernised, and simplified the prose and justified the Bengali alphabet. He eliminated the Sanskrit phonemes and a few marks of punctuation. He wrote many books, but his singularly significant work about Bengali and Sanskrit literature is *Varna Parichay*, which is considered a classic. Vidyasagar simplified and justified Bengali typography into an alphabet of 12 vowels and 40 consonants.

He spent his last two decades in Karmatar (district of Jamtara) Jharkhand among the indigenous Santals because he was unhappy with his family. Later, his health deteriorated, and he died on 29 July 1891 at the age of 70. The Karmatar railway station where he lived has been renamed the Vidyasagar Railway Station in his memory.

III Vidyasagar and Indian education

As a social reformer par excellence, Vidyasagar understood that social reforms could be long lasting if they were imposed from above. And to make the modern/progressive changes permanent, the principal instrument he used was the system of vernacular school education. Contrary to traditional Sanskrit schools, Vidyasagar emphasised the need to establish vernacular schools modelled on the Western/English school system, where all modern/scientific knowledge would be imparted not in English but in vernacular (Bengali) language (Acharya 1995: 670–673).

To make this dream come true, Vidyasagar travelled to many districts of Bengal in his capacity as inspector of schools. This gave him the opportunity to witness the pervading darkness and superstition among the illiterate, uneducated masses of Bengal. He was so distressed by all the malpractices he saw, and especially the exploitation of women in the name of religion, that he hurriedly established 20 model schools in a short period of only two months.

He realised that unless women of the land were educated, it would be impossible to emancipate and liberate them from the terrible burden of the inequalities and injustices imposed on them by the oppressive Hindu society that was blinded by false beliefs and derelict customs. He worked relentlessly and opened 30 schools for girls in Bengal. To promote girls' education, Vidyasagar made door-to-door calls, requesting parents to send their daughters to school. As special inspector of schools, Vidyasagar also used his position to encourage landholders and other wealthy people to establish educational institutions. Within his inspection zone, he was instrumental in founding many schools, several of which were for girls. Some schools were established at his own initiative and with his financial support. Vidyasagar's philanthropy was proverbial. It is said that half the money he got from his salary and the royalties of his published books was reserved for helping the distressed.

His well-documented protests of education department officials testify to the degree of intensity with which he pursued the course of educational reform. He favoured English and Bengali as a medium of learning, alongside Sanskrit, and wanted to offer students a wide range of subjects. He wanted to broaden their horizons in studying and analysing European and Indian conceptual practices so they could judge for themselves and discover the ultimate truth.

He was not afraid of discarding erroneous beliefs of Indian *Shāstras* and preferring European science wherever appropriate. But he also did not blindly accept everything European just by its virtue of being a Western concept. He had an open mind for discovering the truth and truth alone, with an unshakable determination.

IV Vidyasagar: a pragmatist educational reformer

Vidyasagar was a realist as well as a pragmatist. His views are reflected in his educational thought, personal attitude, and social behaviour. He did not believe in re-birth. He claimed there is no other world except the present material world. He asked his mother to help the poor with the fund she used in her religious work. Once at Kashi, the ancient Hindu religious town, he replied to a question from a priest that parents are like Gods to him (Ahmed 2006). In the education reform movement, Vidyasagar initiated many more, which proves his pragmatic view. Though he introduced both the vernacular and English language in the college, he emphasised the vernacular language first.

In the syllabus, he welcomed Western knowledge, such as science and technology, realising the need for modern life. He liked Mill's logic and philosophy, but he did not like Barkley's theory. Before Vidyasagar, only *Brāhmins* were allowed to study in Sanskrit College. Having become the principal of the college, he changed that rule and opened it for everybody. Being a Sanskrit *pandit* (teacher), he realised the traditional Sanskrit learning systems, like *Tola, Chatuspathi* and

Pathshala, or only Sanskrit education were not enough for his countrymen; rather, modern education, such as science, philosophy, etc. were essential to cope with the modern world. To build a modern nation, we are to learn Western science, technology, and values. Vidyasagar felt with his moderated realistic thought that realistic education, instead of spiritualism, is essential to make our society a modern one. He did not desire theoretical excellence or commercial purpose of education; rather, he wanted mundane peace, happiness, and prosperity. Vidyasagar also wanted to set people up to be self-dependent and fit to survive, acquiring the knowledge of realism, social consciousness, modern science, and logic. He found new meaning of life through Western culture. Hence, he did not hesitate to criticise the ancient idealistic Hindu philosophy. His motto was to enrich Indian society with modern science and the best of modern culture. Students would learn through their mother tongue. In the development of Bengali (the mother tongue), it was another attempt of his educational thought. Vidyasagar's education-related works and several types of letters, reports and opinions about educational reforms show his contemporary, creative, and pragmatic sense.

V Vidyasagar: the pioneer of textbooks

Although Vidyasagar had written copiously on subjects like biography, general science, and social ethics, he will be remembered forever in Bengal for his Herculean task of writing textbooks especially for the students. For this, he bought a Bengali letterpress, reformed it and published innumerable textbooks in Bengali, without which it would have been impossible to run the vernacular schools in Bengal, where there had been a dearth of well-written textbooks in Bengali. To achieve this goal, he singlehandedly translated from Standard English and Sanskrit (even Hindi) books. He even invented many scientific terminologies in Bengali, which are still in use. His profound knowledge of Sanskrit came into use here. For example, for the English word "point" he invented the word "*bindu*"; for "coast" he invented the word "*upakool*". These words (and many similar ones) are still used not only in Bengali but also in many Indian languages. By doing this, Vidyasagar helped to develop modern Bengali, like the post-Renaissance European scholars, who helped to develop modern European languages, like French and English, from Latin. On the other hand, through his publication of textbooks, he standardised the modern, "printable", standard Bengali language. To borrow from Benedict Anderson, he pioneered in Bengali "print capitalism" and standardised the modern Bengali language.

Among his textbooks, *Varna Parichay* (in two volumes) will stand first. It is the first primer of the Bengali alphabet to be introduced to children. The word *varna* means "letter" (of the alphabet) and *parichay* means "introduction". Published in 1855, the first part of the book is divided into 25 different lessons on vowels, consonants, words, phrases, and sentences. The second part, split into 10 lessons, teaches conjuncts, phrases and sentences with the conjuncts, *phalas* (dependent consonant forms), numbers, enumeration, and exhortative essays.

Betaal Panchavinsati – 25 tales of a *Betaal* (demon) published in 1847 – a translation from the Sanskrit *Kathasaritsagara* on King Vikramaditya and his *Betaal*, is one of Vidyasagar's most popular works in Bengali prose. Other notable literary contributions include *Banglar Itihaas* (1848), *Jivancharita* (1849), *Shakuntala* (1854), *Mahabharata* (1860), *Seetar Vanavas* (1860), *Bhrantivilaas* (1869), *Oti Alpa Hoilo* (1873), *Aabaar Oti Alpa Hoilo* (1873), *Brajavilaas* (1884), and *Ratnapariksha* (1886). The most far-reaching of his social reform monologues are: The first exposure (1855); *Bidhobabivah* (on widow remarriage), the second book (1855); *Bahubivah* (on the banning of polygamy), the third book (1873); *Balyabivah* (on the flaws of child marriage). There is also an anonymous article published in a journal called *Sarbasubhakari Vidyasagar and Women's Liberation*.

VI Vidyasagar: an advocate for women's emancipation

We have already mentioned Vidyasagar's pioneering efforts towards social reforms, especially his fight for the betterment of women in society. Now let us focus on this in detail. Perhaps Vidyasagar's greatest legacy is his unflinching resolve to change the plight of Indian women, especially in his native Bengal. The enactment of the Act of 1856, which legalised widow remarriage, and the Civil Marriage Act of 1872, which abolished polygamy and child marriage and encouraged widow remarriage, owed a great deal to Vidyasagar, whose writings and activities helped to create public opinion in favour of these social issues.

Being a devout Hindu himself, Vidyasagar sought the transformation of orthodox Hindu society from within. As the principal of Sanskrit College, he encouraged scholars to study ancient sacred texts and interpret them for contemporary usage. His study of ancient texts convinced him that the debilitating status of women in nineteenth-century Hindu society had less legitimacy according to the scriptures but had more to do with the existing power relations in society. The prevailing social custom of *Kulin Brāhmin* polygamy ensured that aged persons (often on the verge of death) married teenage girls and even children. The ill-fated girl used to be widowed very soon because her elderly husband would die in old age. The lives of such girls were full of woes and miseries, such as abstinence, torture, discrimination, and deprivation. These hapless widows were prohibited (as spiritual sanction) to abstain from consuming meat, fish, onion, and garlic. Every day, they had to rise before dawn to conduct their diurnal religious rituals, bathe in icy cold water, wrap a clean white sari around their wet bodies without drying themselves, and pick fresh flowers with dew drops to offer prayers to God. By custom, they were the last ones to eat in the household, or they went without food while observing various religious fasts.

They had to dress in plain white cotton saris and keep their heads shaved for the rest of their lives to render them unattractive to other men. They were usually abandoned soon after their husband's demise and dispatched to their parental homes, with their parents bearing the entire expense of their upkeep in addition to the financial burden of the wedding and dowry. Some widows would even be thrown out of their houses or sent to religious places, like Varanasi or Vrindavan in India, supposedly to pray and purify themselves, but they frequently ended up as prostitutes, rape victims, and unsupported mothers.

Vidyasagar was deeply moved by the plight of these hapless widows. Vidyasagar's heart melted at the pain and suffering imposed by society, often in the name of religion, on Indian women. The problems which saddened him most were polygamy, the ban on widow remarriage, child marriage, gender inequalities, keeping women away from the light of education, and depriving them of property rights (Ghosh 1964: 264). All these malpractices deeply distressed him. He took up his pen, called discussion meetings, ran seminars, and saw government officials. All these efforts were directed to wipe out the evil traditions of the nation. But his call fell on deaf ears. In every instance, dictates from Hindu *Shāstras* were forwarded by the clergy as an excuse. So, Vidyasagar set out to prove them wrong. He conducted extensive research into Hindu scriptures and *Purāṇas* and tried to explain that there was nothing against widows marrying a second time and why polygamy was evil and, hence, unacceptable.

As the principal of Sanskrit College, he encouraged scholars to study ancient sacred texts and interpret them for the times. His study of these texts convinced him that the debased status of women in nineteenth-century Hindu society; the bias in law against female inheritance, wealth, and property and the social prejudice against female autonomy and education was not sanctioned by the scriptures but had more to do with the prevalent power relations in society. He published two volumes of books on the remarriage of widows and another two volumes on polygamy, citing quotes from scriptures and explaining the validity of his arguments.

He compiled a list of "distinguished" polygamous Calcuttans who, unable to control their boundless lust for sex, had married up to 80 times, often marrying under-age girls. For his stern stand against polygamy, he was virulently attacked by the conservative Hindu religious groups and received threats of physical violence and death. But nothing stopped Vidyasagar from what he had set out to do. His iron will be prevailed until the very end. On 26 July 1856, the Government of India legalised widow remarriage.

Due to his courageous entrepreneurship, widow remarriage was ushered in the conservative Hindu *Brāhmin* society of Bengal. To prove that his compassion for widows was not empty rhetoric, as some might have assumed, he even encouraged his son to marry a widow. He also established the 'Hindu Family Annuity Fund' to help widows who could not remarry. He financed many such widow remarriage weddings, often getting into debts himself. With the purpose of gathering people's support for the implementation of the provision of remarriage of widows, he encouraged his only son, Narayan Chandra Bandyopadhyaya, to marry a widow.

Vidyasagar therefore took the task of making the masses realise the reality. He vowed to uplift the status of women and prepared the ground for remarriage. It was not an easy task. But Vidyasagar, who was committed to the noble human cause, succeeded. It was the result of his untiring struggle that the Government of India passed the Widow Remarriage Act in 1856. It was indeed another revolutionary social step taken after the *sati* Regulation Act. Vidyasagar also fought against the evil of child marriage and strongly protested polygamy. Both of these social evils, Vidyasagar argued, had a detrimental effect on women's dignity and self-respect, so he launched a movement against them. Later, legendary Indian figures like Swami Dayānanda Saraswati (1824–1883) and Swami Vivekananda (1863–1902) also worked in this direction, and their cumulative efforts brought about the Child Marriage Prevention Act in 1929. Although various measures were taken for the abolition of polygamy, it was not until India achieved its independence that this tradition could be abolished. It is an irony that a large section of Hindu society still views widow remarriage as taboo.

VII Vidyasagar: the compassionate reformist

Poet Michael Madhusudan Dutta, the eminent Indian/Bengali Poet of the nineteenth century, while writing about Vidyasagar, mentioned him as "the genius and wisdom of an ancient sage, the energy of an Englishman and the heart of a Bengali mother". Though he was very outspoken and blunt in his mannerisms, Vidyasagar had a heart of gold – full of mercy and kindness. He always reflected and responded to the distress calls of the poor, the sufferings of the sick and the injustices of humanity. While a student at Sanskrit College, Vidyasagar would spend part of his scholarship proceeds and cook *paayesh* (rice pudding) to feed the poor and buy medicine for the sick.

Later, when he started earning, he paid fixed sums of monthly allowances to each member of his joint family, to family servants, to needy neighbours, to villagers who needed help and to his village surgery and school. This he continued without break, even when he was unemployed and had to borrow substantially from time to time.

Vidyasagar did not believe money was enough to ease the sufferings of humanity. He opened the doors of the Sanskrit College to lower-caste students, nursed sick cholera patients, went to crematoriums to bury unclaimed dead bodies, dined with the untouchables, and walked miles as a messenger to take urgent messages to people who would benefit from them.

When Michael Madhusudan Dutta fell hopelessly into debt due to his reckless lifestyle during his stay in Versailles, France, he appealed to Vidyasagar (who was also known to all as *daya sagar* – the ocean of kindness – for his immense generosity) for help, Vidyasagar laboured to ensure that sums owed to Michael from his property at home were remitted to him and sent him a large sum of money in France.

VIII Conclusion

To conclude, we reaffirm that Vidyasagar was one of the pioneering figures who played a significant role in all aspects of Indian life – be it education, culture, religion, ethics, or literature. He struggled relentlessly against all forms of corruption, blind superstition, prejudices, and malpractices. He tried his best to emancipate Indian women from the shackles of the biased, patriarchal society and did not want them to live like second-class citizens. He wanted them to be strong individuals with dignity and self-esteem. He was literally a modern man with refined ideas. He fought with the conservative society in the nineteenth century and influenced the government to enact the Widow Remarriage Act. He also fought relentlessly to abolish the practice of polygamy in India.

His acts of supreme kindness and generosity, his fierce determination and courage, his education and social reform, publications and activities have made Vidyasagar immortal. The poet Rabindranath Tagore was hard-pressed to find a comparable personality in the West and, according to him, the closest he found who could come to resemble Vidyasagar in his words and deeds was the English writer Dr Samuel Johnson. Vidyasagar lived his life as a very modest man, a simpleton, but with a generous heart, as he contributed so much to society by dedicating his whole life to uplifting the poor and downtrodden.

Towards the later part of his life, Vidyasagar's health deteriorated considerably because of all the struggles he had gone through those many years of perseverance in order to bring about social reform and justice. Disgruntled with some of his own family members' petty-mindedness and selfishness, he severed all relations with them and lived amongst the tribal people in his last years. Brian Hatcher, a well-known scholar on Vidyasagar, wrote about his reception by the people (Santhal tribe) in Karmatar (at that time a part of Bengal province, now in the State of Jharkhand) in these words:

> The Santhalis tended to be suspicious of any Bengalis who moved into that area, having suffered from the predatory practices of Bengali landlords and moneylenders who migrated to the region a half century earlier. Vidyasagar turned out to be a different sort of neighbour. . . . He often arrived from Calcutta bearing sweets and trinkets to share with local children, who used to greet him at station and ask, 'Uncle, what have you brought for us'?
>
> *(Hatcher 2014: 1–2)*

This great son of India died on 29 July 1891 at the age of 70. Vidyasagar's stature as an educator, reformer, writer, scholar, and philanthropist grew to such great heights that the whole nation, irrespective of race, religion, and caste, mourned his sad demise. Newspapers and magazines were flooded with obituaries and features applauding his deeds and achievements; poets and writers, including the poet-laureate Rabindranath Tagore, wrote poems and prose in his remembrance.

References

Acharya, Paramesh (April 1, 1995). 'Bengali Bhadralok' and Educational Development in 19th Century Bengal', *Economic and Political Weekly*, Vol. 30, No. 13, pp. 670–673.

Ahmed, S. (2006). *Ishwar Chandra Vidyasagarer Sahittya O Shikkha Chinta* (*The Literary and Educational Thought of Ishwar Chandra Vidyasagar*). Dhaka: Rafat Publications.

Ghosh, Binoy (1964). *Vidyasagr O Bangali Samaj*. Kolkata: Orient Longman (Reprint 2011, New Delhi).

Hatcher, Brian (2014). *Vidyasagar: The Life and After-life of an Eminent Indian*. New Delhi: Routledge.

Sarkar, Susobhan (1970). *Bengal Renaissance and Other Essays*. New Delhi: People's Publishing House.

Sen, Asok (1977). *Ishwar Chandra Vidyasagar and His Elusive Milestones*. Calcutta: Riddhi-India.

Tribedi, Ramendra Sundar (1958–59). 'Ishwar Chandra Vidyasagar' [in Bengali], *Charitkatha*. Kolkata: Dasgupta.

Tripathy, Amalesh (1974). *Vidyasagar: The Traditional Moderniser*. Bombay: Orient Longman.

Vidyasagar, *Vidyasagar Rachanasamagra* (Complete Works of Vidyasagar) [in Bengali], Vol. 1 (Parts 1 & 2); Vol. 2. Vidyasagar University Publication Division, Vidyasagar University, West Bengal, 2016–18. See, especially, the 'Introductions' written by Ranjan Chakrabarti & Sibaji Pratim Basu.

3
DAYĀNANDA SARASWATI

Ankit Tomar

> *I have not come to preach any new dogma or religion, nor to establish a new religion, nor to be proclaimed a new Messiah or pontiff. I have only brought before my people the light of Vedic Wisdom, which had been hidden.*
>
> – Swami Dayānanda Saraswati (Satyārth Prakāsh)

I Introduction

Swami Dayānanda Saraswati, also known as *Moolshankar,* was a profound *Vedic* scholar, social reformer, revivalist of *brahmacharya* (celibacy), and a great emancipator of mankind. As an ardent prophet of peace, love, truth, sanctity, and supremacy of the individual, he always stood for the liberation of women and uplifting of the depressed classes. He is known for his greatest contribution towards the reconstruction of Indian society based on humanism. He came as the saviour not only of his motherland but of the world at large. Swami Dayānanda was also a great apostle of the Indo-Aryan culture and civilisation. He boldly hurled India's defiance against the socio-cultural and political domination of the West in India at a time when Indian people were deeply influenced from the superficial aspects of European civilisation and were slavishly copying them on Indian soil. His role can be compared with an intelligent and experienced physician. Before prescribing any remedy for the diseased society, Dayānanda toured the whole of India and then reached to a conclusion that the ills of the subcontinent could be cured only through *Vedic* knowledge. Taking inspiration from *Vedās,* he had not only criticised all the evil practices like idolatry, ritualism, practice of animal sacrifice, the concept of polytheism, the idea of heaven and hell, fatalism, the caste system and untouchability, child marriage, infanticide, etc. which were prevailed during his time, but he also wanted to bring a new social, religious, economic, and political order. Dayānanda believed in the divinity of the *Vedās* manifested at the creation of the universe. According to Dayānanda, the four *Vedās* – the *Ṛigvedā*, the *Yajurvedā*, the *Samvedā*, and the *Atharvavedā* – are the only repositories of true and supreme knowledge regarding God, individual souls, and matter, therefore, the whole of mankind should accept their importance and understand their spirit. He rejected other scriptures and *"Purāṇas"* and argued that the principles of economics, politics, social sciences, and humanities can be found in the *Vedās*. Relying on the *Yajurvedā*, he proved that idol worship is anti-*Vedic* because God does not have any shape, image, or form. Further, the *Ṛigvedā* categorically said that God is one, although people of different religions called it by many names.

To him, the *Vedās* are the basis of humanism. He had a great conviction that the study and understanding of the *Vedās* would be certainly helpful in promoting good in the world and resolving both national and international crises. He ventured hard to acquire and bring back the *Vedās* to mother India and worked tirelessly to provide simple Hindi narrative to the Sanskrit *mantras* (verses); he provided the correct interpretation to the meaning subscribed in the *mantras* of the *Vedās*, thus making the reading, recital, and understanding of the *Vedās* easy and accessible to ordinary people. His clarion call "Go Back to the *Vedās*" created consciousness among the people. Dayānanda also highlighted the spiritual aspect of the man and the importance of religion in the life of man. He believed the only religion is the religion of the *Vedās*. He claimed the *Vedās* are the ultimate source of all religions, and therefore, the religious texts of all other religions are the products of the *Vedās*. He urged that no one should accept religion blindly and must find out how far it is rational. He believed that during the *Vedic* period, observance and performance of religion was considered the highest duty. Dayānanda said that an individual would get maximum happiness if he or she strictly followed the religion.

With the purpose of spreading true *Vedic* religion and culture all over India, he established the *Ārya Samāj* at Bombay on 10 April 1875, which brought a revolution in the field of education and religion. The main objectives of *Ārya Samāj* has been to overcome social suppression of people by educating the masses and liberating them from the shackles of the orthodox society through the propagation of the teachings of the *Vedās*. The *Ārya Samāj* simplified Hinduism and made people conscious of their glorious heritage and superior value of *Vedic* knowledge. The contribution of *Ārya Samāj* in the field of education is commendable. In the praise of Swami Dayānanda, Dr S. Radhakrishnan had rightly said that "among the makers of modern India who had played an important role in the spiritual uplift of people and kindled the fire of patriotism, among them, Swami Dayānanda has occupied the chief place" (Bawa 1979).

II Life sketch

One of the great path makers of modern India, Swami Dayānanda Saraswati (also known as Dayaram and Shuddha Chaitanya) was born in 1824 at Tankara village in Kathiawar (Gujarat) into a deeply religious family. From childhood, he acquired a proficiency in *Vedās* and Sanskrit grammar and language under the highly religious orthodoxy of his father, Karshanji Lalji Tiwari. The loving care of his father and the tender, humanitarian outlook of his mother made him a true devotee of the existing religion and a great *Vedic* scholar. Before reaching the age of 14, he had already memorised the *Yajurvedā* as well as some portions of the three other *Vedās*. Like Gautama became Buddha after witnessing four ordinary scenes of life, Dayānanda's lifestyle was also changed after a single incident when he was 14. It was a day of *Maha Shivaratri* when he kept fast with the other members of the family and experienced a very strange but a unique incident. On the day of the *Maha Shivaratri* fast, he saw that in the sanctorum of the temple of the Lord *Shiva*, a mouse was moving over the idol of *Shiva* and eating the offering that devotees had made to *Shiva*. The doubt flashed in Dayānanda's mind about how the idol could be the omnipotent *Shiva*. To clarify his doubts about idol worship, he made enquiries to his father and asked that "as things stand, is it in any way possible to reach the living omnipotent God through the medium of this image?" In reaction to this question, his father first asked him in a tone of surprise and anger, "why do you ask such questions?" But then he said that in this age of *Kaliyug*, the *Mahadeva* (the great deity) is represented by and invoked only through this image. Later, Dayānanda came to know that the idol was only the symbol of Lord *Shiva* and not the God himself. This incident, which proved as a turning point in Dayānanda's life, had not only aroused his conscience but also led him to think that when the idol could not protect the offering made to it, it could never protect the whole world. Thus, he became convinced about the futility of idol worship and became a staunch crusader against the vices of Hinduism. After the *Maha Shivaratri* festival, at the age of 16, Dayānanda witnessed the cruel death of his younger sister and beloved uncle. Like Buddha, he was also shaken by the phenomenon of death. Thus, three ideas settled in his mind which later shaped his personality and philosophy of religion: disrespect for idol worship, detachment from the world, and disbelief in ritual ceremonies.

In the quest for true knowledge and for the service of mankind, Dayānanda left his home in May 1846 when his father tried to involve him in family life through marriage with a view to put restrictions on his independent mind. Dayānanda was not willing to enter the bondage of family life. He renounced the worldly life as stifling one's life and destroying one's personality. From 1845 to 1860, the young Dayānanda wandered from place to place all over India in pursuit of knowledge. Finally, in 1861, at Mathura, he met with the blind and physically emaciated but spiritually renowned saint Swami Virjananda and became his disciple. Under the able guidance of his *guru*, he studied many things, such as the ancient religious literature, various mythological books, and Sanskrit grammar texts. *Moolshankar* became Dayānanda Saraswati when he entered *Sanyasa* (renunciation) and got true knowledge. As a *guru-dakshina*, he made a promise to his *guru* that he would devote his whole life to disseminating the knowledge of the *Vedās* to mankind and to fight against the conservative Hindu religion and wrong traditions. After receiving his *guru*'s blessings, Dayānanda concentrated all his efforts on propounding the message of the *Vedās*, which, to him, was the last recourse to safeguard humanity. For him, nothing was purer or higher than the truth. It was his ardent love for his *guru* and ceaseless quest for the truth which made him a real *Mahatma*. To fulfil the mission of his life, he founded *Ārya Samāj* at Bombay on 10 April 1875 and passed the rest of his life in establishing branches of *Ārya Samāj* at different places.

From 1874 to 1883, he wrote many books, giving true meaning and direction to *Vedic* life, particularly his great commentary on the *Yajurvedā* and the *Rigvedā*. The philosophy of Dayānanda Saraswati can be known from his three famous contributions, namely, *Satyārth Prakāsh* (The Light of Truth), *Veda Bhashya Bhumika*, and *Veda Bhashyam*. Further, the journal *Arya Patrika*, edited by Dayānanda, also reflects his thought. To stress the importance of animals to the household, he wrote his book *Gaukarunanidhi*, wherein he explicitly talks about the invaluable qualities of the cow and its progeny in relation to the family. Swami Dayānanda had a heart full of love and compassion for the whole of humanity. The outspoken criticism of Hindu tradition and reformative zeal of Dayānanda irritated many orthodox Hindus and conservative circles. However, Dayānanda stood firm and resolute in the face of criticism. He was cruelly poisoned 17 times. On 30 October 1883, the great Swami died of food poisoning.

III *Ārya Samāj*

Maharshi Dayānanda Saraswati spent several years in the dissemination of his doctrines. On 10 April 1875, Dayānanda Saraswati founded the *Ārya Samāj* at Bombay with a mission to spread the teachings of the *Vedās* to the people to bring about self-worth and dignity and overcome oppression and suffering. It was a reformist socio-religious movement of the nineteenth century. It is generally agreed that the *Ārya Samāj*, meaning "society of the nobles" came as a beacon to enlighten the path of humanity. The purpose of the *Samāj* was to move the *Hindu* religion away from the fictitious beliefs. *Krinvanto Vishvamaryam* was the slogan of the *Ārya Samāj* and means, "make the whole world the living place of the noble and the good". The founder ensured that the objectives of the *Ārya Samāj* remained benevolent and prescribed to a total of 28 basic principles and rules to be followed. These were reviewed later in 1877, at Ajmer, to form the 10 main principles that the *Ārya Samāj* subscribed to the whole world. The ten tenets of the *Ārya Samāj* are as follows:

1. God is the source of all true knowledge and of all that is known through knowledge.
2. God is existent, intelligent, and blissful. He is formless, omniscient, just, merciful, unborn, endless, unchangeable, beginning-less, unequalled, the support of all, the master of all, omnipresent, immanent, un-aging, immortal, fearless, eternal, holy, and the maker of all. He alone is worthy of being worshiped.
3. The *Vedās* are the scriptures of all true knowledge, and it is the paramount duty of all *Aryas* to read, teach, and recite them among the people.

4   One should always be ready to accept truth and renounce untruth.
5   Every action should be performed in accordance with *dharma*, that is, after deliberating what is right and wrong.
6   The prime objective of the *Ārya Samāj* is to do well to the world, that is, to promote the physical, spiritual, and social good of everyone.
7   Our conduct towards all should be guided by love, righteousness, and justice.
8   We should dispel *Avidya* (ignorance) and promote *Vidya* (knowledge).
9   No one should be content with promoting his/her good only; on the contrary, one should look for his/her good in promoting the good of all.
10 One should regard oneself under restriction to follow the rules of society calculated to promote the well-being of all, while in following the rules of individual welfare all should be free.

These 10 founding principles (*Niyams*) of the *Ārya Samāj* were the pillar on which Maharishi Dayānanda sought to reform India and asked people to go back to the *Vedās* and its undiluted spiritual teaching. With its opposition to various social evils, the *Ārya Samāj* rendered valuable services to Hindu society. The *Samāj* directs its members to condemn ritualistic practices like idol worship, pilgrimage and bathing in holy rivers, animal sacrifice, offering in temples, sponsoring priesthood, etc. The *Samāj* also encouraged followers to question existing beliefs and rituals instead of blindly following them.

During British rule, illiteracy, ignorance, diversity of faiths, and multifarious social evils were widespread in India. It was a time when the British rulers were not only draining the wealth of India but were also trying to uproot Hinduism through the efforts of their Christian missionaries. At that time, Christian missionaries found a fertile ground for the propagation of Christianity and conversion in India. Indians were converted to Christianity by force or deceit. The growing number of Christian schools played a dangerous role in belittling Hindu religion as Indian culture, history, and social and spiritual heritage were being openly distorted and badly mutilated by the foreign rulers. It was at such a crucial moment when Swami Dayānanda Saraswati emerged as an outstanding religious leader and a saviour of his motherland. Emphasising on the superiority of Hinduism, Dayānanda started the *shuddhi* (purification) movement as a process of converting the people of other religions to Hinduism and also to reconvert those who had changed from Hinduism to other religions. This movement prevented lower-caste Hindus from converting to Christianity or Islam. The *Shuddhi* movement challenged the Christian missionaries who tried to convert the uneducated, poor, and depressed classes of the Hindus.

IV Critique of orthodoxy and social reconstruction

On the question of the social reconstruction of Indian society, Maharishi Dayānanda Saraswati vehemently denounced the practice of untouchability, idol worship, superstitions, blind faith, and the slaughter of animals. Dayānanda also spearheaded his crusade against the caste system and the superiority of the

Brāhmins in the society. He reinterpreted the system of *Varṇadhārma* mentioned in the *Vedās*. He stated that in the *Vedic* period, the ancient sages found that all human beings were not equally fit for all kinds of work, hence, to effect the adjustment between individuals and the society, they allocated different types of duties to different classes of people, as per the doctrines of *guna* (character), *karma* (action), and *swabhava* (nature). They divided the society into four different *varṇas*, namely, the *Brāhmins*, the *Kṣatriyas*, the *Vaiśyas*, and the *Śūdras*. In the *Vedic* period, the *Brāhmins* were given the charge of spiritual and intellectual affairs. The work of political administration and defense was given to *Kṣatriyas*. The *Vaiśyas* were entrusted with the duty of carrying on trade and commerce. The *Śūdras* were given to serve the other three castes. According to Dayānanda, the system of *varṇadhārma* was meant for occupational purpose in the society and the occupations of different classes were based on their aptitude, capacity, or quality, rather than birth. In his words, *varṇadhārma* is:

> A political institution made by the rulers for the common good of the society and not a natural or religious distinction. It is not a natural distinction, for the four castes were not created by God as distinct species of men; but all men are of equal nature, of the same species, and brothers.
>
> *(Arya 1987)*

But Dayānanda later found that the *varṇa* began to be based on birth rather than on deeds and character. According to Dayānanda, the malpractice of the caste system based on birth is an ugly feature of the present Hindu society, and it is mainly responsible for the degradation and degeneration of the Hindus. Therefore, he opposed the caste system and said that all humans are equal in the eyes of God. In his view, it is ridiculous to say that some belonged to a high caste and others to a low caste. Further, he also challenged the monopoly of *Brāhmins* to read the *Vedās* and supported the right of every individual irrespective of caste, creed, and colour to study the *Vedās*. In a similar vein, Dayānanda denounced the practice of untouchability and labelled it as inhumane, unsocial, and as being against *Vedic* religion.

Swami Dayānanda was also against the discriminatory treatment of woman in Hindu society. He was opposed to the evil practices of child marriage, polygamy, *purdah*, and the practice of *sati* (widow burning), which, according to him, did not have the sanction of *Vedās*, and Dayānanda supported legislation to stop the practice. The pitiable condition of child widows in the society, which prohibited remarriage, evoked his deepest concern. He therefore suggested *nigoga* (a non-permanent co-habitation of widow and widowers) and, later, even widow remarriage. On the question of marriage and married life, Swami Dayānanda believed marriage was a religious sacrament, not a social contract. Thus, it should take place between suitable partners, as it is a lifelong tie. Quoting Manu, Dayānanda writes, "it is better that men and women should remain single till death rather than marry unsuitable; i.e. persons of mutually unsuitable qualities, characteristics and temperaments should never marry each other" (*Manusmriti* III: 56–57). He further writes, "if parents arrange a match, it should be done with the consent of the parties. There is nothing but trouble in store for those whose marriage is not of their own choice – they having been simply forced into it" (cited in Bharadwaja 1984: 93).

Moreover, he protested injustice to women and worked for their education. Citing the teachings of the *Vedās*, he proved that women should have equal rights with men. He was in favour of inter-caste marriages and inter-dining. He also supported girls' education and worked tirelessly for the emancipation of women. According to Dayānanda, a society could not prosper without the development of women folk who constituted 50 percent of the population.

Dayānanda also strongly denounced those European scholars and orthodox *pandits* who stated that the *Vedās* preached polytheism and idol worship. He emphasised that polytheism had caused division in Hindu society. Putting emphasis on monotheism and devoting oneself to the formless God, he wrote in the *Satyārtha Prakāsha*:

> There is only one God with all those attributes generally ascribed to him by monotheists. He is the creator, first of the *Vedās*, then of the world, hence; the *Vedās* are eternal as compared with the world, but non-internal as compared with God.
>
> (cited in Bharadwaja 1984: 93)[1]

He quoted many hymns from the *Vedās* to prove that God is one and the supreme God never assumes any human form. Maharishi Dayānanda Saraswati fervently believed in one true God and therefore criticised both those who believed in the existence of many Gods and those who did not believe in His existence. He rejected the Hindu belief of the *avataras* (incarnation) of God, as he found no mention of it in the *Vedās*. Swāmījī, in his masterpiece the *Satyārtha Prakāsha*, has made it clear that though God is one, due to his innumerable attributes, qualities, and activities, he has many names. According to Dayānanda, God possesses the attributes of existence, consciousness, and bliss. He is omniscient, omnipresent, omnipotent, formless, unborn, infinite, merciful, and just. He alone is worthy of being worshipped. As far as the word "*Devatā*" is concerned, Swāmījī states that whatsoever or whosoever possesses useful and brilliant qualities is called a *Devatā*, as the earth, for instance; but it is nowhere said that it is God or the object of our adoration. People are greatly mistaken to interpret the *Devatā* as God.

Maharishi Dayānanda was fully convinced that a lack of knowledge was the main culprit behind the adulteration of Hinduism. Therefore, he prescribed various principles to make the world a happier one. According to him, the revival of *Vedic* culture and civilisation would certainly be helpful in the reconstruction of a society based on humanism. For the "prosperity of *Aryavarta*" (India), Dayānanda also emphasised on compulsory education based on moral and religious foundations and meant for all four classes of men and women. The burden of this education was, according to him, to be shouldered by the king/State.

V Concept of *Vedic swaraj*

Though *Ārya Samāj* had not actively participated in politics, it indirectly helped in the promotion of national consciousness. Dayānanda was the first to advocate *swadeshi* to discard foreign goods. By recognising Hindi as the national language, he promoted the growth of an all-India national spirit. The political philosophy of Dayānanda Saraswati has two central ideas that are somewhat contradictory. The first is the idea of an enlightened monarchy – a concept Dayānanda borrowed from *Manusmṛiti* – that is, a monarchy thoroughly rooted in obedience to *dhārma*. The second is that of elective representation, that is, democracy, where there is no contradiction because in the *Vedās* there are references to assembly and the election of the king. According to Dayānanda, the machinery of the State consists of a king and three assemblies; 1) religious, 2) legislative, and 3) educational. They jointly exercise sovereignty on behalf of the people and with the consent of the people. In the State, the highest office is that of the president (*rājā* or *sabhapati*) of the assembly (*rajsabha*). The office is open to all, and any person can aspire to, and be selected for this office if he fulfils the requisite qualifications. Dayānanda has in detail laid down the necessary qualifications – the type of training and education – the king should have. The *rājā* is neither a hereditary monarch belonging to a particular caste (*varṇa*) nor a representative of God on earth. He is an elected president (*nirvachita sabhapati*) chosen by the learned and able members of the assemblies and approved by the people. The *rājā* is not supreme or absolute, and he derives his authority from the people. He is a trustee and not the sole owner. The *rājā* is appointed by the people, who can remove him from his position if he goes against *dhārma* or fails to perform his duties. In other words, the elected *rājā*, who possesses excellent qualities, is highly trained, and occupies the highest office of the State, is not absolute.

In Chapter 6 of *Satyārtha Prakāsha*, which deals with *rajdhārma* – the science of government – Maharishi Dayānanda has quoted profusely from the *Vedās* and the *Manusmṛiti* to shed light on the qualifications of good rulers. According to Dayānanda, the head of the State must be just, impartial, well-educated, and friendly towards all. He must be as powerful as electricity, as dear to his people as breath, be able to read the innermost thoughts of others, and be merciful in his dealings as a judge. He should enlighten people's minds by spreading knowledge, justice, and righteousness and dispel ignorance and injustice, just as the sun illuminates the world. He should be like fire consuming wickedness, keeping the wicked and the criminals under control like a jailor; he should gladden the hearts of good people like the moon and make the country rich and prosperous as a treasurer keeps his treasury full.

Moreover, in Dayānanda's scheme of government, *dhārma*, public opinion, and assemblies occupy great importance, and they serve as a check on the power of the *rajā*. According to Dayānanda, the people are not under one man or assembly but are under *dharma*, which is the eternal law and the basis of social and political organisation. He believed *dharma* is superior to and independent of the State and that it limits or regulates the power of the ruler.

Swami Dayānanda held the law alone as the real king. He exhorts all to remember the teaching of the *Vedic* text which says, "verily the just law alone is the true king, yes; the just law is the true religion" (Jordens 1978: 20–25). He places the law above the king and over the impersonal law. Quoting Manu, Dayānanda asserts that:

> The law alone is the true governor that maintains order among the people. The law alone is their protector. The law keeps awake whilst all the people are fast asleep, the wise, therefore, look upon the law alone as *dharma* or Right. When rightly administered the law makes all men happy, but when administrated wrongly i.e. without due consideration as to the requirements of justice, it ruins the king. Rightly administered law promotes the practice of virtue, acquisition of wealth and secures the attainment of the heart-felt desires of his people. All would become corrupt, all order would come to an end, and there would be nothing but chaos and corruption if the law were not properly enforced. Both the ruler and the subjects have to fulfil their duties for the nation's prosperity.
>
> *(Dayananda 1978)*

He also places great emphasis on the maintenance of a strong army. He explains that there is no other way of maintaining the independence of the State than the raising up of a strong defensive force within the country. The government, according to Dayānanda, is the guardian and protector of those who are not able to earn their livelihood either because of old age and infirmity or because they are too young to take care of themselves.

His basic effort was therefore directed to attaining the three objectives of *Vedic* revivalism, rationalism, and social reform of considerable contemporary import. He was heavily critical of the West and of Islam. He was equally severe on those who advocated the path of modernisation through Western ideas and attitudes.

The third check imposed on the ruler is the advice of the learned, virtuous, and wise members of the assemblies. In fact, the elected assemblies are the final law-making authority. The government is to be run in accordance with the policies and laws formulated by the assemblies. The king is merely an executor of the law and policies formulated by the assemblies. Dayānanda says that "the king is to execute only those laws and policies that are made by the assemblies. He can do nothing without proper deliberation, consultation and advice of the *sabhas*" (Pandey 1985).

VI Conclusion

The *Ārya Samāj* played a significant role in bringing about socio-religious changes in pre-independent India. Though Dayānanda was criticised as a conservative and sectarian activist who claimed the superiority of Hinduism over and above all other religions, he was one of the makers of modern India. He was not opposed to Christianity or Islam, rather, the evil practices of all religions and their religious imperialism.

Note

1 *Satyārtha Prakāsha* is regarded as a living testament of Swami Dayānanda's teaching. It sheds light on many *Vedic mantras* which had been misinterpreted by Eastern and Western scholars. It enabled scholars as well as laymen to get to the root of *Vedic* knowledge.

References

Arya, Krishan Singh (1987). *Swami Dayananda Saraswati: A Study of His Life and Work*. Delhi: Manohar.

Bawa, Arjan Singh (1979). *Dayananda Saraswati: Founder of Arya Samaj*. New Delhi: Ess Ess Publications.

Bharadwaja, Chiranjiva (1984). *Satyarth Prakash (Light of Truth): The Well Known Work of Swami Dayananda Saraswati*. Allahabad: The Star Press.

Jordens, J. T. F. (1978). *Dayanand Saraswati, His Life and Ideas*. Oxford: Oxford University Press.

Pandey, Dhanpati (1985). *Swami Dayanand Saraswati*. New Delhi: Publications Division, Ministry of Information and Broadcasting, Govt. of India.

Saraswati, Dayananda (1978). *Autobiography of Dayanand Saraswati*. New Delhi: Manohar.

4
JYOTIRAO GOVINDRAO PHULE

Basanta Kumar Mallik

> *Without education, wisdom was lost; without wisdom, morals were lost; without morals, development was lost; without development, wealth was lost; without wealth, the Śūdra were ruined; so much happened through lack of education.*
>
> – Jyotirao Phule

I Introduction

Jyotirao Govindrao Phule was a prominent social reformer and thinker of nineteenth-century India. He led the movement against the prevailing caste restrictions in India. He revolted against the domination of the *Brāhmins* and struggled for the rights of peasants and other lower-caste people. Mahatma Jyotirao Phule was also a pioneer for women's education in India and fought for the education of girls throughout his life. He is believed to be the first Hindu to start an orphanage. In the social and educational history of India, Mahatma Jyotirao Phule and his wife, Savitribai Phule, stand out as an exceptional couple. They were engaged in a passionate struggle to build a movement against the caste system, for equality between men and women, and for social justice. Recognising that knowledge is power and that the progress of women and lower castes was impossible without it, they dedicated their entire lives to spreading education.

II Life sketch

Jyotirao Govindrao Phule, also known as Mahatma Jyotiba Phule, was born in 1827 into the *Mali* (gardener) caste in Maharashtra. He was an activist, thinker, teacher, educationist, and social revolutionary from Poona and occupies a unique position among the social reformers of Maharashtra in the nineteenth century.

He lived and worked in Maharashtra. His father, Govindrao, used to supply flowers to the Peshwa families and others in Poona. Since Jyotirao Phule's father and two uncles served as florists under the last Peshwas, they came to be known as Phules. Jyotirao's mother died when he was hardly one year old. He was brought up by a close relative named Sagunabai.

The Phule family belonged to the *Mali* (gardener) community, which was forbidden from seeking education and other rights that were enjoyed by upper castes. The *Malis* belonged to *Śūdra varṇa* and were placed immediately below the peasant caste of Maratha. The orthodox *Brāhmins* used to preach that *Śūdras* and women were not allowed to receive education and that it would be considered an act of sin if they did so. In this background, in a city like Poona, which was the centre of *Brāhminical* orthodoxy, Jyotirao was not given admission to an Indian school. So, his father sent him to a missionary school where children from all communities were admitted. But due to threats from some *Brāhmins*, Jyotirao's father discontinued his education, and Jyotirao was assigned gardening work on the farm. Jyotirao was unhappy with the work and was extremely eager to continue his studies. Impressed by Jyotirao's intelligence and his love for knowledge, two of his neighbours, one a Muslim teacher and the other a Christian gentleman, persuaded Govindrao to allow Jyotirao to study in a secondary school. In 1841, Jyotirao was admitted to Scottish Mission High School, Pune. After completing his secondary education in 1847, Jyotirao decided not to accept a job in the government.

In 1848, Jyotirao Phule began his work as a social reformer. Interested in the education of boys and girls of lower castes, he started a school for them. Since no female teachers were available, Phule asked his wife, Savitribai, to teach in the school. He opened two more schools for girls in 1851. The following year, Phule was honoured by the board of education for the work he did for girl's education. Phule also established a school for untouchables and a night school in 1852. By 1858, he gradually retired from the management of these schools and entered the broader field of social reform. He supported the movement for widow remarriage in 1860, and in 1863, he established a home for the prevention of infanticide. In a memorial address to the Education Commission, popularly known as the Hunter Commission, in 1882, he described his activities in the field of education.[1] The government appointed him as a member of the Poona Municipality in 1876. Phule continued as a member until 1882 and fought for the cause of the oppressed.

Perhaps Phule's biggest legacy is the thought behind his perpetual fight against social stigmas that are enormously relevant still. In the nineteenth century, people were used to accepting these discriminatory practices as social norms that needed to be enforced without question, but Phule sought to change this discrimination based on caste, class, and colour. He was the harbinger of unheard ideas for social reforms. He started awareness campaigns that ultimately later inspired Dr B. R. Ambedkar and Mahatma Gandhi, stalwarts who undertook major initiatives against caste discrimination. He was also inspired by Mitchell's arguments on caste, religion, and psychological similarities. These factors made him think about reforming the Indian social system (Omvedt 1971: 79).

Phule was not only a leader and organiser of the movement for the emancipation of lower castes; he was also an original thinker who had revolutionary ideas which he expressed through his books. Some of his major works include *Tritiya Ratna* (1855), *Brahmananche Kasab* (1869), *Gulamgiri* (1873), *Shetkaryacha Asud* (1883), *Satsar* Vols. I and II (1885) *Ishara* (1 October 1885), and *Sarvajanik Satyadharma Pustak* (1891). In all of his writings, Phule worked to achieve his motive of universal education, education for women, and the uplifting of people who had been ostracised by the caste system. In *Brahmananche Kasab*, Phule exposed the exploitation being meted out by *Brāhmin* priests. In *Gulamgiri*, he gave a historical account of the slavery of lower castes. In 1883, Phule published a collection of his speeches under the title *Shetkaryarcha Asud* (The cultivator's whipcord) in which he analysed how peasants were being exploited in those days. A text of his philosophical statement can be found in *Sarvajanik Satyadharma Pustak* (A Book of True Religion for All) published in 1891, a year after his death. From Phule's writings, we come to know that his thinking on social and political issues was influenced by Christianity and the ideas of Thomas Paine (1737–1809), who was known for his religious radicalism in England. Phule himself has recorded that he was influenced by Paine's ideas. As a recognition of his great work for the uplifting of the oppressed, Phule was conferred the title of 'Mahatma' in 1888.

Phule devoted his entire life for the liberation of untouchables from the exploitation of the *Brāhmins*. He fought against *Brāhminism* and its evils during the period of Peshwa Bajirao-II (Mani 2005: 253). Apart from being a social activist and reformer, Phule was also a businessman. He was a cultivator and contractor for the Municipal Corporation. He served as commissioner of the Poona Municipality between 1876 and 1883. Phule suffered a stroke in 1888 and was rendered paralysed. On 28 November 1890, the great social reformer Mahatma Jyotirao Phule passed away.

III Views on primary education

Phule's submission to the Hunter Commission is a document of immense importance in the history of educational reform in India. The document contains ideas such as free and compulsory education to all, which is now enshrined in the Constitution of India. It is probably the first document of its kind that speaks of creating a taste for education among the masses and making it accessible to all. Phule had expressed his views on primary education and primary school teachers in a statement forwarded to the Hunter Commission. In his view, it was necessary to bestow prime importance to primary education, rather than higher education, as it was the urgent need of the masses. The British government, which was gaining revenue from taxes paid by commoners, did not provide any resources for giving primary education in return. Phule's argument was that the amounts the masses paid to the government should be invested in their education in proportion to what the government was gaining and that education should be prioritised in government expenditure. The public needed to receive an education that helped them perform their jobs and carry on their day-to- day activities. To reform Hindu society, Phule argued that education was critical because it enabled people to differentiate between good and bad (O'Hanlon 1985: 106).

The British government's focus was on higher education, rather than primary education. Though Phule was not against higher education, he was of the firm opinion that the common masses were less connected to this level of education. Their urgent need, Phule argued, was primary education that had relevance to their lives. He wanted educated persons of high vision and intellect to direct their attention towards ensuring humanism in education. Phule was a visionary who was also interested in educational policies. Therefore, in a statement presented to the Hunter Commission, he argued that the present number of educated men is very small in relation to the country at large and we trust that the day may not be far distant when we shall have the present number multiplied a hundred fold – all taking themselves to useful and remunerative occupation not looking after service (Hunter Commission 1882). Through education, Phule was not just interested in temporarily raising the standard of living for a few persons. He was, in fact, thinking of the future of education for an independent India. His goal was to give Indian society an education that would not only have a permanent value but also cultivate in the people a free mind and liberty of action. Phule concentrated on the fact that the two important needs of an effective system of primary education were quality teachers and a good curriculum. In his view, a primary teacher plays a pivotal role in the education process. According to Phule, a primary teacher must be a trained person receiving a sufficient salary. He wanted teachers to be drawn from lower castes so that they could be given employment opportunities. Phule was also of the view that efficient primary school teachers should be paid higher salaries than others.

Phule related education with access to justice and equity and growth for lower castes and women, and he asserted that only through education could growth be possible. Phule's thoughts on education can be summarised as follows: a lack of education leads to a lack of wisdom, which in turn leads to a lack of justice. This leads to a lack of progress, which leads to a lack of money and results in the oppression of the lower castes. Phule was fully conscious of the importance of education as a tool for social justice and equality. In fact, he saw education as the harbinger of a social revolution. The essence of Phule's educational philosophy was that he considered education a human right. He was indeed the protagonist of the universalisation of educational opportunities, which basically means accepting and extending facilities of education to all, irrespective of caste, creed, religion, sex, and physical or mental disability. Article 45 of the Indian Constitution[2] and now Article 21a are the symbol of victory for Phule's philosophy of equal educational opportunity. Phule also worked for the education of women and virtually laid the foundation for opening opportunities for women to seek formal education. This was especially true of women from the marginalised sections of society. To achieve his aims, Phule opened a girl's school in 1848 at

Budhwar Peth in the residential building of Tatya Sahib Bhide. He opened two more schools in 1851, one of which was for girls of backward classes. Phule had revolutionary ideas about different aspects of education.

IV The educational philosophy of Mahatma Phule

Since all human beings are equal, Phule believed access to education must be uniform and monopolistic controls over education must be curtailed. The universalisation of opportunities and compulsory education must be ensured. While educating individuals, religion, race, caste, and sex should not be considered. Education should develop humanistic values. The education of women and other deprived groups must be given top priority for establishment of social justice. Education must serve as a binding force in society. Curriculum must be utilitarian and practical to cover the needs of the society. Preliminary knowledge about agriculture and health should be included in the curriculum. There should be a differentiation between the curricula of rural and urban schools. Values that stand the test of time, such as freedom, equality, fraternity, kindness, self-respect, devotion to one's nation, and internationalism, should be developed through education. Professional ability and efficiency should be developed so knowledge may be properly linked. The downward filtration theory advocated by Lord Macaulay is not philosophically sound, as it ignores the common masses. Practical knowledge is superior to bookish knowledge. Hence, primary knowledge in accounts, history, grammar, agriculture, ethics, and health should be imparted. Though quantitative growth in primary schools is important, it should not be at the cost of qualitative growth. The government must formulate the scheme of scholarships and rewards for deserving students and those in need of support (Marwaha 2010).

Phule believed the low status of *Śūdras* was due to the denial of education, so he decided to provide them with education (Panday 1986: 59). Phule's bold efforts to educate women, *Śūdras*, and the untouchables had a deep effect on the values, beliefs, and ideologies relating to the movement for social justice through education. His efforts unleashed the forces of awakening among the common masses. Education made women more knowledgeable. They became conscious of the differences between right and the wrong and analysed these differences with a scientific approach. They began to question the age-old customs which degraded them. Similarly, *Śūdras* started claiming equality with upper castes in all areas of life. In short, through education, Phule launched a movement for liberating women and *Śūdras* from the control of vested interests and laid the foundation for a backward class movement in India.

V Phule on British rule in India

British rule had ended the tyranny and chaos of the regime of the last Peshwa in Maharashtra. The colonial rulers had not only established law and order but also the principle of equality before law. The earlier regime of *Brāhmin* Peshwas had imposed strict limitations on education, occupation, and living standards of the lower castes and women. British rule opened opportunities in education and mobility in occupations for the members of all castes. Missionary schools and government colleges were ready to admit any student, irrespective of caste origins. New ideas of equality and liberty could reach the lower castes. Phule was probably the best product of this process. High-caste reformers and leaders also had welcomed the colonial rule. It is not surprising that Phule, who was concerned with the slavery of the lower castes, also favoured the British rule. He hoped the new government, which believed in equality, would emancipate lower castes from the domination of the *Brāhmins*.

The British rule provided new employment opportunities in the administration. Political power at the local level was also being given to Indians. Phule, who had worked as a member of the Poona Municipality, could visualise how lower castes would be able to acquire power at the local level during the period of British rule. He believed in the benevolent attitude of the British rulers towards the lower castes and therefore asked them for several things. He was not sure how long the British rule would continue. Therefore, he wanted lower castes to exploit the opportunity and get rid of the tyranny of the *Brāhmins*. Upper-caste rulers used to collect huge wealth out of taxes levied on the poor, lower-caste population but never used to spend even a *paisa* (one hundredth of a rupee) for their welfare. On the contrary, the British government showed signs of doing good things for the deprived people. Phule assured the colonial rulers that if the *Śūdras* were made happy and contented, they need not worry about the loyalty of the subjects. He wanted the British government to abolish the *Brāhmins'* position and fill the post of village headman (*Patil*) based on merit. In fact, Phule would have liked the British government to put an end to the *balutedari* system, which was connected with caste-specific occupations in the villages. He asked the government to make laws prohibiting customs and practices which gave subordinate status to women and untouchables. Phule wanted *Brāhmin* bureaucracy to be replaced by non-*Brāhmin* bureaucracy. But if the non-*Brāhmins* were not available, the government should appoint British men to these posts. He believed the British officers would be impartial and more likely to side with lower castes.

He knew education had not yet percolated to the lower castes. The masses had not yet become politically conscious. The high-caste elites were claiming that they were the true representatives of the people and therefore were demanding political rights. This process, Phule thought, would re-establish the political supremacy of the high castes. He argued that the Indian National Congress or other political associations were not national in the true sense of the term because they represented only high castes. Phule warned his followers against the selfish and cunning motives of the *Brāhmins* in forming these associations and advised them to keep themselves away from such associations. In his *Satya Shodhak Samaj* (Truth-Seeking Society), he had made it a rule not to discuss politics. In fact, he had expressed more than once a complete and total loyalty towards the new government. He firmly believed the almighty God had dethroned the tyrannical rulers and had established in their place a just, enlightened, and peaceful British rule for the welfare of the masses. It does not mean that Phule did not understand the significance of politics. In fact, he has said that the conditions of lower castes had deteriorated because they were deprived of political power. His efforts to organise lower castes under the banner of *Satya Shodhak Samaj* should be considered a political activity. It is true that he gave preference to social reform rather than political reform, but that does not negate their demand for political rights. Phule advised the lower castes (*Śūdras* and *Ati-Śūdras*) to unite and dethrone the *Brāhmins* and establish their own supremacy. His writings were directed towards this effort.

Though Phule preferred British rule to the regime of the *Brāhmins*, he was aware of the shortcomings of the former and never hesitated to point them out openly. Since his mission was to bring about an egalitarian society where all men and women would enjoy liberty, Phule criticised the British if he felt that their policies went against this idea. He was mainly interested in permanently destroying the supremacy of the *Brāhmins* in social, economic, and political fields. Therefore, he used to attack the British government whenever its policies favoured the *Brāhmins*, even indirectly.

It was the educational policy of the British government which came under severe attack from Phule. He complained that the government was providing more funds and greater facilities to higher education and neglecting that of the masses. He brought it to the notice of the government that the greater portion of the revenue of the government was derived from the labour of the masses. The higher and richer classes contribute little to the State's exchequer. The government therefore should spend a large portion of its income on the education of the masses and not of the higher classes.

Because the educational policy favoured the upper castes, upper-caste members virtually monopolised higher offices. If the government wished the welfare of the lower castes, according to Phule, it was its duty to reduce the proportion of high-caste people in the administration and increase that of those in lower castes. Phule's object in writing a book on slavery was to open the eyes of the government to the pernicious system of high-class education. This system, Phule said, was keeping the masses in ignorance and poverty. The government used to collect a special cess (tax or levy) for educational purposes, but the funds derived were not spent on the education of the masses. Phule criticised the primary schools run by the government by saying that the education imparted in these schools was not satisfactory. It did not prove practical or useful in the future career of the students. He also criticised on similar lines the higher secondary schools, colleges, and the system of scholarships. The scholarship system, he observed, was unduly favourable to literary castes while there was a need to encourage lower-caste children.

He observed that the British officers were concerned about their own comfort and salaries. They did not find sufficient time to know about the real conditions of the peasants nor did they understand the language of the peasants.

The *Brāhmin* officers thereby used to get an opportunity to mislead the British officers and exploit the poor and illiterate peasants. Phule's biographers tell us that when he was a member of the Poona Municipality, he showed rare courage in opposing a move to spend 1,000 rupees upon the viceroy's visit. In 1888, a dinner was organised in honour of the British at Poona. Phule went there in the typical dress of a poor peasant and delivered a moving speech after the dinner. He told the audience that the people of the country were to be found in the villages. He had intentionally come in that dress so that the British guests would come to know how a common peasant lived. He also told them that it was the duty of the government to formulate policies for the welfare of these peasants. In his writings, we also come across a criticism of the government's policies which went against the peasants. We will take note of it while discussing his views on economic issues.

VI Critique of the social order

Phule's criticism of the British government emanated out of his concern for the welfare and status of the lower castes in contemporary society. According to Phule, Indian society was based on inequality between man and man and the exploitation of the ignorant masses by the cunning *Brāhmins*. Phule believed God, who is the creator of the universe, has created all men and women free and capable of enjoying their rights. The creator has created all men and women as the custodians of all human rights so that a man or a group of men should not suppress an individual. The maker has bestowed upon all men and women religious and political liberty. Therefore, no one should look down upon anyone's religious faith or political opinion. Every individual has a right to property. The maker, Phule thought, has given all human beings the liberty of thought and expression, but it should not be harmful to anybody. The creator has made all men and women capable of claiming a position in civil service or municipal administration according to their ability. No one should encroach upon the equal liberty of other human beings. Phule believed all men and women are entitled to enjoy all the things the maker has created. All men and women are equal before law. Phule developed a critique of Indian society in light of these fundamental principles.

Attack on *varṇa* and the caste system: Indian society was founded on the *varṇa* system. Phule challenged the view that it was God-ordained. He held that this claim was made to deceive the lower *varṇas*. Since this claim was made by the religious texts of the Hindus, he decided to expose the falsehood of these texts. Phule depended upon the contemporary theories and his own creativity to interpret these texts. Accordingly, he believed *Brāhmins*, who were known as *Aryans*, descended upon the plains of North India a few thousand years back, possibly from Iran. They came as conquerors and defeated the original inhabitants of this land. Under the direction of leaders such as *Brahmā* and *Parshuram*, *Brāhmins* fought protracted wars against the original inhabitants. They initially settled on the banks of the Ganges and eventually spread out over the other parts of the country. To keep a better hold over the masses, they devised the mythology, the *varṇa*, and the caste system as well as the code of cruel and inhuman laws. They founded a system of priest craft, which gave the *Brāhmins* prominence in all rituals.

The caste system was a creation of the cunning *Brāhmins*. The highest rights and privileges were given to the *Brāhmins*, whereas *Śūdras* and *Ati-Śūdras* (untouchables) were regarded with hatred and contempt. They were even denied the commonest rights of humanity. Their touch, or even their shadow, was considered pollution. Phule reinterpreted the religious text of the Hindus to show how *Aryans* had conquered the original inhabitants. Phule saw the nine avatars of *Viṣhṇu* as various stages of *Aryan* conquest. From those days, the *Brāhmins* had enslaved the *Śūdras* and *Ati-Śūdras*. For generations, they carried the chains of slavery of bondage. Many *Brāhmin* writers, such as Manu, have added to the existing legends which enslave the minds of the masses. Phule compared the system of slavery fabricated by the *Brāhmins* with slavery in America and pointed out that *Śūdras* had to suffer greater hardships and oppression than the blacks. He thought this system of selfish superstition and bigotry was responsible for the stagnation and all the evils from which India was suffering for centuries.

The *Brāhmins* continued to exploit the *Śūdras* from birth to death. The *Brāhmins* tried to exploit the *Śūdras* not only in their capacity as priests also intervened and meddled in other ways. Due to the *Brāhmins'* higher education, they had monopolised all the positions in the administration and judiciary, social, religious, and political organisations. In a town or village, the *Brāhmin* was all in all. He was the master and the ruler. The *Patil* (village headman) at the village had become a nonentity. Instead, the *Brāhmin* village accountant, known as *Kulkarni*, had acquired power in the village. He was the temporal and spiritual adviser of the people, a moneylender and a general referee in all matters. Same was the case at the tehsil (township) level, where a tehsildar used to harass the illiterate masses. Phule tells us that the story holds at all levels of administration and in the judiciary, as well as various other departments of the government. The *Brāhmin* bureaucrats used to exploit the poor and ignorant masses in every case by misguiding the British superiors.

It is essential at this stage to note that Phule, who belonged to the gardener (*Śūdra*) caste, was concerned about not only *Śūdras* but also *Ati-Śūdras*, that is, the untouchables. He advocated that these lower castes and untouchables should organise against the dominance of the *Brāhmins* and strive for an egalitarian society. It is therefore not surprising that Ambedkar regarded Phule as his *guru*.

Equality between man and woman: Other than the *Śūdras* and *Ati-Śūdras*, another oppressed group in the Indian society was women. Phule always mentions the equality of women along with men. He did not assume that when men are mentioned, women are automatically included. He makes a special reference to women when he discusses human rights. Just as *Śūdras* were deprived of rights by the *Brāhmins* by keeping them ignorant, Phule thought selfish men had prohibited women from taking education to continue male domination. The Hindu religious texts had given several concessions to man but had imposed severe restrictions on women. Phule was mainly concerned about the marriage system of those days. He attacked customs and practices such as child marriage, marriage between young girls and old men, polygamy, objection to the remarriage of widows, prostitution, harassment of widows, etc. He advised *Śūdra* peasants not to have more than one wife and not to marry their young children. He had given serious thought to the institution of marriage and had devised a simple and modern contract-type ritual for the marriage ceremony of the members of *Satya Shodhak Samaj*. It is interesting to note that Phule did not stop at visualising equal status to women in marriage, family, education, and religion but claimed that women were superior to men in many respects.

VII Views on economy and the agrarian problem

In caste and social terms, Phule was concerned with the status of *Śūdras*, untouchables, and women in Indian society, while in economic terms he was interested in peasantry and its problems. The high-caste nationalists viewed industrialisation as the only solution to the economic problem of India. Phule, on the other hand, advocated for improving agriculture since he perceived Indian economy primarily as an agricultural economy. He observed that Indian agriculture was going through a crisis, and he identified the following factors as its causes.

First, the size of the population dependent on agriculture had increased. Earlier, at least one person from a farmer's family was employed in the army or the administration of the Indian States. Farmers who owned a small piece of land used to make their living on fruits, flowers, fodder, grass, and wood from nearby forests. The new government had started the department of forests, which covered all hills, valleys, waste lands, and grazing grounds, thereby making the lives of farmers who used to depend upon them difficult. British officers had increased the rate of land tax, even though farmers' incomes had declined.

Farmers were being exploited by moneylenders and *Brāhmin* officers of the revenue and irrigation departments and from the judiciary. Due to severe poverty and the declining conditions of the lands, farmers could not get out of debt. In these cases, the lands were transferred to the moneylenders. Another problem the rural economy faced was that of unfair competition from British goods. Because of the inflow of these cheap and superior goods in large quantities, the indigenous craftsmen of the villages and towns suffered great losses, and in many cases, they had to close their businesses. Those who worked in cottage workshops lost their jobs, thereby increasing the rate of unemployment in rural areas.

Based on his in-depth knowledge of the rural economy and the agriculture sector, Phule suggested certain solutions to these problems. The first and most important solution was the construction of tanks and dams so farms could receive sufficient water supplies. Phule wanted the government to take up schemes such as soil conservation, animal breeding, the teaching of modern farming techniques, annual agriculture exhibitions, etc. He pointed out that unless agriculture was made profitable, the agricultural banks which were talked about in those days would not succeed. Phule asked the government to reduce the burden of taxes on farmers to make agriculture profitable. After paying land cesses and local funds, each person in a farmer's family was left with less than three rupees a month, when an ordinary *Brāhmin* or British officer used to get 15 rupees a month for his miscellaneous expenses. Thus, Phule had shown a rare understanding of the economic problems of Indian society. Though he had welcomed British rule, Phule had realised how the Indian economy, especially its rural sector, was being ruined by the colonial connection. The high-caste elite nationalists had shown how wealth was being drained to England from India. Phule, who was looking from the viewpoint of farmers and lower castes, could see another way wealth was being drained, that is, from the rural sector to the urban sector, from the peasant economy to the *Brāhmin* domain. It should be pointed out here that Phule did not made any class differentiation with the peasantry.

VIII Ideas on universal religion

The idea of the emancipation of the lower castes and the untouchables required a critique not only of the Indian social order or that of the colonial economic policy but also of Hinduism and an attempt to visualise some kind of emancipatory religion. Phule, influenced by the radical religious ideas of Thomas Paine, could succeed in doing this kind of theoretical exercise.

Phule believed in one God. He regarded God as the creator of this world and all men and women as His children. Phule discarded idolatry, ritualism, asceticism, fatalism, and the idea of incarnation. No intermediary between God and devotee was considered essential by him. Phule never believed any book was ordained by God. Apparently, it might appear that Phule's approach was similar to that of M. G. Ranade and his *Prarthana Samaj*. However, Phule differed from Ranade significantly and on very important issues. Ranade wanted to work within the structure of Hinduism. He was proud of the Hindu tradition and never thought of breaking from it. He looked to reformist activities as a continuation of the Protestantism of saints and similar efforts. On the contrary, Phule visualised *Sarvajanik Satya Dhārma* (public true religion) as taking the place of Hinduism. His true religion broke from Hindu tradition altogether (Deshpande 2002: 34). Moreover, Phule differed from reformers like Ranade when he severely criticised the mythology and sacred books, like the *Smṛitis* and *Vedās*, of Hindus. He tried to prove that the history of Hinduism was in fact the history of *Brāhmin* domination and the slavery of *Śūdras*. He found cunningness, selfishness, and hypocrisy in sacred scriptures rather than a discussion of true religion. The elite reformers criticised the contemporary degenerated form of Hinduism, while Phule attacked it from its very inception and showed that *Brāhmins* had deceived lower castes throughout history. Phule interpreted Hinduism as a relation based on *varṇa* and the caste system devised by the cunning *Brāhmins* to deceive the lower castes. While rejecting the notions of high and low, pure and polluted, and the inhuman, aggressive, and oppressive nature of *Brāhminism*, Phule preached his idea of universal brotherhood according to the principles of human equality and dignity. This brotherhood transcends all artificial divisions of social position, language, religion, and nationality. That is why he felt closer to liberal foreigners than to self-serving conservative compatriots (Deshpande 2002: 264).

In fact, Phule accused the *Prarthana Samaj* and the *Brahmo Samaj* for their cunning motives. These *Samajas*, according to Phule, were established by the *Brāhmins*, who were educated because of the revenue collected from lower castes. The activities of these associations were intended to conceal the superstructure built by their politically motivated ancestors in the name of religion. They were formed by the *Brāhmins* for their own defence and deception of *Śūdras* and untouchables. But though he dismissed Hinduism altogether, Phule did not reject the very idea of religion or *dhārma*. He tried to put in its place, a universal religion based on the principles of liberty and equality. His *Sarvajanik Satya Dhārma* emphasised on truth seeking without the aid of any *guru* or text. His religious ideas were definitely influenced by Christianity, but he never advocated conversion because he was also influenced by the radical religious argument of Paine, who had shown a number of defects in Christianity.

His universal religion was liberal and in many respects different from traditional religions. His religion was mainly and primarily concerned with secular matters. Phule had visualised a family where each member of that family might follow his own religion. In this ideal family, a wife might embrace Buddhism while her husband might be a Christian, and their children might follow other religions because Phule believed there might be some truth in all religious texts and scriptures; therefore, one of them could not claim the ultimate truth. He thought that the government should not close its eyes to inhuman religious customs or the unjust traditions and practices of Hinduism. At one place, Phule criticised the colonial government for its policy of continuing the practice of giving grants to temples since he claimed that the money had been collected from lower castes in the form of taxes. Thus, there was no place for any communalism or unwarranted neutralism in matters of religion as far as Phule's religious ideas were concerned.

IX *Satya Sodhak Samaj* and the movement against caste and gender discrimination

In 1848, an incident sparked off Phule's quest against the social injustice of caste discrimination and incited a social revolution in the Indian society. Phule was invited to attend the wedding of one of his friends who belonged to an upper-caste *Brāhmin* family. But at the wedding, the relatives of the bridegroom insulted and abused Phule when they came to know about his caste. Phule left the ceremony and made up his mind to challenge the prevailing caste system and social restrictions. He made it his life's work to hammer away tirelessly at the helms of social majoritarian domination and aimed at emancipation of all human beings that were subjected to this social deprivation. After reading Thomas Paine's famous book *The Rights of Man*, Phule was greatly influenced by his ideas. He believed the enlightenment of women and lower-caste people was the only solution to combat the social evils.

Endeavour for women's education: Phule's quest for providing women and girls with education was supported by his wife, Savitribai Phule. Phule taught Savitribai to read and write, and she was one of the few literate women of the time (Thom and Andrade 2008). In 1851, Phule established a girl's school and asked his wife to teach there. Later, he opened two more schools for girls and an indigenous school for the lower castes, especially for the *Mahars* and *Mangs*.

Phule realised the pathetic conditions of widows and established an *ashram* for young widows, eventually becoming an advocate of widow remarriage. Around his time, society was patriarchal, and the position of women was especially abysmal. Female infanticide was a common occurrence as was child marriage. During that time, young girls were being married to much older men. These girls often became widows before they even hit puberty and were left without any family support. Phule was pained by their plight and established an orphanage in 1854 to shelter these unfortunate souls from perishing at the society's cruel hands.

Efforts towards the elimination of caste discrimination: Phule attacked the orthodox *Brāhmins* and other upper castes and termed them hypocrites. He campaigned against the authoritarianism of the upper castes and urged the peasants and proletariat to defy the restrictions imposed upon them. He opened his home to people from all castes and backgrounds. He was a believer in gender equality, and he exemplified his beliefs by involving his wife in all his social reform activities. He believed religious icons like *Rāma* are implemented by the *Brāhmin* as a means for subjugating the lower castes. The orthodox *Brāhmins* of the society were furious at the activities of Phule. They blamed him for vitiating the norms and regulations of the society. Many accused him of acting on behalf of the British Christian missionaries. But Phule was firm and decided to continue the movement against caste and gender discrimination. He exposed the *Brāhminical* pretensions and appreciated the Christian missionaries for their noble work in school education (Omvedt 1971). Interestingly, some *Brāhmin* friends supported Phule to make the movement successful.

Satya Shodhak Samaj : In 1873, Phule formed the *Satya Shodhak Samaj* (Truth-Seeking Society). He undertook the systematic deconstruction of existing beliefs and history, only to reconstruct a version that promoted equality. Phule vehemently condemned the *Vedās*, the ancient holy scriptures of the Hindus. He traced the history of *Brāhminism* through several other ancient texts and held the *Brāhmins* responsible for framing the exploitative and inhuman laws to maintain their social superiority by suppressing the *Śūdras* and *Ati-Śūdras* in the society. The purpose of the *Satya Shodhak Samaj* was to decontaminate the society from caste discrimination and liberate the oppressed lower-caste people from the stigmas inflicted by the *Brāhmins*. Phule was the first person to coin the term "*Dalits*" to apply to all people considered lower caste and untouchable by the *Brāhmins*. Membership of the *Satya Sodhak Samaj* was open to all irrespective of caste and class. Some written records suggest that they even welcomed participation of Jews as members. In 1868, Phule decided to construct a common bathing tank outside his house to exhibit his embracing attitude towards all human beings and wished to dine with everyone, regardless of their caste.

Aims and objectives of Satya Shodhak Samaj

Phule's main aim behind establishing *Satya Shodhak Samaj* was to free the lower classes from the shackles of religious and social slavery. With the establishment of *Satya Shodhak Samaj*, Phule laid the foundation of the movement of social equality. Truth and humanity were the breath of the *Satya Shodhak* movement. Phule made it clear that all people are the children of God, so they are equal. Therefore, the religious, social, and economic rights must be the same for everybody. Eradication of the injustice done to the lower caste, to free the workers from the exploitation of the exploiters, to establish and raise healthy social lives were the various objectives of *Satya Shodhak Samaj*. The society's main aim was to stop the exploitation of the *Śūdras* and *Ati-Śūdras* by the *Brāhmin* priests and to make lower-caste people conscious of their human rights and free them from psychological and religious slavery. Therefore, *Satya Shodhak Samaj* advocated for true religion and the equality of all people in the universe. To oppose the *Brāhmin* domination and role of the priest, *Satya Sodhak Samaj* arranged simple marriages without any *Brāhmin* priests or rituals. It preached the fatherhood of God and brotherhood of man based on equality and fraternity.

X Contemporary relevance of Phule's philosophy

After 70 years of India's independence, caste and untouchability remained a reality despite constitutional provisions and a set of legislation prohibiting it. Whereas the world has entered the third millennium and is progressing towards accomplishing the goals of liberty, equality, and fraternity, India has failed to eradicate untouchability, caste, and descent-based discrimination. Though some *Dalits* reach higher levels in professions, business, and politics, and some are economically well off, others still suffer from social stigma and reactionary political discrimination. Discriminations against *Dalits* typically manifest in the private sector with respect to employment and social mobility. Prejudices against *Dalits* are reinforced by casteist views and have been identified in caste-related violence. *Dalits* are often denied the basic rights of education, housing, property rights, freedom of religion, choice of employment, and equal treatments in many parts of the country. Even today, caste mindsets still exist in our country. This kind of mindset should be removed from the society. Every *Dalit* and woman should be educated in the society, and then only our society will progress.

As a visionary, Phule had realised the importance of education for women and lower castes, and he did work for that. Phule was a great social philosopher who worked for the emancipation of the oppressed, and his social philosophy has relevance even today. Phule's wife, Savitribai, was his first biographer, and she internalised his vision and philosophy as a devoted supporter of his work. Phule's social thoughts are based on humanism, on the values of equality, justice, and tranquillity. He spread a value-based system through his work and thought. India is an independent country; still, independent values are not there in our society because *varṇa* and the caste system still exist in some parts of the country. Phule was a humanist and a champion of women and lower castes. In modern civilisation, every individual should follow his humanism. Today, education has been reduced to transmitting information. There is a fear of examination because of bookish education. We must be practical and bring life-oriented education. In this context, Phule's education system is still relevant. For him, knowledge is not just information. It involves questioning, understanding, and critiquing knowledge. Interpretation, critique, and values are central to Phule, who gave an alternative to the information approach to knowledge. For Phule, knowledge matters because it can question, change, and transform the individual and society. Thus, for Phule, like John Dewey, education can empower and make society more democratic. It can help in reconstructing, rethinking, and interpreting tradition. This aspect of Phule is extremely relevant in the paradoxical context of caste in contemporary India – where despite constitutional provisions, caste discrimination is widespread.

XI Conclusion

Mahatma Jyotirao Phule was the first Indian educationist whose pragmatic views on education were honoured by the British rulers in India. He was a practical man with a profound philosophical background. The Indian educationists of his period and after were deeply impressed by the richness and originality of Phule's thought. His educational ideas and principles, especially in the field of women's education and universal, free, and compulsory primary education, are most relevant in modern Indian society as elsewhere. It is not an exaggeration to say that the history of women's education in India would be incomplete without making a reference to Phule's contribution. He is rightly called Mahatma.

Notes

1 The full article can be accessed at http//ghalibana.blogspot.com/. . ./memorial-bymahatma-phule-to-hunter.html.
2 Article 45 of the Constitution of India has made a provision for free and compulsory education for children where Article 21a made it a fundamental right.

References

Deshpande, G. P. (Ed.) (2002). *Selected Writings of Jyotiba Phule*. New Delhi: Manohar Publishers and Distributers.

Mani, Braj Mani (2005). *The Debrahmanising of History: Dominance and Resistance in Indian Society*. New Delhi: Manohar Publishers and Distributers.

Marwaha, Navjoti (2010). Mahatma Jyotiba Phule: An Educational Philosopher. *The Primary Teacher*, XXXV (3 and 4), July and October.

O'Hanlon, Rosalind (1985). *Caste, Conflict and Ideology: Mahatma Jyotirao Phule and Low Caste Protest in Nineteenth Century Western India*. Cambridge: Cambridge University Press.

Omvedt, Gail (1971). Mahatma Jyotirao Phule and the Ideology of Social Revolution in India. *Economic and Political Weekly*, 6(37), September, pp. 1969–1979.

Panday, Balaj (1986). Educational Development among Scheduled Cates. *Social Scientist*, 14(2/3), February–March. http://links.jstor.org/sici/7sici

Thom, Wolf and Susan Andrade (2008). Savitribai and India's Conversation on Education. *Oikos Worldviews Journal*, 8.

5

RAMAKRISHNA PARAMHANSA

Praveen Kumar

> *What a scholastic philosopher would call the 'accidents' of Ramakrishna's life were intensely Hindu and therefore, so far as we in the West are concerned, unfamiliar and hard to understand; its 'essence', however, was intensely mystical and therefore universal. To read through these conversations in which mystical doctrine alternates with an unfamiliar kind of humour, and where discussions of the oddest aspects of Hindu mythology give place to the most profound and subtle utterances about the nature of Ultimate Reality, is in itself a liberal, education in humility, tolerance and suspense of judgment.*
> – (Aldous Huxley, Foreword, *The Gospel of Sri Ramakrishna* by Mahendranath Gupta)

I Introduction

Sri Ramakrishna Paramhansa (1835–1897) and his thoughts and ideas had a profound influence on both Indian and Western society. This happened during his lifetime and, through his principal disciple and messenger, Swami Vivekananda, after his death. It would not be wrong to state that his thoughts and ideas continue to exercise influence on Indian and Western minds in the form of the spiritual legacy he and Vivekananda have left behind and the cultural legacy that comes through various Ramakrishna Missions in India and abroad. All these were the result of Ramakrishna's singular strength, which lay in his great religious and spiritual power.

An effort to bring out Ramakrishna's thoughts and ideas requires putting together what exists in the form of his sayings, gospels, and teachings. This is because Ramakrishna has not left behind any systematically produced document or literature that would be based on his thoughts, and the literature must be constructed out of his sayings and teachings. Ramakrishna was not a philosopher in the conventional sense of the term. He was not a social reformer who aimed at bringing an end to the evils of Indian society. He was not even educated in a formal sense. The contents of his teachings or sayings would be of a deep, mystical nature and describe the inner experiences of the great *saint*.[1] Thus, language may not adequately express the "super sensuous perception" of Ramakrishna, who was almost illiterate. He never expressed his thoughts in formal language (Gupta 1941: 4).

The teachings of Ramakrishna also have had practical orientations. Although he never claimed he had founded a religion, his teachings became the "religion" of chosen ones, including in the United States. He preached the old religion of India, which was founded on the *Vedās*, more particularly on the *Upaniṣhads* (Muller 1898: 11). Ramakrishna's philosophy, not being a "philosophy" in the conventional sense of the term, is "borne out of his realisation and [is] in the form of rather spiritual truths". His thoughts can better be understood "not only as a result of intellectual speculations but also of mystical intuition" (Harshananda 1987: 101). His sayings, or *Logia*, were collected and written down by his pupils in Bengali, and some were translated into Sanskrit and English (Muller 1898: 95–96). In the following pages, an endeavour will be made to discuss and analyse Ramakrishna's teachings and sayings including his interactions with his disciples in the form of some social and religious thoughts.

A study of Ramakrishna's sayings or teachings leads us to an understanding that the realisation of God or attainment of spirituality lay at the core of his philosophy. Other things are to be understood in light of the knowledge of this core. Thus, this chapter will focus on the four central aspects of Ramakrishna's teachings, which are knitted closely to his understanding of the Absolute, or *Brahman*, and *Ishwar*, or God. The four aspects are: 1) knowing religion and the *Brahman* or God; 2) the reasons behind a person's inability to identify and know the *Brahman* and which constitutes bondage in this world, that is, *Maya*, spiritualism, and equality; 3) freedom from this bondage in the form of God realisation; and finally 4) the form of knowledge itself. This chapter will deal with the last aspect first because it involves understanding what constitutes valid knowledge and God realisation and, in Ramakrishna's vision, it is only through knowledge that one can identify and realise God.

II Life sketch

Swami Ramakrishna Paramhansa was born on 18 February 1836 in the small Kamarpukur village in Hooghly district of Bengal. His original name was Gadadhar Chattopadhyay, and his parents were Khudiram Chattopadhyay and Chandramani Devi. He hailed from a poor *Brāhmin* family. He did not take interest in studies, but from an early age he was very spiritually inclined. Later, Ramakrishna became the head priest at the Dakshineshwar Kali temple and attained God realisation, or spirituality. Many believed Ramakrishna was a true *avatar* (incarnation) of Lord *Viṣhṇu*. Over the years, many believed Ramakrishna had spiritual powers, and he was respected as a true spiritual figure. He gained several disciples, including his chief disciple, Swami Vivekananda. Many believe Ramakrishna was a man beyond religion. His teachings have become tenets of Hinduism. At the same time, they have also become a kind of life advice for many. Ramakrishna is still the most celebrated mystic in Bengal. He died of throat cancer on 16 August 1886.

III Knowledge, or *jñāna*

Knowledge, generally understood, depends on what has been grasped through sensory experiences. However, to qualify as valid knowledge, it must be scientific. This means it should withstand the scrutiny of logic and rationality. It is required to be proved when its validity is questioned, and there should be regularity in terms of the establishment of a cause-and-effect relationship. It is this form of knowledge, which Vivekananda held as valid during his initial interactions with Ramakrishna. However, under Ramakrishna's guidance, Vivekananda realised existence beyond sensory perceptions, and this is what would constitute true knowledge. This knowledge is real and is based on what can be realised. It is based on true experiences and is an outcome of the spiritual power that a person has developed within.

There are a few things which need to be added here to further explain the mode and method of attaining the knowledge Ramakrishna was maintaining. Vivekananda often contradicted Ramakrishna's statements or assertions on the grounds of scientific validity or acceptability. Ramakrishna, in fact, encouraged his disciples to question his assertions. At times, even he would be ridiculed by Vivekananda while discussing issues such as the existence or realisation of God. Ramakrishna would advise Vivekananda to apply reason and intellect before accepting what was being told to him. Ramakrishna would often tell his disciples, "Test me as the money changer tests their coins. You must not believe me without testing me thoroughly" (cited in Nikhilanand 2015: 44). Reason and intellect, which depend more on senses, have a role to play in terms of moving towards what would constitute knowledge. The knowledge, being a quest for truth or what is real, would, according to Ramakrishna, rather be based on superior understanding. This superior understanding is "acquired through firsthand knowledge of the essence of the things" (Nikhilanand 2015: 37). This goes beyond reason. It is rather based on belief or faith, which always has a solid foundation which cannot falter. A knowledge acquired through reason can be proved wrong; however, knowledge which is based on consciousness of the real cannot be proved wrong. Thus, Ramakrishna would hold that "reason is weak, but the faith is stronger". Vivekananda also accepted this form of knowledge as real once he experienced it in the form of truth or reality. Later, applying this understating to religion, Vivekananda held that religion, too, could be scientific.

If senses cannot reach out to what is real, it is the limitation of the senses, not the inexistence of reality. The same would be applicable to religion or knowing God. As Ramakrishna would say, "if one cannot see stars during the day time that would not mean that there are no stars" (Muller 1898: 98). Vivekananda aptly put this idea in the following words:

> Sciences were but secondary. That which made us realise the *Brahman* was supreme, the highest knowledge. This idea we find in every religion, and that is why religion always claimed to be supreme knowledge. Knowledge of the sciences cover, as it were, only part of our lives, but the knowledge which religion brings to us is eternal, as infinite as truth it preaches.
>
> *(Vivekananda 2006: 366)*

However, a caveat may be added regarding Ramakrishna's views on who can attain the true knowledge. It may be understood that not everyone may be able to attain the ultimate spirituality. Suitability, possibly, may be the most important aspect of the seeker when it comes to the realisation of God. In addition, a true and dedicated master, or *guru*, is the necessary condition for the attainment of this form of knowledge. Only the one who is destined to attain the spirituality can attain it. This was best exemplified in the relationship between Swami Ramakrishna and Swami Vivekananda.

IV Religion, *Brahman*, and the existence of God

> If the room is dark, do you go about beating your chest and crying, 'it is dark, dark, dark?' No, the only way to get the light is to strike a light and then the darkness goes. The only way to realise the light above you is to strike the spiritual light within you, and the darkness of sin and impurity will feel away. Think of your higher Self, not of your lower.
>
> *(Vivekananda 1971: 10)*

Religion, to Ramakrishna, was a spiritual way to realise God. This must be understood in the "wholeness" of everything that exists. Existence of God is a reality, and religion is what makes one experience this reality. One need not be dogmatic regarding which path would lead to God. God, in fact, can be realised through several spiritual paths and disciplines. According to Ramakrishna, *sādhanā*, *jñāna*, *bhakti*, *yoga*, and *karma* all have a place when it comes to the realisation of God. All could be practiced either singly or in combination. However, the only thing that is required is "great earnestness" to realise God (Harshananda 1987: 105). This understanding of religion and God was based on Ramakrishna's spiritual experience. And, to realise God, one must rise above sensory experiences.

Ramakrishna had reached this conclusion after knowing and experiencing the religions of Islam, Christianity, and Buddhism. He understood that all the religions are the same in terms of their objectives or goals. They are to be understood as different paths which lead to the same destination. Followers of different religions may be calling God by different names, as the same person may have different identities, given the way relations are defined by the society. There cannot be different experiences of spirituality. There is oneness when it comes to spirituality or attaining spiritual experience, what Ramakrishna had called "God realisation". Thus, there could be diverse ways and means but only one result, that is, the "realisation of God consciousness" (Nikhilananda 2015: 29).

According to Ramakrishna, reality is one. It may occur in different ways at different places; however, in his message, we find that the essence of everything is the same. The foundation of Ramakrishna's religious teaching is the ancient Indian *Mahavakyas* of *Aham Brahmasmi* and *Tatvamasi*. Ramakrishna synthesised *Advaita Vedānta* with the *Vaishnava* cult of *bhakti*. As stated, he preached that the essentials of all religions are the same (Sharma and Sharma 2017: 165). For the realisation of God, human desire had to be brought under control. He preached discarding desire for material prosperity. This, however, did not require escaping a worldly life. What was required was constant meditation upon God. Human passion or desire must be redirected towards God, which would lead to the elimination of worldly passions and desires (ibid.: 164).

Thus, what we can understand from Ramakrishna's ideas is that there is an omnipotent, omniscient, and omnipresent element that is the cause and result of everything, and this can be called God. God is existent, and can even be seen, but we need to develop the spiritual elements within us to realise and experience God. In a way, one must rise above sensory experiences to realise God. Second, there could be diverse manifestations of this reality, but there is oneness in what we search for as God. Religions are nothing but diverse ways and means to realise God. This is the spiritual way and requires constant meditation upon God. The realisation of God requires the renunciation of material desires and not the renunciation of a worldly life.

Ramakrishna had experienced this truth, meaning the realisation of God directly and spoke of that experience. Ramakrishna accepted *Brahman*, God, or the ultimate truth as the only and highest reality. For him, God has aspects that exist with form (*sakara*) and with attributes (*saguna*). The *Brahman* may even have aspects that can be *nirguna* (without attributes) and *nirakara* (without form). God, for Ramakrishna, is both formless and possessed of form (Harshananda 1987: 102). According to Ramakrishna, "God with form is as real as without form" (Gupta 1941: 238). Ramakrishna compared the formless God to a man playing a single note on his flute, though the instrument has seven holes. But on the same instrument another man plays different melodies (ibid.: 239). According to Ramakrishna, as the sun and its rays, fire and its burning power, and milk and milky whiteness cannot be thought of independent of each other, the absolute cannot be thought of apart from the idea of God with attributes, that is, a personal God and vice versa. Thus, according to Ramakrishna, "God is formless and is with form too, and He is that transcends both the form and formlessness. He alone can say what else He is" (Muller 1898: 105).

Thus, for Ramakrishna, *Brahman* and God may be the same. However, at times, God may be treated as different from *Brahman*. As stated, God is an aspect of *Brahman* that exists in its wholeness. The role of *Brahman*, when involved in creation, preservation, and destruction, is *Ishwara*, or God. Ramakrishna identified the *Ishwara* with *Kali* or *Shakti*. At the same time, Ramakrishna understood *Brahman* and *Shakti* as one and inseparable. According to him:

> The distinction between *Brahman* and *Shakti* is really a distinction without a difference. *Brahman* and *Shakti* are one [*abheda*], just as fire and its burning power are one. *Brahman* and *Shakti* are one, just as milk and the whiteness of milk are one. *Brahman* and *Shakti* are one, just as a gem and its brightness are one. You cannot conceive of the one without the other, or make a difference between them.
>
> (cited in Harshananda 1987: 102)

Thus, for Ramakrishna, "That which is *Brahman* is also Goddess *Kali*, the *Adyasakti*, who creates, preserves, and destroys the universe. He who is *Krishna* is the same as *Kali*. The root is one-all these are His sport and play" (Gupta 1941: 1157). The diverse manifestations of God with forms or without forms, with attributes or without attributes, are all made acceptable by Ramakrishna. Also, different religions, and diverse ways and means to achieve God realisation within the religion, too, are valid. However, all this should happen without any dogma attached to the path that one may opt for God realisation. The only qualification that is required is that one should be earnest in realising and experiencing God. This was the message Ramakrishna gave to the world.

V *Maya*, or bondage

The realisation of God is not possible for most humans. However, a few may be able to develop the spiritual capacity to reach that stage. Ramakrishna would accept that potentially every man could not experience or realise God because of the *Maya*, or the veil that keeps God out of sight of the humans. God, as stated, is located nowhere but in *Brahman*, according to Ramakrishna. However, *Maya* is also located in the *Brahman*. *Maya* in *Brahman* is like poison in a snake; the snake holds the poison within, but the poison does no harm to the snake. Similarly, the *Brahman* holds *Maya* within but remains unaffected by the *Maya*. According to Ramakrishna, all that exists is *Narayana*. "God is in all men, but all men are not in God; that is why they suffer" (Muller 1898: 147). Thus, those who can overcome this "veil of ignorance" can realise God. God manifests in every being, but not every being finds its place in God or *Brahman*. *Maya*, nonetheless, could be the *Vidya Maya* and the *Avidya Maya*. While the former helps a captivated soul to get liberation by giving him discrimination and non-attachment, the latter, however, is manifested as lust and egoism that really binds him (Harshananda 1987: 103).

Being human is being in bondage. Every *jiva* (or man) in essential nature is God himself. Thus, the soul enchained is man, but when free from chains (*Maya*), it is *Siva* (Lord) (Muller 1898: 145). The cause of bondage is *Maya*. Thus, what is required is that the man who aims for liberation or freedom from bondage must cultivate *Vidya Maya*. This is reflected in the egoism, or "I", of human beings. Ego, too, has two sides: the ripe ego and the unripe ego (Harshananda 1987: 104). The ripe ego should be cultivated. The diverse devotional practices (*bhakti-sadhana*) are valid, according to Ramakrishna, as *Ishwara* is real and responsive. Similarly, Ramakrishna also believed the *avatar* (incarnation) of God is also real.[2] God is omniscient and omnipotent. God can be born as a human being. In the words of Ramakrishna, "Since the incarnation is God Himself, seeing Him is equivalent to seeing God" (ibid.: 103).

VI Equality, inequality, and freedom

The understanding of equality co-exists with the concept of inequality in Ramakrishna. However, these concepts have meaning only in a spiritual sense, not in a socio-political sense. Everything that exists is the manifestation of *Narayana*, or God, which is *Shakti* or *Kali* for Ramakrishna. Also, among human beings, everyone can cultivate the self in such a manner that each person can realise God or spirituality. Understood in this sense, every person has equality of status, in terms of manifestation of the same Being or Absolute and being part of the same whole. Also, everyone is equal in terms of capability, as potentially everyone can find his way back to the Origin. However, this equality is co-existent with the inequality of the soul. As discussed, *Avidya Maya*, or the unripe ego, is the cause of bondage, but according to Ramakrishna, "only pure souls are capable of rising above *Avidya Maya* or unripe ego or cultivating *Vidya Maya* or ripe ego. God may dwell in all things, but he was especially manifest in pure soul like Naren" (Nikhilanand 2015: 38).

Thus, not everyone was destined to be free. Only pure souls could achieve this status. This was something given. And this knowledge of Ramakrishna was based on his spiritual experience, which cannot be wrong. This was a conviction which had to be true, and nothing else. As Ramakrishna would state, "divine mother reveals to me nothing but truth" (Nikhilanand 2015: 38). The difference of perceptions regarding God and His existence was also because the devotee who has seen God in only one aspect knows him in that aspect alone. However, he who has seen Him in manifold aspects is alone in a position to say all these forms are of one God, for God is multiform. This is like a person who has seen the chameleon in one colour or in all its colours. He has forms and no forms, and many are His forms which no one knows (Muller 1898: 98). Achieving this knowledge, too, would constitute the realisation of God and hence would be an aspect of freedom as well. Eventually, the relationship between man and God has to be understood in Ramakrishna's statement, where he has said, "as the lamp cannot burn without oil, so man cannot live without God" (Muller 1898: 103).

VII Conclusion

To understand the philosophy that can be made out from the teachings or sayings of Ramakrishna, it requires that one should understand the purpose of life. Ramakrishna has been considered the most influential religious figure of nineteenth-century India. He was a mystic and a true *yogi*. A worshipper of Goddess *Kali*, Ramakrishna is considered a central figure in the revival of Hinduism in nineteenth-century India. The true success and influence of his teachings is best manifested in the life, works, and teachings of Swami Vivekananda, who being an atheist in his early life, became Ramakrishna's most devout disciple, follower, and messenger.

Notes

1 At the outset, it must be made clear that Ramakrishna never propagated a system of philosophy of his own. He experienced the truth directly and then spoke out of the fullness of that experience. Hence, we must piece together his teachings on these aspects of philosophy given at random in his conversations (Harshananda, Swami (1987).
2 So long as one does not become simple like a child, one does not get divine illumination. If you forget all the worldly knowledge you have acquired and become as ignorant as a child, you will gain true knowledge. (Quoted in Muller, Max F. (1898).

References

Gupta, Mahendranath (1941). *Gospel of Swami Ramakrishna*. Translated from Bengali by Swami Nikhilananda. Available at https://www.ramakrishnavivekananda.info/gospel/gospel.htm. Accessed November and December 2018.

Harshananda, Swami (1987). The Philosophy of Sri Ramakrishna. *Vedanta Kesari*, March Issue.

Muller, Max F. (1898). *Ramakrishna: His Life and Sayings*. London: Theosophical Publishing Society.

Nikhilananda, Swami (2015). *Vivekananda: A Biography*, Reprint Edition. Kolkata: Advaita Ashram.

Sharma, Urmila and Sharma, S. K. (2017). *Indian Political Thought*. New Delhi: Atlantic Publishers and Distributors (P) Ltd.

Vivekananda, Swami (Ed.). (1971). *What Religion Is: In the Words of Swami Vivekananda*. Kolkata: Advaita Ashrama.

Vivekananda, Swami (2006). *The Complete Works of Swami Vivekananda*. Kolkata: Advaita Ashrama.

6

PANDITA RAMABAI

Avneet Kaur

> *A life totally committed to God has nothing to fear, nothing to lose, nothing to regret.*
> – Pandita Ramabai

I Introduction

A study of ancient Indian literature reveals that the position of women was not very satisfactory. The status of women was considered equal to that of the *Śūdras*, and the killing of women was also not considered a disgraceful act. Information on the traditional status and role of women in India is derived from historical accounts and classic texts (Altekar 1983: 319). The literature on Indian history abounds with contradictory and conflicting views on the status of women. It can properly be understood within the socio-cultural condition of the society. Our ancient holy literature, such as *Ṛigvedā*, shows evidence that women are men's equals as regards access to and capacity for the highest knowledge, even the knowledge of the absolute *Brahmā*. The *brahmavadinis* were products of the educational discipline of *brahmacharya*, for which women were also eligible (*Rig-Veda*, Verses 7 & 9). The *Ṛigvedā* refers to young girls completing their education as *brahmacharinis* and then gaining husbands, with whom they were merged like rivers in the ocean. The *Yajurvedā* also states that a daughter who has completed her *bramhacharya* should be married to one who is similarly learned (The *Yajurveda* [VIII.1]). *Ṛigvedic* society was patriarchal and based on monogamy. The institution of monogamy is a recognition of the high social status of women. The *Brihadaranyaka Upaniṣhad* mentions a ritual by which a person prays for the birth of a daughter to him, who should be *Pandita*, or "learned lady" (The *Brihadaranyaka Upaniṣhad*, Vol. 1, 4, 17).

As the society got much more settled and was not subjected to the pressure of continuous invasion, the position of women became subject to deterioration.

The majority religion in India, Hinduism, assigned a lower status to women. The ancient law giver *Manu* prescribed, "a women must never be independent". The life of an ideal Hindu wife is to be spent in the service of her husband; she ought to be a *pativrata*. A Hindu woman was expected to be an obedient daughter, faithful wife, and devoted mother. Marriage was the single most important event in her life, and it took place soon after puberty. Thus, child marriage came to be a norm which implied that young girls were not involved in the decision-making process of selecting their husbands. The custom of *sati*, the proscription of widow remarriage even when she is widowed as a child, the insistence on dowry, etc. rendered a Hindu woman a non-person. In addition, the prohibition of inter-religious and inter-caste marriages compelled some women into prostitution or to commit suicide. The contradictory view about women's status is a cause of the emergence of the ideals of womanhood at different times. The concept of *ardhangini* suggests there was equality between men and women, neither of the two being superior to the other. There is recorded evidence to show that for many centuries a woman's position continued to be one in which she did not have either legal or social rights to make her independent of the family into which she was born or married. There are, however, greater evidences to show that the contrary was equally true; that is, woman was not always without rights nor was she constantly in subjection (Mehta 1970: 16–113). Due to the prevalent practices in society, there was a need to reform and empower women.

Pandita Ramabai (23 April 1858–5 April 1922) was an eminent Indian social reformer and activist and a champion of improvement in the plight of Indian women. As a social reformer, she championed the cause of the emancipation of Indian women. A widely travelled lady, she visited most parts of India and even went to England (1883) and the United States (1886–1888). She wrote many books, including her widely popular *The High Caste Hindu Woman*, which showed the darkest of subject matter relating to the life of Hindu women, including child brides and the treatment they receive by the government. She had a strong view of what should be accomplished so women would have more freedom, including the protection of widowed women and child brides, and she was also against the practice of *sati*.

Ramabai was one of the early pioneers in the field of women's education and a champion of women's rights. Her upbringing was such that it was conducive to her later role as a women's rights activist. The Kolkata elite were enchanted by her revolutionary and learned ways and bestowed on her the name *Saraswati* and called her *Pandita* because she seemed as learned as other *Brāhmin Pandits*. Some recent scholarly analyses of Ramabai's contribution tend to focus on a static period of her life. Ramabai was a renowned social reformer in nineteenth-century British India whose life was a prototype of feminist aspiration to succeeding generations of Indian women. She offered an unyielding critique of Hindu orthodoxy, caste, and patriarchy and argued that education would raise the status of Hindu women. Ramabai was a social thinker and reformer who valued and advocated freedom of thought and action and worked tirelessly so equality and progress for women could be achieved. Her critique of Indian and British society was carried in her overt confrontation of Hindu orthodoxy, patriarchy, and British imperialism. Ramabai's overseas travels produced reflections about the places she visited and the cultures she encountered. These writings document her observations about the societies she experienced and embody her critique of slavery, racism, patriarchy, and institutionalised religion, including religious structures in Christianity and her comparative observations about the status of women in India, England, and the United States. After discussing some of the important themes and issues relating to the cause of women, it is imperative to understand Ramabai's life and other issues, such as patriarchy, gender equality, and rights.

II Life sketch

The social context for Ramabai's life was the traditional upper-caste Hindu society which mandated pre-pubertal marriage and immediate post-pubertal consummation of marriage for girls and which denied education to women, which disprivileged their status and curbed their freedom of communication. The salient issues in gender reform, therefore, were the abolition of child marriage, support for widow remarriage, and the introduction of women's education. These initiatives were radical enough to trigger occasional open conflict between the reformist minority and the conservative majority. Reform and religion intersected repeatedly because the multiple oppression of women was justified by sacralising the patriarchal ideology which treated women as inferior and subservient to men, as born solely for a wife–mother role, and as the legal wards and property of their husbands. The reform issues therefore posed a direct challenge to both patriarchy and religion in varying degrees.

The strongest challenge of all came from Pandita Ramabai herself, who interrogated patriarchy through her nationally and internationally famed championship of women's education and the Hindu religion, through her conversion to Christianity and overt missionary activity. Ramabai was born into a Hindu, Marathi-speaking, *Chitpavan Brāhmin* family who hailed from Karnataka. Ramabai was the youngest child of Sanskrit scholar Anant Shastri Dongre and his second wife, Laxmibai. Anant Shastri taught Sanskrit and sacred scriptures to Laxmibai despite strong opposition from the society. Anant Shastri and Laxmibai settled down in the forests of Gangamul in Karnataka to lead a simple life. Even here, in an assembly of learned *gurus* and *pandits*, he had to defend himself for teaching Sanskrit to his wife. He convinced those *gurus* and chief *pandits* that it was not wrong for women and lower castes to be taught Sanskrit *Purāṇic* literature.

During this era, when teaching was denied to women, Ramabai was taught at home. This was especially remarkable considering that in those times women were denied even the basic right to literacy. Her unconventional upbringing facilitated the rejection of a rigid gender-specific role unlike other girls who were forced into wife- and motherhood at an early age, denied education, and made to restrict their lives within the private domain of a joint family. After the death of her parents and sister in the mid-1870s, Ramabai, along with her brother, travelled throughout India until she reached Calcutta (now Kolkata). Ramabai received a formal invitation to lecture in Calcutta before a few learned *pandits*. Ramabai's remarkable scholarship, and especially her in-depth knowledge of the Sanskrit scriptures, created a great impact on the audience. They called a public assembly in the city's town hall and conferred upon Ramabai the highest title possible in India for a woman, that of *Saraswati*, meaning "Goddess of wisdom". In Calcutta, Keshab Chandra Sen, a supporter of *Brahmo Samaj*, suggested to Ramabai that she read the *Vedās* and *Upaniṣhads*. This was the beginning of a new phase in her life, a period in which she grappled with several contradictions in her life which later fructified into liberal feminism.

Ramabai married at the age of 22. She not only departed from the practice of early marriage but also ignored caste restrictions by marrying Bipin Behari Medhvi, a man of *Śūdra varṇa* (lower caste) and an active member of *Brahmo Samaj*. The marriage was criticised, and Bipin Behari was promptly excommunicated. Bipin Behari died within two years of their marriage, leaving Ramabai alone with their young daughter, Manorama. Ramabai wore a white cotton *saree* and cropped her hair, as widows did at that time. Ramabai returned to her native land, Poona, where she was welcomed by the leaders and social reformers. Instead of following widowhood, she turned once more to a public career, with a mission to serve the oppressed women of India. Here, she decided to set up an institution for widows. Ramabai decided to go to England to seek British support for her widow's home (Mudgal 2013).

There, Ramabai enrolled as a student at Cheltenham Women's College to study natural science, maths, English, and in return she taught Sanskrit (Kosambi 1988). After reaching England, Ramabai sought a meeting with Sir Bartle Frere, who was the former governor of Bombay Presidency, and followed the meeting up with an appeal for help, written originally in Marathi and published in 1883 as *The Cry of Indian Women*. The book contained details of Indian women's oppression through early marriage, desertion by husbands, and widowhood. She also appealed on behalf of the *Arya Mahila Samaj* for a widow home in India (Jha 2011).

At the same time, disillusionment with elite liberalism and *Brāhmanic* tradition began to lead her away from Hinduism. In England, Ramabai encountered Christian missionaries. Influenced by their message of love and forgiveness and egalitarian treatment of all, in 1883, along with her daughter, Ramabai accepted Christianity. In 1886, after Ramabai failed to find much support from England, she went to the United States on an invitation by the Dean of the Women's Medical College of Pennsylvania, to attend the graduate ceremony of Anandibai Joshee, a cousin of Ramabai and the first Indian woman to travel to the United States to become a doctor. Ramabai got acquainted with the feminist and other reformist circles in Boston. She soon contacted various church groups and women's welfare groups in fundraising campaigns for her long-lived dream of a women's home in India.

The High-Caste Hindu Woman was India's first feminist manifesto with an agenda for women emancipation and empowerment. During these years, Ramabai also worked on a Marathi book, *Lokesthiti Ani Pravasvritta*, published in Bombay in December 1889, a few months after her return to India. In this book, Ramabai described society, the political system, culture, and activities in the United States. Through this book, Ramabai focused on the importance of social movements for reforming the lives of women. Pandita Ramabai's association with the United States resulted in the December 1887 formation of the Ramabai Association, which pledged ten years of financial support for her proposed secular school for high-caste widows in India (Jha 2011). In February 1889, Ramabai returned to India and opened the school, which she named *Sharda Sadan* (Home of Learning), in Bombay. However, to gain more direct access to orthodox *Brāhmin* families, she shifted the school to Pune, where she was criticised by conservative Hindu society. Consequently, high-caste Hindu widows started distancing themselves from *Sharda Sadan*, forcing Ramabai to increasingly alienate herself from Hindu society and exposing her bonds with Christianity. This led her to open a new Christian body, the *Mukti Sadan*, to house the victims of the Gujarat famine in 1896. With native support dwindling, Ramabai depended almost exclusively on overseas donations to run the *Sadan*, which were eventually amalgamated into a missionary body called Christian *Mukti* Missions. Significantly, the institutional intervention of Pandita Ramabai in ameliorating the conditions of women demonstrated her activities. The Christian *Mukti* Mission, later renamed the Ramabai *Mukti* Mission, turned out to be the women bastion through which numerous activities for women empowerment were carried out. Hence, it provided a home for high-caste Hindu widows, as they were the most marginalised women in the country (Chakrabarty and Pandey 2009).

III Patriarchy and the structure of Indian society

The word "patriarchy", which is frequently used by feminists and writers, literally means the rule of the father, or the patriarch, in a family where the eldest male is the head of the family and controls his wife, children, other members of the family, and slaves (Bhasin 1994: 3). According to Gerda Lerner, "the period of the establishment of patriarchy was not one event but a process which developed over a period of nearly 2500 years from approximately 3100 to 600 B.C." (Lerner 1986: 8). As time passed, the word "patriarchy" came to be generally used to refer to male domination in the family, society, polity, etc. whereby men are the decision-makers in all aspects of life. It is a system of social structures and practices in which men selfishly dominate and exploit women to their own satisfaction. It can also be said to be an ideology in which men are seen as superior to women, that women are and should be controlled by men, and that they are part of men's property (Lerner 1993: 3–4).

Patriarchy can be seen in almost all societies in the world. But it should be noted that its nature is different across societies, in different classes within the same society, and in different periods of history. The term "patriarchy" was taken up by the sociologist Max Weber to describe "a particular form of household organisation in which the father dominated other members of an extended kinship network and controlled the economic production of the household". Its resonance for feminism, however, rests on the radical feminist theory as propounded by American writers, such as Kate Millet, who viewed patriarchy as an over-arching category of male dominance. To Millett, patriarchy as an institution, is a social constant, so deeply entrenched as to run through all other political, social, or economic forms, whether of caste or class, feudality or bureaucracy, just as it pervades all major religions. Millett terms this "sexual politics". She argues that our society, like all other civilisations, is a concept where women are becoming empowered, and a very uniform approach is being adopted to understand the question of patriarchy. Millet's theory of patriarchy resembles that of Shulamith Firestone, in so far as it gives analytic primacy to male domination. Firestone, however, grounds her account more firmly in biological reproduction. Hence, there are different interpretations to understand and analyse the conceptual dimension of patriarchy.

Ramabai was an Indian reformer who was critical of the conception of male dominance which led to the suppression and subjugation of women. Ramabai's aim was gender reform, particularly reforming the lives of upper-caste women, who were the most oppressed. Ramabai held patriarchy, particularly *Brāhminical* patriarchy responsible for the vulnerable condition of women. She held that the low account of women's nature described in *Manusmṛiti* was responsible for women's dependence and suppression. The more she read, the more she became convinced that Hindu scriptures – *Purāṇas, Dharmaśāstras,* and *Vedās* – were strengthening patriarchy. In her words:

> There were two things on which all those books, *Dharmaśāstra*, *Purāṇas* and modern poet, the popular preachers of the present day and orthodox high caste men, were agreed that women of high and low caste, as a class were bad very bad and worse than demons and they could not get *Moksha* as men. The only hope of getting desired liberation was the worship of their husbands. He is her God. The extraordinary religious acts which help women to get into the ways of getting *Moksha* are utter abandonment of her will to that of her husband. Women have no right to study *Vedās* and without knowing them no one can know the *Brahmā*; hence women were not able to attain *Moksha*.
>
> (Kosambi 1988)

Her book *The High-Caste Hindu Woman* was based on the miseries of girls and women in high-caste Hindu families. Even during their marriage, they were not allowed to express their opinion. Ramabai understood that Hindu patriarchy placed women within the domestic sphere as a wife, mother, or housewife according to their role in homemaking. She held the view that patriarchal ideology in India regarded widowhood a punishment for horrible crimes committed by a woman in her previous birth, including disobedience or disloyalty to her husband. Several social practices which degraded widows, such as requiring a widow to wear a plain-borderless *saree* and no jewelry; shave her head; and keep her head carefully covered to make her less attractive to men. If she escapes such a situation, where will she go? She is completely ignorant of any art by which she may make any honest living. The lower castes, like women, were also treated with contempt. They occupied the lowest place in the hierarchical division of the society. They were forbidden to perform religious rites and rituals (Mudgal 2013). They had to serve the upper castes with much dedication, and by true commitment to their duties, there was chance they could attain salvation and be reborn into an upper caste.

The reform movements of those times focused on caste and gender issues. Gender issues had become the preoccupation of the upper castes, whose women were the most oppressed. In Poona, Ramabai, working towards the aim of gender reform, formed the *Arya Mahila Samaj* in 1882 and established branches throughout the Mumbai region. The object of this institution was to promote education among native women and to discourage child marriage. Ramabai urged women to free themselves from the tyranny of Hinduism. She made use of lectures and writing as a medium to bring about change in the lives of Indian women. The earliest available text from Ramabai's literary output was her Sanskrit poem "Lamentation of Divine Language", submitted to the Oriental Conference at Berlin in 1881 and highlighting the violence of colonialism.

Ramabai's role as a spokesperson for the glory of the *Vedic* age created dilemmas. The more she read and reflected on her experiences, the more she was exposed to the subtle patriarchal structure of society. It was during these young days that Ramabai's political thoughts started getting firmly grounded and expressed. She connected the teachings of the ancient literature with the inferior status of women in society. The caste system that was prevalent in the society during those times did not have any impact on Ramabai's progressive thinking. She firmly believed that in ancient times, people were assigned to the four castes according to their work and merit and not on the basis of their birth. It was much later that the caste system became identified with birth and became discriminatory. These caste-based differences, coupled with gender-based differences, deeply affected Indian women. Ramabai understood that the patriarchal ideology of the society placed women within the domestic sphere as a wife/mother/housewife according to her sexual, reproductive, and home-making roles. In this caste-ridden, patriarchal society, the highest status for a woman was that of a *saubhagyavati* (or blessed woman whose husband was alive) and a mother of sons, rather than daughters. A woman who only had daughters or did not have any children had a lower status and lived under the fear of being deserted by her husband. A widow had the lowest status, especially a child widow or one without children. In addition to wearing a plain *saree*, not wearing jewelry, and keeping her shaved head covered, a widow was expected to sleep on the floor, spend time in ritual acts, and eat little food.

Ramabai's study of *Upaniṣhads*, *Manusmṛiti*, and the *Vedās* made her realise how the caste system, the Hindu *Śhāstras*, and social customs helped patriarchy to not only thrive but to grow larger. She thought the low account of women's nature and character depicted in *Manusmṛiti* was, to a large extent, responsible for their seclusion and suppression. Manu's laws deprived women of the house of all their freedom. Ramabai soon realised all sacred books in Sanskrit literature shared hateful sentiments about women. Child marriage, polygamy, and enforced widowhood thus turned out to be great social evils in India which were responsible for the pathetic condition of Indian women and which needed to be changed. It was in this context that Ramabai also shared her views on religion, which, according to her, had two distinct natures in the Hindu law: the masculine and the feminine. Both these kinds had their own peculiar duties, privileges, and honours. For women, it was believed to be her duty to look upon her husband as God, to always obey him, and seek salvation only through him.

Ramabai's most popular academic venture, *The High-Caste Hindu Woman*, contained a critical account of miseries that were faced by girls and women in the domain of a high-caste Hindu joint family system. Daughters were taught to do all household works right at the tender age of nine or ten so that they were well trained to adjust to the life of a young married woman. They were married off without getting a chance to express their opinions. Women in these families were not permitted to read the sacred scriptures and were found fit only for housekeeping work. As a class, women were never to be trusted. Through this book, Ramabai tried to become the voice of these millions of women. She had particularly drawn people's attention towards what she considered the biggest curse for a Hindu woman – her becoming a widow, especially a child widow. The hardships that a Hindu widow had to face were highlighted, and an appeal was made to help them to become independent identities. The plight of a Hindu widow was such that even families of lower castes would not have them as a servant. She was left with no option of making an honest living. Pandita Ramabai considered women of lower castes to be much better off in terms of self-reliance and freedom since they were obliged to depend upon themselves. Ramabai suggested three areas where focus had to be made to improve the condition of these widows: self-reliance, education, and native women teachers.

IV Gender justice and civil rights

It is not wrong to say that Ramabai entered into the feminist discourse through her book *Stri Dharma Niti* (Morals for women). This book turned out to be a guide of women's morality, asking illiterate, ignorant women to recast themselves in a more cultural mould through self-reliance and self-education. Through this book, Ramabai advises the women of India on how to prepare for marriage by choice; be a companion to her husband, who is worthy of trust; achieve ideal motherhood by nurturing sons who would free India; and attain spiritual welfare. It needs to be understood here that Ramabai's feminist consciousness itself began to be questioned through this book. Her endorsement of the *sati–Savitri* model of femininity could be easily debated within the gender discourse of India. However, by advocating late marriages for women and marriages by choice, Ramabai turned out to be a radical, nevertheless. Her next academic venture, *Cry of Indian Women*, more explicitly reflected her feminist thinking and her desire to seek gender justice (Kosambi 2000: 105).

The change in the approach between *Stri Dharma Niti* and the *Cry of Indian Women* was the result of many factors. Her proximity to early feminists like Tarabai Shinde, Anandibai Joshee, and Rakhmabai is clear in latest book. Another influence that impacted on Ramabai's feminist consciousness was her exposure to the more progressive and less asymmetrical gender relations in America and England. Imparting education to women was thought to be the best remedy of the problems. Pandita's hope was that women's education would lead to the rejection of *Brāhminism* and realise the deception of sacred literature. But Ramabai was aware of the mindset of the Indian society which was sceptical of educating women. The few schools that were available were often run by missionaries and, as a rule, a high-caste Hindu woman would prefer death than go to such schools where there was fear of losing their caste. In her testimony before the Education Commission set up in 1882, Ramabai demanded women teachers for girls and schools. She noted that "women being one half of the people of this country are oppressed and cruelly treated by the other half". She also asked for training women as medical doctors to save women who could not consult male physicians. Later, Dr Hunter was invited by Ramabai and the *Samaj* to attend its special meeting, which was attended by about 280 native ladies all stressing the need for women doctors (Kosambi 2000: 340).

Within this context, Ramabai raised the issues of oppressed Indian women – widows, deserted wives, and sexually exploited women. Her main contribution was her desire to protect the upper-caste widow, who was the symbol of Hindu patriarchal oppression. In this regard, she played an important role in the Congress convention demanding civil rights for these women. The first meeting of the national Congress in Bombay in 1889 consisted of around 2,000 delegates, of which three were women, largely because of Ramabai's influence. The purpose of this meeting was to address the need for unity among different races in India and to turn the attention of the British government towards the existing grievances and needed reforms. Ramabai spoke largely on two resolutions: one relating to marriage and the other to the shaving of widows' heads. She brought to notice the injustice meted to the widows by depriving them of property if they married again. Both the resolutions were passed by a large majority, and the request that the members of the conference pledge themselves not to allow marriage until the girl had completed her 14th year was also supported by a large majority. Ramabai's activity during the conference made her a popular national image, and she received many invitations to lecture on education and problems faced by child widows. By this time, Ramabai had made her efforts towards the achievement of gender equality loud and clear.

V Women's education and emancipation

Pandita Ramabai's life struggles visualise the face of cultural chauvinism and radical institutionalisation of man's hegemonic tradition in the whole Indian social system. In other words, the exposure of women's silent suffering for centuries at the hands of a patriarchal system which was the by-product of *Brāhmins'* barbarism. As a widow, Ramabai had undergone all the pain and horrors meant for Indian widows.[1] She had vivid experiences with Hinduism from her childhood into widowhood, and it was rather indicative of the rigid culture implemented in a diabolical manner by the men in that society. When she exposed the flaws and fallacies of a patrilineal system through her lived experience, all the self-style protectors of Hinduism, along with the *Brāhmins*, turned against her. Despite the hostility, Ramabai unearthed the bias of patriarchal society towards women and campaigned to save women's fate with help from around the world.[2] As part of her mission, Ramabai delivered lectures to different people at different places from the perspective of a solitary widow.

Having demonstrated how profoundly *Brāhmins* embedded in the discourse of cultural practice and attacked women with naive ideas, Pandita Ramabai, without much discouragement, continued her movement and propagated that the early marriage of girls denied them proper education as they were getting married at best age to acquire knowledge. The very conjecture of this exclamation was that in the nineteenth century, child marriage was hugely prevalent in India and it resulted in many widows. Moved by this plight of widowhood, she firstly concentrated on widow education with an aim to make them self-reliant. It is rhetoric to share of the painstaking efforts Ramabai had undergone in the process, and to make them independent, she constructed an institution that taught girls formal education, nursing, housekeeping, and other vocational training.

Within a few years, Pandita Ramabai had opened schools and numerous training centres and working units for women, with special emphasis on widows' livelihoods. In the process, she also unearthed the lack of lady doctors, which led to great numbers of premature death, and the numbers of widows suffering from different sicknesses, which was accounted for in approximately 2 million widows, who had no access to medical treatment. Hence, Ramabai formed *Arya Mahila Samaj* in 1882, and the essence of this foundation was more precisely to protect and promote the rights of women in India. The complexity of her position had become evident when Ramakrishna astonishingly said that Pandita Ramabai was too ambitious – and represented a kind of egoism and idealism which has no good as it was a mere pursuit of name and fame (Dietrich 1992: 93). Whatever the criticism may be, the dialectic of Ramabai was to attain emancipation for women whose lives were subjected to inhuman badgering from those exclusivist orientations – Hindu, patriarchal, and upper caste.

In such a situation, it has become precarious for her to be within the principle of inhuman dogmatism and combat against such insensitive practice without compunction. When her movement to educate women rose, hatred among the religious leaders grew like a bonfire in an enchanted forest. The society saw her mission not as a personal quest and struggle but as a betrayal of religion already threatened by alien rule and as a desertion of the fledgling social reform movement. As a result, in 1883, Ramabai converted to Christianity in protest against the inherent discrimination against women in Hinduism. Although her conversion was due to her disillusionment with Hinduism and the heterodoxies of patriarchal monotheism, Ramabai remained silent without developing into a social protest. Thus, she felt the publicity of her actions would lead to social tension and direct reaction against her.

In the same year, Ramabai set her foot in England to study medical with the deep aim to support the miseries of women and girls, but unfortunately she could not continue because of hearing loss. Thereafter, she went to the United States in 1886, travelling coast to coast and propagating her idea in search of philanthropists to support her in opening a residential school for Hindu widows in India. Subsequently, she established a Ramabai Association in Boston, and under the paraphernalia of this association she had collected funds from different philanthropists to fulfil her long-cherished dream. Thus, Ramabai immediately returned to India and opened *Sharda Sadan* in Bombay in early 1889 (Stealin 1977; Celarent 2011: 353). It was the first ever residential school for the high-caste Hindu widows and unmarried girls of Maharashtra (Kosambi 1992: 61). The school imparted both secular education and vocational training to the women so they could become economically self-reliant and slowly lead to structural change of the patriarchal system.

In the beginning, the realisation of this idea into action had faced undaunted difficulties, as there was fear and stigma among women of the cultural bedevilment. Despite the polemic segregation, discrimination, and destitution, few women turned out dauntlessly to receive secular education and skills training. In 1891, the *Sharda Sadan* shifted its centre to Pune, with the objective to facilitate more widows in the orthodox heartland of Maharashtra (Kosambi 1992: 63). But there were many from different segments who feared and scrutinised the *Sharda Sadan* and asked not to propagate any religious faith to the inmates, particularly upon the *Brāhmin* women. Ramabai remained tight-lipped on secular education and did not profess any religious faith in abidance of the society's demand. However, some girls expressed a desire to embrace Christianity, so Ramabai sent them to Christian missionaries for proper instruction. This led to swift reaction from the local Advisory Committee and the public; as a result, the *Sharda Sadan* was alienated from the mainstream and left with a small number of poor, homeless widows (ibid.: 65).

By the subsequent year, Ramabai also extended her mission in famine areas of central India and Gujarat, directly and indirectly, to save hundreds of vulnerable women who were starving and engaging in moral degradation. Her increasing preoccupation with missionary activity combined with the outbreak of plague in Pune resulted in the shift of *Sharda Sadan* from Pune to Kedgaon in 1898; soon after, the Ramabai Association was converted to Christianity and became known as the *Mukti* Mission. It was two years later that the number of inmates increased at *Sharda Sadan*. The new inmates were mostly famine victims from depressed castes, and their needs ranged from creature comforts to character building to secular and spiritual education (Nicol 1996). The *Mukti* Mission of Kedgaon had enormously expanded with a diversification of its activities. In addition to the original *Sadan* meant for Hindu widows, there was another *Mukti Sadan* specifically meant for Christian women; many small sections or centres were also opened for old women and for the blind. Practically, all the work of this large establishment was done by the inmates who received schooling up to the level of matriculation as well as vocational training. Ramabai's dream of self-reliance for women had come true but remained outside the reach of upper-caste widows, whom she had desperately tried to help all her life until she breathed her last in 1922.

Ramabai expressed her concern over the belief among high-caste women that their husbands would die if they read or held a pen in their fingers. The few schools available were often run by missionaries, and high-caste Hindu women avoided going to such schools because they feared losing their caste. It was because of her concern for women's education that the Education Commission invited over 300 women of Ramabai's *Arya Mahila Samaj* in Poona. She advocated trained women teachers, women inspectors for girl's schools, and women medical doctors for women because Indian women would rather die than speak of their ailment to a man (Mudgal 2013). The need for female inspectors was stressed because male inspectors would intimidate the women and magnify their faults since in 99 cases out of 100 the educated men of the country were opposed to female education.

Ramabai had a significant role in the Congress convention in demanding civil rights for women. She brought to notice the injustice meted out to widows by depriving them of property if they married again. It was Ramabai's achievement for gender equality. Salvation for women, especially high-caste widows, was Ramabai's aim. After raising funds for such a salvation house in America, Ramabai built her *Sharda Sadan* in Poona in 1889. Women in this community were taught the doctrines of Christianity, though they were also free to continue in their Hindu beliefs. Ramabai ran into problems in India when she was considered part of the Christian missionary effort, though the same perception was useful when fundraising in the United States. The *Sharda Sadan* was only one of her many initiatives working for the education of women (from young girls to adults) and for the security of widows.

She not only defied gender distinction but also discrimination based on caste. The mark of the Enlightenment anti-caste reformers was in their vision of an anti-caste, anti-class utopia; Ramabai not only added gender to this but attempted to put the vision into practice in a real utopian community. At *Mukti Sadan* in Kedgaon, women of different categories were to be included. The *Sadan* envisioned providing liberation to the deep-seated role of women carved out by the patriarchal order. It provided space to women to be economically independent and empowered. Thus, Ramabai's effort was to make life more meaningful for women as teachers, nurses, or workers. At *Mukti Sadan* in Kedgaon the women did everything from weaving to dairy farming to cooking to gardening to running a printing press and even farming.

The need for the right kind of education is necessary for women because education is the pillar of change in a society. It is something no one can take or give away. In other word, education enlightens confidence in the powers of reason and liberates the sceptic mind to assert the fundamental truth. The hermeneutic idea of Ramabai was to transform the condition of women's education in modern India. She imbibed a conglomerate growth of education as well as a movement for the cause of women in different parts of the country. As a result, the then government took equivocal steps to impart education for women and eventually set up not just a co-educational institution but an institution specifically for women so that young and old could receive unbiased education and know the quintessential rights for all citizens.

This paradigm shift has altered the image of orthodox India, and the untold misery of women is driven away from the prism of parochialism. In the aftermath of independence, the man has no room per se in every sphere, as the Constitution guarantees the right to education for all citizenry. Even the first Prime Minister of India, Jawaharlal Nehru, enounced that educating a man is a step towards educating one person, but imparting education to a woman is building the whole family. Hence, priority should be given to women for they inculcate good moral values, and this is how a nation would progress in the long run. Beyond a doubt, India did extremely well on the literacy front that is, rather, an encouraging development, but there is much more to be done at the governmental level – to provide equal opportunity and ensure that all benefit from education. The central and state governments should ensure the implementation of primary and secondary education programmes for women with free sponsorship. Furthermore, measures to ensure the availability of teachers for girls, the appointment of women teachers, and the development of women will not only be a social benefit but also an economic one. The overall success of women's education lies in the sincere conduct and reactive actions of the government officials and civil societies.

VI Conclusion

Ramabai was a liberal feminist and had a secular outlook. She was concerned with social evils such as female infanticide, child marriage, the *sati* custom, and criticised the oppressive condition of women, especially Hindu widows, and worked to improve them. She used many innovative methods to ensure the participation of women in society. She encouraged many women speakers to speak on a public platform. She also opened up *Mahila Samaj* and *Sharda Sadan* to empower women. She was a nationalist thinker, and her contribution to the cause of Hindu widows is commendable. As Uma Chakravarti says, "Ramabai had reconceptualised widowhood and womanhood in such a way that no male reformer could even think of" (Chakravarti 2008). Thus, her ideas made her far ahead of her times and tremendously influenced political thinking in India. It needs to be stressed here that, despite everything, she strove relentlessly to achieve her goal – the emancipation of Indian women. Given the limitations of family support, funds, and social acceptance, Ramabai did the best she could in those circumstances. The kind of sorrows which she had to face right from her childhood no doubt made her appear as a rigid, tough, but practical person for whom emotions had little meaning. As far as her role of a social reformer is concerned, Ramabai triumphs as a leader who had a futuristic and modern outlook that was much ahead of the times.

The issue of her religious conversion and her not being active in national struggles have all come up from within the Hindu patriarchal society, which could not easily grasp a woman riding high on success, not only nationally but also internationally. Ramabai's love for liberalism and feminism thus rules over all her other political thoughts and establishes her as one of India's earliest liberal feminists – liberal because she loved and supported the notions of freedom and equality and feminist because she was all for women's rights on the same terms as those of men.

Notes

1 Pandita Ramabai was a *Brāhmin* woman married to a man named Bipin Behari Medhvi of Bengal, but unfortunately the marriage ended abruptly with Bipin Behari's death in 1882, leaving Ramabai a widow with an infant daughter.
2 So long as she praised the monotheism and patriarchy of Hinduism, Ramabai was treated as a living example of all great Hindu women and the greatness of Hinduism towards its women, but when she spoke about the hard reality of women, all voices turned against her.

References

Altekar, A.S. (1983). *The Position of Women in Hindu Civilisation: From Prehistoric Time to the Present*. New Delhi: Motilal Banarsidass.
Bhasin, Kamla (1994). *What Is Patriarchy*. New Delhi: Kali for Women.
Celarent, Barbara (2011). The High Caste Hindu Women. *American Journal of Sociology*, Vol. 117(1), pp. 353–360.
Chakrabarty, Bidyut and Pandey Rajendra Kumar (2009). *Modern Indian Political Thought*. New Delhi: Sage.
Chakravarti, Uma (2008). *Pandita Ramabai: A Life and a Time*. New Delhi: Critical Quest.
Dietrich, Gabriele (1992). *Reflections on the Women's Movement in India: Religion, Ecology, Development*. New Delhi: Horizon Indian Books.
Jha, Madhu (2011). "Gender and Caste", in M. P. Singh and Himanhu Roy (Eds.), *Indian Political Thought: Themes and Thinkers*. New Delhi: Pearson.

Kosambi, Meera (1988). Women, Emancipation and Equality: Pandita Ramabai's Contribution to Women's Cause. *Economic and Political Weekly*, Vol. 23(44), October, pp. 38–49.

Kosambi, Meera (1992). Indian Response to Christianity, Church and Colonialism: Case of Pandita Ramabai. *Economic and Political Weekly*, Vol. 27(43/44), pp. 61–71.

Kosambi, Meera (Ed.) (2000). *Pandita Ramabai: Through Her Own Words*. New Delhi: Oxford University Press.

Lerner, Gerda (1986). *The Creation of Patriarchy*. New York: Oxford University Press.

Lerner, Gerda (1993). *The Creation of Feminist Consciousness*. New York: Oxford University Press.

Mehta, R. (1970). *The Western Educated Hindu Women*. London: Asia Publishing House.

Mudgal, Alka (2013). Pandita Ramabai. *Indian Journal of Political Science*, Vol. LXXIV(2), April–June, pp. 347–356.

Nicol, Macnicol (1996). *Pandita Ramabai: A Builder of Modern India*. New Delhi: Good Books.

Stealin, C. D. (1977). *The Influence of Missions on Women's Education in India: The American Marathi Mission in Ahmadnagar, 1830 to 1930*. London: University of Michigan.

7

PERIYAR E. V. RAMASAMY

Debi Chatterjee

> *Is India a single country? Absolutely not! What we have is just a collection of various castes, religions and languages.*
> – Periyar E. V. Ramasamy on India, May 1930 (XIV: 122)
> cited in Bala (2013: 166)

I Introduction

In the Sangam age, that is, the early centuries of the Christian era, *varṇaāśhrama dhārma* had been planted in the Tamil region, in a Tamilised form. As per the presentation of Tolkappiyar, the earliest Tamil grammarian, there existed the *Antanars* (*Brāhmins*), *Arasars* (kings, or *Kṣatriyas*), *Vaisyars* (*Vaiśyas*) and the *Vellalars* (*Śūdras*) (Pillai 1978: 412). By the eighteenth and nineteenth centuries, *Brāhmins* firmly entrenched their position of dominance in the region vis-à-vis the non-*Brāhmins*. The advent of political non-*Brāhminism* in the Tamil region took place with the formation of the South Indian Liberal Federation, or the Justice Party, as it is popularly known. It was formed in 1916. Men like Theagaraya Chetty, Dr T. M. Nair, and others who went ahead to form the South Indian Liberal Federation had on their agenda four lines of action. Firstly, non-*Brāhmins* were to educate themselves in vast numbers. Secondly, they were to work for their country's economic advancement. Thirdly, they were to come together and work to ensure proportional representation for all communities in administration and in the legislative councils. Fourthly, they were to form, through their unified actions, a grand fraternity of people over whom, at some future period, the doctrine of *varṇaāśhrama dhārma* would no longer hold sway. It was with respect to proportional representation that the Justice Party secured its greatest victories. It was against that backdrop that E. V. Ramasamy entered the political scene (Geetha and Rajadurai 1998: 128).

Erode Venkatappa Ramasamy (spelt also as Ramasami), better known as EVR or Periyar[1] (the Great One) can be well rated as second only to Ambedkar in the crusade against caste in modern India. As a result of his contempt for the inequalities created by the caste system, Ramasamy spearheaded radical social reform movements in south India. He was active in politics, which was conditioned by his social vision.

Ramasamy had a dream, the dream of an egalitarian civil society. For the establishment of such a society, certain pre-conditions were necessary. Many of his movements were steps towards the fulfilment of such requirements, or so he believed. Beginning with temple entry and movements for access to public places and progressing to campaigns for women's empowerment, Ramasamy's actions were all aimed at challenging *Brāhminical* dominance. It was the conference of the Progressive Women's Association held in Madras in 1938 that gave the honorific title of 'Periyar' to Ramasamy "for his unparalleled activism to transform the south Indian society".

II Life sketch

Erode Venkatappa Ramasamy, commonly known as Periyar, also referred to as Thanthai Periyar, was an Indian social activist and politician who started the Self-Respect Movement and Dravidar Kazhagam (D.K.). He is known as the "Father of the Dravidian Movement". Ramasamy was born in Erode, in Coimbatore district, in 1879. His parents belonged to the non-*Brāhmin* Balija Naidu community. His father, Venkata Naicker, had originally been a stone mason but later became a fairly rich merchant. His home was the meeting place of many *pandits* and religious propagandists. However, young Ramasamy did not benefit from this, as in his early childhood he stayed with a maternal aunt of his father who happened to be a childless widow. Ramasamy, however, was growing up as a naughty and undisciplined boy. Dissatisfied with his son's upbringing, Ramasamy's father sent him to an English primary school. However, Ramasamy spent barely five or six years in school and learnt very little. When complaints against him in school were becoming too loud, he was withdrawn from school altogether. He was merely a boy of ten. At that age, he was inducted into the family business with which he remained engaged for several years. In 1904, following a quarrel with his father, Ramasamy became a religious mendicant and toured different religious places in the country. While in Benaras, he learnt more about the inequities of the caste system, witnessed the exploitation of the illiterate masses by crafty priests, and noted the absence of morality. Disgusted, he returned home and rejoined his father's trade (Viswanathan 1983: 20–21). Apart from trade, he involved himself in public activities. In 1910, he became a member of the Erode Municipal Council and, in 1918, its Chairman. His activities in the context of the Municipal Council brought him to the attention of the leaders of the Indian National Congress.

From an early age, Ramasamy demonstrated an uncompromising attitude towards the religious practices of the Hindus and the caste system. In a lifetime that spread well into his 90s, Ramasamy kept up his rationalist campaign. On 23 December 1973, he attended his last public meeting which was held at T. Nagar in Madras to spread awareness against superstitions. As his already frail health condition worsened at the meeting itself, he died the next day, that is on 24 December 1973 (Jeyaraman 2013: 96–97).

III Entry into politics and the Congress era

Ramasamy had a deep sense of commitment towards the cause of the depressed castes. And in this respect to start with, his expectations from the Congress leadership were high, only to be disillusioned in the course of time. Ramasamy made an early entry into public life. His first direct contact with political figures in Tamilnadu was probably made when the Madras Presidency Association was founded in 1917. The non-*Brāhmin* members of the Tamilnadu branch of the Congress formed this association to represent and safeguard their interests in the national organisation and at the same time repudiate the claims of the Justice Party to be the sole representative of the non-*Brāhmin* community in the Presidency (Viswanathan 1983: 22).

Following the Jallianwala Bagh massacre, Ramasamy's political involvement increased as he became a regular member of the Indian National Congress. Ramasamy joined the Congress in 1920. The Party's professed ideals – nationalism, emancipation of the oppressed, and social reform – appealed to the reform-minded Ramasamy. Congress on its side was searching for non-*Brāhmin* leaders who could effectively counter the Justice Party charge of *Brāhmin* domination in the party. On joining the Madras Pradesh Congress, Ramasamy had initially "fanatically" supported Gandhi's agitational techniques (Viswanathan 1983: 38) and had aligned himself with the group led by Rajaji. For four years after joining the Congress, Ramasamy held important positions in the regional organisation. During 1923–1924, Ramasamy was the president of the Tamil Nadu Congress. In the following year, he became the secretary. As a matter of fact, when Gandhi launched the Non-cooperation Movement, Ramasamy was the president of the Tamil Nadu Branch of the Congress and, as such, had a prominent role to play in its implementation in the region. Yet, even as he was getting more and more involved in the Non-cooperation Movement and the Constructive Programme, he was drifting from the Congress on questions of policies.

Ramasamy's main commitment was to the cause of the *Śūdra* castes. But very soon, he realised the Congress was letting him down. In 1924, he had successfully participated in the Vaikom agitation and earned the reputation of being the *Vaikom Veer*, or Vaikom Hero. The movement was a movement of the lower castes, the *Ezhavas* and the *Adi Dravidas*, for the right to walk along the streets of Vaikom. It had been organised by the Kerala Congress leadership. As the agitation began, the frontline leaders were arrested, and it fell upon Ramasamy to lead the movement. His credentials as a leader of the oppressed castes were thus established.

Between 1920 and 1924, Ramasamy's political ideas were crystallising. Gradually, he was realising that his objectives could not be achieved through any of the existing political parties. The sharp divide between the *Brāhmins* and the non-*Brāhmins*, which afflicted almost every dimension of social existence, was clearly visible in the field of politics as well. Ramasamy was not prepared to tolerate this silently. Thus, he eventually parted ways with the Congress. In fact, his disillusionment with the Congress had begun as early as the 1920s, when he had attempted to move a resolution on Communal Representation at the Tamil Nadu Congress Conference. His resolution had been disallowed on the ground that it would generate communal tension. Until 1925, he made repeated attempts, but failed. Thereafter, he severed his links with the Congress. Even though Ramasamy dissociated himself from the Congress in 1925, he retained a measure of weakness for Mr Gandhi for another couple of years.

By mid-1927, his break with Gandhi had come. From this time onwards, Ramasamy, in his tirade against caste, took up a clearly anti-Gandhi position. He was convinced that the latter was propagating *Brāhminical* values among the masses of Tamil Nadu. Ramasamy's exit from the Congress to start a new movement for social awakening which he undertook was in a sense his continuation of the Constructive Programme on the lines he desired. The organisation through which he sought to arouse that social awakening was the Self-Respect Movement. It was his parallel to the Gandhian Constructive Programme. The emphasis in his scheme of construction was, however, on the destruction of the old social order. The Self-Respect Movement had been launched by Ramasamy in 1925. With a large middle-class base, it grew to the stature of a popular movement in the 1930s and 1940s. The goal was a total transformation of Tamil society, the destruction of *Brāhminism*, and the liberation of the *Śūdras*.

IV The Self-Respect Movement and Tamil nationalism

It is pertinent to recall that, following his dissociation with the Congress, even as Ramasamy's movement developed along political lines involving a denunciation of Congress and Gandhian politics, it went well beyond the political discourse and encompassed the entire gamut of society. His efforts were directed towards re-structuring Indian culture, weaning it away from the *Brāhminical* stranglehold with the aim of non-*Brāhminising* society and creating a suitable cultural milieu. Ramasamy structured his alternative culture in terms of the Self-Respect Movement. He raised the slogan of *Cuyamariyātai* (self-respect). As for the genesis of the movement, Ramasamy stated:

> I resolved to eradicate the evils of casteism. I decided to crusade against Gods and superstitions. . . . I took it as my full time work to reform society. I started the self-respect movement with the same motive.
>
> *(Naicker 1981: 10)*

The Tamil weekly *Kudi Arasu* became the principal organ of the movement. It was launched in 1925. Through its columns, *Brāhminism* was attacked, and the notion of a casteless society was upheld. Ramasamy's passionate speeches delivered in simple, straightforward fashion succeeded in drawing a sizeable following of the Self-Respect Movement. It became one of the most powerful protest movements recorded in south India to date. The First Self-Respect Conference was held at Chengalpattu on 17 and 18 February 1929. It was an outright war cry against the caste system. The significant points raised in the resolutions were as follows:

1 The restrictions placed on people in the name of *varṇaāśhrama* should go. The classification of society into *Brāhmins, Kṣatriyas, Vaiśyas, Śūdras* and *Panchamas* is highly objectionable and should be got rid of. All people should have the right to walk along any road and make use of any tank or well or choultry (a resting place, an inn or caravansary for travellers) found anywhere. People should avoid wearing caste marks on their foreheads and their bodies.

(Gopalakrishnan 1992: 22)

2 People should not spend any money for worship in temples and they should not recognise middlemen or *pujaris* (priests) that is abolition of *Purohit* system. The intrusion of Sanskrit or any of the north Indian languages in matters of worship and prayer should be got rid of. People should be discouraged from building new temples, mutts, choultries or *Vedic* schools. People should drop their caste titles in their names.

(Gopalakrishnan 1992: 22–23)

At the Second Self-Respect Conference, which was held at Erode, similar resolutions were adopted. In addition, it also condemned idol worship in temples. Speaking at the conference, Ramasamy criticised caste ideology and religion in the strongest terms. He said:

> Have you heard of a *Brāhmin* donkey, a *Brāhmin* dog, a *Brāhmin* monkey, a *Brāhmin* buffalo among the animals? Why have men alone allowed some of their fellow-men to call themselves *Brāhmins*? This is of course due to religion. If religion is used to boost the position of some men and degrade others why should we have this religion at all?. . . . Should we not develop our sense of reasoning and get rid of this evil practice?
>
> *(Gopalakrishnan 1992: 23–24)*

Some of the most sustained struggles which came to be launched by Ramasamy and the Self-Respect Movement were in relation to temple entry, access to public spaces and institutions, gender equality, the abolition of untouchability, anti-*Brāhminism*, anti-caste, and anti-religion. Ramasamy was extremely outspoken in his atheistic beliefs. He strongly expressed his rejection of the idea of God, as well as idol worship, and used sharp language and agitational methods for expressing that opposition.

An important facet of the Self-Respect Movement was the introduction of self-respect marriages. These special types of marriages were conducted in a simple manner without any *Brāhminical* rituals and without the presence of a *Brāhmin* priest. The self-respect marriage vow required man and woman to abide by each other's views, needs, and concerns. The self-respect marriage vow thus allowed and enabled the bride and groom to come together on an equal basis; it thereby indicated that the family which, after all, functions and is built on the basis of conjugal relations, may be re-imagined (Geetha and Rajadurai 1998: 382).

From its very beginning, the Self-Respect Movement considered it necessary to work for the emancipation of women, freeing them from age-old traditions and other irrational chains of bondage and exploitation. In the process, historical and mythological fallacies narrating the necessity of women's subjugation to men in society was challenged. The Self-Respect Movement insisted on the equality of women with men in all matters, including education, the right to ancestral properties, and government jobs. It encouraged widow remarriage, upheld women's right to divorce, and condemned prostitution, the *devadasi* system, and child marriages. The establishment of a separate women's wing to propagate the ideals of the Self-Respect Movement was a clear indication of its commitment to the women's cause. It is pertinent to note here that it was the women's wing of the Self-Respect Movement that made Ramasamy a 'Periyar' (Chandrababu 1993: 177).

The Self-Respect Movement may be said to have passed through four distinct phases in the evolution of its policies between 1925 and 1937. During the first four years, Ramasamy confined himself to advocating social reform by attacking superstitious beliefs and customs. The second phase may be said to have started with the First Provincial Self-Respect Conference held at Chengalpattu in 1929. The third phase, beginning around 1932, followed Ramasamy's European tour when he began to argue in favour of socialism. By the beginning of 1935, under pressure from the British government, Ramasamy changed his stance, moving away from the propagation of socialism and joining hands with the Justice Party leadership (Arooran 1980: 185).

V Formation of the Dravidar Kazhagam

Ramasamy took up the lead of the Justice Party after the party's electoral debacle in 1936. The setback of the party at the polls was so great that it seemed as though the party was on the verge of total extinction. It was at such a juncture that Ramasamy took the lead of the party first as a virtual *de facto* leader and then gaining *de jure* recognition in due course. In 1938, he was unanimously elected the president of the Justice Party. For some time, the Self-Respect Movement and the Justice Party came to function in close association with each other. Thereafter, out of the collaboration of the Justice Party and the Self-Respect Movement, the Dravidar Kazhagam (Dravidian Conference), or the D.K., was born. The goals and regulations of the D.K. were formally adopted in September 1945. Important among these were:

1. (a) Dravida Nadu should have complete autonomy on its social, economic, industrial, and commercial spheres.
   (b) Dravida Nadu and its citizens should be protected from the exploitation and influence of others.
2. The citizens of Dravida Nadu should be given the opportunity to live and prosper without the distinctions of caste, class, and hierarchy.
3. The differences and superstitions that plague the Dravidian people in the name of religion and tradition must be eradicated. Dravidians should be transformed into a society filled with generosity and knowledge.

(Jeyaraman 2013: 52–53)

In 1949, in the aftermath of Ramasamy's second marriage with a much younger girl, Maniammai, a split in the movement took place. A sizeable section of the D.K. under the leadership of Annadurai, formed the Dravida Munnetra Kazhagam, or the D.M.K.

VI On independence: the Constituent Assembly and the Constitution

Ramasamy was very sceptical about what the plight of the *Śūdras* would be in an independent India. Like many other oppressed class leaders, including Ambedkar, Ramasamy was inclined to regard British rule in somewhat favourable terms. The logic was that "Britishers at least consider us as men with equal rights". As such, in his perception, independence was not just a change but a change for the worse. Along such lines, he declared India's Independence Day, 15 August 1947, as a day of mourning for the backward castes.

Both the Constituent Assembly and the Constitution were unacceptable to Ramasamy. He considered the former to be unrepresentative of all sections of the population, while the latter, he felt, entrenched all safeguards for casteism. The overall scenario, in his vision, was as follows:

> The *Brāhmins* have stuck to the seats of government. Power has been transferred into the hands of *Brāhmins*. I blame Gandhi for that. A big conspiracy was hatched to keep us eternally as '*Śūdras*'. Today, everything is in their hands. . . . most of the luminaries in public life want to safeguard casteism, *Śhāstras, Purāṇas*, religion and God.
>
> *(Chatterjee 2010: 245)*

Ramasamy carried his opposition to the Constitution to a point of mass agitation, when in 1957 he instructed his followers to publicly burn copies of the Constitution. It is reported that on the occasion of the agitation, thousands of agitators were arrested throughout Tamil Nadu.

VII The anti-Hindi struggle (1937–1940)

After Ramasamy's showdown with the Tamil Nadu Congress in 1925 and Gandhi in 1927, the Self-Respect Movement became more identity-based and rational in its tirade against *Brāhmins* and *Brāhminism*, Sanskrit and Hindi, the languages of the *Aryans* and of northern India. Several resolutions were passed at the Tirunelveli district. The Self-Respect Conference, held in November 1927 under Ramasamy's presidentship, spoke against the use of Sanskrit in academic institutions (Chandrababu 1993: 155).

In a 1929 editorial of the *Kudi Arasu*, Ramasamy strongly criticised the efforts of Congressmen in Tamilnadu to propagate Hindi, a north Indian language which was essentially an *Aryan* and *Brāhminical* language. Alongside denouncing Hindi, the Self-Respect Movement was advising its followers to study English (Chandrababu 1993: 155).

Anti-Hindi agitation was launched by the Justice Party under Ramasamy's leadership in 1937, as the Congress ministry in Madras planned to introduce the subject in the first three forms in the academic curriculum. It opposed the introduction of Hindi in Tamil Nadu schools and saw it as a scheme of dominance perpetrated by the Government of India from Delhi. Ramasamy viewed such imposition of Hindi as a threat to the Tamil region. The agitation gained the support of scholars, activists, and many Tamils. The teaching of Hindi was considered an attempt by Congress to glorify Hindi and Sanskrit and denigrate the Tamil language.

The fear that Tamil would suffer because of compulsory Hindi became a rallying point for the Tamils. The anti-Hindi agitation had dual dimensions. First, there was a linguistic side to it. Secondly, there was a cultural side. In the political sphere, the agitation led to a revival of the Justice Party which had been inactive since its defeat in the 1936 polls. The lead provided by Ramasamy earned him the leadership of the Justice Party in 1938, and since then the Self-Respect Movement and the Justice Party merged into one. The identification of Hindi with Sanskrit and of the Congress Party with *Brāhminism* led to the revival of similar arguments which had been put forward in the 1920s.

> The introduction of compulsory Hindi was regarded as an attempt of north India to dominate south India, or *Aryan* culture to dominate over Dravidian culture and of Sanskrit over Tamil, and in continuation of such arguments, arose the demand for a separate Tamil land or *Dravidanad*.
>
> *(Arooran 1980: 218)*

VIII The Statehood demand (1940–1944)

The anti-Hindi agitation contained the seeds of the subsequent movement for *Dravidanad*. The notion of a separate *Dravidanad* was linked with the linguistic proposition that the four major languages spoken in south India constituted a separate Dravidian group. With the founding of the non-*Brāhmin* Movement and the Justice Party, the linguistic term "Dravidian" was widely extended to indicate a racial group. The pleas for a separate *Dravidanad* came to be based on those linguistic and racial grounds (Arooran 1980: 233).

Since the Lahore Session of the Muslim League in 1940, in which the demand for a separate Muslim State was raised, the Justice Party began to work closely with the Muslim League to derive strength for the demand for *Dravidanad*. It may be observed that Ramasamy and other leaders of the Justice Party fully endorsed the demand of the Muslim League for a separate State of Pakistan and in return expected the League's support for *Dravidanad*. In 1941, presiding over the Muslim League Conference at Madras, Jinnah readily extended his support, but subsequently he hardly referred to *Dravidastan* (Arooran 1980: 248).

Regarding the concept of *Dravidanad*, Ramasamy had pointed out that it was nothing new but rather an extension of the Congress Party's idea of dividing India into linguistic provinces once independence is attained. While the Congress Provincial Committees had been formed on a linguistic basis in 1920, it was Ramasamy who extended the philological family name "Dravidian" to connote a separate political entity comprising the land and the people where the four major Dravidian languages were spoken (Arooran 1980: 250).

Ramasamy felt that Tamils could receive fair treatment only if they had a separate land of their own. Thus came the demand for *Dravida Nadu*. It envisaged a federation of areas where four major Dravidian languages were spoken, namely, Tamil, Telugu, Kannada, and Malayalam. Ramasamy declared that all people living in those areas, other than the *Brāhmins*, were Dravidians. Ramasamy's conception of *Dravidanad* rested on the presumption that the Dravidian non-*Brāhmins* who spoke the four Dravidian languages were of a racial stock and culture which marked them out as separate from the *Aryan-Brāhmins*. Another important presumption of Ramasamy in the formulation of his scheme of a Dravidian State was that it would be a haven for non-*Brāhmin* Dravidians, securing them against the domination of the *Aryan-Brāhmins*. Thus, Ramasamy's anti-*Brāhmin* principles, too, were the basis of the demand of a Dravidian Federation (Arooran 1980: 250).

IX Rationalism and the struggle against *Brāhminism*

In his uncompromising struggle against caste, Ramasamy's main tool was rationalism. Using that tool, he analysed society and diagnosed its ailments. The chief maladies of Indian society as Ramasamy saw them were God, religion, and caste. In different speeches, throughout his lifetime, Ramasamy demonstrated logically how these institutions were dysfunctional to Indian society. They were nothing but creations of a class in its own narrow self-interest, aimed at duping and exploiting the common man. The deep-rooted damaging effect of religion was all too obvious to Ramasamy. Rationalism made him a non-believer; he was an atheist. But his contempt for all religions was not equally intense. The main target of his attack was Hinduism, and that was due to its caste ideology.

On the social plane, Ramasamy sought to counter caste ideology through a multi-pronged awareness programme. Boycotting priests, condemning the Hindu scriptures, celebrating self-respect marriages without *Brāhminical* rituals, and denying caste norms were just some of Ramasamy's tactics aimed at defying the *Brāhminical* social ethos (Chatterjee 2004).

X The socialist connection and the *samadharma* agenda

Ramasamy was a widely travelled man. Particularly, since the late 1920s, he travelled extensively in India and abroad. Among the foreign countries he visited were several Western States as well as the Soviet Union. Such exposures probably contributed towards his socialist inclination. In 1930, at the Erode Self-Respect Conference, Ramasamy declared that socialism should be the country's goal. In 1932, he placed before the Self-Respect Movement the proposal of forming the *Samadharma* Party. It may be noted that the term *samadharma* was the closest Tamil equivalent of socialism. During this period, Ramasamy was closely associating with Singaravelu, who was a union leader hailing from a fishermen's caste and who is considered the first communist of south India. From 1931 onwards, Singaravelu's articles started appearing regularly in the *Kudi Arasu*. Between 1932 and 1933, the *Kudi Arasu* published a series of articles on Bolshevism, Communism, and the Russian Revolution.

The leftism of the Ramasamy movement, however, was toned down as pressure from the British authorities and from the conservatives within the non-*Brāhmin* Movement. Cutting a long story short, it was not long before Ramasamy decided to tone down his socialist line and revive and radicalise the already existing Justice Party. Even as Ramasamy was giving shape to his ideas of self-respect, he was maintaining close connections with the Justice Party, which at that time was the only non-*Brāhmin* party in Tamil Nadu.

XI Women's liberation and emancipation

Ramasamy repeatedly spoke about the need for the liberation of women. His attention in this respect was focused on questions relating to love, chastity, prostitution, marriage, women's education, property rights, and birth control. Ramasamy regarded women's liberation to be as important as the removal of untouchability for becoming fit for self-government (Saraswathi 1994: 194). He observed that:

> The situation of women in our country continues to be very bad . . .' In giving advice to women he said, women must realise that human society involves the living together of people and that it does not mean that every man must carry away a woman and keep her at home under lock and key.
>
> *(Viduthalai, 15.6.43, cited in Veeramani 1996: 81)*

Ramasamy's emphasis was on educating women, which he believed was more important than educating men. To him, marriage was a partnership of equals. It was not *kanika danam*, where the daughter is gifted in marriage, but was a life partnership agreement. He felt the term *kanika danam* was not a Tamil word but drawn from the language of the northerners and meant that ladies should be treated as slaves to be arbitrarily given to others as a giftable commodity. The notion of life partnership, Ramasamy believed, was integral to the *Kural* of Thiruvalluvar (Ramasami 1983: 18). Within the family, Ramasamy believed the husband and wife should have equal rights. In this line of thought, he strongly advocated self-respect marriages and birth control measures. In the ultimate analyses, he felt that the institution of marriage itself should be abolished. In the 1920s, Ramasamy was advising women not to bear children, and in the 1930s, he came out strongly in favour of birth control. He saw women's right to abortion as a necessary ingredient of women's freedom (Saraswathi 1994: 195).

Several of the issues feminists take up today were perhaps addressed by Ramasamy decades ago in a similar vein. His views were not only extremely radical for his time but even today draw strong criticisms from the orthodox. It may be noted that the honorific title of 'Periyar' was in fact conferred on him by women at one of their conferences in 1936.

XII Revolution and communism

Ramasamy's visit to the Soviet Union stimulated in him a general interest for socialism. And this interest was clearly reflected in his ideas and activities on his return to India in November 1932. When Ramasamy and S. Ramanathan returned from the Soviet Union, they published a series of articles in translation in the *Kudi Arasu* containing Vladimir Lenin's views on religion.[2]

Between the years 1933 and 1936, the self-respecters articulated much of their ideas on religion, caste, and social reform within the broad parameters of socialist logic (Geetha and Rajadurai 1998: 246–247). It is significant to note that much of Ramasamy's admiration for the Soviet Union rested less on the economics of the socialist agenda and more on the latter's experiments in abolishing religion (ibid.: 424). In this context, it is pertinent to note that when Ramasamy had visited the Soviet Union he had registered as an honorary member of the atheists' association, and on his return to India he had published a series of articles in the *Kudi Arasu* which contained Lenin's views on religion. Subsequently, as *Puratchi* came to replace *Kudi Arasu*, in the very first editorial of the new weekly it was stated that the present capitalist State was held captive by the clutches of the priests (ibid.: 424). This class of priests would have to be destroyed before the capitalist class could be destroyed. In an article serialised in the *Kudi Arasu* between 1930 and 1931, Ramasamy noted that:

> Though given the horrors and deprivations of Indian society, a Russian type revolution should have occurred, it did not so happen because the

caste system functions as a protective force and helps in preserving and perpetuating the notion of economic inequality.

(Kudi Arasu, 4.10.31)[3]

XIII Humanism

Ramasamy considered himself a humanist – *manida dharmavadi* – and asserted that all that he preached was based on the humanist approach. He believed that a good society had to be a human society and a human society should be rational and have the capacity to think. Existing society he felt to be irrational and akin to an animal society. Ramasamy has been regarded as the Voltaire of South India, particularly Tamil Nadu. Both Voltaire and Ramasamy were rationalists. Both sought to generate amongst the people a realisation that all persons are equal and that every individual has the birth right to enjoy liberty, equality, and fraternity. Ramasamy spent his whole life trying to awaken the people to their needs of education and to make them conscious of their backwardness, misplaced faith in superstitions, deception, and exploitation by some scheming individuals. He sought to generate in them the desire for self-respect and self-confidence. Ramasamy's self-respect encompassed the concepts of liberty, equality, and fraternity as exhorted by the French revolutionaries. He felt that the principles governing public life should not hamper personal freedom and should be such as not to provide room in their application for partiality or discrimination between the high and the low (*Kudi Arasu*, 26.10.30). Throughout his life, Ramasamy focused on self-respect for all people of India.

XIV Conclusion

Ramasamy was exceedingly wary of State power. This was evident in his overall aversion to electoral politics and his efforts to keep the Dravidar Kazhagam as essentially a radical social organisation focusing on the radical social movement. In the Tamil region, Ramasamy's legacy lives on – from the political to the cultural to the literary fields. The iconisation of Ramasamy as a phenomenon is clearly visible. There are statues and busts of Ramasamy adorning every other road, lane, and bylane in Tamil Nadu. At the foot of the pedestals can most frequently be found the phrases "There is no God; whoever believes in God is a fool". A stereotype of Ramasamy is thus firmly etched in the public mind, a rather simplistic reading no doubt of a radical, multi-dimensional character.

The Self-Respect Movement had an impact not just in Tamil Nadu but also in overseas countries with large Tamil populations, such as Malaysia and Singapore. Among Singapore Indians, groups like the Tamil Reform Association and leaders like Thamizhavel G. Sarangapani were prominent in promoting the principles of the Self-Respect Movement among the local Tamil population through schools and publications.

Nonetheless, today Ramasamy's rationalism-based cultural norms and practices remain restricted to a limited number of committed followers, failing to replace the *Brāhminical* order. In fact, the political impact of his social ideas seems to be more pervading. As lamented by a contemporary author:

> I look here at aspects of the Self-Respect Movement, a radical anti-caste movement begun by E. V. Ramasamy Periyar in 1925, and which convulsed the Tamil country into eruptions of defiance, anger and subversion for the next two decades. The Dravidar Kazhagam (DK) was formed in 1944 by Periyar himself, and the Dravida Munnetra Kazhagam (DMK) in 1949, by a group of men who were dissatisfied with the DK. Both organisations continue to be vocal and active in Tamil politics today. However, in different ways, both have compromised and even reneged on the founding ideals of the Self-Respect Movement. This is so particularly with reference to the women's question, the resolution of which was quite central to the self-respecters' anti-caste agenda.
> *(Geetha and Rajadurai 1998: 180)*

As Ramasamy sought to make self-respect a mass movement, building up a powerful force involving activists drawn from all castes and from both men and women, he projected a Dravidian identity rooted in what was perceived as the culture of the Tamil people. In doing so, he indeed succeeded in giving a powerful political thrust to this social alternative (Omvedt 2010).

Several political parties in Tamil Nadu, such as D.M.K. and A.I.A.D.M.K., owe their origins to the Self-Respect Movement, the latter being a 1972 breakaway from the D.M.K. Yet the Dravidian movement failed in establishing itself as an effective alternative to the *Vedic Aryan-Brāhminic* force it despised. Not only did it lose its radical social thrust, which would have included the liberation of women and the securing of full human rights to the *Śūdras* and *Dalits*, it remained confined as a movement to Tamil Nadu. As it focused on Tamil national identity, the concept of a Dravidian civilisational identity was lost. Even the people of the other southern States were not ready to accept their identity as Dravidians, let alone the vast majority of people in Maharastra, Orissa, Gujarat, or elsewhere (Omvedt 2010).

Efforts to engineer a culture are by no means new. In India, political and social activists have, with diverse intents, undertaken such attempts at different points in time. In challenging *Brāhminism*, the cultural world of the *bauls*, *sahajiya vaishnavas*, and the *matuas* of Bengal are but a few examples. However, none could develop a wide sustained base for a durable duration nor offer a comprehensive theoretically structured rationalistic alternative, as most of these movements visualised the challenge in terms of alternative religious discourses. In terms of developing a holistic, rationalist alternative to *Brāhminism* in modern times, Ramasamy's scheme is perhaps one of the most comprehensive of such efforts, as it takes note of the inseparable links of the social, economic, cultural, and political realities and posits an integrated alternative theory.

Notes

1 *Kudi Arasu*, 11.12.32; 18.12.32; 25.12.32; 8.1.33; 15.1.33.
2 Ramasamy was also referred to as *Tantai*, or Father, and *Talaivar*, or Leader.
3 *Kudi Arasu*, 4.10.31 and 26.10.30 in V. Anaimuthu, edited and compiled, *Periyar E.V. Ramasamy. Chinthanaigal, Thoughts of Periyar E.V.R.*, Thinker's Forum, Tiruchirappalli, 1974, vol. 3, 1974, pp. 1677–1680.

References

Arooran, Nambi (1980). *Tamil Renaissance and Dravidian Nationalism, 1905–1944*. Madurai: Koodal Publishers.
Chandrababu, B. S. (1993). *Social Protest in Tamil Nadu; With Reference to Self-Respect Movement (From 1920s to 1940s)*. Madras: Emerald Publishers.
Chatterjee, Debi (2004). *Up Against Caste: Comparative Study of Ambedkar and Periyar*. Jaipur: Rawat Publications.
Chatterjee, Debi (2010). *Ideas and Movements Against Caste in India: Ancient to Modern Times*, 2nd Edition. New Delhi: Abhijeet Publications.
Geetha, V., and Rajadurai, S. V. (1998). *Towards a Non-Brahmin Millennium, From Iyothee Thass to Periyar*. Calcutta: Samya Publications.
Gopalakrishnan, M. D. (1992). *Periyar: Father of the Tamil Race*. Madras: Emerald Publishers.
Jeyaraman, Bala (2013). *Periyar: A Political Biography of E.V. Ramasamy*. New Delhi: Rupa Publications Pvt. Ltd.
Naicker, E. V. Ramasami (1981). *The Genesis of My Self-Respect Movement*. Madras: Arivukkadal Achagam.
Omvedt, Gail (2010). *Round Table India*. 4 October, available at: https://roundtableindia.co.in/index.php?option=com, accessed on 7.7.17.
Pillai, K. K. (1978). "The Non-Brahmin Movement in South India", in S. P. Sen (Ed.), *Social Contents of Indian Religious Reform Movements*. Calcutta: Institute of Historical Studies.
Ramasami, Periyar E. V. (1983). *Self-Respect Marriages*. Madras: Periyar Self-Respect Propaganda Institution, translation By A. S. Venu.
Saraswathi, S. (1994). *Towards Self-Respect: Periyar EVR on A New World*. Madras: Institute of South Indian Studies.
Veeramani, K. (1996). *Periyar on Women's Rights*. Madras: Emerald Publishers.
Viswanathan, E. S. (1983). *The Political Career of E. V. Ramasami Naicker*. Madras: Ravi and Vasanth Publishers.

8

BHIMRAO RAMJI AMBEDKAR

Narender Kumar

> *No one can hope to make any effective mark upon his time and bring the aid that is worth bringing to great principles and struggling causes if he is not strong in his love and his hatred. I hate injustice, tyranny, pompousness and humbug, and my hatred embraces all those who are guilty of them. I want to tell my critics that I regard my feelings of hatred as a real force. They are only the reflex of the love I bear for the causes I believe in.*
> – Dr B. R. Ambedkar in Preface to "Ranade, Gandhi and Jinnah",
> (Dr Babasaheb Ambedkar *Writings and Speeches 1979*,
> Vol. 1 pp. 208–209)

I Introduction

Dr B. R. Ambedkar has been a towering personality of the twentieth century encompassing various personas. Popularly known as Babasaheb, he remains among the few thinkers who continue to inspire those seeking radical but peaceful transformation in the existing social, political, and economic spheres. Popular and academic focus has been on his role as chief architect of the Constitution of India and as guardian of ex-untouchables' emancipation, but his contribution for common women through the Hindu Code Bill and for his labour in different capacities during the British period have no parallel.[1]

Ambedkar started his journey in public life through intervention in the Southborough Committee in 1919 and tried to differentiate between touchables and untouchables in the Indian society. Additionally, probably for the first time among any of his contemporaries, he argued for the universal adult franchise and self-representation of the communities instead of other representation. Later, before the Simon Commission and during the Round Table Conferences, Ambedkar tried to convince the British and Indian delegates that *Dalits* needed Separate Electorates for which he opined only after writing in detail about different electoral systems during those times. Until 1946, Ambedkar kept his efforts to bring changes in the lives of marginalised groups, including religious minorities, from outside and inside the decision-making structures and finally kept arguing for their rights in the Constituent Assembly and beyond.

In this chapter, we examine and analyse Ambedkar's understanding of *Brāhminical* Hinduism, better known as the Hindu social order; the curse of caste and untouchability Ambedkar faced and challenged throughout his life; the ideas of nation and nationalism, which continue to threaten to engulf Indian society in the twenty-first century; democracy, for which Ambedkar remained perturbed about whether it would take root in the unequal Indian/Hindu society infested with graded inequality; and, finally, interface between religion and politics, which forced Ambedkar to take refuge in Buddhism during his last days.

II Life sketch

Bhimrao Ambedkar was born on 14 April 1891 in the town Mhow, Madhya Pradesh, where his father was a soldier in the British Army. Having born into the family of a soldier, Ambedkar may not have faced the kind of humiliation that any other untouchable child would, but as time passed while interacting with the society around him, Ambedkar started realising his unique social status, first in the school and then elsewhere. Having sharp mental capabilities, Ambedkar first passed his primary and secondary schooling, then college, and finally got a scholarship to study abroad for further higher education and acquired the highest of degrees. Comprehending his intellectual and representative qualities, Ambedkar was consulted on various occasions by the British government on the question of untouchable rights, starting from 1919 with his first representation to the Southborough Committee until the caste-Hindus under the leadership of Gandhi realised his genius and offered him to be the chief architect of the Constitution of India. He became the first law minister of independent India and resigned from the cabinet of Nehru after flouting the passing of the Hindu Code Bill, his second most important legal document (after the Constitution) on the rights of women. During his last days, Ambedkar converted to Buddhism with around half a million of his followers and got *Mahaparinirvana* (salvation in death) on 6 December 1956.

III Critique of *Brāhminical* Hinduism (Hindu social order)

Ambedkar's first major academic intervention was at the age of 25 when he wrote a paper, *Castes in India*, about caste and its genesis and features. Later, he wrote one of his most popular papers, *Annihilation of Caste*. Ambedkar opined that caste is an essential feature of Hindu religion which created a well-defined social order, the Hindu social order. He discussed in detail the essential principles and unique features of this order in BAWS, Vol. 3.

Ambedkar identified some attributes of the caste system which were exclusive and peculiar to Hindu society, such as dividing the population into groups as castes, making it endogamous (restraining marriage among the castes) not as a custom but as a rule. Several rights, like civil, cultural, educational, and economic, were assigned to each caste differently without freedom of change, leaving no space for individual choices and capability. Unequal entitlements of various rights within the castes being one of the fundamental features, attributed the lowest rights at the bottom and the highest at the top, depriving many the right to choose their occupation, acquire property, and receive education. Furthermore, rights have been so distributed that the privileges of higher castes became disabilities for the lower ones. For example, the teaching of *Vedās*, receiving grants and gifts, and officiating at sacrifice, have been the exclusive domains of the *Brāhmins*. Additionally, they had no restriction to adopt the occupation of their choice, a benefit denied to other castes/*varṇas*. Nevertheless, the *Brāhmins* were not to adopt the impure occupations fixed for the Untouchables.[2] It was in this light that the untouchables had to face isolation and exclusion of a severe kind, which is a unique feature of the Hindu social order.

One might wonder why the untouchables accepted the impure occupations and why there was no major revolt against such a system. Thus, the question is, how does the social order sustain and maintain itself? It was in terms of social and economic penalties, wherein instruments of social and economic boycott laid down against violation of codes, became central to sustain and maintain the order. Those who defied the order faced the wrath of the dominant sections of the society.

Thus, Ambedkar termed the Hindu social order as a system of governance, production, organisation, and distribution based on fixed rights; graded rights and penalty against violation that not only sustained the order but also provided philosophical justification. Deepak Lal (1988) writes that "what is important is that the economic and non-economic aspects of the 'system' (Hindu social order) mutually reinforced each other".

Among the essential principles, one was making the individual an end in him/herself, thus denying the recognition of other individuals. Therefore, it leads to the denial of individual merit and non-consideration of individual justice. The matter does not end here, but it also does not recognise fraternity and equality among the members. The doctrine that the different classes were created from different parts of the divine body has generated the belief that it must be divine will that individuals should remain separate and distinct. It is this belief which has created in the Hindu an instinct to be different, to be separate, and to be distinct from rest of his fellow Hindus.

The question of inequality among the different *varṇas* is another departure that becomes part of the problem. The inequality is an essential part as it does not simply have inequality of classes but graded inequality, making the inequality vertical. In other words, caste members stand one above the other, not horizontally, where mobility could be easier. This difference is not merely conventional but spiritual, moral, and legal, and Ambedkar argued that no sphere of life is untouched that is not regulated by the principle of graded inequality (BAWS,

Vol. 3). Another essential principle identified is the fixity of occupations for each class and its continuance by heredity, which was codified by Manu. Yet, another principle is the fixity of people within their respective classes, banning free interchange and intercourse between different classes of Hindu society and leading to bars against inter-dining and inter-marriage, the defying of which attracts punishments of different kinds.

IV Caste and Ambedkar – Gandhi debate

As Gandhi and Ambedkar remain major thinkers of twentieth-century India, similarly, caste and untouchability remain the two conceptions which have produced complications and solutions and which continue to do so. Many people endorse that *Annihilation of Caste* has been Ambedkar's most profound text.[3] It remains most profound not because it challenges the Hindu right-wingers or the conservative elements in Hinduism but for its contestation posed to those who are better known as left-liberals.

This debate was not a new one. Both men were their generation's emissaries of a profound social, political, and philosophical conflict that had begun long ago and has still by no means ended. Ambedkar, the untouchable, was heir to the anti-caste intellectual tradition that goes back to 200–100 B.C.E. Gandhi, a *Vaiśya*, born into a Gujarati *Bania* family, was the latest in a long tradition of privileged-caste Hindu reformers and their organisations (Roy 2014).

A few fundamental differences need to be understood between Ambedkar and Gandhi. One, their location in the Hindu social structure; two, their views on *varṇa*, caste, and untouchability separately and jointly; three, the solutions they produced to address these social proscribes; and four, what could have been their stands on these in contemporary times. When we look at their location it becomes quite obvious that Gandhi comes from high social order and Ambedkar from a lower one as imagined and imposed in the Indian society. Gandhi was second in the *varṇa* hierarchy, and Ambedkar had no place in this hierarchy as a *Panchama*, officially a non-existent category in the *varṇa* system.

The views on *varṇa* are very distinct for both. Gandhi did not find any problem in observing the *varṇa* system and performing the tasks assigned to different *varṇas*; however, Ambedkar had serious objection to it and considered it the fundamental basis for the inequality in the Hindu society which Ambedkar termed as parent to caste differences. Ambedkar supported the complete annihilation of caste, whereas Gandhi initially wanted and emphasised no inter-dining and no inter-caste marriages among different castes. Rajmohan Gandhi, Mahatma Gandhi's grandson argued that in the later phase of Gandhi's life, he reconsidered the view and advocated inter-caste marriages. Both Ambedkar and Gandhi were for the abolition of untouchability. Though Gandhi did make it part of his schedule to visit untouchables, Ambedkar considered it shallow reform without getting into the cause and philosophy behind the practice.

Thus, Ambedkar had a much different take on this and argued that *varna*, caste, and untouchability are interlinked and produce rationale and justification for each other, even if the abolition of untouchability is attempted, it won't help unless and until the foundation provided by caste and *varna* are annihilated and wished away for which Gandhi was not ready. However, during his last days, Gandhi supported inter-dining and inter-caste marriages. His ideas and support for the *varna* system based on worth and not on birth are well grounded. Countering and understanding the incongruity of this idea, Ambedkar argued:

> How are you going to compel people who have achieved a higher status based on their birth, without reference to their worth, to vacate that status? How are you going to compel people to recognise the status due to a man in accordance to his worth who is occupying a lower status based on his birth?
>
> *(BAWS, Vol. 1: 59–60)*

In a recent intervention on the debate, Arundhati Roy remarks on the position of Gandhi regarding his belief in *chaturvarna*:

> Gandhi never decisively and categorically renounced his belief in *chaturvarna*, the system of four *varnas*. Still, why not eschew the negative and concentrate instead on what was good about Gandhi, use it to bring out the best in people? It is a valid question, and one that those who have built shrines to Gandhi have probably answered for themselves. After all, it is possible to admire the work of great composers, writers, architects, sportspersons and musicians whose views are inimical to our own. The difference is that Gandhi was not a composer or writer or musician or a sportsman. He offered himself to us as a visionary, a mystic, a moralist, a great humanitarian, the man who brought down a mighty empire armed only with truth and righteousness.
>
> *(Roy 2014: 42)*

Questioning further she asks:

> How do we reconcile the idea of the non-violent Gandhi, the Gandhi who spoke Truth to Power, Gandhi the Nemesis of Injustice, the Gentle Gandhi, the Androgynous Gandhi, Gandhi the Mother, the Gandhi who (allegedly) feminised politics and created space for women to enter the political arena, the eco-Gandhi, the Gandhi of the ready wit and some great one-liners – how do we reconcile all this with Gandhi's views (and deeds) on caste? What do we do with this structure of moral righteousness that rests so comfortably on a foundation of utterly brutal, institutionalised injustice?
>
> *(Roy 2014: 42–43)*

Rajmohan Gandhi, who has written a critique to Roy's claims, argues that:

> It may be true that for a long time, Gandhi did not attack caste and remain confined to abolition of untouchability that "was an excellent strategy for undermining caste" and finally in 1935 in a journal he wrote *Caste Has to Go*.
> (Gandhi 2015: 83)

However, one can argue that Gandhi did not speak against the *varṇa* system for which Ambedkar had no mercy.

When we examine the contribution of Gandhi and Ambedkar then, we need to keep their backgrounds and the philosophies of their socialisation that influenced them to reach to the solutions that they both strived for the upliftment and empowerment of those on the margins of society. It is interesting to note that the ideologies and the supporters of such ideologies that were against Gandhi's and Ambedkar's opinions on caste and untouchability are now appropriating aspects of both. Nevertheless, their stances on the cardinal features of the Hindu social order, namely, caste and untouchability, need to be analysed. One needs to question how many leaders of contemporary India are in a position to speak against these issues with the same force and commitment as even Gandhi did in his time.

V Constitution-making, rights, and citizenship

The rule of law was very dear to Ambedkar, and that is why he generally opined against the societal customs and conventions which influenced the rule of law. Because Ambedkar was the chief architect of the Indian Constitution, it is generally assumed that every article, clause, etc. in the document had his consent. However, if one looks at his writings and the kind of discourse reflected there, it becomes obvious that his ideas on many of the issues in the Constitution were much different, which reveals the apprehensions with which he became part of the Constitution-making process.

Even in the Constituent Assembly, Ambedkar was critical of Nehru's Resolution, which initiated the process of formal Constitution-making and argued that the part dealing with the fundamental rights of the citizens was a hollow in the absence of remedies. It was those remedies which were essential "whereby people can seek to obtain redress when rights are invaded". He observed that even the principle that describes "that no man's life, liberty and property shall be taken without the due process of law, finds no place in the Resolution". In the absence of it, the option was left to the executive or the regime of the day that might decide about the way it imagined the rights of the citizens (BAWS, Vol. 13: 8–9).

In the beginning of the Constitution-making process, Ambedkar might have been critical of Nehru's Resolution, which did not mention explicitly remedies against the violation of the fundamental rights of the citizens, but at the same time he believed rights could not be absolute. While concluding the debate on the draft Constitution, he again argued that rights are not absolute and need to be qualified by certain conditions. Thus, Ambedkar wanted a balance where the rights of the citizens could not be unconditional, but at the same time if rights were violated, they needed remedies. Responding to the queries and comments of the members of the Constituent Assembly on the draft Constitution, Ambedkar said:

> In the opinion of the critics, Fundamental Rights are not Fundamental Rights unless they are also absolute rights. The critics rely on the Constitution of the United States and to the Bill of Rights embodied in the first Ten Amendments to that Constitution in support of their contention. It is said that, the Fundamental Rights in the American Bill of Rights are real because they are not subjected to limitations or exceptions. . . . I am sorry to say that the whole of the criticism about fundamental rights is based upon a misconception. In the first place, the criticism in so far as it seeks to distinguish fundamental rights from non-fundamental rights is not sound. It is incorrect to say that fundamental rights are absolute while non-fundamental rights are not absolute. The real distinction between the two is that non-fundamental rights are created by agreement between parties while fundamental rights are the gift of the law. Because fundamental rights are the gift of the State it does not follow that the State cannot qualify those.
> *(BAWS, Vol. 13: 63)*

The incorporation of Directive Principles of the State Policy was not so popular in different Constitutions in those times (1940s), and Ambedkar termed these "novel features of parliamentary democracy". There was no certainty as to what kind of regime or party might come to power since it was left to the people in a democracy to have a regime of their choice, and Ambedkar knew the implications of the conception of "tyranny of the majority" coined by J. S. Mill and how that was destructively reflected in Nazi Germany, where an elected regime implemented the genocide of millions of Jews and other minorities. In this light, Ambedkar argued that "whoever captures power will not be free to do what he likes", and in such situations the regime or party will have to respect these "instruments of instructions which are called Directive Principles". He argued very categorically that though those in power may not have to answer the breach of these instructions in the form of Directive Principles of State Policy in a court of law, but it would be the election that would certainly make such powers to respond. He could very well visualise the value of these when he said that "What great value these Directive Principles possess will be realised better when the forces of right contrive to capture power" (BAWS, Vol. 13: 65).

The Constitution-making period had the shadow of partition, which created India and Pakistan. The fallout of the partition did not deter the drafting committee from making certain essential provisions for the protection of the minorities, and Ambedkar was clear about the need to include certain fundamentals even in the Fundamental Rights. The reactionaries of the times criticised such provision, and Ambedkar responded with the following:

> Speaking for myself, I have no doubt that the Constituent Assembly has done wisely in providing such safeguards for minorities as it has done, in this country both the minorities and the majorities have followed a wrong path. It is wrong for the majority to deny the existence of minorities. It is equally wrong for the minorities to perpetuate themselves. A solution must be found which will serve a double purpose. It must recognise the existence of the minorities to start with. It must also be such that it will enable majorities and minorities to merge someday into one.
>
> (BAWS, Vol. 13: 62)

This statement shows that Ambedkar was concerned with the rights of the minorities and wanted the majority to recognise and initially give special treatment and rights to the minorities, but at the same time minorities also needed to realise that they could not perpetually and notionally remain minorities in national life. They would have to merge with the larger majority and become one so that the divide between the majorities and minorities could be bridged. Nevertheless, the complexity of the issue was so tricky that it may not have been so easy to transcend the differences. The way minorities' issues are being handled even today, despite Ambedkar's warnings, that the merging of the majority and minorities seems a far-off dream.

VI Women's rights and the Hindu Code Bill

Hindu society did not have merely unequal characteristics in terms of *varṇa*, caste, and untouchability but, like almost all societies, also in terms of the low status of women. One may argue that women across the world face inequality and discrimination. So, what is so unique about Indian, especially Hindu, women? If one looks at the customs and conventions inflicted upon Hindu women by the laws of Manu that ruled societal behaviour, one will find them on a distinct plane, more so when one is reminded of the practices of *sati* and child marriage. In the *Annihilation of Caste*, Ambedkar refers to these problematic issues with reference to caste but while working upon the Hindu Code Bill, he suggested remedies.

It was obvious that traditionally society did not give rights to women, as codified through some texts. As Ambedkar's concern was to bestow rights to women, he did not hesitate to refer to some of the traditions that granted Hindu women rights, and it is in this context that his contribution in terms of the Hindu Code Bill becomes a milestone in the lives of Hindu women, for whom almost no constitutional expert in modern India tried to contribute as much as did Ambedkar. It is revealing to note that he faced opposition not only from Hindu males but Hindu females as well.[4] It is probably in this light that Sharmila Rege argued that Indian feminists need to reclaim Ambedkar for his forthright contribution regarding women's rights, and especially Hindu women's rights (Rege 2013). Deliberating upon the major characteristics of the Bill in the Parliament of India, Ambedkar said:

> The points which arise out of this Bill for consideration and which are new are these: First, the abolition of birth right and to take property by survivorship. The second point that arises for consideration is the giving of half of share to the daughter. Thirdly, the conversion of the women's limited estate into an absolute estate. Fourthly, the principle of monogamy and fifthly the principle of divorce.
> *(BAWS, Vol. 14 [I]: 11)*

Looking at the opposition to the Hindu Code Bill, Ambedkar went to the extent of calling himself a conservative to persuade the conservative elements in the House (Parliament) and cited the instance of Edmund Burke, who had written against the French Revolution for being too radical and advised his own countrymen, who were very conservative, that "those who want to conserve must be ready to repair". It was against this backdrop that Ambedkar appealed, "if you want to maintain Hindu system, the Hindu culture, the Hindu society do not hesitate to repair where repair is necessary". Ambedkar went on to emphasise that the Hindu Code Bill asks for nothing more than repairing those parts of the Hindu system which had become dilapidated (BAWS Vol. 14 [I]: 283).

It would be interesting to note that this Bill could not be passed despite the progressive elements, like Nehru at the helm of affairs, in the government, and Ambedkar resigned from the Cabinet as first Law Minister of independent India for blaming Nehru's regime for having buried the Bill "untold and unsung". Emphasising the significance of the Bill, he said:

> No law passed by the Indian legislature in the past or likely to be passed in the future can be compared to it in point of its significance. To leave inequality between class and class, between sex and sex which is the soul of Hindu society, untouched and to go on passing legislation relating to economic problems is to make a farce of our Constitution and to build a palace on a dung heap. This is the significance I attached to the Hindu Code.
> *(BAWS, Vol. 14 [II]: 1325)*

This statement tries to introduce a comprehensive bill on the rights of women in general, and Hindu women in particular, that was passed by Indian Parliament in bits and pieces starting from 1955 and remains unfulfilled today.

VII Democracy, State, and society

Democracy became the most aspired system of government in the twentieth century. India became one of the first countries to adopt democracy and continues to have it and strengthen it today. As democracy was one of the major desires of the builders of modern India, Ambedkar also contributed in this regard, making it part of India's political history. For him, democracy meant "a form and method of government whereby revolutionary changes in the economic and social life of the people are brought about without bloodshed" (BAWS, Vol. 17 [III]: 475). Parliamentary democracy was his favourite variant of this political system, rather than a presidential regime in which there is concentration of power in the hands of one man leading to a kind of hero worship where "the principle of self-government expresses the desire of the people to rule itself rather than be ruled by others whether the rulers be absolute monarchs, dictators or privileged classes. It is called democracy" (BAWS, Vol. 10: 39). Thus, in a democratic system, the government needs to be of the people and by the people rather than for the people, as in the latter case the prominence is taken by the government and not by the people.

A leader coming from a background as an untouchable, Ambedkar tried to use democracy to ensure the representation of his caste fellows in elected assemblies through positive discrimination and the forming of political parties. As a believer in law, Ambedkar promoted constitutional arrangements; as a progressive statesman, he argued in favour of equality and socialism as pre-conditions for sustainable democracy. His socialist inclination and resistance to his proposal on adopting constitutional socialism in the Constituent Assembly made him settle for an alternative solution in liberal democracy. Political reservation through reserved seats in place of separate electorates, reservation in only the public sector rather than both in public and private sectors, and Directive Principles of State Policy for social and economic democracy through liberal policies in place of state socialism are some of the adjustments and compromises Ambedkar had to make. However, his broader understanding and desire of constitutional measures are stored in his major contributions outside the Constituent Assembly, namely, in States and minorities, on the eve of Constitution-making and in the manifesto of the Republican Party of India after the completion of the Constitution-making process. The influence of pragmatism, a conception of Ambedkar's teacher John Dewey of Columbia University, is clearly reflected in some of these adjustments and accommodations. Ambedkar's pragmatism reflects his inclination towards liberal ethos, where the individual becomes the focus, and it is probably this individual who needed to be freed from the clutches of societal and economic disparities in Ambedkar's model. Without addressing the latter, the former was not feasible, which comes out distinctly in Ambedkar's contribution at several junctures of his life.

Apart from providing larger contours of democracy, Ambedkar also remained an advocate for group rights within the democratic design. His consistent focus on minority rights in a democracy and his search for the best alternative finally brought him to the conception of *relative majority* to ease the influence of absolute majority in the legislatures and *principle of unanimity* in choice of Cabinet, including the Prime Minister, for addressing the questions of minorities. He was categorical and blunt in saying that the question of minorities was dwindling from one method to another, and in the lack of principle, one after another method was being employed as one method failed and another was implemented without adhering to some fundamental principles. Elaborating about the principles for the minorities' question, Ambedkar underlined the following:

1. Majority rule is untenable in theory and unjustifiable in practice. A majority community may be conceded a relative majority of representation, but it can never claim an absolute majority.
2. The relative majority of representation given to a majority community in the legislature should not be so large as to enable the majority to establish its rule with the help of the smallest minorities.
3. The distribution of seats should be so made that a combination of the majority and one of the major minorities should not give the combination such a majority as to make them impervious to the interest of the minorities.
4. The distribution should be so made that if all the minorities combine they could, without depending on the majority, form a government of their own.
5. The weightage taken from the majority should be distributed among the minorities in inverse proportion to their social standing, economic position, and educational condition so that a minority which is large and which has a better social, educational, and economic standing gets a lesser amount of weightage than a minority whose numbers are less and whose educational, economic, and social position is inferior to that of the others.

(BAWS, Vol. 1: 373–374)

The conception of relative majority would remain among some of Ambedkar's original contributions in the successful functioning of a democracy. Though he believed in an institutionalisation mechanism for the success of democracy, it was not a one-way street; rather, citizens should interrelate with others and allow others to do the same. Thus, Ambedkar did not fix meanings to democracy beyond a certain level but expected future generations to evolve by defining and redefining their own democracy.

Ambedkar's functioning as chairperson of the drafting committee gave him a central role in the making of the Constitution that defined not only the position and powers of the three organs, namely, the legislature, the executive branch, and the judiciary, but also defined the rights of the citizens to impose limitations on the authorities of these organs. In the absence of limitation, there could be "complete tyranny and complete oppression". While defining the objective of the Constitution, Ambedkar stated that "while we have established political democracy, it is also the desire that we should lay down as our ideal economic democracy". This was argued to be emphatic advice to those who form the government.

Though Ambedkar had been concerned with individual rights and the individual remained central to his thinking, he was equally concerned with the role of the State in the democratic system. Inequalities and discrimination as societal norms prevailed in all societies, but it was too entrenched in Indian society, wherein not inequality but graded inequality characterised Hindu society. This special inequality required a more nuanced solution, which led Ambedkar to suggest State socialism. While speaking on Nehru's Resolution in the beginning of the formal Constitution-making process, Ambedkar argued:

> Sir, there are here certain provisions which speak of justice, economic, social and political. If, this Resolution has a reality behind it and a sincerity, of which I have not the least doubt, coming as it does from the Mover of the Resolution, I should have expected some provision whereby it would have been possible for the State to make economic, social and political justice a reality and I should have from that point of view expected the Resolution to state in most explicit terms that in order that there may be social and economic justice in the country, that there would be nationalisation of industry and nationalisation of land, I do not understand how it could be possible for any future Government which believes in doing justice socially, economically and politically, unless its economy is a socialistic economy.
>
> (BAWS, Vol. 13: 8–9)

The word "socialism" has been inserted into the preamble of the Constitution after more than two decades of its coming into force, which indicates a lack of consensus among the founding fathers for inclusion of the word, despite Nehru and a few others' inclination towards including it. While debating the right to property as a fundamental right, Ambedkar in 1955 said:

> The Article 31, with which we are dealing with, in this amending Bill, is an Article for which the Drafting Committee and I can take no responsibility whatsoever. We do not take any responsibility for that. That is not our draft. The result was that the Congress Party, at time when Article 31 was framed so divided within itself that we did not know what to do? What to put and what not to put? There was a section in Congress Party; one section was made by Sardar Vallabhbhai Patel, who stood for full compensation in the sense, enacted as our land acquisition, namely, market price plus 15 percent solatium. That was his point of view; our Prime Minister was against compensation. Our friend, Mr Pant who had conceived his *Zamindari* Abolition Bill before the Constitution – wanted a very safe delivery of baby. So he had his own proposition. There was this struggle and left the matter to them to decide in any way they like and nearly embodied what their decision was in Article 31. The Article 31 in my judgement is very ugly thing, something, which I do not like to look at.
>
> (BAWS, Vol. 15: 948)

This statement on the floor of the House depicts the unease with which Ambedkar had to make some compromises which had major implications for future generations. By becoming part of the Constitution-making process, he might have seen an opportunity to work not only for the welfare of the marginalised, including the Scheduled Castes, but also to serve the country as he acquired a central role in the Constitution-making process as the chairperson of the drafting committee. When one goes through the debates in the Constituent Assembly and Ambedkar's overall interventions, one realises that he not only got that opportunity but also deserved it, as reveals his acumen on diverse issues as an expert of the jurisprudence.

VIII Nationalism and nation-building

Ambedkar has been largely portrayed as if he had no commitment towards nation and lacked an inclination towards nationalism.[5] He could visualise the implications of the tendency of (caste and religious) communal nationalism reflected in the caste and religious differences and assertions have implications for nation-building. The feeling of nationalism that inspired common masses marked the whole movement against the British. However, during the first half of the twentieth century, this was disturbed by the developments of religion and caste identity-based interests arriving on the political scene. In this context, Ambedkar observed:

> A nation is not a country in the physical sense, whatever degree of geographical unity it may possess. A nation is not the people synthesised by a common culture derived from common language, common religion or common race. . . . Nationality is a subjective psychological feeling. It is feeling of corporate sentiment of oneness which makes those who are charged with it feel that they are kith and kin. . . . It is a feeling of 'consciousness of kind' 'which bind together those who are within the limits of kindred. It is longing (a strong feeling of wanting added) to belonging to one's own group. . . . This is the essence of what is called a nationality and national feeling.
>
> *(BAWS, Vol. 1: 143–144)*

Nation for Ambedkar is not something that already exists, but it is to be created with the efforts by those who want to make nation a reality. There may be different identities reflected through different communities, but nation does not mean suppressing those distinct and separate communities. Considering historical experience, he opined "neither race nor language or territory" makes a nation, but it is a spiritual reality that binds them. In this light, Ambedkar stated:

> Nationality is social feeling of a corporate sentiment of oneness. It is a feeling of consciousness of kind, like-mindedness, possessing things in common in life of communication, participation and of sharing with all those who constitute one nation. In this sense nation is a society where there is

an unlimited scope for 'social endosmosis', Nation is a democracy, a mode of associated living, of conjoined communicated experience.

(BAWS, Vol. 1: 57)

Thus, effective interface through communication, participation and sharing among those who constitute one nation is key to nationhood. Most of Ambedkar's writings and interactions reflect his major inclination to address the challenges of inequality and discrimination and his striving for economic and social equality. However, while the independence of the country was to become a reality, he did not hesitate to advise that it is not merely economic and social equality that stand as a force for a country aspiring to be independent. Ambedkar argued that fraternity is also a necessary condition for making political democracy function efficaciously and making a nation sturdy, lacking exclusivities of various kinds. Therefore, the absence of social and economic equality and a lack of fraternity are bound to emasculate not only the democracy that was being established but also the nation itself that was to be created after the British left.

Possibly, Ambedkar warned of the way the majority in India was handling the minorities' question in the context of nation and nationalism during his own time and even during the British rule. One may argue that the game of "divide and rule" was at work between the majority and the minority. Nevertheless, that explanation may not be sufficient, as there were several facts coming to the fore which needed attention. The following excerpt is testimony to this:

Unfortunately, for the minorities in India, Indian Nationalism has developed a new doctrine, which may be called the Divine Right of the Majority to rule the minorities to the wishes of majority. Any claim for the sharing of power by the minority is called communalism while the monopolising of the whole power by the majority is called Nationalism.

(BAWS, Vol. 1: 427)

IX Buddhism, religion, and politics

Religion was a sneaky proposition for Ambedkar. He vehemently opposed Hinduism and its precepts and declared that he would not like to die a Hindu, and during his last days he embraced Buddhism. The question then is whether he can be called a religious man. His expressions indicate that he had a much different notion of religion that was not *dhārma* of Hinduism, which was personal, but *dhamma* of Buddhism, which was social and propagated a society of equals.

Ambedkar was not anti-religion, as was Marx, but he was also not religious in the literal sense of the term. He used to observe the significance of religion in the lives of people and understood that humans needed some kind of conception of religion, and he identified four characteristics of religions:

1   The society must have sanction of law or the sanction of morality to hold it together; without either the society is sure to go to pieces.

2   Religion if it is to function must be in accord with reason, which is another name for science.
3   It is not enough for religion to consist of a moral code, but its moral code must recognise the fundamental tenets of liberty, equality, and fraternity.
4   Religion must not sanctify or ennoble poverty.

(Keer 1954: 421)

Ambedkar differentiated even between *dhārma* and *dhamma* by saying that the first is more personal and its purpose is to explain the origin of the world, whereas *dhamma* is social and its purpose is to reconstruct the society (BAWS, Vol. 11: 322). Usually, morality is considered an essential part of any religion, and probably every religion claims to be standing on morality, but Ambedkar countered those who argued that Hinduism was founded on the conception of morality and asserted the following:

> Hinduism is a religion, which is not founded on morality. Whatever morality Hinduism has it is not an integral part of it. It is not embedded in religion. It is a separate force, which is sustained by social necessities and not by injection of Hindu religion. The religion of Buddha has morality. It is embedded in religion. Buddhist religion is nothing but morality. It is true that in Buddhism there is no God. In place of God, there is morality. What God is to other religions morality is to Buddhism.
>
> *(BAWS, Vol. 17 [II]: 98)*

If we looked at Ambedkar's conception of the relationship between religion and politics, there are two perspectives which emerge: 1) if religion brings morality in politics, then it is desirable, and 2) if religion is perceived as a division in terms of majority and minority, high and low, then such a religion is not only undesirable but should also be discarded, as the purpose of religion is to bind the society. He could very well anticipate the role of religion in politics and more so when Hinduism claimed to be the religion of the majority.

Ambedkar considered Hinduism not a religion but a political ideology. Finding the chronology of religion in India, he argued that there have been three major transformations of religions, namely, *Vedic* religion, *Brāhminism*, and Hinduism, and that it was during the *Brāhminic* period that Buddhism was born.[6] Instead of calling Hinduism a religion, he categorised it as a political ideology and argued:

> Hinduism is a political ideology of the same character as the Fascist or Nazi ideology and is thoroughly anti-democratic. If, Hinduism is let loose, which is what Hindu majority means, it will prove a menace to the growth of others who are outside Hinduism and are opposed to Hinduism. This is not the point of view of Muslims alone. It is also the point of view of the Depressed Classes and also of non-*Brāhmins*.[7]

He could visualise that Hinduism could have a major influence on the Indian masses and its protagonists could well become powers to reckon within the democratic system due to its majoritarian tilt and warned against it in the following terms:

> If Hindu *Raj* does become a fact, it will, no doubt, be the greatest calamity for this country. No matter what the Hindus say, Hinduism is a menace to liberty, equality and fraternity. On that account, it is incompatible with democracy. Hindu *Raj* must be prevented at any cost.
>
> *(BAWS, Vol. 8: 358)*

Ambedkar's visionary ideas reflect how he could visualise the unfolding of history in post-independent India. His apprehensions about the Hindu *raj* probably are becoming true, as the majority rule is giving way to rightist tilts in the contemporary polity.

X Conclusion

It is in this context that the reading of Ambedkar becomes significant. However, one needs to understand how thinkers like Ambedkar or Gandhi become part of appropriation and campaign by the right, and the answer lies in the selective and subjective reading of their ideas and texts. The far right may appropriate Ambedkar's position on the idea of Pakistan and Muslims only in the particular context of partition, but if one looks at the larger framework within which Ambedkar was operating and arguing, then one cannot miss his concerns for the annihilation of caste and his critique of the Hindu social order, his fight for rights to minorities based on principles and not on methods, his strong inclination towards democracy with its transformative variant, and his non-compromising attitude towards the creation of nation and a feeling of nationalism complemented by the principles of equality and fraternity and not of hollow nationalism of hooligans attacking the dissenting voices. It is hoped that the discussion on Ambedkar in this chapter will keep inspiring the generations seeking transformation through peaceful and constitutional measures without compromising the basics of a revolt, that is, considerable social and economic transformation.

Notes

1 The substance and volume of the draft of the Hindu Code Bill is testimony to Ambedkar's concern for women, namely, the way he described their existing status and did not shy away even to bring instances of women's better status espoused in different and rare Hindu scriptures, comparing it with those which popularly denied equality to women. Secondly, for labourer, Ambedkar fought for equal wages and the betterment of women labourer as a member in the Bombay Legislative Council and as a member of the viceroy's executive council.
2 This phenomenon can be observed even today if one looks at the number of persons engaged in scavenging, of which the majority are untouchables and *Brāhmins* are non-existent or a miniscule minority.

3 Gandhi responded to the text during his lifetime and triggered the debate. Kanshi Ram, the founder of the Bahujan Samaj Party, read the text many times and produced a most formidable alternative to the politics of his times. Recently, Arundhati Roy, a celebrated contemporary writer, tried to contemporise and contextualise the debate further.
4 Hindu women protested the introduction of the Hindu Code Bill at the India Gate, claiming that Dr Ambedkar was interfering in the personal affairs of Hinduism and that they did not want any rights through the Bill.
5 Not only in popular image but even in literature Ambedkar's contribution and perspectives are absent, as could be observed by a comprehensive writing called "Worshiping False Gods" by Arun Shourie, which detailed Ambedkar's interactions with the British as if no other Hindu leaders had such an interaction with them.
6 For details see BAWS Vol. 17 (III): 406.
7 This is quoted by Y. D. Sontakke in *Thoughts of Babasaheb Ambedkar*, Samyak Prakashan, New Delhi (Source material on Ambedkar and his movement).

References

Babasaheb Dr. Ambedkar Writings and Speeches [BAWS] (2014). Vol. 1–17. Reprint by Dr. Ambedkar Foundation. New Delhi: Ministry of Social Justice and Empowerment, Government of India.
Gandhi, Rajmohan (2015). Response to Arundhati Roy. *Economic and Political Weekly*, Vol. L, No. 30, pp. 83–85.
Keer, Dhananjay (1954). *Dr. Ambedkar: Life and Mission*. Bombay: Popular Prakashan.
Lal, Deepak (1988). *Hindu Equilibrium: Cultural Stability and Economic Stagnation*, Vol. I. Oxford: Clarendon.
Rege, Sharmila (2013). *B.R. Ambedkar's Writings on Brahmanical Patriarchy: Against the Madness of Manu*. New Delhi: Navayana.
Roy, Arundhati (2014). *The Doctor and the Saint*. New Delhi: Navayana.
Sontakke, Y. D. (2004). *Thoughts of Babasaheb Ambedkar*. New Delhi: Samyak Prakashan.

9
JAGJIVAN RAM

Meena Charanda

You can chain me, you can torture me, you can even destroy this body, but you will never imprison my mind.[1]

– Jagjivan Ram

I Introduction

Jagjivan Ram, who is famous as *Babuji* in Indian history, was a man of great charisma and capacity. He was a messiah of social justice and social equality. His meteoric rise in the public sphere saw him emerge as a great and popular political leader, a leader who devoted his life to the development and welfare of the nation and its people. A champion of the depressed and underprivileged classes, Ram had a long career in Indian politics as an outstanding leader. His enduring and quintessentially twentieth-century political legacy reminds us of the courageous, idealistic spirit of India's political leadership which not only fought the freedom struggle movement during that time but also planned the foundation of this great and modern democratic republic. Ram played a major role in scripting the political, constitutional, and social development of India. A man of great deed and stature, he enjoyed respect from all sections of society. The leaders of opposition also praised him. Even today, he remains an outstanding figure in the map of Indian politics, his values and principles guide us as a light in the darkness of political social and public life (Sharma 1974: 21–31).

Ram was an activist who fought against the social discrimination that prevailed during that era. He was instrumental in forming many institutions for the depressed classes. His activity in the social and political spheres was rewarded after India gained independence, when he became the fourth Deputy Prime Minister. Ram was endowed with a sensitive soul; he was filled with anguish when he witnessed discrimination in his society. This anguish found practical expression in his works. The evolution of the social reformer into a nationalist politician was the outcome of mature reflection. He had a vision, a vision of a casteless and democratic Hindu society. He always tried to establish democratic policies which would be beneficial for all. As a member of the Constituent Assembly of India, Ram ensured that social justice would be enshrined in the Constitution (Chanchreek 1978: 105).

Ram served his country for more than 40 years as a proud member of the Indian National Congress. He set a benchmark in every ministry in which he worked. As defence minister, he was instrumental in the creation of Bangladesh. As union agriculture minister, his contribution to the green revolution is still remarkable. He worked continuously for equality in the society, although he witnessed the atrocities towards *Dalits*; still, he followed the path of peace and harmony for their empowerment. This is why the anniversary of his birth is celebrated as *Samta Diwas* because he believed in equality, human dignity, and individual freedom.

II Life sketch

Jagjivan Ram was born on 5 April 1908 in Chandwa, a small village situated in Shahabad district, which is now known as Bhojpur in Bihar State. His father, Shobhi Ram, was in the British Army. Due to family tradition, Shobhi Ram learned English and became proficient in it. He was posted in Peshawar, but due to differences with his seniors, he resigned. After that, Shobhi Ram returned to Bihar, bought land in Chandwa, and settled there with his family. At the age of six, Jagjivan Ram was sent to the village *pathshala* to start his elementary education in Barely. Soon after he started schooling, his father passed away, leaving the young Jagjivan in the care of his mother, Vasanti Devi, who despite the social and economic problems, insisted Jagjivan continue his education.

Babu Jagjivan Ram was an exceptional and marvellous student. The deep and abiding thoughts and impressions of his late father and the religious atmosphere at home, as well as his love and affection for his mother and the village schoolmaster, Pandit Kapil Muni Tiwari, were instrumental in shaping and nurturing Ram's character as a youth. He worked day and night to learn English until he mastered the language. He was advised by many friends and fellows to avail the scholarship offered to *Harijan* students, but Ram was confident in his ability to compete with the students in the general category, so he refused the scholarship. He competed with the other students on equal standing and earned the scholarship based on his meritorious academic performance.

Ram was admitted in Arrah Town School in 1922. It was here for the first time that Ram came face to face with the oppressive caste discrimination and bigotry of the upper castes that had suppressed his community for centuries and placed abhorrent limits on him as a person and his community as a whole. The school had separate water pitchers for Hindu and Muslim students. Some upper-caste boys refused to drink water out of a pitcher which Ram had touched. A separate pitcher was installed for the Schedule Caste students. Ram refused to tolerate this insult and broke the pitcher; when it was replaced, he destroyed it again. Taking note of his protest, the headmaster ordered that a common pitcher be installed for all students. Although Ram got the victory in that instance, the discriminatory treatment he felt at school filled his heart with both grief and anger. Despite these incidents and the discriminatory treatment, he passed his matriculation in first division. By the time he passed out of secondary school, he had earned the reputation of being a strong, principled human who could not tolerate injustice in any form.

In 1925, when Pandit Madan Mohan Malaviya came to Arrah, Ram, because he was the best student in the school, was asked to read the welcome address. Deeply impressed by the erudition and panache of the young Ram, Pandit Madan Mohan Malaviya invited him to study at Banaras Hindu University. However, the Christian Mission of Chandwa also offered to bear the expense of Ram's education and urged his mother to send Ram to Lucknow and then to America for higher studies. But Vasanti Devi turned down this proposal. She felt that changing religion was not an answer to the arrogant caste system, and she advised Ram to join Banaras Hindu University. Ram also faced caste-based prejudices and hostility at Banaras Hindu University. The servants in the hostel would not serve him or place his order, and they also refused to wash his plates in the student mess, a place which was common to all. But even as a new student, he had earned respect and loyalty from the entire students' Union Council, who stood up in his defence and resolved the situation, dictating that every student will wash his own plate. Ram did not want to inconvenience the entire hostel, so he decided to transfer out of it.

When Ram was a child, he dreamed of being a scientist. But as he grew up, he was unable to ignore the socio-political situation developing in the country, so he scarified his personal objectives and goals to address the problems of his motherland. Ram's student years strengthened him to fight on two fronts, first for the freedom of the country and second for social reforms and social equality. In 1934, Ram established the *Akhil Bhartiya Ravidas Mahasabha* in Calcutta. The other organisations he established for social reforms were *Khetihar Mazdoor Sabha* for agricultural labour and the 'All-India Depressed Classes League'. Through these organisations, Ram convoluted the depressed classes in the freedom struggle movements and also appealed that all *Dalit* leaders should unite not only for social reform but also to demand political representation on an equal basis (Chanchreek 2013: 51–55).

The date of 19 October 1935 will remain an historical day in the history of modern India. On this day, Ram appeared before the Hammond Committee at Ranchi and demanded voting rights for *Dalits*. In 1936, when he was just 28 years old, Ram started his parliamentary career as a nominated member of the Bihar Legislative Council. In 1937, he contested as a candidate of the Depressed Classes League and was elected unopposed to the Bihar Legislative Assembly from the East Central Shahabad (Rural), and he also ensured the unopposed victory of his Depressed Classes League candidates in all 14 reserved constituencies. With this form of unopposed and critical victory, Ram emerged as the kingmaker for all. Afterward, the Congress invited him to join the party. The British were keen to set up a puppet government in Bihar, and for their policy of divide and rule, they needed Ram's support. They offered a large sum of money and a ministerial berth as well as other political benefits to buy his support, but he did not even consider it. All national leaders and the entire nation praised his act of patriotism and integrity. Gandhiji said that Jagjivan Ram had a pure heart and that he emerged as a pure form of gold in this test when the attempt to establish a puppet government failed. A Congress government was then formed. Ram was appointed the parliamentary secretary in the Ministry of Agriculture, Co-operative Industry and Village Development. In 1938, he resigned along with the whole Cabinet on the issue of the Andaman prisoners and the British policy of involving India in the Second World War without the consent of all leaders, who were active in the national freedom struggle movement during that time.

Ram's participation in the freedom struggle and his activities as a Congress leader are inseparable; they cannot be divided. As a leader of the party, Ram strengthened the national cause by his strong organisational work and his policies. In 1942, the Congress party launched the Quit India Movement under the leadership of Mahatma Gandhi. On that occasion, Ram joined the Congress leadership in Bombay. The All-India Congress Committee (AICC) passed the historic 'Quit India Resolution'. When this resolution was passed, many top Congress leaders were arrested, and it was left to Ram to make the Quit India movement a historic success. He came back to Bihar to organise a mass movement against the British rule. Due to his revolutionary and multidimensional activities and the impact he had on the masses for supporting the Quit India movement, Ram was arrested from his home in Patna. When he was released, he organised many meetings and rallies and criticised the British rule for their suppression of the Indian freedom movement by violent means. He won unopposed in the 1946 central elections from the constituency of East Central Shahabad (Rural). In the same year, he was a representative of the depressed classes before the Cabinet Mission in Shimla. There he strongly defended the cause of the depressed classes and the unity of the nation. He rejected the designs of the British and other factious forces to further divide the country.

III Independence and after

After India became independent, Ram's contribution for nation-building left a mark. As one of the founding fathers of the Constitution and as an important leader of the Constituent Assembly, he ensured the importance of social justice as one of the ideals enshrined in the Constitution. When he was appointed labour minister, he introduced time-tested policies and laws for labourers' welfare on a great scale. He was instrumental in enacting some of the most important legislation for labourers. As the defence minister, he changed the political map of the world and made history by liberating Bangladesh and forcing the Pakistani Army to surrender unconditionally, without any major losses. This war was unlike any other. Ram kept his promise that the war would not be fought on a single inch of Indian territory. When Ram took charge as the minister of agriculture and irrigation, he organised the public distribution system in such a way that food was available to the masses at a reasonable price. As a minister, he had great ability to look after the affairs under his sphere of influence and had his priorities well defined to take on such challenges. In all the ministries and departments at the centre where Ram held the charge, he left his mark as a leader of the masses. He utilised his political power as an opportunity to transform people's lives and promote their welfare (Kalhan 1980: 130–135).

In a turn of events, Emergency was declared on 26 June 1975. The fundamental rights as enshrined in the Constitution were suspended. Prime Minister Indira Gandhi recommended the dissolution of the Lok Sabha to hold fresh general elections. The impact of the Emergency was felt on a broad level, and everyone was affected. Ram subsequently resigned from the Cabinet and formed his own party, the Congress for Democracy (CFD). He fought the election and emerged victorious once again to Lok Sabha in the general elections from the Sasaram constituency in Bihar. After that, he joined the Janata Government and became defence minister. He merged his party with the Janata Party and became the deputy Prime Minister of the country. He continued to handle the charge of defence minister until 28 July 1979. There were many internal conflicts in the Janata Party, which resulted in the party losing its majority in Parliament, and the government, led by Shri Morarji Desai, collapsed in 1979. Chaudhary Charan Singh was given opportunity to prove his majority in the House, but he failed. After the fall of his government, many members of Lok Sabha rallied around Ram and asked him to claim the post of Prime Minister. The President, however, dissolved the Lok Sabha on 22 August 1979 and ordered fresh elections. In the year of 1980, the people of Sasaram re-elected Ram to the Lok Sabha and for the first time he was a member of the opposition. When the Janata Government failed, Ram launched his own party, the Congress (Jagjivan), and in the general election of December 1984, he once again returned victorious to the Lok Sabha. His long tenure as a Member of Parliament is a vibrant example of his dedicated life in political as well as social life. From his first term as a Member of Parliament to his last term until his death, Ram represented the same constituency. His uninterrupted legislative career, spanning more than half a century, is a record in itself. Leaving behind the message of equality, for which he fought his entire life, he breathed his last breath on 6 July 1986.

Ram believed education was one of the greatest and most effective means for the downtrodden sections to stand up for their own rights. He believed that if all classes had equal access to education, their natural abilities would flourish. He supported reservation for the Scheduled Castes and Tribes in educational institutions because, according to him, it was the one way in which they could escape the burden placed upon them by their economic backwardness. Since they did not have proper financial resources, they were unable to access education; if they could not access education, they could not get jobs, so the vicious circle would continue. From his own personal experience as well as from his observations over the years of incidents within and outside the country, Ram realised education is a powerful tool for empowerment and is a source of sure and steady socio-economic advancement. The disadvantaged sections ought to develop a spirit of self-reliance and self-respect through their hard work, which would, according to Ram, avert the syndrome of dependency (Ram 1977: 155–158).

IV Social justice and uplifting of the downtrodden

Ram showed complete solidarity with the depressed classes beginning early in his life. He firmly believed there was an urgent need to improve the situations of the oppressed and downtrodden sections of society. The most remarkable fact of Ram's political life is that he is appreciated nationwide as one of India's tallest leaders. He was committed to dealing with the wound of casteism, which had deep roots in Indian society from ancient ages. Many people were denied equal opportunities in political and economic spheres due to casteism. This concept was inconsistent with a modern democratic society and was against basic human dignity. Ram experienced firsthand the dark side of untouchability, and he believed it was the basic reason for the marginalisation of the *Dalits* and was a barrier in the full development of individual calibre. Deeply hurt by the existing situation in the country at that time, particularly the practice of caste-based discrimination, Ram dedicated his leadership prowess and all effort to uplift the depressed and marginalised classes (Singh 1977). Promoting people's welfare in general and the uplifting of the oppressed in particular, became Ram's life goal, about which he was very passionate.

During his early years, Ram witnessed the sufferings of the depressed classes under the feudal caste system. However, he did not surrender to the unjust order of the society; rather, he made it his mission to solve the social problems in every possible way. His negative experiences toughened his resolve to fight for justice, and he made it his life-long goal to strive for eliminating the social sickness that crippled and was halting the development of a vast section of the Indian population. For his support and persistent struggle for the cause of the downtrodden, Ram has been rightly called the messiah of the *Dalits*. He always suggested that for Hindu *dhārma* it is an urgent need to respect and give a right place to the *Dalits*.

Ram realised that conversion to another religion was not the answer, nor was it a solution for casteism. According to him, casteism was a molder which had affected all religions and the only way to get away from it was to reform the Hindu religion and change the social attitudes prevailing in the society. The temple entry movement gained momentum largely due to his efforts, and today the doors of Jagannath temple at Puri, Vishwanath temple in Kashi, and Meenakshi temple in Madurai, are opened for upper and lower castes alike. He was a symbol of hope and aspiration of the backward and depressed classes. He never criticised the Hindu religion and boldly advocated the path of self-reliance for *Dalits*. He advised them to carry on a stern struggle against social prejudices and the unequal treatment meted out to them by society. He made clear the fact that it was necessary to end the social orthodoxy.

Ram symbolised the morning of a new era of averment, equality, and empowerment for the depressed classes. His life was a positive statement for the depressed classes, who were clearly inspired by Ram's continuing presence in the national political scene. His earnestness, dedication, and political punch instilled confidence and courage among them. His achievements were considered part of a noteworthy procession for his community (Sinha 1973). As a member of the Constituent Assembly, Ram played an active role in creating provisions for the safeguarding of the depressed classes in the Constitution. He also ensured that the Constitution had strong provisions to prohibit any practice of untouchability and discrimination of persons on the grounds of caste. The provision for State intervention for the advancement of socially backward classes by way of reservation in public employment and reservation of seats in legislatures for the Scheduled Castes and Tribes also owes its success to leaders like Ram. He was instrumental in drafting the Protection of Civil Rights Act of 1955. These provisions were of great meaning, and they resulted in instruments of socio-political empowerment and economic progress. All these provisions have resulted in offering a better deal to the depressed classes and bringing social changes in India with a new approach and social outlook. Ram did not nurture any utopian hopes that the caste system would be eliminated at once. His strategy and approach to the curse of casteism was based on his enduring faith in the values of our great democratic society and the process of transformation through that system, which is established by the Constitution. He tried to debate the issue of the depressed classes' welfare with a broad mindset. In breaking the barriers of the caste system and transforming society, he believed that with the use of education, people would come to know their rights, which would promote their welfare. Throughout his life, Ram believed in human dignity and individual freedom of choice.

V Political and economic vision

Throughout his life, Ram stood firm for democratic values and believed in his principles, never compromising his values even in disruptive political situations. Despite being a senior Congress member and a close confidante of Smt. Indira Gandhi, he never hesitated to differ from her views. Ram tried to sway Smt. Gandhi to overturn the Emergency and restore a normal atmosphere in the country. When he failed in this effort, he resigned from the Cabinet.

Ram believed in a planned economy. He believed it was the only way in which not just the narrow interests of one section of society, who held all power in their hands, but the interests of all sections of society could be served on a broader and larger scale. He said it was the only tool through which destruction of scarce resources could be prevented. It is of great importance to hear the lengthy reply which he gave to a question on whether the adoption of democratic socialism in India had been correct. He always supported the process for equity and egalitarianism in the economy and society for the poor, depressed, and marginalised classes.

VI Conclusion

Ram believed in non-violence and *satyāgraha* (holding firmly to truth) for his whole life. It is a misconception that he was only a leader of *Dalits*. His appeal had nationwide effect. He urged the uplifting of *Harijans* and all backward classes. He worked towards the restoration of a rightful place for all of them in society. It was an elephantine task, but Ram's determination was strong. He did not believe in any magic wand for the betterment of lower castes; he was confident it would happen by making them realise their full rights, first by infusing confidence in them and second by removing the shackles that throttled or trammelled their mental horizons. This clearly showed his pre-vision farsightedness as a great leader and also his capacity to sense the general attitude of the suppressed masses that he was spearheading for social equality and a rightful place in all aspects of human rights.

Ram passed away from illness on 6 July 1986 in Delhi at the age of 78. As an outstanding and remarkable leader who shared his political career with many generations, Ram has left a remarkable impression on the polity of India. He was a stout leader of his time and a bright star of Indian Parliament. When he died, leaders, media, and the whole nation expressed their grief. He was treated with national honour. All the respective members of the Cabinet, including the President and Prime Minister, attended his funeral. With Ram's passing, came the end of an era which represented perhaps the most important phase of India's transition from pre-independence to independence. He has left the legacy of a sincere and dedicated political leader, a committed public servant, freedom fighter, social reformer, revolutionary, and a true humanist.

He will be remembered in Indian history for a long time to come for his wide contributions towards socio-economic development. He was a democrat from the core and scrupulous to Indian politics with his mature ideas and philosophy. He was a pillar of strength for the Indian polity during a period of great challenges and transition. He played a substantial role in the uplifting of the backward and depressed classes and ensured justice for them, enhancing the country's infrastructure of development and accelerating its march to emerge as a strong power in the world. When he passed away, the country lost a unique leader, a nationalist, and a great visionary.

His legacy will live on forever and continue to inspire the coming generations for his social and political activities. In every role, Babu Jagjivan Ram carved out a special milestone for himself in India's modern political history. During his long and remarkable political career, he had become a legend. He earned respect and admiration from all sections of society, including from the opposition. His contribution to our nation-building is invaluable in the political, economic, and social sectors. His life and work will undoubtedly continue to inspire future generations.

Note

1 The quote originally belongs to M. K. Gandhi but frequently used by Jagjivan Ram.

References

Chanchreek, K. L. (1978). *Jagjivan Ram Crusade for Democracy*. New Delhi: Sultan Chand Publication.

Chanchreek, K. L. (2013). *Jagjivan Ram Selected Bibliography. 1903–1975*, New Delhi: Sultan Chand.

Kalhan, Promila (1980). *Jagjivan Ram and Power Politics*. New Delhi: Allora Publication.

Ram, Jagjivan (1977). *Vital Role in Restoring Democracy*. Patna: Celebration Committee.

Sharma, Devendra Prasad (1974). *Jagjivan Ram: The Man and the Times*. New Delhi: Indian Book Company.

Singh, Nau Nihal (1977). *Jagjivan Ram: Symbol of Social Change*. New Delhi: Sundeep Prakashan.

Sinha, A. C. (1973). *Struggles and Achievements; Babu Jagjivan Ram Commemoration Volume*. Kanpur: Alka Prakashan.

PART II
Moderate-Gandhian thought

10
DADABHAI NAOROJI

Radha Kumari

> Let us always remember that we are all children of our mother country. Indeed, I have never worked in any other spirit than that I am an Indian, and owe duty to my country and all my countrymen. Whether I am a Hindu, a Mohammedan, a Parsi, a Christian, or any other creed, I am above all an Indian. Our country is India; our nationality is Indian.
> – Dadabhai Naoroji (Presidential Address, INC Session, Lahore, 1893)

1 Introduction

Dadabhai Naoroji (1825–1917) was a pioneer of the Indian nationalist movement who is remembered for his economic analysis of the British rule in India which led to the formulation of his drain of wealth theory, which discusses the flow of wealth to Britain that was bleeding dry India and her self-sufficient small-scale industries. Although Naoroji was not the first to draw leaders' attention to the economic exploitation of India under colonial rule, as two centuries before him (in 1776) Adam Smith in *The Wealth of Nations* had called the British colonists "plunderers of India" (Smith 1776/2007: 582). Naoroji also cites many British intellectuals who had admitted the economic burden on India, calling it a drain (notable among them being Sir John Shore, James Mill, Montgomery Martin, Sir George Wingate, and Lord Roberts, to name only a few),[1] and then Karl Marx in *On Colonialism* (1857)[2] had described the situation in almost similar terms. Naoroji was the one who theorised the economic drain and presented it with facts and figures in his *Poverty and Un-British Rule in India* (1901).

This does not mean, however, that he wished for an immediate end to British rule in India as some of his contemporary radical nationalists, such as Bal Gangadhar Tilak, Bipin Chandra Pal, and Lala Lajpat Rai, did. He was a moderate and liberal politician who wished for better representation and more power for common Indians in public affairs within the British rule in India through petitioning the British authorities and cultivating a culture of dialogue and discussion, though it is also true that towards the end of his life he suspected the efficacy of moderate political thought and supported the radical thinkers' ideology of *swaraj* (self-rule) for India. It is worth noting here that Naoroji was one among only a few Indians who had been educated in English from a young age and who imbibed English culture to the full, appreciated the benefits of the British colonial rule in India, and fully realised the significance of colonial modernity for the Indian masses. He lauded the colonial masters for their active contribution towards the eradication of social evils from India, such as the *Sati* tradition, child marriage, infanticide, armed banditry (the ill famous *pindaris*), and thugs; for allowing the remarriage of widows (especially Hindu widows); for introducing a modern education system, peace and order, freedom of speech, freedom of the press, and modern social and political institutions; for reassuring security of life and property; for bringing Western enlightenment to Indian soil with a scientific outlook; for rediscovering the great ancient Indian literature and philosophy; for developing railways, posts, and the telegraph; and for industrially developing some valuable Indian products, such as coffee, tea, indigo, cotton, and silk. Naoroji also admired the British for their good intentions in India, hoping for equal treatment of the native Indians, and he was sure that it was only in British hands that the glory of India could be achieved (Naoroji 1887: 131).

Yet Naoroji criticised the British rulers for their apathy towards the poor, suffering Indian masses who toiled day and night but still found it difficult to keep their body and soul together since the largest share of their earnings was being siphoned off to England. Naoroji made all attempts to bring it to the notice of the British rulers of India as well as to the notice of the common and influential people in England that, as regarded the cause of humanity, the English rule in India had contributed nothing; their contribution to India's civilisation was negligible. They repeatedly broke their pledges to give Indians a fair share in the administration of their own country and thus displayed utter disregard for the feelings and opinions of the Indian natives; that they were more interested in collecting taxes from people than in developing the infrastructure and creating the means to pay those taxes was apparent. Naoroji vehemently criticised the British government in India for establishing an inequitable financial relationship between England and India which was solely responsible for India's poverty (ibid.).

It is in this backdrop that we need to study Naoroji's ideas on the economic and political atmosphere in the country at that time, especially his moderate and liberal political views and his means of achieving social justice for his countrymen. Thus, in the following sections we shall briefly chart out Naoroji's political and economic ideas based on his books, papers, and speeches given on various occasions.

II Life sketch

Dadabhai Naoroji was born in Mumbai on 4 September 1825 into a poor Parsi family who spoke Gujrati at home. His father, Naoroji Palanji Dordi, died when

Naoroji was only four years old. The family fell upon difficult times, but his mother, Maneckbai, was a determined lady and despite herself being illiterate, she wished to provide her son the best quality education. The Native Education Society School became his primary education provider, and then he received further education from Elphinstone Institute. Naoroji was a brilliant pupil from early childhood, and at the age of 15, he was selected for the Clare's Scholarship. At the age of 25, he was appointed assistant professor of mathematics and philosophy at Elphinstone Institute and became a professor at the age of 30. At the same institute, he also served as treasurer of the Students' Literary and Scientific Society. The society was founded in 1848, primarily for the education of girls (*The Hindu* [Madras], March 13, 1886). The Bombay Association was founded in 1852, to meet the political needs of the people (*Report of the Indian National Congress*, Second Edition, 1886: 56). Naoroji hailed from a Zoroastrian community, and to clarify the principles of the religion to common people, he founded a fortnightly publication, *Rast Goftar* (the truth teller). In addition, to re-establish the past grandeur of his religion, he actively took part, along with J. B. Wacha, S. S. Bangali, and Naoroji Furdonji, in founding the *Rahnumae Mazdayasnan Sabha* (Religious Reform Association) at Mumbai in 1851, a society that is still in operation. The *Sabha* did not confine itself to mere religious reforms but worked for social reforms too, and with the unanimous support of the Parsi community in the region, advocated for uniform education, specifically Western education, for priests and the Parsi youth. Girls were also encouraged to pursue education. "Marriageable age for girls and boys was increased which led to their early emancipation. Interestingly, Dadabhai Naoroji was married at the age of 11, while his wife Gulbaai was just 7 years old at that time" (Encyclopaedia of World Biography, Encyclopedia.com, September 8, 2017).

The Parsi community had been primarily a mercantile community, and Naoroji's family was no exception. He worked as a partner in Cama & Co. (London) for a while but didn't like their unethical practices and resigned. In 1859, he founded his own cotton-trading firm, Naoroji & Co. He also had a partnership in a textile mill. Maharaja Sayajirao Gaekwad III of Baroda was his patron, and his public life began with his appointment as the *dewan* (minister) of the Maharaja in 1874. Moreover, he served as a member of the Legislative Council of Bombay from 1885 to 1888. In 1867, he helped to establish the East India Association, which later took the shape of Indian National Congress (I.N.C.). He also served as the president of the I.N.C. in 1886, 1893, and again in 1906. It was in the Calcutta session of the I.N.C. in 1906 that four resolutions – on self-government, the boycott movement, *swadeshi*, and national education – were passed. Naoroji was a British citizen, and in the 1892 general elections in England he won a seat in the Parliament from Finsbury Central for the Liberal Party, becoming the first British Indian MP (Member of Parliament). His interest in the lives of the poor people of India inspired him to formulate his drain of wealth theory, and gradually he developed an interest in politics (Masani 1939: 413–414). Though Naoroji gave full credit to his mother for the success he achieved in his life, it may be safely concluded that the genesis of his personality lies in his family background, in the education he received, his upbringing, the spiritual atmosphere at home, his involvement in various organisations and movements, the prevalent economic situation in India, and the influence of great people and personalities on his thoughts. Educated in English, Naoroji was acquainted with the Western progressive ideas of liberty, nationalism, democracy, equality, fraternity, and justice, which led him to desire the same socio-political conditions for India. But his loyalty to the British crown did not allow him to be a vociferous and vehement or radical critic of the British rule in India, and therefore, at times, we notice contradictions in his views regarding colonialism and freedom.

III Socio-economic and political views

As mentioned, Naoroji is primarily known for his economic nationalism illustrated in *Poverty and Un-British Rule in India*, published in 1901. But he was a prolific writer and a distinguished speaker. His essays and speeches are collected in book form. His notable political works are *The European and Asiatic Races: Observations on the Paper Read by John Crawfurd* (1866),[3] *Admission of Educated Natives into the Indian Civil Service* (1868), *The Wants and Means of India* (1870), and *Poverty of India* (1878). In addition to politics, Naoroji also wrote extensively on the Parsee religion in *The Parsee Religion* (1861b) and *The Manners and Customs of the Parsees: A Paper Read before the Liverpool Philomathic Society* 1861a.

In his early career as a parliamentarian and as a political activist, Naoroji was wholly influenced by the British character and system of governance, and therefore, what he wanted in India was an Indianisation of the British administration, that is, more representation of the Indian educated class in the British administrative machinery in India.[4] With this moderate objective in mind, Naoroji did take part in the activities of the I.N.C., which was founded in 1885 by Allan Octavian Hume, along with William Wedderburn, Pheroze Shah Mehta, and Dinshaw Wacha. The objective of the I.N.C. was to create a way for educated Indians to have a greater say in the British administration by creating a forum from where there would be a continuous dialogue between the British high officials and the English-educated Indians concerning civic and political matters in the daily lives of Indian people. The prominent English-educated Indians who joined the I.N.C. and had faith in the British system to grant their demands were Gopal Krishna Gokhale, Motilal Nehru, Madan Mohan Malaviya, and Badruddin Tyabji. Their feelings are aptly summarised by Ashu Pasricha (2008: 72), who writes that these moderate Congressmen believed the British nation was essentially just and good and that if it could be acquainted with the true state of Indian affairs, all their grievances would be redressed. Their way of achieving this was sending petitions, having discussions, attending conferences, and pledging solidarity and loyalty to the government. The Bombay Legislative Council, founded in 1961 as the Legislature of the Bombay Province in British India, had the provision of nominating four (which was later increased to five) non-English

Indian natives as non-official members into it. These members were allowed to move their own bills and vote on the bills introduced in the Council, but they were not allowed:

1   To question the executive,
2   To move resolutions,
3   To examine the budget, or
4   To interfere with the laws passed by the Central Legislature.

Although in 1892, under the Indian Councils Act, the role of the Council was boosted and the number of non-English members was increased from 5 to 20, the Council, and especially the Indian non-official members in it, lacked teeth. Owing to their limited powers of participation in the administration, the Indian members resorted to what is now termed "politics of moderation". They were totally dissatisfied with their role in the Council and petitioned the governor, who acted as the president of the Council, as well as the official members (all Englishmen) from time to time for reforms in the Council to allow better representation of Indians. What these moderate thinkers wanted from the British administration can be summarised as follows:

1   **Constitutional reforms:** Allow more participation of Indians through expansion of the Council; the Council should allow Indians more control over finances.
2   **Administrative reforms:** The executive and judiciary must be separated; Indian civil services must be Indianised; the Arms Act was to be protested; public welfare schemes should be undertaken; better primary, technical, and higher education for the masses should be implemented; Indian labourers should be protected against exploitation; the passing of the Calcutta Corporation Act should be opposed.
3   **Economic reforms:** As Naoroji had shown in his analysis, the members alleged that the ever-increasing poverty in India was directly linked to exploitation of Indian economy by the British and that while a major portion of India's wealth was being transferred to Britain, there were no equivalent returns in terms of social and industrial development work in India.

The imperial government in India displayed a liberal face in its initial days, taking up numerous civilising missions based on universal racial characteristics to be carried out through Western cultural education, but late in the nineteenth century, the discourse of racial similarities changed into that of racial differences and cultural inferiority, as argued by Catherine Hall (2002) and Jennifer Pitts (2005). Naoroji adhered to his argument on the liberal civilising mission of the British Empire to demand self-governance for Indians and thus laying bare the partisan politics of England. He made it clear that he stayed in England solely to carry out his political aspirations. Once he was interviewed by a press correspondent from the *Daily Graphic* on this issue (He was a Liberal Party MP in the UK House of Commons in the British Parliament between 1892 and 1895), and he said:

> What I should most like to see would be the direct representation of the Indian people at Westminster. But as that privilege has not yet been offered to us, the next best thing we can do is to invite English constituencies to send natives of India to Parliament, when they are otherwise qualified for the trust.
>
> *(Daily Graphic, August 9, 1892)*

The interview was reproduced in India. In his Introduction to *Poverty and Un-British Rule in India*, he remarks that "The present system of government is destructive and despotic to the Indians and un-British and suicidal to Britain. On the other hand, a truly British course can and will certainly be vastly beneficent to both Britain and India" (Naoroji 1901: v).

Moderates, such as Dadabhai Naoroji, Gopal Krishna Gokhale, Surendranath Banerjee, Pherozeshah Mehta, Madan Mohan Malaviya, Badruddin Tyabji, and Justice Ranade had put in decades of struggle to obtain greater political representation and power in public matters for the common Indian people. Actually, these people were not full-time politicians nor was the I.N.C. a full-fledged political party; therefore, the British government never took them seriously. They would hold an annual meeting for three days at a prominent city in India, such as Bombay, Calcutta, Madras, or Lahore, deliberate upon and adopt a few ineffectual resolutions, and disperse to meet again the next year! Of course, they did cultivate a process of dialogue and discussion with the hope of yielding greater British respect for the rights of Indians in their own land. Naoroji being one of them did succeed in kindling the flame of economic and political nationalism among the future Congress leaders despite their moderate and extremist differences of opinion. An interesting fact about Naoroji which indicates a change in his political views is that he became Indian representative in the Socialist Second International at their 1905 Congress in Amsterdam. Two years later, his assistant, Mrs Bhikaiji Rustom Cama attended the 1907 International Socialist Conference in Stuttgart (Germany) where she hoisted the "flag of Indian independence" and presented a vivid picture of famine in India (the reason for which was British exploitation of the country) with the sole intention that her appeal would lead to human rights intervention and autonomy for India from Great Britain (Gupta 2003).

Naoroji personally believed in constitutional agitation and campaigning for demands for India within the British parliamentary system. The major issues concerning the problems in India, according to him, were much needed reforms at various levels, such as in civil services and the councils. As he viewed, Anglo-Indian civil service officials work well, but even the best of administrators is not heard by a little parliamentary publicity, while such detailed questions were beyond the functions of the Parliament. They must be fought out in India itself, where we have our Legislative Councils and our own press. The cost of an

English civil servant working in India is very high, and moreover, the Englishmen never made India their home. The remedy therefore was to hold civil service examinations simultaneously in India and England so that natives of India may have a better chance of getting appointment.

Regarding the election system followed at the time, Naoroji was in favour of a popular election so that a few members of each Legislative Council should be elected by the same electorate which now choose Municipal Councils. But Naoroji didn't want the elected members to outvote the government, nor did he visualise the Indian legislature to be exactly like the British Parliament. What he wanted was power for the members to advise the government (*Daily Graphic*, August 9, 1892/India, August 26, 1982: 214–215).

IV Theory of moral and material drain

Naoroji's work focused on the drain of wealth from India into England through colonial rule. He put in perspective what was happening to the financial resources and revenues collected in India under British rule over time, especially during the nineteenth century. Through a thorough calculation of the total production of India and the total food production in different provinces of British India (the Central Provinces, Punjab, North-West Provinces, Bengal, Madras, Bombay, and Oudh), and taking into consideration other items of India's wealth, its necessary consumption, its production compared with cost of living, and its imports and exports, Naoroji calculated the exact drain to England. In his words:

> These evils have ever since gone on increasing, and more and more counterbalancing the increased produce of the country, making now the evil of the 'bleeding' and impoverishing drain by the foreign dominion nearly or above £30,000,000 a year in a variety of subtle ways and shapes; while about the beginning of the last century the drain was declared to be £3,000,000 a year – and with private remittances was supposed to be nearly £5,000,000 – or one-sixth of what it is at present. If the profits of exports and freights and insurance, which are not accounted for in the official statistics, be considered, the present drain will be nearly forty than thirty millions; speaking roughly on the old basis of the value of gold at two shillings per rupee
>
> *(Naoroji 1901: viii).*

According to Naoroji, the large-scale poverty of the Indians and the recurring famines in the land were the direct results of the British exploitation of the Indian economy. He boldly associates India's economic problems to this exhaustive drain and even chides the Anglo-Indian community for their utter selfishness:

> The utter exhaustion and destruction from all these causes is terrific, and cannot but produce the present famines, plagues, etc. What would Britain's

condition be under a similar fate? Let her ask herself that question. The Anglo-Indians always shirk that question, never face it. Their selfishness makes them blind and deaf to it.

(Naoroji 1901: x)

Thus, it was Naoroji's skilful handling of statistics (one of the sub-headings in the book is *How Statistics Should be Compiled*) in arriving at the exact facts and figures (though some of the British officials disagreed with his figures and criticised his theory of exploitation) that opened people's eyes to the reasons behind the large-scale poverty in India and made him the most popular leader among the English-educated Indians. "The whole produce of India is from its land", said Naoroji. And then he calculated that the whole domestic product of India in 1870 was roughly £168,000,000, which with the aid of opium, salt, and forest revenues would be roughly £200,000,000, while the population of British India at the time was 150,000,000. The reason behind the poverty of Indians was "giving, therefore, less than Rs. 27 per head for the annual support of the whole people" (Naoroji 1901: 2). The six factors that contributed to the drain of wealth from India, in his opinion, were: 1) India was governed by a foreign government; 2) no immigrants came to India who would have brought the labour and capital required for economic growth; 3) British administrators in India and the occupational army were paid from the revenues collected from India; 4) the British Empire, in and outside of India, was being built using Indian money; 5) free trade policy was just an eyewash, it was meant to thrust in Indian foreign goods at high prices and offer high-paying jobs to foreign officials; and 6) the British officials did not make India their home, they would buy property in England and leave with money from India.

Mahatma Gandhi strongly believed in Naoroji's theory of the drain of wealth, and to counter this drain he launched his *swadeshi* movement. He urged Indian people to use only home-made goods and items so that Indian cottage industries, which were dying because of lack of support at home and industrialisation in England, could be revived and so the hungry and poor, but industrious, masses of India could earn enough for their livelihood in a respectable manner. Gandhi encouraged people to boycott not only foreign goods (e.g. clothes coming from Britain manufactured in Manchester and tools coming from Germany) but also to spin sufficient yarns at home and to wear only clothes made in India, however coarse they may be, called *khadi* clothes. The Congress Working Committee encourage people to spin, distributed free spinning wheels and provided free cotton for the first month.

Naoroji saw India in chains and the Indian masses as demoralised. They accepted British hegemony and superiority in all spheres of life. That's how it was possible for a small number of Europeans to rule a vast country like India. The exertion of British superiority led to a moral drain, that is, it was given out that the British officials working in India had a moral right to enjoy higher status and consequently higher pay. Thus, India had to pay approximately

Rs 200,000,000 annually to the Europeans in the Indian Civil Service, adding to the nation's poverty. Moreover, under the euphemism of free trade, English merchants opened the country to exploitation and open loot through unbalanced trade and unjustified currency exchange rates. The additional objective was to open up the country to create exorbitant and highly paid jobs for the European personnel sent to work in India. This income– a cost to British India (ultimately paid by the poor) – was a moral drain on Indian resources.

V From economic nationalism to political nationalism

The previous section discussed Naoroji's analysis of the disastrous economic condition of India under British rule that led to seven severe famines and scarcities in India between 1860 and 1880, taking not less than 10 million human lives. Naoroji openly blamed the unjust and ill-conceived land revenue policy and the greedy British system of governance in India for all these disasters, which, according to him, "did not care whether we live or die, but £30 million worth of produce must be annually carried away from this country with the regularity of seasons" (Naoroji 1917: 238–239). Naoroji opened the eyes of hundreds of future nationalist leaders who fought for India's freedom. His nationalist sentiments inspired his vehement criticism of the British system of (economic) governance in India: "You are bleeding the people", he said. He made it clear that British Empire building and the growing riches in England were solely founded on Indian blood:

> Hundreds of millions of India's wealth have been spent to form your British Empire. Not only that but you have taken away from India all these years millions of its wealth. The result is obvious. You have become one of the richest countries in the world. . . . And we have become the poorest country in the world.
>
> *(Naoroji 1917: 232)*

Naoroji strongly believed in the secular and democratic nature of the British political and social institutions created for public good, but he was aghast to realise that the same British ruling machinery worked differently in India, especially as the machinery was let loose to extract as much wealth as possible from India, giving in return only a paltry development, such as a network of railways, a postal service, and educational services, and that in Naoroji's eyes was the fundamental evil of the otherwise benevolent British rule in India. It seemed that Britain was forcibly extracting wealth as if she believed India had to pay the price for being ruled by her. The revenues raised by the rulers through taxes were not fully spent in India on developmental works as happens in democratic countries, as was the case in Britain. From the total revenues raised in India, according to Naoroji's estimates, roughly one-fourth was transferred out of the country to be added to England's resources. How Britain, which claimed to believe in the sanctity of democratic political and economic institutions, could do that to India was a surprise to Naoroji and is what he termed "un-British" practice.

Since he had a very favourable impression of the British character, Naoroji did not consider the British rule in India a foreign dominance to be overthrown at any cost but as an extension of the great British Empire where the administrative authorities happened to indulge in malpractices, which, in his opinion, could be set right through persuasive petitioning. In *Poverty and Un-British Rule in India*, he is found reminding the British officials in India of their pledges, assurances, and promises made to the people of India:

> In the 'faithful and conscientious fulfilment' of solemn pledges, India expects and demands that the British Sovereign, People, Parliament, and Government, should make honest efforts towards what the Bishop of Bombay described as the aspirations and necessities of India 'Self-government under British paramountcy' or true British citizenship.
>
> *(Naoroji 1901: xiv)*

Another example of his faith in the perceived British character and the British democratic system of governance is witnessed in his address to the second session of the I.N.C. in which he reminds the members that the Congress was not a platform for sedition and rebellion against the British government but rather yet another stone in the foundation for the stability of the British government. Moreover, in the Lahore Session of the Congress in 1893, Naoroji reiterated his support for the British government in India (Zaidi 1985: 44). But there occurred a gradual shift in emphasis in his ideas when he realised that his tactics were not producing any favourable results and that the actual British character was different from his initial perception. He started expressing his disenchantment with the British rule in India. He realised that the real objective of the colonisation of India was not to create an Indian India but a British one, which he expresses in his 1895 speech (Naoroji 1917: 153). Naoroji started opposing British policies and rule in India, which is especially reflected in his 1904 and 1905 speeches in which he asserted that self-government was the only panacea for India's miseries (Zaidi 1985: 440).

VI Role in the Indian freedom struggle

Naoroji realised, though a little late in his life, that the policy of moderation and persuasion in a democratic fashion did not work with the British administration in India. Petitioning, representations, discussions, conferences, and appealing the British officials' morale to realise their step-motherly behaviour with India produced no significant results in the end. When this realisation dawned upon Naoroji, his attitude towards the British government changed. For instance, in his address to the I.N.C. at its *Benaras* session in 1905, he supported the radical nationalists, declaring that "self-rule was the only alternative to solve the miseries of the Indian masses, without self-government, the Indians can never get rid of their present drain, and the consequent impoverishment, misery, and destruction" (Zaidi 1985: 440). In this session of the I.N.C., a resolution to boycott British goods was put forward. In the Calcutta session of the I.N.C. in 1906, over which Naoroji presided, four resolutions – self-government, the boycott of foreign goods, *swadeshi*, and national education – were passed. In his presidential address, Naoroji declared:

> We do not ask for favours, we want only justice. Instead of going into any further divisions or details of our rights as British citizens, the whole matter can be comprised in one word – 'self-government' or *Swaraj*, like that of the United Kingdom or colonies.
>
> *(Zaidi 1985: 76)*

In addition to his demand of self-government, the boycott of foreign goods, *swadeshi*, and national education, Naoroji gave six factors contributing to the flow of wealth from India to Britain:

1. Rule of a foreign government
2. No foreign immigrants to India who might have brought their capital as well as labour
3. India paid for Britain's civil administration and the occupational army on Indian soil
4. India paid for the empire building within and outside India
5. Free trade resulted in offering high-paying jobs to foreign personnel
6. The principal income earners were not Indians; they bought properties outside India or left the country with large sums of money

VII Conclusion

To sum, the drain of wealth theory is ascribed to Dadabhai Naoroji, as he discussed these ideas in detail with enough facts and figures providing a thorough statistical analysis in *Poverty and Un-British Rule in India* (1901). His work is primarily focused on bringing the attention of the British government towards the ill effects of colonial rule in India and the Indian economy drained into England through a smooth system of economic exploitation. He had arrived at a rough estimate of the net national profit of India in 1901, which helped him to calculate how much wealth was flowing annually from India to Britain. His political ideas, too, were purely concerned with economics as he made an attempt to prove that Britain was a burden on the Indian economy, but at the same time he wanted a greater representation of Indians in the British administrative machinery in India through several reform measures.

According to Naoroji's estimates in 1870, there was roughly £30,000,000 lost in annual revenue to Britain for which there were no chances of return. It was, according to Naoroji, just blood-sucking vampirism, and Britain's actions were monstrous. Of course, Britain did bring some services to India, such as railways, a postal service, the telegraph, and English education, for which it deserved some tribute. But Naoroji mentioned that money for such services was already being drained out of the country; for example, the money earned by railways did not belong to India, and it was not spent on any services in India. Therefore, such revenues did not bring any direct profit to the Indian economy. For such services, other countries were paying off foreign investment, whereas, despite the fact that railways were earning profits for Britain, Indians were paying for the services rendered. For the drain of wealth, there were other gateways, too. For instance, British workers earned wages that were never equivalent to the work they did in India. The British government encouraged her subjects to take up lucrative jobs in India, and the government allowed them to take a large part of their income back home. The other instance is of trade imbalance, that is, Indian goods were undervalued, so they were purchased cheaply, while goods coming from Britain were overpriced and sold at exorbitant prices in India. The East India Company was buying raw materials from India with the money drained from the country to export to Britain and then the products produced in Britain were imported to sell at higher prices, adding further dimension to exploitation through so-called free trade.

Thus, Naoroji's nationalism was of an economic nature in its initial phase, but it gradually acquired a political form with the passage of time and with his disillusionment with the British governance in India. His ideas helped to develop a strong political nationalism among the next generation of I.N.C. leaders, and thus the Indian independence movement gained further momentum during his lifetime.

Notes

1 Naoroji, Dadabhai. (1901). *Poverty and Un-British Rule in India*. London: Swan Sonnenschein & Company, pp. vii–ix.
2 The publishers of this book remark: When a national revolt against British rule broke out in India in 1857, Marx and Engels, who followed the struggles of the Indian for their freedom with great attention and heartfelt sympathy, came out with a series of articles in the *New-York Daily Tribune* in which they analysed the progress of the uprising, showed its causes, its nation-wide scope, and its connection with "a general dissatisfaction exhibited against English supremacy on the part of the great Asiatic nations" (p. 8).
3 Naoroji points out the common mistakes made by European travellers on the intellectual capabilities of the Asiatics because of their superficial observation and imperfect knowledge of the natives.
4 Before dealing with the evil qualities of the British rule in India, in *Poverty and Un-British Rule in India*, he gives a brief sketch of the benefits India had derived from the British connection, that were of utmost importance to Indians – the abolition of *Sati* and of infanticide, the introduction of English education, the maintenance of law and order, and freedom of speech and press (p. vi).

References

Daily Graphic, August 9, 1892 / *India*, August 26, 1982: 214–215. https://www.webmaster@graphic.com.gh

Encyclopedia of World Biography. https://www.encyclopedia.com/people/history/south-asian-history-biographies/dadabhai-naoroji, accessed on September 8, 2017.

Gupta, Indra (2003). *India's 50 Most Illustrious Women*. New Delhi: Icon Publications.

Hall, Catherine (2002). *Civilizing Subjects: Colony and Metropole in the English Imagination*. Chicago, IL: University of Chicago Press.

The Hindu [Madras], March 13, 1886. www.thehindu.com

Marx, Karl, and Engels, F. (1857). *On Colonialism*. Moscow: Foreign Languages Publishing House.

Masani, R. P. (1939). *Dadabhai Naoroji: The Grand Old Man of India*. London: George Allen & Unwin.

Naoroji, Dadabhai (1861a). *The Manners and Customs of the Parsees: A Paper Read Before the Liverpool Philomathic Society*. London: S. Straker & Sons/Bombay: Union Press.

Naoroji, Dadabhai (1861b). *The Parsee Religion*. University of London. https://archive.org/details/cu31924031767779/page/n3/mode/2up?view=theater

Naoroji, Dadabhai (1866). *The European and Asiatic Races: Observations on the Paper Read by John Crawfurd*. London: Trubner & Company.

Naoroji, Dadabhai (1868). *Admission of Educated Natives into the Indian Civil Service*. London: Macmillan.

Naoroji, Dadabhai (1870). *The Wants and Means of India*. London: Vincent Brooks, Day and Son.

Naoroji, Dadabhai (1878). *Poverty of India*. London: Vincent Brooks, Day and Son.

Naoroji, Dadabhai (1887). *Essays, Speeches, Addresses and Writings*. Bombay: Caxton Printing Works.

Naoroji, Dadabhai (1901). *Poverty and Un-British Rule in India*. London: S. Sonnenschein.

Naoroji, Dadabhai (1917). *Speeches and Writings of Dadabhai Naoroji*. London: Nateson.

Pasricha, Ashu (2008). *Encyclopaedia of Eminent Thinkers: Vol. 11: The Political Thought of Dadabhai Naoroji*. New Delhi: Concept Publishing.

Pitts, Jennifer (2005). *A Turn to Empire: The Rise of Liberal Imperialism in Britain and France*. Princeton, NJ: Princeton University Press.

Report of the Second Indian National Congress, Held at Calcutta, Second Edition, 1886, pp. 52–56. https://dspace.gipe.ac.in/xmlui/handle/10973/19465

Smith, Adam (1776/2007). *An Inquiry into the Nature and Causes of the Wealth of Nations*. Digital edition from Meta Libri. Originally published by W. Strahan and T. Cadell, London, in 1776. https://metalibri.incubadora.fapesp.br

Zaidi, Moin A. (1985). *Dadabhai Naoroji: Speeches and writings*. New Delhi: Indian Institute of Applied Political Research.

11
GOPAL KRISHNA GOKHALE

Abha Chauhan Khimta

> *Public life must be spiritualised. Love of country must so fill the heart that all else shall appear as of little moment by the side.*
>
> – Gopal Krishna Gokhale

I Introduction

India has produced several eminent people during the last century, and they have each shaped the destiny of this ancient country. It has presented to the world great and gifted people in arts, science, history, education, religion, economics, politics, and more. These people have laid sound foundations for a bright future for India. At the same time, they have tried to glorify the great old Indian civilisation to revitalise the dormant spirit of the people. Gopal Krishna Gokhale was born amongst these great men and women who strove for the fulfilment of India's destiny. He worked at a time when there was unrest in the social and political milieu.

A new era began in 1858 with the transfer of power from the East India Company to Queen Victoria. It was a period of new thinking and challenge to Indian thinkers and leaders. They felt that British rule had uprooted Indian tradition, culture, history, religion, and social and political order. On the other hand, Britishers claimed that Indians' backwardness was due to social customs, caste distinctions, the treatment of women, and many other evils, real or imaginary, which had contributed to their own fall (Deogiribar 1992: 1–2).

Gokhale began his career in the field of education and ended with the constitutional agitation for India's independence. His courage, sincerity, and singleness of purpose have inspired many Indians. After Gokhale's death, Gandhi wrote and spoke on him from time to time. In one message he said:

Gokhale's life was that of a man of religion. Everything he did was done in the spirit of a devotee. Gokhale once called himself an agnostic. Even so, I could discern a religious strain in his work. It would not be improper to say that his very doubt was inspired by religion. A man who leads a dedicated life, who is simple in habits, who is the very image of truth, who is full of humanity, who calls nothing his own–such a man is a man of religion whether he himself is or is not conscious of it. Such was Gokhale as it. Such was Gokhale as I could see during the twenty years of my friendship with him.

(Singh 2008: 75)

II Life sketch

Gopal Krishna Gokhale was born on 9 May 1866 in a village named Kotluk in the Ratnagiri district of Bombay Presidency (Maharashtra). The village belonged to his mother, Satyabhama. Gokhale was born into a *Chitpavan Brāhmin* family. The family commanded considerable prestige and originally belonged to a village called Velaneshwar in the Ratnagiri district. Gokhale's forefathers had moved to an adjoining village, Tamhanmala (Deogiribar 1992: 2). Gokhale's father, Krishnarao, was a rent collector and was supported by his wife in his struggle to maintain the family. Krishnarao was keen to give the best possible English education to both of his sons, Govind and Gokhale. Both of them completed their elementary education at Kagal and were sent to the high school at Kolhapur in 1876. In 1885, Gokhale joined the Fergusson College as a lecturer in English. He had a deep interest in British history and political economy. He explained the principles of economics as applicable to Indian conditions and became the chief spokesman of the Deccan Education Society (D.E.S.). He became the Secretary of the *Sarvajanik Sabha* and later of the 'Deccan Sabha' under the guidance of Justice Ranade. Gokhale developed a style of his own while under Ranade's able guidance. He joined the Indian National Congress (I.N.C.) in 1889 under the leadership of Ranade, Dadabhai Naoroji, and Sir Pherozeshah Mehta. Gokhale met Ranade in 1887, and their relationship continued until the latter's death in 1901.

In 1903, Gokhale said that the caste system could not be defended. He bluntly stated that Indians could not complain of discrimination by Europeans in South Africa or elsewhere unless they ceased to discriminate against their own low-caste countrymen. Following Ranade, he asked Indians to turn the searchlight inwards (Ghose 1980: 69). Gokhale believed in secularism and was a great supporter of Hindu–Muslim unity. Gokhale joined the D.E.S. in Poona at the age of 19. He cultivated a lucid English style during his college days and was impressed with his Principal Wordsworth and Professor Howthorn Waite. Wordsworth taught him English, while Professor Howthorn was his mathematics teacher. Gokhale joined the New English School as an assistant master in Poona. The New English School had been started by a band of patriots which included Bal Gangadhar Tilak, V. K. Chiplunkar, G. G. Agarak, and V. S. Apte. Their papers

Kesari and *Maratha* were vehicles of a new spirit for leaders like M. G. Ranade, K. T. Telang, and R. G. Bhandarkar. During 1886, Gokhale contributed a series of articles to the *Maratha* (Gupta and Gupta 2000: 10).

III Constitutionalism and *swadeshi*

Throughout his life, Gokhale worked for one-nation ideals. For promoting a homogeneous India, he was an ardent advocate of Hindu–Muslim harmony and unity. Gokhale observed that there could be no future for India unless a spirit of cooperation was developed and established (Das 2005: 214). Like Naoroji, Mehta, Ranade, and Surendranath Banerjee, Gokhale made it a condition of the membership of the 'Servants of India Society' that those who would dedicate themselves to the service of this country must rise above the narrow communal considerations and set aside the prejudices that divide man from man (Goyal 1965: 19). Gokhale did not demand complete independence (*purna swaraj*) for his country; rather, he desired self-government without severing the British connection.

In 1905, Gokhale advocated *swadeshi* as the only resort of the people to fight the adverse economic forces in the country. According to him, the *swadeshi* movement was both a patriotic and an economic one. He rejected the word boycott and only advocated the use of word *swadeshi* to describe their movement. According to him, "For when you boycott foreign goods you must not touch even a particle of imported articles; and we only make ourselves ridiculous by taking of a resolution which we cannot enforce" (Goyal 1965: 30). Gokhale believed in the adoption of constitutional agitation. According to him:

> Constitutional agitation was agitation by methods, which they were entitled to adopt to bring about the changes they desired through the sanction of constituted authorities. Thus, defining the field of constitutional agitation was very wide one. But there were two essential conditions; one that the methods adopted were such as they were entitled to employ, and secondly, that the changes desired must be obtained only through the action of constituted authorities by bringing to bear on them the pressure of public opinion.
> *(Goyal 1965: 40)*

Gokhale believed in the adoption of passive resistance and believed the passive-resistance movement must be moral and spiritual. Gokhale justified the adoption of passive resistance only when all other means of redress have failed.

IV Social regeneration

In 1905, Gokhale founded the 'Servants of India Society' to create love for the motherland and a spirit of sacrifice, to encourage cordial relations between the communities, to assist education movements, and to work for the elevation of the depressed classes (Gupta and Gupta 2000: 10). In matters of party organisation and technique, Gokhale was largely indebted to Mehta. Like Ranade and Naoroji, Gokhale was a great admirer of Western traditions and British rule. Therefore, he considered the introduction of British rule the fortuitous dispensation of divine providence sent to rouse India from the lethargy of centuries and to teach her how to remodel her institutions in the image of the most advanced nation in the world at that time (Wolpert 1990: 297). At the same time, Gokhale also demanded amelioration of the helpless conditions of the depressed and downtrodden countrymen condemned as low castes. In his words:

> Modern civilisation has accepted greater equality for all as against privilege and exclusiveness, the larger humanity of these days requires that we should acknowledge claims by seeking the amelioration of the helpless condition of our down trodden countrymen.
>
> *(Natesan 1916: 1057)*

Gokhale was inspired by Western and Indian traditions. Though he disliked the evils of Hinduism, he never thought of giving up his own religion. It was in this line that Gokhale established the 'Servants of India Society' in 1905. The necessity for such an organisation was for nation-building in India. He felt that for success in this work, it was necessary that "a sufficient number of our countrymen must now come forward to devote themselves to the cause in the spirit in which religious work is undertaken. Public life must be spiritualised" (Goyal 1965: 15). Gokhale sought to raise politics to the level of religion. He understood religion in the sense of ethics and morals. Thus, truth and honesty characterised all his utterances and actions (ibid.: 16). Gokhale was an optimist and an idealist. He believed in the progressive perfectibility of all mankind through the agencies of education, the accurate dissemination of information, and social and material amelioration. In voicing the political demands of his people, he was eminently practical, moderate, and invariably constructive (Wolpert 1990: 300).

Gokhale inherited the traditions of the early Congress, which struggled mainly for recognition by the government and followed the principles of moderation and loyalty in its dealings with foreign rulers. He realised the importance of the role of education in nation-building and became associated with the D.E.S. He was convinced that education could play an important role in nation-building.

V Ethics and politics

The word "ethics" has unfortunately lost much of its relevance. If we look at the political scenario prevailing in our society, it is noteworthy that almost everything in the settlement of immoral matters is a mixture of selfish desires. When citizens enjoy or appreciate moral stuff, they are also served with bitter and unethical motives from which they lose hope, and with that the urge for progress and development has sadly disappeared. A particular word in the present situation has lost its relevance. However, the worrying fact is that if ethics loses its value in a particular field, that field will definitely impose a negative trait on the evolution and formation of society.

Gokhale was a noble man. His dedication to public life and the freedom of movement was consistent and was the foundation of the 'Servants of India Society'. Gokhale said:

> Public life should be made spiritual. The love for the motherland must fill the heart in such a way that everything else will be appearing from its side for a moment. An ardent patriot who rejoices at every opportunity to sacrifice for the motherland, a hard-hearted man who refuses to deviate from his goal – deep faith in the goal of providence, which cannot be shaken by trouble or danger – these workers, equipped to begin their mission must and respectfully enjoy the pleasure spent in the service of their country.
>
> *(Mahajan 1944: 18)*

In the meantime, two clear trends were to be seen. Although the origins of moderate philosophy can be traced back to the changes brought about in India by Western liberal education, one group sought to liberate India from the dark ages of history, while the other sought to integrate the good aspects of other religions and cultures with the desire to revive a better Indian culture and was essentially a conservative approach (Karve and Ambedkar 1966: 22).

> It was a case of love at first sight; it was so severe in 1913. It felt like everything I wanted as a political activist – crystal clear, I felt good not to be one of those things. For me it was enough that I was not found guilty of making a complaint. He was and remains the most perfect man in the political arena.
>
> *(Gandhi 1955: 55)*

Thus, Gokhale is better known as a moderate thinker and a moderate leader who played a major role in the Congress during the period of its formation. It was agreed that there was no need to agitate for social and religious reform as well as economic reform of the people. Thus, the first Congress was of elite character and from Western education and culture. The affected small educated minority, loyal to the regime with a zeal for social upliftment, was never considered a dangerous organisation (Das and Patro 1988: 2).

The tradition of the first Congress was inherited by Gokhale, who fought primarily for recognition by the government and adhered to the principles of moderation and loyalty in dealing with foreign rulers. But he had a special attitude towards the British rule. Sometimes he supported the government and wanted to learn the administrative process of the British government. But he was not a blind supporter of the government. When he discovered government malpractices which were against Indian interests, he opposed them (Karve and

Ambedkar 1967: 57–58). He vehemently opposed the salt tax, excise duty on cotton products, and many other illegal activities of the government. He filed a case for the eradication of poverty before the Welby Commission, for which he went to London. He spoke out against social and economic ills, such as poverty and hunger, alcoholism, and prostitution. The rise of socially backward classes, the education of women, mass education, and other similar issues were facing the nation. Gokhale's life as a political leader can be understood against many aspects, namely, his role in nation-building activities, his views on political progress and self-government, his humanity, and finally his economic views. He believed in constructive government intervention, especially for the benefit and development of the Indian economy (Mohanty 2015: 102).

Gokhale believed the national character of a people and their ability as a community were synonymous with public life and that for public life to be an efficient and effective project of the common spirit, "there must be a distinction between matters of conscience and matters of judgment". To qualify all life as public life, there must be two prerequisites: first, "it must be in the public interest"; and second, "that life should be shared and participated in, if not by whole people, at least by a very large number of people" (Gokhale 1922: 2–3). For an ambitious India, Gokhale turned to public life in the West and pointed out that in general it represents three different yet interrelated areas: national public life, political public life, and social and humanitarian public life. The result, in their own words, seems to be that they are bound to enjoy political liberties, to echo the voice for freedom, and to guarantee more freedom and the end of public life which guarantees liberties. At any time, they were to further expand the constraints of freedom, to achieve more political freedoms, and to effectively fulfill the obligations that come with political freedoms (Sitaramayya 1946: 91).

Gokhale mentioned that in the past, public life sometimes meant service to the British government, but with the change of time, for the Indian people, it became "voluntary service in the interest of our fellow companions". Gokhale also warned that public life in India was the result of a relatively recent acquisition and that it could not be understood if it were different from the problems and limitations that would naturally come to the nation in slavery (Dhawan 1946: 139). And so, Gokhale said, "Now we must make it a matter of our public life, now we must make it a matter of our public service". To the officer, Gokhale said:

> This person can claim to be equipped with a single spirit. Willing to sacrifice for personal comfort and personal convenience. . . . We must be willing to subordinate our own personal judgment in the consideration of public affairs, which is necessary for good.
>
> *(Gokhale 1902: 51)*

With patience and autonomy the public servant should cultivate and strengthen the power of the people, who understand the needs and responsibilities of public life. Gokhale believed that by dedicating creative public service through cooperation, discipline, and inseparability, people would be "trained". What has been given or what it can give us has been fully and effectively assumed by us. Gokhale's wish that the public worker, in the face of his constitutional capacity, dedicate himself to the cause of public education in a unified manner:

> Public life in India and the shortage of reliable and willing workers and that time was about to begin. He implied from country councils to village unions, to city councils and local bodies, to the press and forum, and to the various movements that we have inaugurated for the education of public opinion.
> *(Patwardhan and Ambedkar 1962: 80)*

There are ample opportunities for public activists who will advance Gokhale's cause.

Gokhale's understanding of British rule in India was a decisive factor in his political goals and agenda. As stated, Gokhale sincerely believed India's relations with the British would help her in many ways in the long run, and therefore he condemned any idea of severing those ties. The political objective he suggested was Indian self-government. The early leaders of Congress were satisfied with the idea of "good government", which meant an efficient and enlightened government (Wolpert 1990: 98–99). But like Naoroji, Gokhale gradually realised that no good government is possible without self-government. Moreover, they felt that the British had given good government in the sense that they had established law and order in the society, but the time had come for the Indians to be involved in the work of the government, and this was possible only with the permission of the British (Mathur 1966: 112–113). Addressing the Banaras Congress (1905), Gokhale said, "In the interest of the Indians, the Congress wants all this to change and rule India". This result can only be achieved by the government gaining more and more vocal power in our country.

The liberation of man was the idea Gokhale gave to Indian politics. He believed nation-building was possible only through the development of the people through their nationalist capacity and values. In his 1902 speech, he said:

> What is needed is for us to feel that we have a government, "national in spirit though foreign in personnel" – The government, which subordinates everything else for the welfare of the Indian people, will do its utmost to enhance the moral and material interests of the Indian people.
> *(Sadanandan 2013: 22)*

Gokhale and Ranade tried to bring about a change in Indian politics by emphasising surrender, full dedication to the cause of the country, and observation and purity of action. Gokhale's attitude towards social reform was essentially humanistic and liberal. He said that "morality is always based on secular matters and does not refer to any religious belief. His concept of secularism speaks of respect for the methods of worship and culture that enable people to understand the various ways of life" (Patwardhan and Ambedkar 1962: 77).

Gokhale adhered to the philosophies of logic, spiritual and moral liberation, and universal tolerance. He appealed that such sections of the society should be subjected to severe socio-economic disabilities due to the bad practices of the caste system and discriminatory policies pursued by the government. He encouraged them to adopt a moral approach to political questions and public responsibilities. It is true that no progress is possible in our society without enjoying minimal basic freedoms, the denial of which means to deny the development of human personality (Noda 1961: 87). Gokhale placed great emphasis on national unity and saw it as the first precondition for the growth and development of Indian nationalism. He called for uniting people of different communities into a single unit, excluding caste and religious considerations. He advocated Hindu–Muslim unity and argued that the future of India would not be possible without the cooperation of these two communities.

He also believed in the priority of the means. He emphasised the spiritualisation of politics and wanted to use it as a tool to serve the people. He advocated moderation, logic, and compromise as a political technique. He placed more emphasis on character-building and stressed that the nation should get freedom before applying (Barman 2013: 29). He stressed the need to raise moral and social standards to fully involve the people in national development. He believed the individual could not be moral or immoral. However, a person in society could be moral or immoral. Personal freedom is a duty of the State, while social morality, surrender, complete devotion to the cause of the country, and purity are the duty of the individual (Dhawan 1946: 139). In addition, he suggested ways and means of raising funds, financing the functions of the development of welfare in an underdeveloped economy. He suggested focusing on State borrowing and reducing spending on State policing functions to use the money saved for development functions (Bhagwan 2018: 231).

Gokhale's political ideas insisted on personal freedom, the liberation of man with secularism, sacrifice for the cause of the nation, and surrender. A politician like Gokhale who can inspire people with his thoughts and deeds always does great service to the nation and will always have a place in the hearts of the people (Barman 2013: 30).

VI Conclusion

Gokhale was devoted to racial equality and harmony and considered equality, freedom, justice, and the rule of law to be essential for universal progress and peace. Gokhale was a humanist, and he had faith in the good nature of man. His ideas on humanism are close to those of Locke and Rousseau. He believed in the protection of rights of all the communities and creeds. He also advocated the desirability of education through his mother tongue. He also boldly said that the government should allocate more funds than what it was hitherto allocating for the spread of education. Gokhale was among those moderates who during the closing years of the nineteenth century laid the foundations of Indian economic thought. He was also the founder of the framework of the basic concepts of the welfare State in India.

References

Barman, Shrutilekha (2013). Political Ideas of Gopal Krishna Gokhale. *The International Journal of Humanities & Social Studies*. Vol. 1, No. 6.
Bhagwan, Vishnoo (2018). *Indian Political Thinkers*. Lucknow: Atma Ram & Sons.
Das, Hari Hara (2005). *Indian Political Thought*. Delhi: National Publishing House.
Das, Hari Hara, and P. S. N. Patro (1988). *Indian Political Tradition*. India: Stosius Inc/ Advent Books Division.
Deogiribar, T. R. (1992). *Gopal Krishna Gokhale*. New Delhi: Publication Division, Ministry of Information and Broadcasting, Government of India.
Dhawan, G. N. (1946). *The Political Philosophy of Mahatma Gandhi*. Bombay: Popular Prakashan.
Gandhi, M. K. (1955). *Gokhale: My Political Guru*. Ahmedabad: Navajivan Pub. House.
Ghosh, Sankar (1980). *Leaders of Modern India*. New Delhi: Allied Publisher.
Gokhale, G. K. (1922). *Public Life in India-Its Needs and Responsibilities*. Crawfordsville: National Literature Publishing Company.
Gokhale's Farewell Speech: Fergusson College, September 19, 1902: Speeches, Poona, India.
Goyal, O. P. (1965). *Political Thought of Gokhale*. Allahabad: Kitab Mahal Private Ltd.
Gupta, V. P., and Mohini Gupta (2000). *The Life and Legacy of Gopal Krishna Gokhale*. New Delhi: Radha Publication.
Karve, D. G., and D. V. Ambedkar (1966). *Speeches and Writings of Gopal Krishna Gokhale*, Vol. 11. Bombay: Asia Publishing House.
Karve, D. G., and D. V. Ambedkar (1967). *Speeches and Writings of Gopal Krishna Gokhale*, Vol. III. Bombay: Asia Publishing House.
Mahajan, Vidya Dhar (1944). Some Aspects of Gokhale's Political Thought. *The Indian Journal of Political Science*. Indian Political Science Association. Vol. 6, No. 1, July–September, pp. 18–27.
Mathur, B. (1966). *Gokhale: A Political Biography*. Bombay: Manaktalas.
Mohanty, D. K. (2015). *Indian Political Tradition: From Manu to Ambedkar*. New Delhi: Anmol Publications Pvt. Ltd.
Natesan, G. A. (Ed.) (1916). *Speeches of Gopal Krishna Gokhale*. Madras: Natesan and Co.
Noda, Fukuo (1961). Political Ideas of G. K. Gokhale. *Journal of the Society for Asian Political and Economic Studies*. Vol. VII, No. 4.
Patwardhan, R. P., and D. V. Ambedkar (1962). *Speeches and Writings of Gopal Krishna Gokhale*, Vol. I. Bombay: Asia Publishing House.
Sadanandan, G. (2013). *Modern Indian Social and Political Thought*. Thrissur: School of Distance Education, University of Calicut.
Singh, M. K. (2008). *Gopal Krishna Gokhle*. New Delhi: Anmol Publisher.
Sitaramayya, B. P. (1946). *History of the Indian National Congress*, Vol. I. Bombay: Padma Publications.
Wolpert, Stanley A. (1990). *Tilak and Gokhale: Revolution and Reform in the Making of Modern India*. Delhi: Oxford University Press.

12

MOHANDAS KARAMCHAND GANDHI

Ambarish Mukhopadhyay

> *For me the only training in Swaraj we need is the ability to defend ourselves against the whole world and to live our natural life in perfect freedom, even though it may be full of defects. Good government is no substitute for self-government.*
> – (Mahatma Gandhi, *Young India*, 22 September, Vol. II, No. 38, 1920: 1)

I Introduction

Mohandas Karamchand Gandhi, commonly known as Mahatma Gandhi, was an Indian political and civil rights leader who played a significant role in India's struggle for independence. Gandhi is also known as *Bapuji* (endearment for father in Gujrati) and Father of the Nation and was one of the most outstanding men the twentieth century produced. Gandhi made the techniques of non-violence and *satyāgraha* powerful weapons in his fight against British imperialism. Both the doctrines of non-violence and *satyāgraha* are linked to Gandhi's innate attachment to truth, which is described as "truth force". With these powerful political tools, Gandhi inspired several other political leaders all over the world, including Nelson Mandela, Martin Luther King Jr., and Aung San Suu Kyi, among others. He inspired movements for civil rights and freedom across the world. The honorific *Mahatma* (meaning "great-souled" or "venerable"), first bestowed upon him in 1914 in South Africa (Gandhi, Rajmohan 2010: 172), is now used throughout the world. Gandhi, apart from helping India triumph in its struggle for independence against British rule, also led a simple and righteous life, for which he is often revered. Gandhi's early life was pretty much ordinary, and he became a great man during his life. He proved that one can become a great soul if one possesses the will to do so.

The next section of this chapter will contain a life sketch of Gandhi, focusing on his childhood, early life, education, and career. This will be followed by an analysis of the central themes of Gandhi's social, economic, and political thoughts.

II Life sketch

Childhood

Mohandas Karamchand Gandhi was born on 2 October 1869, in Porbandar, a coastal town of the Kathiawar district (in modern-day Gujarat). He was born into a Hindu merchant-caste family to Karamchand Gandhi and his fourth wife, Putlibai. Karamchand served as the *diwan* of the then Porbandar State. The Gandhis had been in government service for more than a generation, although strictly speaking they were merchants and farmers of the *Vaiśya* caste (Byrne 1984: 4). Karamchand was not highly educated. He could read and write and knew little history and geography. But he had a reputation for being incorruptible and tactful. Putlibai, Gandhi's mother, belonged to an affluent *Pranami Vaishnava* family. She never learned to read and write, but she was a simple, kind-hearted, and extremely devout woman. The two most important things in her life were her family and her religion. Gandhi was deeply influenced by his mother. As a child, Gandhi was as restless as mercury, either playing or roaming about. One of his favourite pastimes was twisting dogs' ears. The Indian classics, especially the stories of Shravana and King Harishchandra, had a great impact on Gandhi in his childhood. In his autobiography, Gandhi admits that they left an indelible impression on his mind. Gandhi's early self-identification with truth and love as supreme values is traceable to these epic characters. Gandhi's lifelong struggle against the idea of untouchability began with an act of youthful rebellion. He used to play with a sweeper boy called Uka, who was an untouchable. When one day Putlibai caught the two boys playing together, she was very angry with her son and scolded him for playing with an untouchable. Gandhi listened but was unconvinced. Whenever his mother was not looking, Gandhi continued playing with Uka because he treated him just like a brother.

Thus, quite early in his life, Gandhi began his long campaign to break down the barriers of caste and to get rid of untouchability. He even found a new name for the untouchables. He called them *Harijans*, or the "Children of God" (Byrne 1984: 7).

Early life and schooldays

When Gandhi was seven years old, his father left Porbandar for the smaller State of Rajkot, where he became a counsellor to its ruler, the Thakur Sahib. His family joined him later. At the age of nine, Gandhi was enrolled at a local school in Rajkot where he studied the basics of arithmetic, history, geography, and the Gujarati language. Two years later, he joined Alfred High School. He was an average student, won some prizes, but he was a shy and tongue-tied student with no interest in games; his only companions were books and school lessons. At the age of 13, Gandhi was married to Kasturba (who was also of the same age), the daughter of a Porbandar merchant. It was the custom at that time to marry young, and marriages were arranged by the parents, often when the children were little more than babies. Later in life, looking back on how he had behaved as a "schoolboy husband", Gandhi spoke out strongly against the "cruel custom of child marriage". But at the time, he was pleased and excited by the prospect of having a wife. It was fun, rather like getting a new playmate (Byrne 1984: 9). Due to the marriage, Gandhi lost a year at school, but he was later allowed to make up by accelerating his studies.

In late 1885, Gandhi's father died. In the same year, Gandhi and Kasturba had their first baby, who survived only a few days. The two deaths anguished Gandhi. Later, the couple gave birth to four more children, all sons: Harilal, Monilal, Ramdas, and Devdas. In 1887, Gandhi graduated from the high school in Ahmedabad. In the next year, he enrolled at Samaldas College in Bhavnagar State but eventually dropped out and returned to his family at Porbandar.

The London years

Later, Gandhi was advised by a family friend, Mavji Dave Joshiji, to pursue the study of law in London. The idea must have seemed fanciful at the time because Gandhi had finished school with mediocre marks. There were monetary constraints also; Gandhi came from a poor family, and his father had not left the family well off when he died. Gandhi's mother was also against Gandhi leaving his wife and family and going so far from home. In fact, she was scared, as she heard too many stories about the bad habits young men acquired there: eating meat, drinking alcohol, and going out with women. But Gandhi was excited by the idea of studying in London. To convince his mother and wife, Gandhi made a vow in front of his mother that he would abstain from eating meat, drinking alcohol, and having sex with women in London. Gandhi's brother Laxmidas, who was already a lawyer, cheered Gandhi's plan to study in London and offered to support him. Putlibai also ultimately gave Gandhi her permission and blessing.

On 10 August 1888, Gandhi left Porbandar for Bombay (present-day Mumbai). After arriving there, he stayed with the local *Modh Bania* community while waiting for the ship travel arrangements. Ultimately, Gandhi sailed from Bombay to London on 4 September 1888. In London, Gandhi attended the University College, which is a constituent college of the University of London. In this college, Gandhi studied law and jurisprudence and was invited to enrol at Inner Temple with the intention of becoming a barrister. During his stay in London, Gandhi joined a vegetarian society and was soon introduced to the *Bhagavadgītā* by some of his vegetarian friends. The contents of the *Bhagavadgītā* would later have a massive influence on his life. In fact, it was in London that Gandhi first began to take a serious interest in religion.

Through his study of the *Gītā* Gandhi first began to develop his ideas on detachment from material possessions. The religious text influenced him to become a man of action – a spiritual man who *acts* rather than sits and reflects. At the same time, he also read other great religious texts, like the *Qurʾān* and the *Bible*. Meanwhile, he continued with his legal studies and passed his final examinations. On 10 June 1891, Gandhi was called to the Bar and he enrolled in the High Court on 11 June. The following day, Gandhi sailed for India. It was as if he had taken all he wanted from England and had no wish even to spend another day there (Byrne 1984: 23). Gandhi's London days had quite a significant impact on his mental make-up and ideas. His new-found ideas on diet and religion had begun to shape his thinking. In a short while, he would get the opportunity to put some of these ideas to the test.

When Gandhi returned to India, he came to know that his mother had died while he was in London and that his family had kept the news from him. He now faced the most pressing problem: to earn money to support his family. He decided to try his luck in Bombay and establish himself as a lawyer, but he failed because he was psychologically unable to cross-examine witnesses. He returned to Rajkot to make a modest living by drafting petitions for the litigants. In 1893, a merchant in Kathiawar named Dada Abdullah, who owned a shipping business in South Africa, contacted Gandhi and asked him if he would be interested to serve as his cousin's lawyer in Johannesburg, South Africa. Gandhi accepted the offer and left for South Africa, which later served as a turning point in his political career.

Gandhi in South Africa (1893–1914)

Gandhi sailed for South Africa in April 1893 at the age of 23. Immediately after arriving in South Africa, Gandhi faced discrimination because of his skin colour and heritage, like all people of colour (Parekh 2001: 7). South Africa at that time was a glaring example of racial discrimination between whites and blacks. Gandhi faced humiliation in South Africa on many occasions. He was not allowed to sit with European passengers in the same coach and was told to sit on the floor near the driver; he was beaten when he refused. In another instance, Gandhi was thrown off a train at Pietermaritzburg station for travelling in first class. He sat in the platform shivering in the cold for the whole night and pondering whether he should return to India or protest for his rights. He chose to protest. Such incidents turned Gandhi into an activist, and he took upon him many cases that would benefit the Indian and other minorities living in South Africa. Indians were not allowed to vote or walk on footpaths, as those privileges were limited strictly to the Europeans. In 1894, the Natal government proposed a discriminatory bill to deny Indians the right to vote. Gandhi planned to assist Indians in opposing the bill. Though unable to halt the passage of the bill, Gandhi's campaign was successful in drawing attention to the grievances of Indians in South Africa. He managed to establish an organisation named Natal Indian Congress, and through it moulded the Indian community in South Africa into a unified political force (Tendulkar 1951: 21).

In 1906, the Transvaal government promulgated a new Act compelling registration of the colony's Indian and Chinese populations. A mass protest meeting was held in Johannesburg to resist the Registration Act – The Black Act, as it later came to be called. Gandhi stressed that there must be no violence during the protest: the Indians had to fight their oppressors without weapons, even at the risk of death. This idea, which was not completely new, of course, was sometimes called passive resistance. Gandhi, however, did not like the term, as he did not see resistance as something passive. He rather settled for a new word: *satyāgraha*. In Sanskrit, *sat* means truth, while *agraha* is firmness. *Satyāgraha* is, thus, "firmness in truth" or a kind of "soul force". Gandhi spent the rest of his life developing and refining this concept (Byrne 1984: 47). According to Anthony Parel, Gandhi was also influenced by the Tamil text *Tirukkural*, which was later translated into many languages. Leo Tolstoy mentioned it in his correspondence with Gandhi that began with *A Letter to a Hindu* (Parel 2002: 96). In 1910, Gandhi, with the help of his friend Hermann Kallenbach, established an idealistic community named Tolstoy Farm near Johannesburg. There, Gandhi nurtured his idea of peaceful resistance. Gandhi's ideas of protests, persuasion skills, and public relations developed during his 21 years in South Africa. During these two decades, Gandhi fought for civil rights and was transformed into a new person. He carried back with him to India his ideas when he returned in 1915.

III Gandhi, Indian National Congress, and the struggle for India's independence (1915–1947)

During his stay in South Africa, Gandhi had earned a reputation as a nationalist, theorist, and organiser because of his activism against the racist policies of the British. Gopal Krishna Gokhale, a senior leader of the Indian National Congress (I.N.C.), invited Gandhi to join India's struggle for independence against the British rule. Gokhale thoroughly guided Gandhi about the prevailing political situation in India and the social issues of the time. Gandhi joined the I.N.C. with Gokhale's invitation, and in 1920 he took over the leadership of the Congress. After assuming the leadership of the I.N.C., Gandhi led nationwide campaigns for easing poverty, expanding women's rights, building religious and ethnic amity, ending untouchability, and achieving *swaraj*, or self-rule, for India. He led numerous agitations and protest movements (which he named *satyāgrahas*) against the British colonial rule. The Champaran *satyāgraha* (1917), the Kheda *satyāgraha* (1918), and the salt *satyāgraha* (Dandi march, 1930) were some of the most significant.

Gandhi urged his fellow countrymen to stop cooperating with the British. He believed the British succeeded in India only because of the cooperation of the Indians, so he gave the call for non-cooperation. In fact, the non-cooperation movement became one of Gandhi's most important political strategies in his fight against British rule. Gandhi cautioned the British rulers not to pass the Rowlatt Act, but they did not pay any heed to his words. As announced, Gandhi asked everyone to engage in civil disobedience against the British which the British started suppressing by brutal force. The worst of such repression was the Jallianwala Bagh Massacre on 13 April 1919.

The concept of non-cooperation gradually gained popularity and spread throughout India. Gandhi extended this movement and focused on *swaraj*. He urged people to stop using British goods and asked them to resign from government employment, quit studying in British institutions, and stop practicing in law courts. However, there was a violent clash in the Chauri Chaura town of Uttar Pradesh in February 1922, which forced Gandhi to call off the movement. In 1922, Gandhi was arrested and tried for sedition. As World War II progressed, Gandhi intensified his protests for the complete independence of India from foreign rule. He drafted a resolution calling for the British to quit India. The 'Quit India Movement' started in 1942 and was the most aggressive movement launched by the I.N.C. under Gandhi's leadership. Gandhi was arrested on 9 August 1942 and was held for two years in the Aga Khan Palace in Pune. The movement came to an end by the end of 1943, when the British gave hints that complete independence would be granted and power would be transferred to the people of India. Finally, Gandhi postponed the Quit India Movement, which ultimately ensured the freedom of 100,000 political prisoners.

Gandhi's vision of an independent India based on religious pluralism was challenged in the early 1940s by a new Muslim nationalism (led by the Muslim League) which demanded a separate Muslim homeland carved out of India. The British Cabinet Mission in 1946 offered the independence of India on the condition of partitioning the country. The I.N.C. accepted the proposal despite being advised otherwise by Gandhi. Sardar Patel convinced Gandhi that it was the only way to avoid civil war, and the latter reluctantly gave his consent. In August 1947, Britain granted independence to India, but it was a fractured one. The country was partitioned into two dominions – India and Pakistan. As many Hindus, Muslims, and Sikhs made their way to their new lands, communal violence and riots broke out, especially in Bengal and Punjab. Gandhi appealed for peace and unity among Hindus and Muslims. He visited the affected areas, attempting to provide solace. In the months following, Gandhi undertook several fasts unto death to stop the religious violence.

The inspiring life of Mahatma Gandhi came to an end on 30 January 1948, when he was shot by Nathuram Godse at point-blank range. Nathuram was a Hindu fanatic, a radical who held Gandhi responsible for India's partition. Godse and his co-conspirator Narayan Apte were later tried and convicted. They were executed on 15 November 1949.

Gandhi's life and works have attracted much scholarly analysis of his ideas, beliefs, principles, and practices. Three books that influenced Gandhi most were Henry David Thoreau's *On the Duty of Civil Disobedience* (1849), William Salter's *Ethical Religion* (1889), and Leo Tolstoy's *The Kingdom of God is Within You* (1894).

Ruskin inspired Gandhi's decision to live an austere life in a commune, first on the Phoenix Farm in Natal and then on the Tolstoy Farm in Johannesburg. The most profound influences on Gandhi were from Hinduism, Christianity, and Jainism. His thought was in harmony with the classical Indian traditions (Parekh 2001: 43).

Gandhi was, however, no armchair theorist. He was a man of action. His social, political, and economic ideas emerged during his action-packed life, and he continuously put those ideas into practice to fulfil his cherished goals. His philosophy and ideas have created a long-lasting imprint not only on our country but in different parts of the world as well. In the next part of the present essay, we will try to analyse the major components of Gandhian philosophy. We will start with the concept of *satyāgraha*.

IV Gandhi's ideas on *satyāgraha*

Gandhi dedicated his life to discover and pursue truth, or *satya*, and called his movement *satyāgraha*, which means appeal to, insistence on, or reliance on the truth. *Satyāgraha* as a principle and political movement occurred in 1920, and Gandhi termed it the 'Revolution on Non-cooperation' before a session of the I.N.C. in September of the same year. By *satyāgraha*, Gandhi meant adhering to truth under all circumstances and considered it the most powerful weapon for fighting against imperialism or another powerful enemy. The concept of *satyāgraha* and its practice in socio-political contexts constitute the essence of Gandhi's philosophy. Gandhi combined the twin ideas of truth and non-violence into the principle of *satyāgraha*. Using the banyan tree as a metaphor, he argued that "*satya* (truth) and *ahiṃsā* (non-violence) together make the parent trunk from which all innumerable branches short out" (Mukherjee and Ramaswamy 1998: 119). Perhaps it was Gandhi's unique contribution, as it opened a new political culture of social activism. It is a new technique of opposing or resisting injustice. But the method of resistance should be non-violent with adherence to truth and justice. This way of resisting injustice with a view to altering social relationships without harm or ill will towards anybody is the essence of the concept of *satyāgraha*. It is a method of direct action against injustice with a firm commitment to truth.

Gandhi distinguished the ideas inherent in his *satyāgraha* campaigns with the concept of passive resistance, which he equated with non-violence of the weak (Gandhi 1968a: 1152). While passive resistance does not carry love for the opponent, *satyāgraha* is based on love, and it abandons any form of hatred. Any individual, whether weak or strong, can resort to *satyāgraha* when he feels injustice is being done to him.

The term *satyāgraha* is composed of two Sanskrit words: *satya* and *agraha*, meaning to hold fast (*agraha*) to truth (*satya*). Thus, *satyāgraha* literally means clinging to truth or insistence on truth. It means "truth force" or "soul force" and entails that non-violence (of the strong) would be adopted as the exclusive means for pursuing truth (Gandhi 1968a: 179) Gandhi states that a *satyāgrahi* will always try to vindicate truth and justice. For Gandhi, violence is untruth and non-violence is truth. By non-violence, he meant that no one should be injured and there should be no hatred in thought, speech, or action. Gandhi believed a true *satyāgrahi* hated evil and loved his opponents because, for him, it was not the man but the institution which was to be hated.

According to Gandhi, *satyāgraha* has three major components or characteristics: 1) converting the views of one's opponents. The goal of converting an opponent's views entailed, in Gandhi's opinion, a preparedness to suffer deprivation, imprisonment, and even death. 2) A consistency between means and ends, which entails that the *satyāgrahis* would view the social and political goals they pursue as inextricably intertwined with the means adopted to achieve them. 3) Non-cooperation with a corrupt political and social system to be distinguished from civil disobedience in that while civil disobedience was a response to laws considered by conscience to be unjust, non-cooperation was a response to an unjust political, social, and economic system. Non-cooperation was therefore more extensive and widespread in its application, and this led Gandhi to believe that it was capable of stopping a government from functioning (Mukherjee and Ramaswamy 1998: 120).

A *satyāgrahi*, according to Gandhi, should have high ideals. To transform himself into an impersonal force, a moral power for removing injustice and transforming relationships, a *satyāgrahi* must discipline himself vigorously for a long time. He must purify himself and purge himself of the last vestiges of immorality. He must impose on himself the five vows – *satya*, *ahiṃsā*, *asteya*, *aparigraha*, and *brahmacharya*. Such vows constitute the minimum *yama*, that is, moral restraint, without which no one is qualified to be a *satyāgrahi* (Bandyopadhyaya 2000: 221).

The various forms of action for organising *satyāgraha* can be divided into five broad categories: 1) fasting, 2) non-cooperation (including strikes), 3) civil disobedience, 4) defiance of violence, and 5) self-imposed suffering other than fasting. All the *satyāgraha* movements, Gandhi and his followers performed fall under at least one of these five categories. However, the classifications remain too vague and intractable unless accompanied by a classification based on the number of people participating in a particular act of *satyāgraha* and its area of operation (Bandyopadhyaya 2000: 228). Accordingly, there can be individual *satyāgraha*, group *satyāgraha*, mass *satyāgraha*, national *satyāgraha*, and even *satyāgraha* at the international level. In a particular form of *satyāgraha*, some, but not all the methods/techniques may be applied. An individual *satyāgrahi* may resort to fasting, defiance of violence, or civil disobedience. But in group *satyāgraha*, the people may defy violence, undertake self-imposed suffering, and resort to civil disobedience or non-cooperation. In mass *satyāgraha*, when many people from different social backgrounds are involved, strategies like non-cooperation and civil disobedience may be employed. For the mass to participate in a *satyāgraha*, strict moral training is required. The leader of the mass *satyāgraha* is to impose discipline and moral restrictions on the people. Gandhi and some of his ardent followers had organised several mass *satyāgraha* to fight injustice and resolve conflicts for ushering in social change.

However, though Gandhi believed *satyāgraha* could also be a technique for a nation facing external aggression (i.e. national *satyāgraha*), there has not been a single instance so far where it has been applied in practice. But Gandhi articulated his view of national defense through non-violence during the Second World War. *Satyāgraha* can also be extended to the international arena. Conflict between countries can be peacefully settled in some international forum. Gandhi was firm in his conviction that any conflict or crisis, whatever its nature or dimension, can be resolved by the method of *satyāgraha*. It can be an effective means to solve any human problem.

The *satyāgrahas* Gandhi organised in South Africa and India were broad social movements involving thousands of people. If we expect that all those people will possess the moral qualities for participation in *satyāgraha*, that will be impossible and impracticable. We should, in this context, keep in mind that there is a difference between an absolute and a workable ideal. The leader of a *satyāgraha* movement must accept the requisite ideals, but the masses should try to follow the leader and make possible efforts to inculcate these ideas. Thus, what is required for a leader is not strictly required for a common man joining in a *satyāgraha* movement. However, the common man must adhere to the ideals of non-violent action. History shows that on several occasions, Gandhi called off *satyāgraha* movements when they deviated from the moral path, even though if a movement was at its peak. Gandhi faced a lot of criticism for it, but he never compromised with his ideals.

However, we should keep in mind that *satyāgraha* is not the panacea to resolve all conflicts, as Gandhi thought. Its success depended on the nature of the social structure and political system to a large extent. For example, a liberal sociopolitical system with systematic adversaries will be more conducive for *satyāgraha* to be successful. In social organisation, Gandhi gave utmost priority to *satyāgraha* for establishing justice. In this Gandhian framework, *satyāgraha* becomes the only means of social control. But such generalisation is founded not on objective truth but on emotional belief.

Yet, notwithstanding these limitations, Gandhi's vision of *satyāgraha* is a novel one. It has opened up many dimensions to develop non-violent and peaceful solutions to many human problems. To Gandhi, non-violent *satyāgraha* was the main instrument or means to attain the goal of independence from alien rule – self-rule, or *swaraj*.

V *Swaraj* and Gandhi's views on State and democracy

The literal meaning of the Sanskrit word *swaraj* is "self-rule" and "self-restraint" (*swa* means "self", and *raj* means "rule"). Gandhi used the term *swaraj* with a definite meaning and significance which usually refers to his vision of India's independence from British colonial rule (Patil 1983: 39). *Swaraj* stresses governance not by a hierarchical government but self-governance through individuals and community-building. The focus is on political decentralisation. Gandhi's concept of *swaraj* emphasised on India discarding British political, economic, bureaucratic, legal, military, and educational systems and institutions. Gandhi used the term *swaraj* for the first time in his writing in 1906 in connection with Shyamji Krishna Verma, an Indian patriot who had risked his profession and security for the sake of *swaraj*. Gandhi gave serious thought to the question of *swaraj* in a series of articles he wrote for the *Indian Opinion* during his return voyage from England to South Africa in 1909 and which appeared subsequently as *Hind swaraj* or "Indian Home Rule". *Hind swaraj* constitutes Gandhi's first blueprint on *swaraj* and conveys a comprehensive notion of the idealistic aspect of his thought.

Swaraj to Gandhi did not mean just the transferring of the colonial British rule, which was power-brokering, favours-driven, bureaucratic, and exploitative in nature, into Indian hands. He warned that such a transfer would be "English rule, just without the Englishman. This is not the *swaraj* I want" (Mishra 2012: 167). The crux of his argument centred on the belief that the British colonial rule in its entirety was inherently unjust, exploitative, and alienating. The real goal of the freedom struggle, to Gandhi, was not only to secure political *azadi* (independence) from Britain but rather to gain true *swaraj* (liberation and self-rule).

Gandhi viewed democracy as more than a system of government; to him it meant promoting both individuality and the self-discipline of the community. Democracy meant settling disputes in a non-violent manner; it required freedom of thought and expression. For Gandhi, democracy was a way of life (Tewari 1971: 225).

Gandhi used the term *swaraj* for both the individual and the nation. By individual *swaraj*, Gandhi meant rule over oneself and control over lust for man cannot rule over himself without conquering the lust within him. Rule over all without rule over oneself is deceptive and disappointing. The great mission in life cannot be fulfilled without rule over the self (Patil 1983: 39). Gandhi used the term "national *swaraj*" in a wider sense. For him, national *swaraj* meant national self-rule in political, social, economic, and moral fields.

Although the term *swaraj* means "self-rule", Gandhi gave it the content of an integral revolution that encompasses all spheres of life. At the individual level, *swaraj* is vitally connected with the capacity for dispassionate self-assessment, ceaseless self-purification, and growing self-reliance. Politically, *swaraj* is self-government and not good government. For Gandhi, good government is no substitute for self-government. In other words, it is sovereignty of the people based on pure moral authority. Economically, *swaraj* means full economic freedom for the toiling masses. In its fullest sense, *swaraj* is much more than freedom from all restraints; it is self-rule and self-restraint.

Swaraj is a kind of individualist anarchism. It warrants a Stateless society. According to Gandhi, the overall impact of the State on the people is harmful; he viewed the State as a "soulless machine" which ultimately does the greatest harm to mankind. A non-violent State is like an "ordered anarchy" (Chakraborty

2006: 138). In a society of mostly non-violent individuals, those who are violent will sooner or later accept discipline or leave the community, stated Gandhi. He emphasised a society where individuals believed more in learning about their duties and responsibilities, not demanding rights and privileges. Gandhi believed *swaraj* could not only be attained with non-violence, but it could also be run with non-violence. A military is unnecessary because any aggressor can be thrown out using the method of non-violent non-cooperation. While a military is unnecessary in a nation organised upon the principle of *swaraj*, Gandhi added that a police force is necessary, given human nature. However, the State would limit the use of force by the police to the minimum, aiming for their use as a restraining weapon.

Adopting *swaraj* means implementing a system whereby the State machinery is virtually nil, and the real power directly resides in the hands of the people. This philosophy rests inside an individual who must learn to be the master of his own self and spreads upwards to the level of his community, which must be dependent only on itself. In such a State (where *swaraj* has been achieved), everyone is his own ruler. He rules himself in such a manner that he is never a hindrance to his neighbours. It is *swaraj* when we learn to rule ourselves.

Gandhi wanted all those who believed in *swaraj*: 1) to reject and wholly uproot the British *raj* (rule) from within themselves and their communities and 2) to regenerate new reference points, systems, and structures that enable individual and collective self-development. This regeneration was to grow from the strengths, perspectives, wisdom, and experiences of people living in villages in India, rather than in cities in Britain, America, and even in India for that matter. This is where Gandhi's most significant concept of *gram swaraj* comes in.

VI *Gram swaraj* (village republic)

Gandhi opined that to serve our villages is to establish *swaraj*. In a series of articles in *Young India* and *Harijan* he elaborated this idea. Gandhi stated that if the village perishes, India will perish too. There will be no more India. Her own mission in the world will get lost. We must make a choice between the India of the villages, which are as ancient as herself, and the India of the cities, which are a creation of foreign domination. Today, the cities dominate and drain the villages so that they are crumbling to ruin. Cities must subserve villages when that domination goes. The exploitation of villages is itself an organised violence. If we want *swaraj* to be built on non-violence, we will have to give the villages their proper place, argued Gandhi.

Gandhi's idea of *gram swaraj* is that it is a complete republic, independent of its neighbours for its own vital wants; yet interdependent on many others in which dependence is a necessity. Thus, every village's primary concern will be to grow its own food crops and cotton for its cloth. It should have a reserve for its cattle and recreation and playgrounds for adults and children. Then, if there is more land available, it will grow useful money crops, excluding ganja, tobacco, opium, and the like. The village will maintain a village theatre, a school, and a public hall. It will have its own waterworks ensuring a clean water supply.

Education will be compulsory up to the final basic course. As far as possible, every activity will be conducted on a cooperative basis. Non-violence, with its technique of *satyāgraha*, and non-cooperation will be the sanction of the village community.

Gandhi identified some basic principles of *gram swaraj*. Those are as follows: 1) *Supremacy of man* – the end to be sought is human happiness combined with full mental and moral growth. This end can be achieved through decentralisation. 2) *Physical labour* – such labour is the highest form of sacrifice. Return to the village means a definite voluntary recognition of the duty of body labour and all it connotes. 3) *Equality* – equitable distribution of resources. Economic equality is the master key to non-violent independence. 4) *Trusteeship* – at the root of the concept of equal distribution must lie that of the trusteeship of the wealthy for superfluous wealth possessed by them. 5) *Decentralisation* – Gandhi believed that if India is to evolve along non-violent lines, it will have to decentralise its social, economic, and political structures. 6) *Swadeshi* – it is that spirit in us which restricts us to the use and service of the British and to promote our own. Every village of India should emerge almost as a self-supporting and self-contained unit, exchanging only such necessary commodities with other villages as are not locally producible. A true champion of *swadeshi* will not express ill will towards a foreigner. *Swadeshi* is not a cult of hatred; it is a doctrine of selfless service that has its roots in the purest *ahiṃsā*, that is, love. 7) *Self-sufficiency* – the unit of society should be a village – a manageable small group of people who would, in the ideal, be self-sufficient (in the matter of their vital requirements) as a unit. Every village must be self-sustained and capable of managing its affairs, even to the extent of defending itself against the whole world. 8) *Panchayati raj* – the government of the village will be conducted by the *Panchayat* of five persons annually elected by the adult villagers, male and female, possessing minimum prescribed qualifications. This *Panchayat* will be the legislature, executive, and judiciary combined to operate for its year of office.

Gandhi recommended two moral weapons for dismantling the existing society and for reconstructing the *swaraj* State: 1) *satyāgraha* and 2) constructive programme. Along with the fight against the civil practices and institutions, Gandhi emphasised on new constructive programmes, like village industries, *khadi*, the unity of religions, the removal of untouchability, a new educational system, a new economic order, a society free from diseases, and so on (Patil 1983: 42–43).

Gandhi, as per his own claim, was a practical idealist. Apart from the idealist aspect of *swaraj* to which he was deeply committed, he had a knack for a practical, utilitarian approach to *swaraj*. Those were expressed in course of his struggle for *swaraj* from 1920 to 1947 and his vision about it after independence. The concept of *swaraj* holds the key to Gandhi's political philosophy. This is not to minimise the significance of other concepts, such as non-violence, *satyagrāha*, and *sarvodaya*. It simply means that the importance and effectiveness of these concepts cannot be fully grasped unless they are located within the paradigm of the concept of *swaraj*. In the following section, we will discuss Gandhian *sarvodaya*.

VII Gandhian *sarvodaya*

Sarvodaya is a Sanskrit word comprising two terms: *sarva* (all) and *udaya* (upliftment). Thus, the etymological meaning of *sarvodaya* is the uplifting/well-being of all, or universal welfare (Chetty 1991: 46). Gandhi first coined the term as the title of his 1908 translation of John Ruskin's essay on political economy – *Unto This Last*. Gandhi used the term for the ideal of his own political philosophy. The ideal was to be achieved by unceasing service to humanity. *Sarvodaya* represents Gandhi's ideal social order. Its basis is all-embracing love. By bringing about a country-wide decentralisation of both political and economic powers, *sarvodaya* provides opportunity for the all-round development of the individual and the society.

Sarvodaya implies the participation of all kinds of people. It also stands for the total blossoming of all the faculties – physical, mental, and spiritual – of the human being. It is an activity in which all may partake and in which all must partake if it is to amount to a full realisation of the human faculties of the human soul (Sharma 1960: 259).

Sarvodaya connotes that all are to be equal members of the social order, all sharing in the produce of their labour, the strong protecting the weak and functioning as their trustees and protectors, each promoting the welfare of all according to their abilities and through all the means at their disposal. *Sarvodaya* is a peaceful and non-violent way of achieving social justice. It is founded on the assurance of meeting basic essential needs and freedoms – physical and moral – of the humblest *antyodaya* (individual last in the line). Gandhi felt strongly that the best foundation on which societies should be built were the qualities of truth, love, and compassion in both our personal and public lives. The theory of trusteeship; the elimination of exploitation in every shape or form; and a classless society, securing the welfare of all without any distinction of race, religion, sex, or political affiliation, are the hallmarks of the *sarvodaya* society, Gandhi envisioned. *Sarvodaya* is both an ideal vision and a praxis action programme for the welfare of all. These two aspects of *sarvodaya* are complementary: as an ideal, it sets sublime goals and inspires people to engage in an action programme to achieve the goals.

Sarvodaya cannot be seen in isolation from Gandhi's other ideas; rather its significance becomes even clearer when it is viewed in the whole spectrum of Gandhi's vision, his worldview. *Sarvodaya* occupies the central place in Gandhi's worldview. The way of life Gandhi practiced in the *ashramas* he founded was known as *sarvodaya* – the well-being of all. The aim of these *ashramas* were "plain living and high thinking", where the well-being of all men could be secured. Through this ideal, Gandhi envisioned the rise of India, which in turn could become a light to other nations. Though Gandhi aimed to uplift Indians, as an advocate of the *sarvodaya* ideal, he never harboured any ill will against the people of other countries. His patriotism and nationalism never made him a sectarian in comprehending Indian welfare at the expense of the rest of the world. It was by serving Indian people that Gandhi aimed at serving the whole of mankind (Chetty 1991: 48).

Gandhi's concept of *sarvodaya* is based on three basic principles:

1   The good of the individual is contained in the good of all.
2   A lawyer's work has the same value as the barber's in as much as all have the same right of earning their livelihood from their work.
3   A life of a labour, that is, the life of the tiller of the soil and the handicraftsman is a life worth living.

Gandhi's vision of a *sarvodaya* socio-economic order was a non-violent, non-exploitative, humanistic, and egalitarian society. This was his vision of the ideal socio-economic order, in the context of which he formulated his economic ideas and principles. The basic components of Gandhian *sarvodaya* include *swadeshi*, bread-labour, *aparigraha* of non-possession, trusteeship, non-exploitation, and *samabhava* (sense of equality). Gandhi's idea of *sarvodaya* has the following characteristics:

1   There will be no centralised authority, and there will be political and economic decentralisation in the villages.
2   Politics will not be the instrument of power but an agency of service, and *rajnīti* will yield place to *loknīti*.
3   All people will be imbued with the spirit of love, fraternity, truth, non-violence, and self-sacrifices.
4   There will be no party systems or majority rule, and the society will be free from the evil of the tyranny of the majority.
5   The *sarvodaya* society is based on equality and liberty; there is no room in it for unwholesome competition, exploitation, or class hatred.
6   There will be no private property, exploitation, or source of social distinctions and hatred.
7   The *sarvodaya* movement is based on truth, non-violence, and self-denial.

Gandhi's concept of *sarvodaya* thus envisages a new humanistic socialist society. Man will be the centre of such a society. Unless the individual cultivates values like love, sincerity, truth, an abiding sympathy, etc., the emergence of a new society will only remain a pious dream. In this process of change, the State has little role to play. The State can, at best, effect change at the level of the external behaviour of man. It fails to influence the inner springs of life.

Sarvodaya visualises a simple, non-violent, and decentralised society. In such a society, the people are endowed with real power. Democracy becomes meaningful and assumes significance only when its structure is reared on the foundation of village *Panchayats*. The idea of *sarvodaya* contains the contents of egalitarianism.

Gandhi's '*sarvodaya* economic model' was quite different from the model of socialism championed and followed in independent India by Pandit Jawaharlal

Nehru. Though the objective of both was to eradicate poverty and do away with unemployment, the Gandhian approach of economic development preferred adapting technology and infrastructure to suit the local situation, in contrast to Nehru's large-scale, socialised, State-owned enterprises (Bhatt 1982: 85). To Gandhi, the economic philosophy that aims at the "greatest good for the greatest number" was fundamentally flawed, and his alternative concept of *sarvodaya* set its aim at the "greatest good for all". Gandhi challenged Nehru and the modernisers in the late 1930s who called for rapid industrialisation on the Soviet model, and he denounced the model as dehumanising and contrary to the needs of the villages, where the great majority of the people lived (Chakraborty 1992: 275). While disagreeing with Nehru about the socialist economic model, Gandhi also criticised capitalism, which was driven by endless wants and a materialistic view of man. To Gandhi, both socialism and capitalism were wrong, in part because both focused exclusively on a materialistic view of man and because the former deified the State with unlimited power of violence, while the later deified capital. He believed that a better economic system is one which does not impoverish one's culture and spiritual pursuits (Parekh 1991: 133).

Gandhi's ideals have lasted well beyond the gaining of India's independence (*swaraj*). His followers in India continued working to promote the kind of society he envisioned. Their efforts have come to be known as the *sarvodaya* movement. The *sarvodaya* movement has its target the establishment of a whole network of self-supporting village communities. Agriculture will be so planned that all people will have enough to consume. Industry will be conducted on a cottage basis until all the people in the village are gainfully employed. The needs of the village will be determined by the people of the village themselves, through village councils representative of the whole village. Gandhi's followers Vinoba Bhave, J. P. Narayan, Dada Dharmadhikari, Dhirendra Mazumdar, and others undertook various projects aimed at encouraging popular self-organisation during the 1950s and 1960s, including the *bhoodan* and *gramdan* movements. Many groups descended from these networks continue to function in India today.

To sum, *sarvodaya* is the application of the principle of non-violence in the transformation of societies from their present forms – which are mostly exploitative and disfavour the most disadvantaged – towards more balanced, inclusive, and egalitarian forms which could be enshrined in the principle of social justice for all. Gandhi's vision of *sarvodaya* embraced a holistic approach to life and remains one of his major and distinctive contributions to India.

Gandhi's penchant for the construction of an indigenous brand of politico-economic theory resulted in the structuring of a specific path of development suited to the requirements of his country. Perhaps for this reason, he was not much attracted either towards the capitalist or the socialist model of development. He was not, therefore, a doctrinaire economist (Kapoor 1993: 2). Gandhi's economic ideas were part of his general crusade against poverty, exploitation, socio-economic injustice, and deteriorating moral standards. Gandhi propounded this socio-economic philosophy with his theory of trusteeship.

VIII Gandhian theory of trusteeship

Trusteeship provides a means by which the wealthy people will be the trustees of trusts that looked after the welfare of the people in general. Gandhi believed that the wealthy people could be persuaded to part with their wealth to help the poor. Gandhi's concept of trusteeship was based on the teachings of *Ishopanishad*, which states that one is asked to dedicate everything to God and then use it only to the required extent. The principal condition laid down in it is that one must not covet what belongs to others. In other words, in the first instance, everything must be surrendered to God and then out of it one may use only that which is necessary for the service of God's creation, according to one's strict needs. The spirit of this doctrine is detachment and service. Gandhi's idea of trusteeship emerged from his faith in the law of non-possession. It was founded on his religious belief that everything belonged to God and was from God. Therefore, the bounties of the world were for his people as a whole, not for any particular individual. When an individual has more than his respective portion, he becomes a trustee of that portion for God's people. Man should live his life day to day without trying to store things for the future. If this principle had been imbibed by people in general, it would have become legalised, and trusteeship would have become a legalised institution.

The centre of Gandhian economic thought is man. He gave importance to the development and uplifting of human life and social values rather than raising higher standards of living. Fundamental ethical values, therefore, had an upper hand in his economic ideas. The concept of trusteeship reflects Gandhi's efforts towards spiritualising economics. Gandhi owes the concept of trusteeship to his studies of the *Gītā* the *Bible*, books on jurisprudence, Snell's *Principles of Equity*, and Ruskin's *Unto This Last* (Kapoor 1993: 4). The development of Gandhi's idea of trusteeship spread through three phases. The first phase was reached when Gandhi returned to India from South Africa. The second phase came during 1934–1946, and the third and last phase ranges between 1946 and 1947.

According to Gandhi, trusteeship was the only ground on which he could work out an ideal combination of economics and morals. In concrete form, the basic principles of trusteeship can be identified as follows:

1 Trusteeship provides a means of transforming the present capitalist order of society into an egalitarian one. It is based on the faith that human nature is never beyond redemption.
2 It does not recognise any right of private property except so far as it may be permitted by society for its own welfare.
3 It does not exclude legislation of the ownership and use of wealth.
4 Thus, under State-regulated trusteeship, an individual will not be free to hold or use his wealth for selfish satisfaction in disregard to the interests of the society.
5 Just as it is proposed to give a decent minimum living wage, a limit should be fixed for the maximum income that would be allowed to any person in society.

6   The character of production will be determined by social necessity and not by personal greed.

Gandhi had great faith in the goodness and perfectibility of man. He favoured the idea that society should be built on need and not on greed, as there is no limit to greed, but there is a limit to our need. He wanted the society to be built on the basic principle that each one of us should work according to his capacity and should receive things according to his needs. Gandhi's idea of trusteeship can be considered in a holistic manner. Once the idea of trusteeship grips the society, then the whole idea of philanthropy and gifts would disappear from the society. A trustee would never entertain the feeling that he has given away something of his own, as he would never have the feeling of exclusive ownership of his property. He would never take himself more than a trustee. Gandhi categorically stated that trusteeship was not philanthropy. Philanthropy is an act of charity by the riches; usually the purpose behind philanthropy is self-glorification. Trusteeship calls for renunciation with the surrender of ownership. Thus the element of attitude is crucial in trusteeship. A trustee is one who holds property or wealth in trust for others who are identified as beneficiaries.

Gandhi envisioned a new industrial relationship in the economic arena. In fact, his trusteeship principle was to keep power (any kind of power) in check. It is not only material possessions or physical labour which produces wealth and power. There is "special talent" (such as that of an artist) which a man or woman has acquired at birth, and such talents make him/her wealthy and powerful. Material wealth can be distributed equally, but what about these talents which also result into power and wealth and their unequal distribution? According to Gandhi, the man with extraordinary talents should hold his talents in trust for society. The man must be ready to share the fruits of his talents with his neighbours, as per the principle of trusteeship. Thus, Gandhi's concept of trusteeship embraced not only material possessions (amenable to equal distribution) but non-material possessions (not amenable to equal distribution) too.

Gandhi, however, did not think of the institution of trusteeship to be imposed by law. To him, it would be against the principle of non-violence. Any law, Gandhi opined, should be sanctioned by the people only. If trusteeship is to be developed, the people's minds need to accept it first; hence an atmosphere of acceptance needs to be created first. When such an atmosphere is created, the State may adopt the statute, giving legal recognition to the institution of trusteeship. To create such an atmosphere, the process may be commenced at the *Panchayat* level, where it may be easier to garner acceptances of the idea.

Gandhi's theory of trusteeship was not conceived as a compromise to enable the rich and the working classes to work together during the struggle for India's independence. It was not a compromise with the rich to the poor. It evolved as an integral part of the theory and dynamics of a non-violent revolution in the field of economic relations. Gandhi, therefore, claimed that his theory of trusteeship was no makeshift or camouflage. He was sure that it would survive even when other theories were proved wanting and discarded.

The concept of a trusteeship economy, which Gandhi built up systematically, was a pioneering effort on his part. His emphasis was on idealism and the innate goodness of human beings, the social concern, the fierce determination, and unshakable dedication which could bring about a socio-economic order somewhat superior to the acquisitiveness of the private enterprise, and the all-powerful democratic socialism in which the individual was scarified at the altar of the State. Thus, Gandhi's notion of trusteeship was an economic thought in itself that differed significantly from both capitalism and socialism – it was a non-violent alternative (Kapoor 1993: 5).

IX Gandhi's critique of modern civilisation

Gandhi condemned modern civilisation not because it was Western or scientific, but because it was materialistic and exploitative. Speaking to the Meccano Club, Calcutta, in August 1925, he said:

> Do not for one moment consider that I condemn all that is Western. For the time being, I am dealing with the predominant character of modern civilisation, do not call it Western civilisation and the predominant character of modern civilisation is exploitation of the weaker races of the Earth. The predominant character of modern civilisation is to dethrone God and enthrone Materialism. I have not hesitated to use the word '*Satan*'. I have not hesitated to call this system of Government under which we are labouring as *Satanic*.
>
> *(Gandhi 1968b: 23)*

On several occasions Gandhi clarified that he was not opposed to science or machinery as such. Far from opposing the progress of science, he admired the modem scientific spirit of the West and maintained that the world needs the marvellous advances in science and organisation that the Western nations have made. One of the basic errors of the Western, post-Enlightenment modernity, he said, was the exploitation of "the weaker races of the earth" and the destruction of the "lower orders of creation" in the name of science and humanism. Modern civilisation, Gandhi said, is based on a faulty concept or model of man as a materialistic or body-centred, limitless consumer of utilities. Such a view of man places sensual or materialistic wants over spiritual or moral values. It regards the individuals as wholly independent or self-centred atoms with no moral or spiritual bonds or obligation. Acting as infinite consumers of utilities, modern, or rather modernist, persons resort to the mechanised or industrial production of articles which are meant not for immediate use but for exchange between town and village and between metropolis and colony. In this exchange, the town and metropolis gain at the expense of the village and the colony. Industrialisation on a mass scale, wrote Gandhi, "will necessarily lead to passive or active exploitation of the villagers as the problems of competition and marketing come in" (Gandhi 1968b: 23). On another occasion, Gandhi wrote, "Europeans pounce upon new territories like crows upon a piece of meat. I am inclined to think that this is due to their mass-production factories" (Gandhi 1968b: 23).

In Gandhi's opinion, modern civilisation seeks to increase our "bodily comforts" through better houses, better clothes, faster modes of travel and transport, mechanised production, etc. These, however, have failed to bring happiness to the people. On the contrary, they have brought about newer diseases, dehumanisation of workers, and more efficient and large-scale means of the destruction of life. In his words:

> Men were made slaves under physical compulsion. Now they are enslaved by temptation of money and of the luxuries that money can buy. There are now diseases of which people never dreamt before. This civilisation takes note neither of morality character nor of religion. Civilisation seeks to increase bodily comforts, and it fails miserably even in doing so.
> *(Gandhi 1968 b: 23)*

Divorced from ethics or morality, the modern self or the individual is left to the play of self-interest, greed, competition, exploitation, brute force, and violence. Modern man feels no moral or spiritual restraints in conquering or colonising other peoples. Imperialism and fascism were to Gandhi the mere political expressions of the *satanic* character of modern civilisation.

X Conclusion

Mohandas Karamchand Gandhi stated that his own life was his message. It was undoubtedly a great life intensely lived at many different levels. A religious man in his personal life, Gandhi was also a great social reformer, one of the greatest political activists the world has ever seen, and a social and political thinker who was profoundly disturbed by the inadequacies of contemporary social organisation and values (Bandyopadhyaya 2000: 3). All his life, Gandhi had striven so that power would eventually come within the grasp of the masses. He proposed the acceptance and practice of truth, non-violence, vegetarianism, *brahmacharya* (celibacy), simplicity, and faith in God. Gandhi's aim had been to fashion out of non-violence an instrument by means of which even ordinary men and women could, by collective enterprise, gain and preserve their freedom. And through such endeavour, each of those who participated would become individually more and more perfect (Bose 1972: 298). Though Gandhi would be remembered forever as the man who fought for India's independence, his greatest legacies are the tools and techniques he used in his fight against the British rule.

Gandhi's life and teachings inspired many who specifically referred to him as their mentor or who dedicated their lives in spreading his ideas. In Europe,

Romain Rolland was the first to talk about Gandhi in his 1924 book *Mahatma Gandhi*. Brazilian anarchist and feminist Maria Lacerda de Moura wrote about Gandhi in her work on pacifism, entitled, *Serviço militar obrigatório para mulher? Recuso-me! Denuncio!*. In 1931, Albert Einstein exchanged letters with Gandhi in which Einstein addressed Gandhi as a role model for future generations. We conclude by citing what Einstein said of Gandhi:

> Mahatma Gandhi's life achievement stands unique in political history (of the world). He has invented a completely new and humane means for the liberation war of an oppressed country, and practiced it with greatest energy and devotion. The moral influence he had on the consciously thinking human being of the entire civilised world will probably be much more lasting than it seems in our time with its overestimation of brutal violent forces. Because lasting will only is the work of such statesmen who wake up and strengthen the moral power of their people through their example and educational works. We may all be happy and grateful that destiny gifted us with such an enlightened contemporary, a role model for the generations to come. Generations to come will scarce believe that such a one as this walked the earth in flesh and blood.
>
> *(Cited in Kumar 2008: 65)*

References

Bandyopadhyaya, Jayantanuja (2000). *Social and Political Thought of Gandhi*. Calcutta: Manuscript India.

Bhatt, V. V. (1982). Development Problem, Strategy, and Technology Choice: Sarvodaya and Socialist Approaches in India. *Economic Development and Cultural Change*, 31(1), pp. 85–99.

Bose, Nirmal Kumar (1972). *Studies in Gandhism*. Ahmedabad: Navajivan Publishing House.

Byrne, Donn (1984). *Mahatma Gandhi: The Man and His Message*. Bombay: Orient Longman.

Chakraborty, Bidyut (1992). Jawaharlal Nehru and Planning, 1938–1941: India at the Crossroads. *Modern Asian Studies*, 26(2), pp. 275–287.

Chakraborty, Bidyut (2006). *Social and Political Thought of Mahatma Gandhi*. New Delhi: Routledge.

Chetty, Rathnam K. M. (1991). *Sarvodaya and Freedom: A Gandhian Appraisal*. New Delhi: Discovery Publishing House.

Gandhi, Mahatma (1920). *Swaraj in One Year*. Young India, 22 September, Vol. II, No. 38, pp. 1–8.

Gandhi, Mahatma (1968a). *The Selected Works of Mahatma Gandhi*. Shriman Narayan (Ed.). Ahmedabad: Navajivan Publishing House,

Gandhi, Mahatma (1968b). *The Collected Works of Mahatma Gandhi*. Vol. XXVIII (August–November 1925). Ahmedabad: Navajivan Trust.

Gandhi, Rajmohan (2010). *Gandhi: The Man, His People and the Empire*. London: Haus Publishing Ltd.

Kapoor, Archna (1993). *Gandhi's Trusteeship, Concept and Relevance.* New Delhi: Deep and Deep Publications.

Kumar, Ravindra (2008). *Gandhian Thought: New World, New Dimensions.* Delhi: Kalpaz Publications.

Mishra, Anil (2012). *Reading Gandhi.* New Delhi: Pearson.

Mukherjee, Subrata and Ramaswamy Sushila (Eds.) (1998). *Non-violence and Satyagraha.* New Delhi: Deep and Deep Publications.

Parekh, Bhikhu (1991). *Gandhi's Political Philosophy: A Critical Examination.* London: Palgrave Macmillan.

Parekh, Bhikhu (2001). *Gandhi: A Very Short Introduction.* New Delhi: Oxford University Press.

Parel, Anthony J. (2002). Gandhi and Tolstoy. In M. P. Malthai et al. (Eds.), *Meditations on Gandhi.* New Delhi: Concept publishing House.

Patil, S. H. (1983). *Gandhi and Swaraj.* New Delhi: Deep and Deep Publications.

Sharma, B. S. (1960). The Philosophical Basis of Sarvodaya. *Gandhi Marg,* 4(3), July.

Tendulkar, D. G. (1951). *Mahatma: Life of Mohandas Karamchand Gandhi.* New Delhi: Ministry of Information and Broadcasting, Government of India.

Tewari, S. M. (1971). The Concept of Democracy in the Political Thought of Mahatma Gandhi. *Indian Political Science Review,* 6(2).

13

VINOBA BHAVE

Suratha Kumar Malik

> Talks on the *Gītā is the story of my life, and it is also my message.*
> – Vinoba Bhave, *Talks on the Gītā*, translated and published
> by Dr Parag Cholkar, Paramdham Prakashan, Pavnar, Wardha

I Introduction

Vinoba Bhave is one of the great thinkers and reformers of India and a source of national pride. He was a man who struggled against evil and turned ills into good. A spiritual visionary with a practical position and with utmost respect for the poor and the law of the country, Bhave's knowledge and ability was to a degree of excellence. His life was full of heroic deeds and dedication, and he was a man of spiritualism, non-violence, love, and human values. As an avid acolyte and follower of Mahatma Gandhi, Bhave's life is his message because he practised what he preached. He was a freedom fighter, a non-violence activist, a spiritual teacher, and a great social reformer. As an ardent believer in Gandhi's philosophy, he preached the doctrine of equality and non-violence. For the poor and downtrodden, he dedicated his total life and struggled for their rights. Like a *sanyasi* (saint), he led an ascetic life of spiritualism and simple living. In addition to being a champion of the non-violence struggle, he is also recognised for his *bhoodan* (gift of land) and *gramdan* movements (gift of village).

In 1958, for community leadership, Bhave received the international Ramon Magsaysay Award, and in 1983, posthumously, he was conferred with the *Bharat Ratna* (India's highest civilian award). He was a brilliant scholar who could bring accessible knowledge to ordinary people. As S. Radhakrishnan pointed out, "Indeed his life represents harmonious blend of learning, spiritual perception and compassion for the lowly and the lost" (cited in Agrawal 2008: 282). Bhave dedicated his life to establish an equal and just society. His *bhoodan* movement, which he started on 18 April 1951, attracted the attention of the world. In fact, his life remains a heroic tale of his struggle for equality and justice, his love for human values, and his belief in truth and non-violence. He is considered the national teacher of India and the spiritual successor of Mahatma Gandhi.

II Life sketch

On 11 September 1895, in a small village called Gagoji (present-day Gagode Budruk) in Kolaba in the Konkan region of what is now Maharashtra, Vinayaka Narahari Bhave, otherwise known as Acharya Vinoba Bhave, was born into a *Brāhmin* family. He was the eldest son of Rukmini Devi and Narahari Shambhu Rao. Vinayak (affectionately called Vinya) had three brothers and one sister. His father, a trained weaver, worked in Baroda. Bhave was much influenced by his mother, who was a spiritual lady. At a very tender age, he was much inspired from the *Bhagavadgītā* (the religious scripture of Hindus). At a young age, he was also interested in the writings of Maharashtra's saints and philosophers and was profoundly interested in the core learning, especially mathematics. His thirst for knowledge was not limited to routine course work. His college life remained full of internal agitation and uneasiness. In March 1916, on his way to Mumbai for the intermediate examination, he put all his school and college certificates in a fire. He then decided to travel to Varanasi (called Benaras or Kashi) instead of Mumbai. The decision was prompted by his hankering for spiritualism and to attain the all-pervading and imperishable *Brahmā* (supreme soul).

Bhave was attracted by the news that Gandhi was going to speak at Banaras Hindu University. Immediately, he wrote a letter to Mahatma Gandhi, and Gandhi advised him during a personal meeting at Kochrab *ashram* in Ahmedabad. The meeting changed Bhave's course of life. His first experience with Gandhi was unique, and he found within Gandhi a great soul. In Bhave's words, "providence took me to Gandhi and I found in him not only the peace of the Himalayas but also the burning fervour of resolution, typical of Bengal. I said to myself that both of my desires had been fulfilled" (cited in Agrawal 2008: 283). Then, Bhave participated in the activities of Gandhi's *ashram*, and slowly the adherence and attachment between Gandhi and Bhave grew stronger. Bhave started studying, teaching, spinning, and ameliorating the life of the community and other activities in the *ashram*.

On 8 April 1921, Gandhi asked Bhave to take charge of the *ashram* at Wardha. He published a monthly called *Maharashtra Dharma* in Marathi in 1923, and it included his essays on the *Upaniṣhads*. This monthly became a weekly and continued for three years, during which time his writings on the *Abhangas* of Sant Tukaram (a saint poet) went popular. With the tide of time, Bhave's quest for spiritualism took him to new heights, and his engagement with Gandhi's constructive programmes relating to village industries, *khadi*, new education (the *nai talim* scheme or Wardha scheme), and hygiene and sanitation also kept on heightening. With the idea of supporting himself by spinning alone, he shifted to Nalwadi (a village about two miles from Wardha) on 23 December 1932. But, in 1938, he shifted to what he called *Paramdham Ashram* in Paunar, where he became sick. Throughout this period, Bhave's engagement in the freedom struggle remained dynamic, and he spent some time in jail. Bhave utilised his jail period for writing and reading. In the Dhulia jail, he checked the proofs of his book *Gitai* (Marathi translation of *Gītā*). He also gave lectures to his fellow colleagues in the jail about *Gītā* which were compiled by Sane Guruji and later published as a book. The book *Swarajya Shastra* and other *Bhajans* (religious songs) of saint Eknath, Gyaneshwar, and Namdev were completed while Bhave was in jail. *Sthitaprajna Darshan* and *Ishavasyavritti* were written in the Seoni jail and the Nagpur jail respectively. He learnt four south Indian languages and created the *Lok Nagari* script at the Vellore jail. Bhave himself had written several books, the most important of which are *Ishavasyavritti*, *Swarajya Shastra*, and *Steadfast Wisdom*. His works include diverse aspects of education, religion, and philosophy and are approachable to the common masses. His competency was profound and was reflected in his editing work of *Sevak* (in Marathi) and *Maharashtra Dharma Sarvodaya* (in Hindi). Bhave was a versatile polyglot, and he had command of more than 15 languages, including Arabic, French, and English.

Rajendra Prasad, Jawaharlal Nehru, and other Gandhian followers had met at Sevagram in March 1948. There, the idea of *sarvodaya samaj* developed and was accepted by all. But other Gandhian followers did not get Bhave's cooperation because at that time he was engaged in activities that would help to recover from the wounds of the partition in 1947. He started the programmes of *kanchan-mukti* (freedom from dependence on gold, that is, money) and *rishi-kheti* (cultivation without the use of bullocks, as was practiced by *Ṛishis*, i.e. the sages of ancient India) in 1950 (Govindan 1985: 18). He started his peace trek on foot in the violence-prone areas of Telangana (now the separate Telangana State) in April 1951, after attending the *sarvodaya* conference at Shivarampally. In the history of non-violent struggle, a new chapter was created when Bhave started the *bhoodan* movement in Pochampalli (Telangana) on 18 April 1951.

Bhave was very much acquainted with the power and strength of *padayatra* (march on foot). Throughout the country, he walked for 13 years and began his *toofanyatra* (journey with the speed of high-velocity wind) using a vehicle. In July 1965, he started the *toofanyatra* in Bihar, which continued for four years. From September 1952 to December 1954, he also received 23 lakh acres of land during his *padayatra* in Bihar. During his *yatra*, he covered thousands of miles and spoke at thousands of meetings and gatherings and mobilised the people of the country, cutting down the obstacles of class, caste, religion, and language. Even in May 1960, some dacoits from Chambal Valley ceded them to Bhave, and that was the victory of non-violence. Bhave had confidence in the power of the people. To develop a positive spirit and confidence among the people, he initiated several programmes, such as *shanti sena* (army for peace), *sampattidan* (gift of the wealth), *shramdan* (gift of the labour), and *sarvodaya patra* (the pot where every household gives a daily handful of grain).

On 7 June 1966, Bhave declared that he wanted to free himself from outer visibility and wanted to enter the inward world of spiritualism. On 2 November 1969, he returned to Paunar after travelling across India. On 7 October 1970, he announced that he would stay in one place. From 25 December 1974 to 25 December 1975, he observed a prolonged year of silence. He also undertook a fast to stop the slaughter of cows in 1976. On 15 November 1982, he breathed his last breath at his *ashram*, and mother India lost her illustrious son who had been a worshiper of truth and non-violence.

III Views on education

For Bhave, the aim of education is the development of human potentialities and qualities. He was much worried about the problems of education. In his view, there are two problems regarding education; the first is a lack of education, and the second is a lack of quality and value education. So, there is lack of education on one side and a lack of the right kind of education on the other. Education in our country is based on memorisation and the ability to argue. Memorisation focuses on bookish knowledge, which is not the essence and aim of education. True education should reflect other human qualities and the development of human potentialities.

It should be a synthesis between *jñāna* (knowledge) and *karma* (practical training and vocational skills). But, unfortunately, there is no scope for all these qualities in the present education system. After spending 15 years in prolonged study, the students are not skilled and trained in any work-oriented education, such as agriculture or carpentry, and it makes them idle and unproductive without self-reliance and productive skills. So, the person will live in the society without any practical knowledge or preparation for practical living. Education should be related to one's practical life and should not be based on mere memory and fact without any practical use in life. It should be value oriented and life oriented.

Therefore, in Bhave's view, "Our education should be work oriented and work centred, and the teachers and students should do an hour of manual labour chanting Lord's name in mind" (cited in Govindan 1985: 18). Basic education is not practical as long as there remains a gap between physical and mental efforts. Physical training and sports activities must have a place in education as any other subjects have. If so, the present system of education can have tall claims. Basic education is not just a process of teaching; it is a scheme of life (*Sarvodaya* 1958: 4). Independence of thought, fearlessness, and self-control are three tests of education and only that country in which these three qualities find expression is educated. The two tests of education are that it should lead to spiritual development and it should correspond to the situation (Bharathi 1995: 132). Every government tries to control the system of education for its own benefit and ideology, which is dangerous to the spirit of democracy. Bhave held that just as the judiciary is independent and the government has no authority over it, the education department should be free and independent from government intervention as well (ibid.: 134).

Bhave's ideas on education are found in his book *Thoughts on Education*, in which he advocates that the present education system be contrasted with the ancient system found in the *Upaniṣhads*. There is a need to completely overhaul the present system which is commercialised and urban oriented. The present system does not really educate the youth for shouldering the responsibilities of life, nor is a genuine urge for knowledge generated. Education is only bookish; it does not have much relation to the reality of life. Education must train students to think for themselves. The basic education professed by Gandhi and developed by Bhave represents a new philosophy of life. Basic education wants to remove division in the society by removing the difference between manual and mental labour. It tries to imbibe among the students the doctrine of the dignity of labour. A great majority of Indian people live in villages, so the scheme of education should be village oriented.

Education should be informal and include the study of nature and understanding practical problems. Students should actively participate in all aspects of the village economy, such as agriculture, animal husbandry, and other cottage industries. Bhave also recommended the revival of the "wandering teachers" system, the spiritual *gurus* who would wander from village to village preaching ideas of human value. As a matter of policy, Bhave opposed the practice of charging fees for education. He never thought the concept of co-education was a controversial issue. His approach to women's problems is also spiritual. With a pure heart, it should be possible for men and women to carry the task of social service. The concept of *bramhacharya* is a virtue to be followed by all, even in the household.

IV Views on Hinduism

Bhave was an ardent follower and preacher of Hindu *dhārma*. He believed Hinduism gives its followers complete freedom. To Bhave, the essence of Hinduism is that it never forces regular prayer or any kind of strictness and rigid regulation. The Hindu religion is liberal and believes in freedom and different ways of life. It only demands the purification of mind, heart, and soul and emphasises on inner purification. Hindu culture believes in integration, co-opting, inclusion, and assimilation. If it becomes limited and narrow, Bhave argued, it will be destroyed. It is a great liberal religion which exists from time immemorial (*sanatan*) to the present with an amalgamation of knowledge and philosophies. Bhave believed there is no difference between religions; though outward forms of religions are different, in essence, they are similar. Hindu religion and philosophy, which is known as *sanatan dhārma*, believes not only in worshiping God but also worshiping animals, birds, snakes, plants, rivers, and every form and source of energy and nature, like earth, sky, water, fire, sun, moon, river, mountain, etc., for natural equilibrium, which is scientific and environmentally friendly. As compared to Western socialism, India believes in a socialism much beyond and broader than the narrow Western concept. Western socialism believes in equal rights and protection of all human beings, but it is silent about flora and fauna. Hindu culture, on the other hand, treats animals with compassion and even worships animals, like cows and bullocks. It also worships plants and trees, such as tulsi (basil), bael, neem, and banyan.

V Views on religion

Bhave was a deeply religious man in a true sense. He studied and analysed various religious texts, but he was not a bigot. He respected all religions. He had been welcomed by all religious sects. In one place, he commented, there could never be any opposition between two religions. We can only expect opposition of two religions against irreligion. Therefore, his concept of religion is not an outward manifestation but an inward feeling. Though a deep devotee, he never stopped criticising outdated customs. But his criticism was based on rationality, not a hatred of the past.

We find an element of liberalism in Bhave's thoughts on religion. He appears to have been a free thinker and grasped the essence of all religions. At one point, he commented that exclusionist and institutionalised religion only divides people. He valued the core of religion. To Bhave, all religions were but partial embodiments of the truth. Humanism must be the primary religion for the whole of mankind. The only religion is the religion of man, and a foundation of that religion is faith in God. He wanted a new religious structure to be built to give humankind spiritual guidance. He felt that this new religion should have the following assumptions. First, it should not be based on rewards and punishments to be given in the afterlife; in other words, it should only be concerned with the present life. Therefore, Bhave wanted religion to have a direct relation to the present life on earth.

Second, new religion should avoid all inequalities, whether social or economic. Bhave's crusade against the caste hierarchy, which is central to the Hindu religion, is certainly revolutionary. Moreover, he professed this at a time when caste feelings were very strong. Bhave also wanted the new religion to value the dignity of manual labour. This was again a bold attempt to change social attitudes towards the people who were doing the scavenger work. In fact, he himself did that work and wanted all *ashram* people to follow his example.

For Bhave, religion is not a private matter of an individual. It is a social force and encompasses the entire social fabric. Religion should be integral and not partial in its application. It is neither sectarian nor confined to modes of worship. It is a transformation of society. A religious reformer should try to preserve and promote what is good in thought and practice, and he must depreciate the superstitions and blind beliefs and introduce innovations. In his words:

> My reliance is on God alone. I have come here for three things: (i) I want to see, (ii) I want to listen and (iii) I want to love. Whatever power God

has given me to love, I would use it all here, if it falls short, I would beg of him for more. Let us pray to God with all our heart.

(Nargolkar 1966: 50)

VI Non-violence and spiritualism

Following Gandhiji, many educated persons participated in the freedom struggle through non-violent means, but people did not fully adhere to non-violence. Even the constructive programmes which Gandhi introduced as a part of his struggle for independence were not fully followed by people and members of the Congress. Neither the constructive programme nor the means of non-violence were implemented as Gandhiji desired; therefore, the freedom struggle was not totally non-violent. Bhave called it the non-violent of the weak. In such a situation, where people are prone to violence, the lesson of non-violence should impart from the school. The lessons of cultural, social, economic, and spiritual equality should be disseminated from the school. The aim of non-violence is not mere political independence; rather, it should include social and economic independence. Without the development of spirituality and spiritual equality among ourselves, we cannot achieve the goal of non-violence. The practices of truth and non-violence should go hand in hand, where non-violence in its complete sense includes both pure and applied aspects which Gandhiji had applied in his *ashram* life.

In the present time, the schools of our country should create such an environment, because in the changing world, only spirituality and science can save the world. People all over the world are fighting in the name of religion; therefore, spirituality will take precedence over religion. Spiritualism should be celebrated, and it will overcome the barriers of caste, race, language, religion, nationalities, economic and gender inequalities. Man is essentially a spiritual being, and all humans are spiritually one. Therefore, human conscience is the domain of spiritualism. To summarise, there are three things which Bhave preached as far as non-violence and spiritualism are concerned: the positive meaning of non-violence; the achievement of economic, social, and spiritual equality in the context of India; and the global feeling of human conscience towards spiritualism.

VII Association with Gandhi and role in the freedom struggle

Bhave was attracted to the principles and ideologies of Mahatma Gandhi, and he considered Gandhi his *guru*, from both a political and a spiritual point of view. He followed Gandhi's leadership without question. The attachment and bond between the two increased with time, and Bhave involved himself with the Gandhian constructive programme for the service of the country. The relation between Bhave and Gandhi was symbiotic because purity of means and morality were of prime importance for both of them. Both dedicated their lives for the service of the poorest. Jayaprakash Narayan made an apt remark about the relationship between the two when he said:

Revolutionary and path finding thinkers in history have usually been followed by mere interpreters, systematisers and analysts. There have been rare exceptions, such as Luxemburg and Lenin in the case of Marx. Vinoba was such an exception in the case of Gandhi.

(cited in Tandon 1981: IX)

The relation and respect between Gandhi and Bhave can be understood from a letter the former wrote to the latter. An extract from the letter reads:

I do not know how to appreciate you. Your character and love enamour me and also your self-examination. I am not a person to evaluate your worth. I accept your own assessment and assume the position of a father to you.

(cited in Jayapalan 2003: 225)

Vinoba spent the better part of his life in the *ashrams*, carrying out the various programmes designed by Gandhi. His political ideologies were directed towards principles of peaceful non-cooperation to attain freedom. He took part in all the political programmes Gandhi designed. Under Gandhi's influence, Bhave also got involved in the Indian freedom struggle. He took part in programmes of non-cooperation and especially the call for use of *swadeshi* goods instead of foreign imports. He took up the spinning wheel, churning out *khadi* and urged others to do so, as well, resulting in mass production of the fabric. Bhave believed in the necessity of India's political independence. He also believed the real independence of the villager is impossible without the constructive programme, of which *khadi* was at the centre (Sukumaran 1997: 254).

For taking part in the flag *satyāgraha* at Nagpur, Bhave was jailed for months in 1923, at the Akola jail and the Nagda jail. Gandhi sent him to Vaikom (in Kerala) in 1925 to supervise the entry of the *Harijans* to the temple. For raising his voice against the British rule, Bhave was again jailed for six months in 1932. He was chosen as the first individual *satyāgrahi* by Gandhi in 1940. As an individual *satyāgrahi*, during 1940–1941, he was jailed thrice at the Nagpur jail. He was jailed for three months the first time, six months the next time, and for one year the third time. He was introduced to the country by Gandhi on 5 October 1940, when Gandhi had issued a statement about Bhave, making him familiar among the countrymen. Bhave was imprisoned again in 1942 for his participation in the Quit India Movement; his three-year sentence was divided between the Seoni and Vellore jails.

Bhave not only followed Gandhian ideas but also further developed them with his own interpretation and concepts. The Gandhian ideas he developed were as follows:

- Bhave developed Gandhi's critique of parliamentary democracy (in the book *Hind swaraj*) through a systematic critique of communism, capitalism, and the welfare State.

- Bhave advocated the concept of *loknīti* in place of Gandhi's concept of *rajnīti* as an alternative to parliamentary democracy.
- By devising the concept of *bhoodan*, Bhave reinterpreted the Gandhian concept of trusteeship.
- Bhave developed Gandhi's idea of the abolition of State and politics through his concepts of *anushasan* and *loknīti*. He also expanded the idea of Gandhian *satyāgraha*.
- Like Gandhi, Bhave reinterpreted the *Bhagavadgītā* as *samyayoga* and emphasised the spirit of *samatva* (equanimity) where Gandhi, in *anasakti yoga*, emphasised on the spirit of detachment.

After India's independence and the demise of Mahatma Gandhi, Bhave tried to provide new orientation and activities to Gandhian philosophy. He began his own activities, like *bhoodan, sampatidan, gramdan*, and *gram swaraj*, and also expanded the concept of *satyāgraha* by incorporating new dimensions.

VIII Sarvodaya and *gram swaraj*

Gandhiji was impressed by John Ruskin's book *Unto This Last*, and he translated it into Gujarati as *Sarvodaya*. It could literally mean good for all. Vinoba, who took this principle from Gandhiji, developed it and gave an institutional structure and also implemented in selective areas through various schemes, such as – *bhoodan* (land gift), *sampattidan* (wealth gift), *shramdan* (labour gift), and *buddhidan* (wisdom gift).

> In the words of Dr Rajendra Prasad, the latter's work is an extension of the efforts of Mahatma Gandhi, and the further application of his method. Actually Vinobaji has built his philosophy on the principles of non-violence and trusteeship subscribed by Gandhiji.
>
> (Srivastava 1967: 206)

Bhave wanted to make villages self-sufficient and economically viable where large-scale industry played a minimum role. The society projected by the *sarvodaya* would be a society consisting of small peasant proprietors along with the small producer and artisans and would be based on mutual cooperation and self-interest (Narayanasamy 2003: 88). Wealth would belong to the whole society and be used for social good. The ideal of "each according to his need" would be achieved without government coercion.

Writing an introduction to Jayaprakash Narayan's book *From Socialism to Sarvodaya*, Bhave asserted that:

> *Sarvodaya* was not a reaction to any ism. It was India's own thought and her own system but not something that could not be applied to any other time or country. *Sarvodaya* affirms the indivisible unity of life. It refuses to

divide people on the line of State, nationality, religion, caste and language. I am convinced that the various one-sided ideologies, groping in wilderness would ultimately merge in the ocean of *sarvodaya*.

(Bhave 1989: 67)

Continuous spiritual development through self-less action with faith in non-violence and truth is the goal of *sarvodaya*. In *sarvodaya*, the interest of the individual became one and the same with the interests of others and finally became one with the supreme interest. No contradictions were left, all conflicts, internal or external, were resolved (Tandon 1981: 105).

Indeed, Bhave formulated three principles. In his words, "*sarvodaya* is our philosophy; constructive programme is our action plan, and following the *vratas* with the blessing from divinity is our *bhaktimarg*" (Bhave 1989: 70). Sarvodaya is the principle of life as well as the principle of the organisation of society and State. *Sarvodaya* emphasised on four principles: first, the importance of village and cottage industry; second, the abolition of the private ownership of land; third, a casteless and classless society; and fourth, emphasis on *nai talim*. The concept of *sarvodaya* is not limited to India but is wider and applicable to the whole world. As per the principles of *sarvodaya* and *vasudaiva kudumbakam* of the *Upaniṣhads*, Bhave changed the slogan *Jai Hind* to *Jai Jagat*.

In fact, Bhave as an anarchist had a deep distrust of government and its administrative apparatus. He wanted all the issues and disputes to be settled by social cooperation. The ultimate aim of *sarvodaya* was to free society from government control; that did not mean, however, that there would be chaos, but the authority would be distributed among villages, and the goal of *gram swaraj* would be achieved. As Bhave mentioned:

> We want an order of society which will be free not only from exploitation but also from every government authority. The power of the government will be decentrailsed and distributed among the villages. Every village will be a State to itself, the center will have only a nominal authority over them. In this way, gradually, we will reach a stage when authority in every form will become unnecessary and therefore fade away giving rise to a perfectly free society.

(cited in Ramabhai 1954: 209)

In such a society, no difference would be made between intellectual and manual labour. Basically, it would be a small-scale unit of production because the use of machinery would lead to the centralisation of production and the concentration of wealth. While some form of industries may be inevitable, there will be social control and democratic management so that these large-scale industries do not result in a concentration of wealth. The production of armaments would be totally banned. Decisions should be arrived at unanimously. If there are differences, the decision will be postponed. An individual who differs from society based on his "inner voice" or conscience can resort to *satayāgraha*. This guarantees an individual's liberty (Narayanasamy 2003: 90).

India that is *Bharat* belongs to its villages. As Gandhi mentioned, villages are little republics. Without ameliorating the conditions of villages, India will not develop. Unfortunately, the villages continued to remain dependent although India had become independent. There is need to create independent villages to fulfil the purpose of independent India, and that is only possible through achieving *gram swaraj*. For constructing a *sarvodaya* society based on *gram swaraj*, Bhave emphasised on the following points:

- Equality in all respects.
- *Ahiṃsā*.
- Simple living.
- Decentralisation.
- Non-attachment.
- Self-dependency and co-operation.
- Bread labour or physical labour.
- Emphasis on village industries and cottage industries.

In *gram swaraj*, there would be no discrimination based on religion, caste, or race; there would be no inferiority or superiority, only love; and no conflict would prevail. It would function as an extended family of small villages, with no scope for power and money. In *gram swaraj*, emphasis should be provided on knowledge of self, humanism, science, and spiritualism. It is not a scheme or plan but contemplation. It will be achieved through *gram samaj* and *gram nirman*. Through *gram swaraj*, Bhave aimed to establish a "republic of *sarvodaya* villages". In his words:

> *Gram swaraj* was the basis of India's *swaraj*. More important was the fact that all the people should feel from the bottom of their hearts that *swaraj* had really been established, only then in real terms, *swaraj* would be established in every village.
>
> (CVVB, XVI: 187)

IX The *bhoodan* movement

The concept of *bhoodan* is an original contribution of Bhave which extended the trusteeship theory of Gandhi. The first step towards the establishment of a *sarvodaya* society is *bhoodan*. As India is a predominantly agricultural country, it had the enormous problem of landless peasants. Under the *zamindari* system, large-scale land holdings were being held by big landlords while the farmers who worked on the land and created wealth could not enjoy it. Under these circumstances, in Telangana, the Communists launched a movement called "land to the tiller". Bhave took up the issue and sought to take a Gandhian approach to the problem. All land belonged to God, and under certain circumstances, there had been unequal holdings. So, something is required to level the holdings. But it should not be based on the violence of landless peasants against landlords and taking over the lands by force. Therefore, Bhave decided to appeal to the good nature of landowners to spare something for the landless. As he mentioned, "in the family, if there are five sons, I want to be considered as sixth. Thus, I claim one sixth of the total cultivable land" (cited in Narayan 1970: 210). The idea is that those peasants who possess more land should donate the surplus land for the use of the landless people. "I want one sixth to big peasants and *zamindars*. My request is to keep a little for themselves and donate rest to me; I would go on demanding till all the landless in the country are provided with land" (cited in Deshpande 2012: 2).

His meeting with the people of Pochampally village of the Nalgonda district in Telangana on 18 April 1951 began a new chapter in the history of non-violent struggle. Communists had established a reign of terror in the region at that time over the land question. Bhave asked the *Dalits* about their problem, and the *Dalits* asked for 80 acres of land for their living. Then, Bhave appealed to the villagers for land donations, and to everybody's surprise, a landlord named Ramchandra Reddy agreed to donate 100 acres of land for the *Dalits*. The incident was described by Babu Ram Misra as follows:

> Vinoba closed his eyes and went into deep meditation. After some careful thinking came the reply: is it possible for any landlords to donate the land to solve the problem of misery, poverty and unemployment in the village? There was utter silence in the meeting. But curiously enough, beyond the expectation of anybody, Shri V. R Reddy, one of the landlords of the village got up and said, 'I will make a gift of one hundred acres of land'. This reply of Shri Reddy was most unexpected and pleasant. Vinoba did not expect such a spontaneous reply and he asked him to repeat it. Shri Reddy in a firm tone repeated exactly what he had said before and further assured them that he was prepared to give a written declaration to that effect.
>
> (Misra 1956: 22)

This incident in the Pochampally village showed the path of non-violence to solve the landless problem without any revolutionary bloodshed, as the Communists had believed necessary, to solve the landless problem. It was the humble beginning of the great *bhoodan* (gift of land) movement; rich and landowning people began donating land as per Bhave's appeal. In Telangana, the gift of land averaged 200 acres per day. On Bhave's journey from Pavnar to Delhi, the average gift was 300 acres a day. Bhave had put five crore acres as the target. While walking in Uttar Pradesh in May 1952, he received the gift of the whole village of Mangrath (Agrawal 2008: 285). Kerala, Orissa, Bihar, and Tamil Nadu also contributed significantly during his trek through these States. In Bihar alone, Bhave received 23 lakh acres of land. He tried to establish the independent power of the people through non-violence. Other than *bhoodan* (land gift) and *gramdan* (village gift), he took other programmes, such as *shramdan* (the gift of labour), *sampattidan* (the gift of wealth), *sarvodaya-patra* (the pot where every household gives a daily handful of grain), *jeevandan* (the gift of life), and *shanti sena* (army for peace). Being influenced by Bhave, Jayaprakash Narayan in 1954 gave the gift of his life, and Bhave acknowledged it by giving the gift of his own life (Sukumaran 1997: 25).

Bhave's deep commitment to spirituality was not appreciated by the Communists, and they criticised his idea of the voluntary donation of land by the rich. They argued that most of the land donated by the rich peasants was uncultivable and questioned the ideology behind the *bhoodan* movement. In reply to the Communists, Bhave said he was not against communism. However, he found fault with the communist approach to social problems. To Bhave, the communist tendency to treat all rich people as bad would only strengthen the unity of the affluent classes against the poor. In contrast, Bhave's approach would be to isolate the good rich people from the bad. About the Communists' argument that the land donated by the rich was uncultivable, he countered by saying that some *rajas* (kings) had in fact donated good land. Even if some gave uncultivable land, they would themselves be exposed before the public, which would be a victory for the poor in its own way. Bhave was firmly committed to the idea that it was possible to change the hearts of people and that if the rich people took up the *bhoodan yajna* movement and donated their property, Communists would vanish.

X The *gramdan* movement

Gramdan is an advanced stage of *bhoodan*. For the cause of establishing *sarvodaya*, Bhave advocated the concept of *gramdan*, in which an entire village would dedicate itself and work together to eliminate poverty. A genuine feeling of love and co-operation among the various sections of society would be created. Man's faith in true religion would be strengthened. The new social order would be one of non-possession. A voluntary manual labour would attend to the various needs of the village. To remove political bitterness, a common platform for all political parties would be formed. It aimed at world peace. Bhave was influenced by ancient Hindu texts, the basis of which formed the moral principles of *gramdan*. These moral principles are: 1) land belongs to God (*Sabai Bhumi Gopal Ki*), and there is nothing called private land ownership, and 2) as the *Smṛitis* have professed that it is a sin to sell land, religious texts, daughters, and cows, it is morally wrong to sell off land which belongs to God. The goal of *gramdan* was to reduce economic inequalities and to wipe out social disparities. Explaining the significance of *gramdan*, Bhave said:

> *Gramdan* means equitable distribution or *samya-yoga*. Without a diffusion of compassion of heart, it is futile. Thus, *gramdan* connotes identification of one and all. In *gramdan*, landholders have to give their land, the landless

labourers have to donate their labour and the intellectuals have to offer their intellect. Dedication from all elements is the key of *gramdan*.

(cited in Ramabhai 1954: 197)

One aspect of this *gramdan* is creating self-sufficient villages. Bhave's ideal is individual production, not that of the co-operative venture advocated by the Communists. His economics are simple and include agriculture, spinning wheels, and village crafts. The villagers should use what is produced in that village to eliminate the exploitation of outside market forces. Again, the Communists criticised this assumption as it cut down consumers' choices. But in Bhave's words, "until and unless the factors of production are completely owned by community and the production is carried on collectively, there would be exploitation in the village" (cited in Ommen 1965: 1035).

XI *Sampatti dan*

The idea of *sampatti dan* envisages a moral responsibility of the wealthy sections towards society. It is not like taxation by the government or the appropriation of wealth, as suggested by the Communists. The householder would be asked to donate one-sixth of his wealth. The amount would be with the owner. He would be asked to spend it on specific things suggested by Bhave or his nominee and to send receipts. Though the primary idea is to finance *sarvodaya* activities, *sampatti dan* has certain broader aims. The rich would win the love and trust of the poor. The wealth would be regarded as a common fund of the entire society. It would foster an ideal that gold or money is of less value than manual labour. The aim of *sampatti dan* is to make people to discharge their social responsibility and become less and less dependent on government agencies. This would generate *lokshakti* (people's power) that could guide social affairs independent of States' supervision (Ommen 1965: 1036). It is clear that this is highly idealistic. There will always be vested interests in society who will be unwilling to share their wealth with others. It is impossible to perceive a situation in which wealth and property would be voluntary given up by the rich. But Bhave's optimism and faith in humans' change of heart was very deep.

XII Views on democracy and party system

There was a remarkable change in Indian politics between the pre-independence and post-independence periods. The pre-independence period was marked with political agitations, movements, and a period of unrest. After independence, the nation faced new challenges. Bhave was bothered by some of the questions about the nation. What should be the attitude of people towards a native government? How far will the newly established political institutions serve the nation? What are the challenges faced by a country which is economically poor but has embraced a democratic set-up? He had witnessed many elections, studied different political parties' manifestos, and observed the workings of some government institutions. With all his experiences, Bhave wrote the book *Lokniti*, which highlights the defects in the formal democratic structure and offers some suggestions. Bhave believed, like many liberals, that the democratic form of government was better than dictatorship, but the Western model as it was being followed in India had many shortcomings.

Bhave had propounded an indigenous theory of State and governance based on India's tradition, culture, social and economic condition. He criticised India's blind imitation of the Western model of democracy. Democracy, according to Bhave, "is one of the best systems, among all the political systems that had existed so far. However it is not an ideal system. It had various drawbacks" (CVVB, XVI: 95). These shortcomings Bhave identified are as follows:

- It provides undue importance to numerical calculations, harming the unity of humanity.
- It does not succeed in curtailing regional and parochial feelings, including nationalism. Competitive election creates hatred among people on different party lines, which also arouses feelings on caste, religion, region, and language.
- Like other systems, it is based on violence; political parties used immoral techniques to win over elections, which have dangerous consequences.
- In democracy, decisions are not taken by the people but by a few individuals as representatives. It also does not provide economic and political freedom in a true sense.

Though he considered parliamentary democracy a better form, Bhave suggested that India's typical condition and specific problems should be considered and that its own model of democracy should evolve. He viewed the idea of a welfare State as a wrongly conceived notion. If the government were to act in a way covering various aspects of citizens' lives, such as education, health, and economic betterment, there would be little incentive for the people. Their freedom would remain a tactical approval of the government's policies in every five years during elections. Sometimes, it could be disapproval. Yet, the fact remained that citizens were far removed from administration in the planned economy of a welfare State.

In the present system, the representatives of the people act as middlemen. As we should get rid of middlemen in business and other activities, we should also implement a system in which these representatives cannot be involved in dealing with people's problems. What, then, did Bhave have in mind? He advocated direct democracy, a policy perceived by Jean Jacques Rousseau in his 'general will' theory in which the community would unanimously arrive at a decision based on the common good. The idea of the *Panchayat* system is one such thing. The villagers would have a *Panchayat* where what is good for the whole village would be discussed. That is why there was a convention that elections here should be held on a non-party basis. But the convention failed. Today, all local bodies' elections are fought on a party basis.

For this reason, Bhave distrusted the party system. He vehemently criticised the party system, which become indispensable for a parliamentary democracy. In his view, the party system was a foreign concept and not suitable to the Indian social system. Parties divide people, while social problems should unite them. Therefore, he was in favour of the dissolution of various political parties and wanted the formation of a united front of all good and honest people in the country carrying out programmes agreed upon by the community (Masani 1957: 97). Political parties, Bhave argued, invariably instigate the people as they are always for power. Once, Bhave remarked, "I do not recognise parties at all. My study of history and my experience all leads to me the conclusion that parties in our country in the long run are going to be disastrous" (cited in Ramabhai 1954: 155). He vehemently criticised the role of opposition. In his words:

> They perform the role of a magnet, i.e., they only point out the drawbacks of the ruling party, and fail to perform the role of constructive opposition. This has primarily happened because all political parties have become power centric, they revolve around politics.
>
> *(Bhave 1999: 29–30)*

Another aspect of modern democracy Bhave criticised was the use of money power in elections. To Bhave, it distorted the picture of public opinion. Votes were being purchased. An eminent and honest worker hardly got a chance of being elected against a rich opponent. Moreover, the election system being fought on a caste basis had perpetuated the caste structure. While *sarvodaya* believed in evolving a casteless society, the elections always divided people based on caste, religion, region, and so on. Bhave's views on many of the political institutions appear to be highly idealistic. But still, his writings are a warning that establishing a political democracy without proper social and moral force is of little use. If we ask whether the present model of parliamentary democracy based on elections and the party system is able to cater the needs of poor people, the answer is far from satisfactory.

XIII Views on planning

In Bhave's view, government planning should aim at food and employment for all, giving priority to the needy. Bhave wanted every village to prepare its own plan, using its own capacity and resources. He believed that if the country planned for small schemes, the country would progress and all would have livelihoods and jobs. Without acquiring skills in doing small works, if the nation planned for a big scheme, it would definitely fail, according to Bhave.

The Prime Minister invited Bhave to Delhi to discuss his ideas with the planning commission. Bhave made the 1,200 kilometre journey on foot. In the meeting, he emphasised on the following points:

- Decentralisation in all fields.
- India should attain self-sufficiency.
- Employment for all.
- Land distribution should be suitable for cultivation.

The preliminary draft of the planning commission was sent to Bhave. After a prolonged discussion, he expressed his dissatisfaction with many issues. The main points he opposed and which differentiated from his views were on the issues of birth control, cottage industry, the prohibition of liquor, basic education, and cooperative agriculture (Bharathi 1998: 25).

XIV Conclusion

Vinoba Bhave was an original thinker. He critically estimated the shortcomings of the Indian social and political system. In his opinion, the social transformation of individuals is more important than political empowerment. He emphasised on the discharging of one's duties rather than agitation for rights. He sincerely believed that real India lived in the country's villages, and he wanted villages to be economically self-sufficient, socially tension free, and morally ideal places. To achieve this, he suggested various constructive programmes.

Bhave was a strong believer in spirituality. For him, non-violence was the ultimate strength. He was critical about Marxist and socialist ideologies of revolution for equality. He wanted the wealthy classes to realise their moral duty towards others. He desired a total transformation of the society through non-violence. The experiments in the *bhoodan* movement encouraged him to follow peaceful methods to change the society and hearts of the people.

Bhave has contributed a lot towards the history of non-violent movements and tried his best to solve the landless problem through non-violence. He remained a true worshiper of truth and non-violence and is considered the national teacher of our great country. As an ardent follower of Gandhi, he dedicated his life for the service of the nation. He fought for the liberation of the society and raised his voice against the inequality prevalent in the society. He was a saint and a moral-political philosopher who connected science with spirituality and the autonomous village with the world movement. As a believer of *swaraj*, Bhave considered the power of people superior to the State power. He was a legend and a true spiritual successor of Gandhiji. His death on 15 November 1982 left a void in the social thought of India. Many of his ideas remain relevant and inspiring in strife-ridden modern times.

References

Agrawal, Lion M. G. (Ed.) (2008). *Freedom Fighters of India* (Vol. 3). Delhi: Isha Books.

Bharathi, K. S. (1995). *Thoughts of Gandhi and Vinoba: A Comparative Study*. New Delhi: Concept Publishing Company.

Bharathi, K. S. (1998). *Encyclopedia of Eminent Thinkers: (Vol. V): The Political Thought of Vinoba*. New Delhi: Concept Publishing Company.

Bhave, Vinoba (1989). *Sarvodava Vichar ani Swaraiva Shastra*. Wardha: Paramdham Prakashan.

Bhave, Vinoba (1999). *Lokniti*. Varanasi: Sarva Seva Sangh Prakashan.

Deshpande, Madhura (2012). Acharya Vinoba Bhave – Father of the Bhoodan Movement. *Time*, the Weekly News Magazine, USA.

Govindan, S. V. (1985). *A Saint of the Modern World*. World Conference of Religion for Peace, Satsang Sadan, Hanumanpur, Varanasi.

Jayapalan, N. (2003). *Indian Political Thinkers: Modern Indian Political Thought*. New Delhi: Atlantic Publishers and Distributers.

Masani, R. P. (1957). *The Five Gifts*. London: Collins.

Misra, Babu Ram (1956). *V for Vinoba: The Economics of the Bhoodan Movement*. Bombay: Orient Longman.

Narayan, Shriman (1970). *Vinoba: His Life and Work*. Bombay: Popular Prakashan.

Narayanasamy, S. (2003). *The Sarvodaya Movement: Gandhian Approach to Peace and Non-Violence*. New Delhi: Mittal Publication.

Nargolkar, Vasant (Trans.). (1966). *The Creed of Saint Vinoba*. Bombay: Bharatiya Vidya Bhavan.

Ommen, T. K. (1965). Problems of Gramdan. *The Economic and Political Weekly*, Vol. 3, No. 8, pp. 1034–1040.

Ramabhai, Suresh (1954). *Vinoba and His Mission*. Sevagram, Wardha: Akhil Bharat Sarva Seva Sangh.

Sarvodaya (1958). Vol. VII, June.

Srivastava, G. P. (1967). The Political and Economic Philosophy of Acharya Vinoba Bhave. *The Indian Journal of Political Science*, Vol. 28, No. 4 (October–December), pp. 206–215.

Sukumaran, N. P. (1997). *Sarvodaya Darsanam*. Kochi: Poornodaya Book Trust.

Tandon, Viswanath (Ed.) (1981). *Selections from Vinoba*. Varanasi: Sarva Seva Sangh Prakashan.

Vinoba Bhave Collected Volumes, (CVVB), Vol. XVI (Tesari Shakti, 1996). Pavnar, Wardha: Paramdham Prakashan, Gramseva Mandal.

PART III
Leftist-socialist thought

14

MANABENDRA NATH ROY

Aritra Majumdar

> *An increasingly large number of men, conscious of their creative power, motivated by an indomitable will to remake the world, moved by the adventure of ideas, and fired with the ideal of a free society of free men, can create conditions under which democracy will be possible. Spiritually free individuals in power will smash all chains of slavery and usher in freedom for all.*
>
> – M. N. Roy (*New Humanism: A Manifesto* 1947: 51)

I Introduction

Narendranath Bhattacharya, or as we know him today, Manabendra Nath Roy, was a man who donned as many ideological caps as he wore disguises and cloaks. In a political life that spanned the first half of the twentieth century, he moved across the world, organising movements in regions as diverse as Mexico and China. This was complemented by an equally diverse range of ideologies, beginning with nationalism, moving onto socialism, and eventually to his own radical humanism. At each stage, Roy's popularity differed, waning and waxing constantly. Yet his indomitable courage gave him fixity of purpose, enabling him to cross ideological spectra that few men have, and in so doing, creates a unique ideology that rings true even today.

Quite naturally, writing about such a complex individual is not an easy task. It becomes a little easier, however, if we try to correlate his actions with his political beliefs, since the two were always intimately connected. To this end, it would be necessary to first go through his life history, underlining his major influences and achievements, as well as his voluminous works, before diving into his political thought. In the second section, we focus more on the Marxist and radical humanist phases of Roy's career since it was during this time that he produced his most thought-provoking ideas and gained the greatest recognition among both his admirers and opponents. This, hopefully, will bring out his critical train of thought, the ideals and goals for which he strove, and make clear the fact that these goals were never constant but changed according to the conditions and his understanding of the forces of history.

II Life sketch

The man who would become M. N. Roy to the world was born as Narendranath Bhattacharya in Kheput in the Arbelia division of 24 Parganas (West Bengal) in 1887. Born into a priestly family, he received education in Sanskrit, English, and Bengali in Arbelia and then Kodalia (Gordon 1968: 200). What truly inspired young Roy was Bankim Chandra Chatterjee's *Ananda Math*, creating in him a love for the motherland (Roy 1964: 568–569).

Following his father's death, Roy and his brothers reached Calcutta in 1905 to find their own fortune. Here, he came into contact with revolutionaries like Jatin Mukherjee, or *Bagha Jatin*, and committed a series of dacoities to raise money for the nationalist cause (Gordon 1968: 203). An attempt to gather arms for an armed revolt with the help of the Germans led him to East Asia twice in 1915, but the plan failed (Roy 1964: 9–13, 569–570). Hoping to persuade the Germans directly in Berlin, Roy arrived in America, eventually becoming Lala Lajpat Rai's secretary. This brought him into contact with American radicals, and thence to socialism (Roy 1964: 28–44).

Roy was forced to flee to Mexico when America joined the war against Germany in 1917. Here, he finally gave up the German arms project. Instead, he joined the Socialist Party of Mexico and began to rejuvenate it as a means of liberating the Latin American masses. With the help of the Bolshevik Michael Borodin, he turned the Socialist Party into the Communist Party, the first such party in the New World (Roy 1964: 70–103, 150–211).

As delegate of the new Communist Party to the Second World Congress of the Communist International (Comintern) to be held in 1920, Roy set off for Russia. Moving through Spain and the Netherlands, he finally reached Berlin (Roy 1964: 270–294). After Roy arrived in Moscow, Vladimir Lenin asked him to read through the draft of his theses on *National and Colonial Questions*. Roy obliged and proposed an entirely new approach to the colonial problem. He remembered expecting Lenin to brush it aside and was surprised when Lenin himself proposed that his own as well as Roy's *Supplementary Theses* be accepted in the Congress. Thereafter, Lenin and Roy would become close comrades and, to some extent, friends. This set the stage for Roy as a Marxist theoretician and also paved the way for his rise in the Comintern (Roy 1964: 330–337, 380–381).

As a leader of the Comintern, Roy was sent to Central Asia to explore revolutionary possibilities there and in Afghanistan and India. Finding *muhajis* inspired by the Khilafat movement in the region, he chose a few of them for Communist education. This eventually led to the formation of the Communist Party of India (C.P.I.) in Tashkent in 1920 (Roy 1964: 407–455). With the formation of the

C.P.I., Roy began to take more interest in India. His *India in Transition* (1922) and *Future of Indian Politics* (1926), along with his appeal to the Ahmedabad Congress, outlined his ideas on India. He saw the bourgeoisie coming to a compromise and betraying the national movement. The proletariat would have to overthrow this imperialist–bourgeois alliance and establish socialism (Ray Vol. III [Part-I] 2005: 20, 38–44).

In 1927, Roy and Nikolai Bukharin were sent to guide a revolution in China. Dissension between the two leaders and the petty ambitions of Mao Tse-Tung and other Chinese leaders ruined this effort, and Roy returned to the U.S.S.R. This failure and more likely his refusal to support Stalin's bid for power in its final stages as well as writing for the German Communist Opposition (KPD-O), estranged Roy from the Comintern. He was finally expelled in late 1929 (Manjapra 2010: 75, 84).

At this juncture, Roy decided to return to India. His writings (mentioned earlier) had won him some recognition; however, he had been indicted in absentia in the Kanpur Conspiracy Case of 1924 and had to move incognito once he arrived in 1930. Roy gathered a loyal group of followers, including V. B. Karnik, Tayyib Shaikh, and Maniben Kara. With their help, he toured extensively under the guise of a Congressman, helping organise peasant and workers' movements in Uttar Pradesh and other regions. These experiences led him to put forth his study of rural India in *Oppression and Rebellion in the Indian Villages* (Ray Vol. III [Part-I] 2005: 146–206).

Unfortunately, the police soon arrested him on 31 July 1931. He was sentenced to 12 years in prison for the Kanpur Conspiracy Case. This was later reduced to six years. In prison, Roy wrote a number of works, including *My Defence*, in which he argued that imperialism was a usurpation of Indians' sovereign rights; *Our Task in India*, which outlined communist goals and ideals; and *Whither Congress; A Manifesto*, in which he tore into *swarajist* policy and demanded a revolutionary leadership to lead the nationalist party instead (Ray Vol. III [Part-I] 2005: 240–257). Roy also developed an interest in eclectic Indian and Western philosophy, paving the way for the philosophical foundations of his later radical humanism (ibid.: 204–318).[1] Meanwhile, his followers had formed the 'Committee for the Action of Independent India', which led the way to the formation of the Revolutionary Party of the Indian Working Class (R.P.I.W.C.). In *The Manifesto of the Revolutionary Party of the Indian Working Class*, he suggested a three-fold alliance of peasants, workers, and petit-bourgeoisie against the big capitalists and the imperialists (ibid.: 256–264).

On 20 November 1936, Roy's prison sentence ended, and he was released. He joined the Congress but didn't get along with Gandhi, Nehru, or Bose. Naturally, his support base within the Congress was limited from the start. Hence, his support never translated into influence within the Congress, and most of his proposals were either rejected or severely watered-down. Realising the entrenched position of the Congress right, led by Sardar Vallabhbhai Patel, Roy formed the 'League of Radical Congressmen' in 1938 at Tripuri. The Indian Federation of Labour (I.F.L.), similarly, was the Royist alternative to the All India Trade Union

Congress (A.I.T.U.C.) (Ray Vol. III [Part-I] 2005: 325–335). Through all this, Roy, with the help of the I.F.L., published a journal called *Independent India*. Along with this journal, Roy published a number of short tracts, including *Our Differences* (1939), *Royism Explained* (1939), *The Russian Revolution* (1937), and *Independent India* (1938) (Manjapra 2010: 119–120, 129).

Roy had been a vocal critic of British imperialism but having seen Nazism rise first hand in Germany, he chose to support the war effort from 1939 onwards. This finally led to his expulsion from the Congress. He formed the Radical Democratic Party (R.D.P.) thereafter, but it failed to win a single seat in the 1946 election. Thereafter, Roy became convinced that India required party-less radical democracy, and to this end, he dissolved the R.D.P. in 1948. Instead, he launched and propagated his ideals of radical humanism and radical democracy (Roy 1964: 583–585, 591–600).[2,3] Sadly, life did not give him many years to pursue this new ideal. Following a prolonged illness after a fall from a hillside, Roy breathed his last breath on 24 January 1954 (Roy 1964: 600–603).

The purpose of this life sketch was twofold; first, to give the reader a broad idea of what M. N. Roy's intellectual development looked like, and second, to impress upon the reader that at each stage, it was praxis rather than just theory that drove him. Keeping these points in mind, it is now time to examine some of the finer details of Roy's political thought.

III Roy–Lenin controversy

As mentioned in the life sketch, the Roy–Lenin controversy arose over Lenin's theses on the *National and Colonial Questions*, which Lenin intended to submit to the Second World Congress of the Communist International in 1920.[4] Lenin was not, as Roy insinuated, a stranger to the colonial question, though the latter was right in that Lenin had no first-hand knowledge of the colonial world (Talwar 2006: 105–109). In 1905, Lenin had written *Two Tactics of Social Democracy in the Democratic Revolution*,[5] and in 1917 he wrote *Imperialism: The Highest Stage of Capitalism*. Following up the arguments in these books, his theses argued that, historically, revolution was likely to occur in two stages:

1   The stage of bourgeois revolution, which would take on an anti-feudal character.
2   The stage of socialist revolution.

(Talwar 2006: 115)

As far as the backward and colonial countries were concerned, the conditions were not yet ripe for socialist revolution. These countries still contained feudal and absolutist forces in power, aided and abetted by a reactionary clergy. In colonial countries, in particular, the imperialist powers were allied to these feudal elements (Lenin 1920: Para 5–7).[6] In such countries, capitalism was still developing, with the nationalist bourgeois being its spearhead. This bourgeois enjoyed broad support, being able to mobilise the peasantry and other groups victimised by feudalism and colonialism in its struggle against feudal and imperial forces. Given the numerical inferiority of communist movements in these countries, alliance with the bourgeoisie was the only option. In this alliance, they would overthrow feudal–colonial relations and establish national democracy, paving the way for social revolution (Talwar 2006: 114–115).

During the period of collaboration, the Communists had to be careful of bourgeois deception. Instead, only those movements which did not demand limiting the proletarian potential would be supported. Special attention had to be given to peasant movements and communist education so that a proletarian movement would be ready to attack the bourgeoisie at the right moment. This would establish the social revolution and the dictatorship of the proletariat (Lenin 1920: Para 8–10).

Roy's *Supplementary Theses* showed that he had three fundamental differences with Lenin on the following issues:

1 The level of economic development in the colonies.
2 The relations between the bourgeoisie and imperialism, given the state of production relations.
3 How revolutionary the situation in the colonies were and how to proceed in relations with the colonial bourgeoisie.

Roy argued that colonial nations such as India had been undergoing industrialisation since the late nineteenth century. Hence, it would be wrong to consider the economic relations in these colonies as pre-capitalist. Prior to the First World War, British capital saw Indian capitalists as a threat to their expansion and hence stymied the latter. However, this attitude had changed in recent years, leading to the further growth of capitalism and the proletariat (Talwar 2006: 122). Further, the proletariat itself was animated not by nationalism but by its own economic and social questions. Hence, an alliance with the class enemies would be artificial and stymy the growth of class consciousness. Instead, the Communist Party of India must lead the proletariat to unleash an organised movement without allying with nationalism (Haithcox 1963: 94).

Roy argued that such a movement was bound to lead to the collapse of the colonial empire as well, since in his view, European capitalism increasingly came to depend upon the colonies for survival. As such, the break-up of the colonial empire would lead to the breakdown of European capitalist States and usher in socialism in Europe. Hence, for socialism to win in the West, it had to first win in the East (Talwar 2006: 122–123).

In his *Memoirs*, Roy complained that in the Second World Congress, his theses, while being accepted, were greatly watered-down. Whereas he had asked for the Communists to focus exclusively upon the workers and peasants, the final thesis asked for them to cooperate with bourgeois nationalism. The decision of which national movement was "revolutionary" enough was left to the individual Communist parties of the countries, provided they existed[7] (Talwar 2006: 125).

IV Transition from Marxism to radical humanism

Roy had become a staunch Marxist during his days in Mexico, and his debate with Lenin and activities in the Comintern followed from staunch Marxist and Communist beliefs.[8] During his incarceration in India, however, he began to argue that Marxism wasn't simply what Marx had said a hundred years earlier. Instead, Marxism was more method than dogma and was open-ended at that (Ray 2005: 250–255).

Eventually, he came to two concrete criticisms of Marx from a philosophical viewpoint. One, Marxist thought needed to consider the discoveries regarding matter made in the field of physics. Second, and much more importantly, he believed Marx had not incorporated any contributions from the Orient, and thus his views needed to be reformulated in light of the arguments and experiences of the people of Asia (Ray 2005: 260–268).

At the same time, Roy's inquiries gradually transformed him into an Epicurean. Holding that happiness was the greatest goal of mankind, he began to champion a vision of freedom which "entailed individuals engaging in unhindered traffic with their material surroundings, and free experience of the pleasure of the senses without the limitation of social codes or taboos". This enjoyment could come through knowledge of causalities, which would free man from fear and anxiety, and this freedom would make man happy (Manjapra 2010: 121).

Further, as early as 1937, we find him arguing that economic critique is not enough. Each civilisation had its own philosophy, and any subversion must be preceded by a critique of philosophy. This would be followed by not just the overthrow of an economic system but a "historical and cultural background" (Manjapra 2010: 142). Most scholars, however, date the real shift in Roy's philosophical underpinnings to 1940, when his work *Materialism* came out. Here, economic determinism is replaced by growing emphasis on the role of civilisation. Roy argues here that it is not the collective that determines the progress of civilisation but the individual who imagines his own dream of civilisation. Such men, who have existed since antiquity, form a philosophical brotherhood stretching across time. The goal of this brotherhood is freedom, which is the highest ideal any man can hope to achieve (Manjapra 2010: 155).

This emphasis on the individual and the philosophical underpinnings of the quest for freedom, which would become the cornerstones of his radical humanism, also led him to a thorough and searching critique of Marxism. In his works *New Humanism: A Manifesto* (1947) and *Reason, Romanticism and Revolution* (1952–1955), he took up the critical tenets of Marxism and demolished them one by one (Manjapra 2010: 155).

Roy begins his *Manifesto* by pointing out that the Marxist utopia of proletarian dictatorship remained confined to one country (Russia) and created the "collective ego of the proletariat", to claim subordination and the sacrifice of individuals composing the classes. Instead of proletarian world revolution, what followed was the era of triumphant reaction and counter-revolution. Since the conclusion of the Second World War, this supposed engine of proletarian revolution is herself pushing the world to the "very brink of the precipice". Hence, he argues, the Marxist view of history is fundamentally erroneous (Roy 1947: 2–3).

1 Surplus value: Roy went beyond the historical experience and looked at the theoretical concepts underlying Marxism. He began with the theory of surplus value. In Chapter 5 of his *Manifesto*, Roy argued that Marx had been wrong in arguing that surplus value was a special characteristic of capitalism. Ever since the dawn of society, it had been a foregone conclusion that for society to progress, all that man produced must not be consumed. What remained after the needs had been met, would be used for further progress. This was surplus value, which he called social surplus (Roy 1947: 23). Quite naturally, social surplus continued to exist under capitalism. Marx was correct in arguing that this social surplus was taken from the proletariat by the exploiters, that is, the capitalists. This exploitation, in the Marxist scheme of things, would stop when the proletariat captured power. They would instead expropriate the exploiters (Roy 1947: 25).

The problem with this scheme is that for any progress to take place, surplus value would have to be produced. Theoretically, this would be appropriated by the worker's dictatorship. However, in practice, this dictatorship became the State. Hence, the worker's surplus went to the State, creating State capitalism instead of the social revolution Marx had envisaged. Under such supposedly socialist State capitalism, the State begins to exploit the workers, replacing the capitalist class (Roy 1947: 25–26). Instead, Roy argued that the sanction for ending of exploitation was not economic but moral. Marx asked for social revolution, which presupposed the moral decision to end exploitation. Hence, he believed that the exploitation of social surplus would end not by economic but moral means (Talwar 2006: 218).

2 Theory of class struggle: Roy argued that Marx's fixation with the theory of surplus value and economic determinism led him to argue that throughout the ages, society had been turned into classes and class struggle. Roy conceded that classes existed, but he also found a cohesive tendency. In mores of culture, dress, food, and faith, there existed powerful integrative factors. Without these cohesive tendencies, society would have collapsed and social evolution would have failed (Talwar 2006: 221). Furthermore, Marx argued that under capitalism there would be only the bourgeoisie and proletariat and no middle class. Roy argued that the middle class had not disappeared but, rather, the intensification of capitalism exploitation had pushed this middle class closer to the proletariat while increasing its numbers (Roy 1947: 26–27).

This consciousness of exploitation, however, is not enough. It must be combined with cultural and educational faculties. Situated between the self-serving capitalists and the proletarians who had little of culture or education, the middle class possessed both the economic and cultural forces required to conceive of a more equitable structure of society. Socialism was essentially a middle-class ideology.[9] Taking Lenin's dictum further, Roy thus argued that a professional party could only come from the middle class since only middle-class persons could be professional revolutionaries (Talwar 2006: 222–225). In practice, the

Communist parties decried culture and bourgeois and forced the middle-class intellectuals to sink to the level of the proletariat. This dissuaded others from joining this proletarianised party structure (Roy 1947: 30–31).

Finally, Roy tore into the concept of classless society. For him, the finality of the resolution of class struggle in a classless society is bogus since if man reached a final state, he would have no option to progress. Inevitably, mankind would stagnate and disintegrate. Marxism would become not a philosophy of freedom but a death sentence for mankind (Talwar 2006: 223).

3 Economic determinism: If a classless society was a death sentence, economic determinism was "a flight from reason on a philosophical level".[10] According to economic determinism, primitive man was engaged in a brutal struggle for survival. This need for economic survival predisposed man to follow the path prescribed by Marx, leading from the formation of society and State all the way to capitalism. It left no space for man's creativity.

Roy argued that man was not simply an economic machine driven by hunger but a creature seeking to emancipate himself to a higher plane. This plane involved moral, intellectual, and social life, which would not be serviced by the bare economic necessities of life. Man's search for such a plane led him to use his brain to produce ideas, which culminated in the formation of State and virtually everything that followed. If there were any deterministic forces involved, they would have to include ideas, beliefs, aspirations, etc. and not simply the need to eat. To argue otherwise, it would be argued that man as economic machine had no capacity to make history (Talwar 2006: 216–217).

4 Future of socialism: Roy's final critique attacked the fact that Marx was a critic. Marx was at his best when he analysed capitalism, but his prescription for the period following proletarian revolution was vague. Marx believed that history being determined by relations of production, these relations would decide what the actual system would be. His only belief was that this future would be a classless one (Roy 1947: 11–15).

In response, Roy argued that this lack of clarity meant that once the Russian revolution took place, the Bolsheviks were found charting *terra incognita*. This confusion led Lenin to found a system that produced State capitalism and then became a socialist version of the nationalist power-hungry modern State. This State placed the Bolsheviks in a different situation from their comrades in bourgeois and colonial countries. The contradiction between post-revolutionary State and pre-revolutionary movement tore apart the international Comintern (Roy 1947: 14).

Despite taking Marx to task on several counts, Roy did not consider Marxian spirit to be utterly sterile. He argued that like many others who came up with ideas of utopia before him, Marx was a romanticist and dreamt of revolution with a burning passion. Firing this passion was a firm moral conviction that a better and more equitable society could be created. This faith, argues Roy, was suffocated when Marx began to use Hegelian dialectics and in doing so claimed that he had found a scientific theory of revolution. This denied the role of morality and romanticism which the earlier believers in socialist utopia had. His dogmatic disciples turned his arguments for scientific socialism into an absolute ideology which denied man any scope for creativity.

Hence, the need of the hour was to rediscover the romantic moralist in Marx and proceed from there on to found a new set of ideals – a Third Force – which would ensure that man achieved the socialist utopia without sacrificing his higher faculties. This force would be radical humanism, or new humanism, capable of ushering in a new renaissance in human society (Roy 1947: 16–22).[11]

V Theory of human nature

Before we talk of the core tenets of radical humanism, it is necessary to understand the foundational assumptions upon which Roy built his system. Central to these is the theory of human nature. According to Roy, human nature was a product of both man's position as the highest evolutionary product in a mechanistic universe, as well as his animal instincts. Like the former, there were many constants in human nature, and it was not an amorphous amalgam of social relations, as Marx would have it.

These constants of the nature of man included the capacity for rationality. For Roy, rationality was inherent because, like the physical universe and all beings on earth, he too was a product of natural laws. Hence, when he came into existence through evolution, he was possessed of a nervous system which inherently told him what was good for him. Today, we call this tendency instinct. For Roy, instinct was simply undifferentiated reason and existed in primitive man due to his immediate biological ancestry (Roy 1952a: 180–192).

This tendency for rationality can be seen in the field of primitive religion. Instead of possessing complex theology, these early systems invented Gods from within the natural surroundings. Since the man was already engaging with these surroundings in a rational manner, he created a rational religion. However, Roy's rational and moral man was not to be found in real life. The source of this deficiency was the "wrong philosophy", which led to moral chaos. For ages, he had been taught to believe in some higher authority, which led to regimentation. Instead, if he could be taught that his urge for freedom buried deep inside him was the fountainhead of a good and just society, he would be a reliable source of socially beneficial behaviour.

To believe without use of one's rational faculties was fundamentally objectionable to rational man. Instead, he developed the concepts of will, intelligence, and emotion from his rational understanding of his environment and himself. Such a view argued that in all this, there was nothing irrational or impulsive, and everything was proceeding according to the law of the cosmos. Since the law of the cosmos is rational, man too is rational, and he only does rational things unless deluded by wrong ideology (Talwar 2006: 263–264).

But rational man was not an amoral mechanical machine. Instead, his rational animal instinct led him to seek out what was good for him. Seeking out such goodness for himself led him to generalise that goodness as good for all. This rational desire for the good of all creates an instinctive ability called conscience. Such conscience leads to morality, which manifests itself as man's desire to seek harmonious and beneficial relations with all (Roy 1947: 36–37).

In Roy's opinion, then, morality arose from a rational desire for the good of all. It was not dictated by religion or brought forth by a mysterious force within oneself. That being the case, he argued that religion itself had represented a rational desire for freedom at one stage since it sought deliverance. But the incomplete store of human knowledge led man astray into dogmatic ideals about God. A morality born of such incomplete knowledge could only create "spiritual terrorism". Morality must and would be borne out of man's free, rational will. Furthermore, such morality would not change with the times. In opposition to the Marxist argument for social conditions determining morality, Roy argued that there were two types of values. One group included variable ones related to the conditions of man. The other, however, involved constant values which were not related to the condition of man. This second group was the foundation of morality and ethics, so morality did not change with time but provided continuity in human life (Talwar 2006: 266–268).

VI Concept of freedom

We have seen how Roy, in his transition from orthodox Marxism to radical humanism, laid great stress on the concept of freedom of the individual leading to the greatest measure of happiness. Furthermore, in his critique of Marxism, Roy took the Marxists to task for creating the collective ego, which hindered the free expression of the potentialities of the individual. In his opinion, this had created the monstrosity of the Soviet Union, where the bureaucratic control destroyed the ideal of social liberty.[12]

Given the unhappy experience of the Soviet Union, Roy's radical humanism defined freedom as the "progressive disappearance of all restrictions on the unfolding of the potentialities of individuals as human beings, and not as cogs in the wheels of a mechanised social organism" (Roy 1947: 54).[13] Thus defined, freedom could be traced back to the rational man's search for a means of survival through the conquest of nature. This was a biological quest that arose out of the fact that man had infinite potentiality for development. Notably, it was not just a negatively defined quest to adapt but a positive search to ensure that nature was modified with a purpose, which was defined using human intelligence (Talwar 2006: 270).

However, freedom was not circumscribed by any specified set of purposes nor guaranteed by a specific type of structure or ideology. Hence, while man must enjoy the greatest amount of economic freedom, this was not to ensure the development of a specific stage of economic development. Neither would economic freedom lead to complete freedom as defined by Roy. Conversely, no single ideology or facet of social or economic reconstruction – even if it provided a certain type of freedom, for example, economic freedom – could provide mankind with all-round freedom. Hence, neither a socialist State structure nor the pursuit of priestly revelation could provide man with the freedom he needed. Instead, they would simply produce dogmatic men who slavishly followed the doctrines from above without applying their rationality (Ray 1956: 25–29).

Such freedom would have to be constantly sought after, breaking down more and more barriers that fettered the unlimited potentialities of man. However, there would be no half-way houses, where compromises would be made with the quest for freedom. Roy made it clear that any person who did not have or did not strive for the most comprehensive form of freedom was in fact not free at all. He was a slave and would open the door for anti-freedom forces, which would enslave all (Talwar 2006: 274).

At the same time, Roy did not move into the polarity of freedom without responsibility. For Roy, freedom being rational and thus moral, it would make man a responsible citizen. He would do everything needed to ensure the betterment and well-being of his fellow citizens. Indeed, if the individual suffered for the greater good, provided that good could be demonstrated, there was nothing repugnant about such suffering. However, this was not a simple nationalist definition. Roy was emphatic in asserting that nation-States, with their formalistic definition of freedom of citizens, failed miserably in providing actual freedom. Rather, Roy envisaged a broader global definition of citizenship in which mankind was the defined populace (Roy 1947: 40–42).

Hence, man was, by his biological heritage, a seeker of maximum freedom. This freedom was comprehensive and allowed him to develop his faculties to the greatest possible extent. No limited freedom, formal or revolutionary, could define or circumscribe this freedom. Instead, man sought to provide freedom to more and more of his compatriots, who included people not limited by a nation-State or ideological or religious system. Such a search for freedom for all would be the logical culmination of the boundless potentiality of man.

VII The concept of political order and the theory of State

To understand Roy's concept of the political order and the theory of State, it is necessary to understand his idea about the origin of human society. Having argued that man arose from a law-bound cosmos and hence had an inbuilt rationality, Roy did not argue that this created in men an ideal society from the very beginning. In the early stages, man lived like the apes that had come before him, eking out a struggle for existence. It was rational for him, therefore, to seek means to achieve a better and safer life. Such means involved joining in with other men, so their combined efforts would be more successful than that of the lone individual. Hence, it was the rational search for existence that produced civil society (Talwar 2006: 280–282).

As society became more complex, two necessities arose. One was to administer social life, including maintaining law and order. The second was to coordinate the different departments of social life. Men, realising these needs, took the next rational step of creating the State to fulfil these conditions. The State, then, was formed as a rational stage in the development of man and hence was not inconsistent with the desire for freedom. In fact, since man himself created the State, the latter was a structure subservient to the wishes of the former, and not the other way around. Hence, the individual could demand changes in the State that allowed for greater achievement of freedom to develop his potentialities, but the State could not demand surrender of freedom by the individual (Roy 1952b: 16–20).

Hence, the Royist State would ensure law and order, defend the citizens against external aggression, and maintain socio-economic institutions, but it would not impinge on the freedom of the individual. How was this to be achieved? Roy's solution was to decentralise the State to the greatest possible extent without utterly dissolving it. To ensure that the people had the greatest amount of control over the State, he argued that there should be people's committees of a voluntary nature which would perform most of the functions carried out by the bureaucracy and the political apparatus in the modern State. Such functions, with the participation of almost all citizens in cooperation with each other, would ensure the greatest amount of freedom for all. Naturally, the central government would be weak and perform only the most basic of tasks required to hold itself and society together (Talwar 2006: 284–288).

Roy's primary concern in formulating this political and social structure was to avoid the dictatorial *Leviathan*. Roy felt that since man created society and State using his own rational senses in his quest for freedom and the realisation of his potentialities, State and society must serve him. Such service precludes any demand for surrender of freedom since they exist primarily to defend and further it. Therefore, man must always guard against any form of regimentation of the political order which infringes upon his freedom. Only then can society and State carry out their true duties (Roy 1952b: 40–43).

VIII Critique of liberal democracy and the concept of radical democracy

Having gone through the concepts of rational and moral man, freedom of the individual, and the concept of political order, it is now time to see how Roy brought them together in a scheme for "real" democracy, which he called radical democracy. In his *Manifesto*, Roy makes it clear that neither Western democracy nor Marxism provide true freedom to man. The reasons for the failure of Marxism were given earlier. For democracy on the other hand, Roy argues that liberal democracy reduces the exercise of sovereignty to a mere formality – a legal fiction. People vote in elections to delegate power to representatives, who then make all decisions for the people. Until the next election, the people have virtually no say in the running of the State or society (Roy 1947: 4–6).

However, since man created the State to serve himself, sovereignty and power must always reside in him. The moment this power was given away, even if temporarily, the ideals behind the creation of the State were defeated. Voting, therefore, became a formality to hand over real power to representatives, thus extinguishing the ability of man to ensure that the State worked for him (Roy 1947: 7–9).

Once the ability of the common man to rule the State was lost, government became by the representatives and for the representatives. Such representatives, however, were in most cases not individuals but candidates of a certain party. Candidates and ordinary members worked for the party and not the people. The party became the de facto ruler. Furthermore, liberal democracy could not be truly democratic, even under ideal circumstances, because the elected candidates were never elected by all. In the 'first-past-the-post system', those whose votes proved to be in the majority got their choice of representative, while the other's votes became meaningless. Roy was equally concerned about the moral corruption of the party system. In his opinion:

> Liberal democracy turned elections into a race for capturing power. Such a race employed all methods, fair and foul, to win. Naturally, the ideals of honesty and sincerity had no chance of survival under this system. The party system thus bred social and political immorality.
> (Talwar 2006: 239–241)

Roy's alternative was radical democracy, or organised democracy. Since man was inherently rational and moral, he only had to return to the right path. Once he did so, he would rediscover his true nature and become an ideal political participant. In other words, he would realise once again that his interest lay in guiding the State in a positive direction in cooperation with others. Thus, he would take an active part in the political structure of the State (Roy 1947: 36–37). Such a politically concerned and active citizen would combine with other similar citizens into people's committees. These committees would include all the citizens of the locality. Thus constituted, they would discharge all functions of local self-government. They would also nominate candidates for State and central legislatures. Once elected, they would be responsible to the committees and their electorate (ibid.: 47–50).

Roy was careful to differentiate these candidates from the existing ones in liberal democracy. For one, these candidates would belong to no party. In fact, Roy's vision was for a *party-less democracy*, where sovereignty would be held by the person and not a party (Talwar 2006: 299–300). Again, the representatives would be constantly in touch with the committees and act according to their wishes. If they failed to do so, they could be recalled by the committees. Hence, they would be forced to respect the wishes of the people, which included every citizen of the country. The result would be a structure of extreme decentralisation, wherein the people's committees would act as miniature republics in their own right. The central government would, in many cases, do nothing more than gather and pass on information. However, Roy did not oppose economic planning, as long as it didn't hamper freedom (ibid.: 247–248, 299–300; Roy 1947: 50).

This structure, however, would not arise in a day. At the local level, the intermediate period would see the formation of people's committees. When elections came and different existing parties put up their candidates, the people's committee may choose to support none of them and instead send their own candidate. This candidate would not be beholden to any party but the people in the committee. He would have to consult the committee on all matters and remain in power only as long as the committee reposed faith in him. Started at the micro level, this would lead to the establishment of a network of people's committees, which would become the foundation for a people's democracy (Roy 1964: 135–141). At the central level, it would require that the Council of States of the Federal Assembly be composed of outstanding men from different professions. These men, by their keen intellect, would set up laws which would break the current mould and usher in a new era of radical democracy (Roy 1947: 59–61).

IX Conclusion

This chapter has sought to show how M. N. Roy developed as an intellectual and contributed to the development of intellectual thought in India and abroad. His vast experiences and boundless energy allowed him to work for the emancipation of the masses, initially under the umbrella of nationalism, then Marxism, and finally his own vision of radical humanism.

Critics may argue that his influence was inversely proportional to his deviation from orthodox political practice. He achieved his greatest successes as an orthodox Marxist, founding two influential Communist Parties and becoming the prime authority on Asia. His influence declined as he moved into the opposition and then founded his own radical democracy. This found few takers, and when he finally dissolved the Radical Democratic Party to focus on the Radical Humanist Movement, his camp was reduced to only his wife, Ellen Roy, and a few ardent followers.

Yet this would be a lopsided assessment. From the very beginning, Roy was at once a devoted member of whichever ideology he championed and a careful reviewer of its internal workings. His shifts out of nationalism and into socialism, then to the opposition, and finally to radical humanism, displayed his deep understanding of the situations and the ideologies which sought to master these situations.

This keen intellect was backed up by indomitable courage. Once convinced of his position, Roy was a passionate messiah who spared himself no pain in working towards the emancipation of the masses. His final and mature ideology – radical humanism – despite its poor popular reception compared to his Marxism, was a major intellectual achievement. Despite its flaws, it exposed some of the most fundamental problems with both liberal democracy and communism at a time when they were becoming two blocs competing for world domination. His solution solved many of the difficulties inherent in those two systems and created a system that could, in theory, return to man the place that religion, Marxism, and even liberal party systems had snatched from him. Giving this place to humanity was indeed a noble ideal, one which was seldom attempted with such devotion and rigour. As Sumanta Banerjee noted on the 50th anniversary of Roy's death:

> Roy's life reads like an adventure on two levels – one of a revolutionary meteor flying up in the skies as it were, be dazzling the observers, and the other of a restless soul down below rowing in the rough sea of politics, moving from one political harbour to another in his ideological odyssey.
> *(Banerjee 2004: 2957)*

Notes

1 For lack of space, Roy's *Prison Diaries* can only be summarised briefly. People interested in this period are advised to go through Sibnarayan Ray's three excellent chapters on Roy's time in prison. The 100-page reference given earlier reflects the sheer amount of writing Roy did during this time but which cannot be discussed here. The texts have also been compiled as *Prison Manuscripts*, and this term may be used interchangeably with *Prison Diaries*.
2 Note that this section falls in the Epilogue of Roy's *Memoirs* and was actually written by V. B. Karnik, who became a close ally of Roy during his days in Berlin and remained a staunch Royist during Roy's life in India.
3 Term used by Manjapra. See Chapter 4: Interstitial Politics in Manjapra, pp. 111–152.
4 See previous section for details.
5 Talwar, p. 115.
6 The present *Draft* has been procured from Marxist.org. The date of publication is not mentioned, so the original date of the thesis has been used. See the References section for details.
7 A lively debate exists regarding the impact of the Roy–Lenin controversy. See Haithcox pp. 94–96. For the full list of possible readings on the topic, see References.
8 See previous section. It may be argued that during his final days in Europe, Roy was no longer "orthodox" in the Stalinist sense; he remained a staunch Communist as part of the German Opposition (KPD-O).
9 Talwar, pp. 221–222. Later, in *Beyond Communism*, he argued that romanticism about revolution was another critical aspect of a revolutionary. Since only the middle class could possess such romanticism, this class was the perfect recruiting ground for revolutionaries. Talwar, pp. 225.
10 Roy, Quoted from Talwar, p. 214.
11 Roy summarises his conception of Marx's ideas in the initial phase and then his obsession with Hegelian dialectics, in Chapter 4 of his *Manifesto*.
12 See previous sections "Transition from Marxism to radical humanism" and "Critique of Marxism".
13 See Thesis 3 of his 22 Theses, which are reproduced as part of the *Manifesto*.

References

Banerjee, S. (2004). Remembering M. N. Roy. *Economic and Political Weekly*, 39(27), 2957–2958. Retrieved from www.jstor.org/stable/4415221
Gordon, L. (1968). Portrait of a Bengal Revolutionary. *The Journal of Asian Studies*, 27(2), 197–216. https://doi.org/10.2307/2051747

Haithcox, J. (1963). The Roy–Lenin Debate on Colonial Policy: A New Interpretation. *The Journal of Asian Studies*, 23(1), 93–101. https://doi.org/10.2307/2050635

Lenin, V. I. (1920). *Draft Theses on National and Colonial Questions for the Second Congress of the Communist International*. Retrieved from www.marxists.org/archive/lenin/works/1920/jun/05.htm

Manjapra, Kris (2010). *M. N. Roy: Marxism and Cosmopolitanism*. New Delhi: Routledge.

Ray, Sibnarayan (Ed.) (1956). *M. N. Roy: Philosopher-Revolutionary (A Symposium)*. Kolkata: Renaissance Publisher.

Ray, Sibnarayan (2005). *In Freedom's Quest: Life of M.N. Roy* (3 Vols.). Kolkata: Renaissance Publisher.

Roy, M. N. (1947). *New Humanism: A Manifesto*. Kolkata: Renaissance Publisher.

Roy, M. N. (1952a). *Reason, Revolution and Romanticism* (2 Vols.). Kolkata: Renaissance Publisher.

Roy, M. N. (1952b). *Radical Humanism*. New Delhi: Eastern Economist Pamphlets.

Roy, M. N. (1964). *Memoirs*. Bombay: Allied Publishers Private Limited.

Talwar, Sadanand (2006). *Radical Humanism: Political Philosophy of M.N. Roy Revisited*. New Delhi: K. K. Publications.

15
NARENDRA DEVA

Satrajit Banerjee[1]

> Socialism seeks to establish a classless society. Socialism wants to restructure society in such a way as to bring to an end the mutually opposite interests of the various classes consisting of the exploited and the exploiter and the tyrant and the tyrannised. And the society may become a collection of co-operative individuals in which the advancement of one member may naturally mean the advancement of the others, so that all members may collectively lead a life directed towards common progress.
>
> – Acharya Narendra Deva, *Towards Socialist Society* (1979: 209)

I Introduction

Socialism as an idea and a form of constructive movement for social change was developed and operated under the broader platform of the Indian National Congress (I.N.C.) during the colonial period in India. It is a well-known fact that the idea of socialism evolved as a universal doctrine from the West. However, the ideology of socialism was adopted and modified by several Indian nationalist thinkers and activists as an alternative and tangible way in the anti-colonial struggle. Socialism as an ideology and as a form of activism got divergent connotations by different thinkers and practitioners based on the historical necessity of a given country or the pursuit of imminent goals. Similarly, in the Indian context, the ideology and practice of socialism was differently interpreted and upheld by various nationalist thinkers. Indeed, different forms of socialism in India were largely influenced by different doctrines, such as scientific socialism, Marxism, and Fabianism. Acharya Narendra Deva, a pioneer of Indian socialism, blended the basic principles of Marxism, Leninism, and the Gandhian method of non-violence in formulating his notion of socialism for reconstructing the Indian social system and emancipating India from British colonial domination. This chapter highlights the notion of socialism as conceptualised by Narendra

Deva and will consider the major political and philosophical sources, both Indian and Western, which left a formative impact upon Narendra Deva. Further, the chapter endeavours to present different facets of Narendra Deva's vision of socialism and to illustrate and analyse, in vivid detail, his articulation of socialism as an idea and a tangible method of social transition and reconstruction and a viable form of anti-colonial struggle in India.

II Life sketch

Acharya Narendra Deva was born on 31 October 1889 in Sitapur, Uttar Pradesh. He obtained a post-graduation degree from Allahabad University in 1911 and got an honorary bachelor's degree in jurisprudence from Banaras Oriental College in 1917. He was associated with political activities on one side and various educational institutions on the other. Narendra Deva was associated with the Kashi Vidyapeeth since its inception and served this institution as professor and subsequently as principal for almost two decades. After India's independence, he was appointed at Lucknow University and Banaras Hindu University respectively. Narendra Deva was drawn to politics from his early childhood. He attended the Lucknow conference of Congress with his father in 1899 at the age of ten. From 1906 to 1910 and from 1916 to 1948, Narendra Deva attended all conferences of the I.N.C. The events of contemporary India and world politics deeply influenced him. He was also moved by Dadabhai Naoroji's speech on total *swaraj* in the Calcutta session of the I.N.C. in 1906 (Dhar 1986: 53–54).

Narendra Deva's political activities were versatile and full of contradictions. At the initial stage of his political career, he was inspired by the extremist leaders of Congress. Throughout his political life, he relentlessly advocated and supported socialism. Yet he actively participated in the non-cooperation movement and the civil disobedience movement led by Mahatma Gandhi. Although Narendra Deva believed in the socialist revolutionary mass movement, he joined Gandhian non-violent demonstrations. Indeed, to him, a supporter of total *swaraj* should support all nationalist movements. In his praxis of socialism, Narendra Deva combined non-violence with the extreme principles of socialism. He was closely attached with several farmers' movements. He was one of the founding members of the All India *Kisan Sabha* (Dhar 1986: 54).

Narendra Deva opposed the split of the I.N.C. In 1910, when the extremists left Congress, he refused to attend the conference at Allahabad. He further joined Congress in 1916 as the extremists were reunited with the Congress. Narendra Deva formed the 'Congress Socialist Party' in 1934, following a prolonged disagreement with the stance of I.N.C. regarding ideological pursuit and strategy regarding anti-British struggle. Narendra Deva assumed the Congress would lose its versatile character after independence and turn into a centralised and authoritarian party. In 1934, he convened in the All-India Congress Socialist Conference and was lauded as a prominent nationalist leader after his election as the president of the Congress Socialist Party. He was welcomed by Jawaharlal

Nehru as a member of the Congress Working Committee in 1936 and was selected as a member of the Legislative Assembly in Uttar Pradesh twice, first in 1936 and then in 1946. Narendra Deva resigned from the Legislative Assembly as soon as the Congress Socialist Party left from the same. For the promotion of socialism and the expansion of a mass base of the party, he opened the membership to the public. In 1952, the Congress Socialist Party and the Kisan Mazdoor Praja Party of J. B. Kripalani were merged into the Praja Socialist Party (P.S.P.). He presided over the national Conference of the P.S.P. at Gaya in 1955, where his thesis on democratic socialism, also known as his "Gaya thesis", was endorsed. Narendra Deva breathed his last on 19 February 1956 in Madras (Mehtora 1986: 158; Verma 1990: 519).

III Sources of Narendra Deva's political philosophy

Narendra Deva was influenced by the Indian intellectual tradition and socialist thought of the West. He sought to commingle Marxism and Gandhism in his articulation of political philosophy. It was clearly reflected in his speeches and efforts that his ultimate objective was to realise socialism through non-violent means. Narendra Deva emphasised on the humanist aspect of Marxism. One of his major concerns was to spread the idea of cultural socialism in India. Narendra Deva's approach heavily relied on Marxist ideology. Although he emulated the theory and techniques of dialectics, Narendra Deva did not adopt unequivocally the materialist interpretation of Marxism. He mentioned that contemplation of the objective and principles of socialism and the essence of Marxist dialectics were required to realise the objective condition of India. He had unflinching faith in the validity of the materialist interpretation of history expounded by Marx. Hence, he considered this method of explicating history as a reliable approach to understand the development of world history as well as the objective condition of Indian society (Verma 1990: 519–520).

He mentioned that only scientific socialism could rescue mankind from the catastrophic outcome of warfare. In the All India Socialist Party Conference, held in 1949 at Patna, Narendra Deva presented a new articulation of Marxism. He argued, following the Marxist enumeration, that history always advanced towards a definite direction. From the Marxist understanding of historical evolution, Narendra Deva was convinced that capitalism accelerated worldwide the growth of narrow individualism and egoism. In a capitalist system, the labour force had been conceived as a commutable product like other commodities, and the labourers were compelled to dispose of their labour almost unconditionally. He sought to put an end to all sorts of domination over the working class and stressed on the human aspect of the labour force. He envisioned for creating a welfare collective order based on the principle of righteousness in place of a competitive capitalist system relying on profit and maximisation. He reaffirmed that the revolutionary proletariat would be the vanguard of humanity. In the Patna conference, Narendra Deva eulogised Marxism as a philosophy of humanism.

Indeed, he conflated the ideology of Marxism with the notion of altruism in his political philosophy (Dhar 1986: 54–56).

Narendra Deva was also deeply influenced by the ideas of Friedrich Engels, Karl Kautsky, Rosa Luxemburg, and Vladimir Lenin. Engels' interpretation of history and his views on the conditions of the cultivators and employing a democratic method in revolution left a deep imprint on the mind of Narendra Deva, whose socialistic ideas were further enriched by Kautsky's illustration of morality and Luxemburg's humanistic and cultural approach. In Luxemburg's opinion, socialism fulfilled the basic and primary needs of individuals. It was an embodiment of worldwide cultural struggle. Moreover, Lenin's enunciating of the role of the middle class for propagating socialist ideals and advancing socialist movements and the inevitability of conscious human effort for attaining ultimate socialist objectives also had tremendous influence on Narendra Deva (Dhar 1986: 55). The book *Historical Materialism*, written by Nikolai Bukharin, had significant bearing on Narendra Deva as well. He appreciated Bukharin's approach of classifying classes in the society. Like Bukharin, Narendra Deva also believed society was not constituted of only two classes, viz., bourgeois and proletariat; rather, mixed class, transitional class, and middle class were also considered important elements of social stratification. Narendra Deva also maintained that the working class would establish, at certain stage of history, absolute control over the industrial sector (Mehtora 1986: 161).

Further, he borrowed the idea of general strike as a strategy to be employed in the socialist revolution from the syndicalist theory propounded by George Sorel. Narendra Deva was aware of the ideological and strategic implications of general strike. He pointed out two important features of general strike: firstly, it forced the alien ruler to retreat from a country by crippling its economy, and secondly, the strong organisational basis required for general strike would enhance the scope of a socialist revolution. Narendra Deva asserted that the strategy of general strike might fail to yield the desired outcome in the mass movement; nevertheless, it would be used as an effective weapon by the working class to wield their political power in the nationalist struggle (Verma 1990: 522). Narendra Deva pursued a secular perception regarding the nature of nationalist politics and discarded the idea of revivalism. However, he was not at variance with the formative role of spiritualism in politics, as he endorsed Buddhism as a pragmatic form of religion (ibid.: 519). Therefore, Narendra Deva sought to redefine socialism with an objective to bring about social transformation in India.

IV Ideas on socialism

According to Narendra Deva, the main purpose of socialism is to establish a classless society. In fact, socialism sought to eliminate the sources of class antagonism through the process of social reconstruction. Socialism endeavoured to create a social order based on mutual cooperation among individuals where the uplifting of an individual was regarded as an indicator of social progress, thereby leading to the general development of all. Socialism claimed to establish an open and exploitation-free social order which would rescue mankind from their vulnerabilities and plight. Like Marx, Narendra Deva also believed socialism elevated an individual from the domain of narrow self-interest to the sphere of ultimate emancipation. Indeed, socialism appeared to offer freedom to the whole world, and it diligently remained engaged in eradicating the hindrances detrimental to the growth of individuals (Deva 1979: 209).

Narendra Deva devised a blueprint of socialism at the 1934 Congress Socialist Party Conference in Bombay. He regarded that the national industries in this order would be controlled by the working class. In such a society, no one would be allowed to accumulate an uncountable amount of property and monopolise over it. Property, like other social institutions, would be regulated by social norms and the needs and demands of individuals. Rights entitled to individuals contained the elements of social obligations. The State would be entitled to own private properties to serve the greater public interest, and the Parliament would be entrusted to carry out the responsibility of compensating individual loss. The State would be actively involved in economic activities and would be directed towards planned economic development. The main purpose of the State-run economy would be to ensure optimum and proper use of human resources and material wealth. Narendra Deva suggested certain measures, such as the promotion of small industries, the nationalisation of big industrial enterprises, and the introduction of a cooperative system in agriculture for implementing socialist ideals in the society. He was enthralled by the initiatives of economic planning pursued in Russia and advised to his socialist compatriots to take such measures suitable for India by reviewing the achievements of Russia.

Narendra Deva had set certain specific programmes for socialist groups. In the proposed land reform policy, he announced that the ownership of land will be handed over to cultivators. He actually wanted to eradicate the *zamindari* system to eliminate inequality in India. He believed that the fundamental prerequisite of establishing a socialist society was to recognise individual freedom. Narendra Deva, like Kautsky, believed socialism was not only a social organisation associated with the production system but was a democratic system, too. Socialism and democracy were complementary to each other; none of them would flourish without the other. According to him, socialism should be grounded on democratic means and democratic values. He also identified the inevitability of class struggle in the process of the transition to a socialist society. He, realising the nature of contradictions in capitalism, like Lenin, firmly believed in the antagonist relation between labour and capital. Narendra Deva upheld the importance of resorting to non-violent means in class struggle. He strongly claimed that socialism and class struggle would aim at the economic reconstruction of the society and establishing a classless and exploitation-free socialist democracy based on moral principles for eradicating inequality and the exploitation of the people (Dhar 1986: 57–58).

V Socialist transformation and elevation to socialism

Narendra Deva delineated that the potential of class struggle was embedded in the existing asymmetric, coercive, and exploitative economic order. He enumerated, following Lenin, "A socialist movement had every chance of breaking out first in a country where the masses had been ruined by economic exploitation, even though the country is not sufficiently developed industrially, if a revolutionary situation is present" (Mehtora 1986: 161). The prevailing economic structure in India, creating a gulf between the have and have-not, divided the population into two clear-cut classes, viz., the exploited and the exploiter. Narendra Deva admitted that radical transformation of an economic order required a revolutionary impetus. On one hand, the depressed class would struggle to overturn the existing order; while on the other hand, the dominating class would strive hard to maintain the status quo. Therefore, the privileged class consequently thrashed every attempt of the oppressed class. According to Narendra Deva, socialism resolved to attain an order conducive for the emancipation and development of the exploited class and ensured equal access to opportunities to the have-not. The doctrine of socialism conceived, as he mentioned, class struggle as a manifestation of the anti-colonial struggle. However, the efforts of the exploited class had certain moral contents which made them aware of the higher moral objectives and principles to be pursued through class struggle (Deva 1979: 291–292).

Indeed, the idea of a socialist revolution was based on moral conscience and humanist values. Narendra Deva considered that a movement of the people would reach its ultimate goal when it adhered to moral conduct. In his opinion, non-violent strategy should be followed for conducting class struggle. In the programme of the "Praja Socialist Party", it was enshrined that non-violent class struggle would be employed in the socialist revolution. Therefore, *satyāgraha* and strike were to be employed as amicable and democratic manoeuvres of the social transformation movement. He further iterated that *satyāgraha* and strike would be the last resort if the other peaceful means failed to yield the desired result. The Congress anticipated that strike would be proved otiose in a planned economic production and distribution system as existed in India under British rule. For the ceaseless economic growth and reconstruction, peace and stability should be restored in the industrial sector. Narendra Deva retorted that peace could not endure in a system of exploitative economic order. He further argued that the demand of the Congress to maintain peace in the industrial sector had failed to ensure security of employment, adequate wage, and having a fair share of profit and even the proper treatment of workers. Moreover, it had proved propitious for capitalist interests by overlooking the main sources of conflict and antagonism. Even the Congress could not provide a suitable mechanism for the equal distribution of national income. Therefore, Narendra Deva argued that the oppressed classes would be able to protect their interests by organising strikes and *satyāgraha*. He envisioned that these two methods could be used against the foreign domination as establishing a classless socialist society (Deva 1979: 293–294).

Narendra Deva also mentioned the significant role of the trade union for carrying out socialist agitation. The trade unions devoted their energy to garnering the economic interests of the workers and neglected organised political actions. Although they lacked the capability to exterminate capitalism alone, they were likely to earn social recognition through their persistent struggle for the economic rights of the workers and other exploited classes. Narendra Deva believed the process of social restructuring would not be successful without formulating an effective political programme for consolidating oppressed classes and capturing political power by constitutional and democratic means. Narendra Deva stressed on adhering to parliamentary means, apart from discarding armed insurrection and other violent methods, for social transformation. He further argued that the parliamentary process would not only be used in the struggle against imperialism but also could be applied to instilling socialist values among the masses. He suggested that by taking part in electoral politics and assuming a place in the legislature, the socialists might get a greater opportunity to inculcate socialist principles in the society. The "Praja Socialist Party" should have to spearhead the initiative of proliferating socialist ethics in the society (Deva 1979: 294–296). Indeed, Narendra Deva envisaged that "the socialists desire to build up a powerful anti-imperialist front to achieve independence of the country and to establish a democratic regime wherein the economic life of the people would be organised on socialist lines" (Deva 1946: 115). Narendra Deva clearly asserted that the socialist transformation demanded the liquidation of the distorted system and discarded personal vengeance against any individual.

Regarding the class character of the socialist revolution, Narendra Deva mentioned that the society was not merely divided into two classes, namely, the bourgeoisie and proletariat, but there were other important classes, like the middle class, intelligentsia, declassed masses, and common people. The ultimate purpose of the socialist movement was to include the intermediary class and declassed masses within the broader framework of class struggle. He observed that the middle-class population played a dominant role in the national struggle. But he felt that expansion of the popular base of the national movement would turn it into a more formidable struggle against imperialism. He visualised that the working class would provide leadership in the anti-imperialist struggle. He perceived that the native princes, capitalists, and feudal lords together with the British, formed an imperial coalition. He urged for constituting an alliance among peasant workers, intelligentsia, and the common masses against the imperial coalition. He firmly believed that the economic struggle of the working class would, in time, assume the character of political movement. However, he was aware of the lack of cooperation among the peasants and their inability to articulate demands and move together in a coherent and organised way. The peasants did protest on several occasions against the land reform policy of the British government, but those demonstrations were sporadic and short-lived. With the expansion of the mass base of the national struggle, Narendra Deva assumed, the peasant agitation would get a larger platform. He considered the development of widespread class consciousness as the essential prerequisite for class solidarity. He further mentioned that two elements which made a class self-conscious were propaganda and organisation. In his opinion, the revolutionary intelligentsia would carry forward the task of implementing those instruments for generating class consciousness (Deva 1979: 184–186).

Narendra Deva emphasised on the pioneering role of organisations like *Kisan Sabha* for the restoration of Indian agriculture. He advocated for the improvement of the farmers and development in rural areas through the promotion of public education. Like Stalin, Narendra Deva believed farmers should be motivated towards socialist ideals. To attract the peasants towards socialist ideas, Narendra Deva thought, it was imperative to establish strong cooperative society. Moreover, it was necessary to take such policy to provide the farmers loans and relieve themselves from debts. He also considered the urgent need of abolishing middleman between the State and the tiller of the land by revising the existing land policy. Narendra Deva never viewed nationalism from a narrow, parochial, or sectarian perspective. In his opinion, the effect of agrarian reconstruction might give rise to the narrow peasantism which was likely to be proved counterproductive to the interests of the farmers. Even this peasantism might lead to division and conflict between the rural and urban areas. He insisted on introducing a new life movement for overcoming the social backwardness of the rural population and making socialist ideas more acceptable to them. However, he was aware of the impediments of consolidation of the agricultural class. Narendra Deva rightly assumed that the main obstacle of developing class consciousness and unity among the farmers was casteism, religious differences, diversity of agricultural patterns in different regions, and the predominance of the wealthy class in the I.N.C. (Verma 1990: 522).

He realised there was a gradual rise of political consciousness in the working class of India which resulted in the rise of pro-worker political party in some provinces of India. In addition to this, positive steps were taken for the establishment of the 'All-India Working Party'. The working class of India would eliminate capitalism and had taken the pledge to resist all imperialist-capitalist exploitation. The 'All-India Working Party' identified the aim of achieving ultimate national liberation to improve the condition of the working class. This group decided to give leadership to the nationalist movement. Some of the demands of the peasantry would be incorporated within the demands of workers' movement. Even though Narendra Deva believed the movement of the pro-people was being driven sporadically due to internal discrimination, in many cases, opportunist leadership misguided the workers and created division among their ranks. The lack of good revolutionary leadership in the direction of the movement was clearly visible, and organisational weaknesses were also being noticed. For this reason, the workers' strike programs often failed. According to Narendra Deva, "if the organisers of the movement can ensure reliable and appropriate leadership, this movement can become larger and fruitful" (Deva 1979: 186–187).

VI Socialism and morality

Narendra Deva considered that the modern foundation of socialism was humanist, social, and historical in nature. The genuine humanist morality emerged only in that social order that was free from all forms of exploitation, suppression, and misery. Even the existence of class conflict and class domination devalued the principles of morality in society. The pursuit of profit maximisation degraded the moral condition of society and facilitated the expansion of corruption in the prevailing economic order. Therefore, Narendra Deva contended that the notion of morality should be contemplated from the socialist perspective. From the social aspect, it had been apprehended that the conscious initiative of individuals led to their moral elevation and the growth of social morality. He argued that humans were social beings and thus could develop moral virtues as an inseparable part of society. Therefore, Narendra Deva argued that individuals' moral qualities were germinated within a righteous and suitable social order. He believed most of the moral principles that prevailed in society protected the interests of the dominant class. The exploited class wanted to highlight the nature of social inequality and oppression and tried to rescue themselves from the separation of the predominant class. As a result, certain alternative moral principles came into practice. Hence, the working class claimed for their social recognition through equality and freedom. In a class-divided society, at a certain phase of social evolution, an alternative moral order emerged out of clashes among opposing moral forces (Deva 1979: 302–303).

In human society, the moral qualities of an individual emanate from sociability. But in a class-stratified society, class consciousness preponderates over the social consciousness and hence, the interest of the dominant class evades social responsibility. Narendra Deva felt that it would be imperative to pursue the revolutionary transformation of the social order to dispense justice to the exploited class. The prime objective of this radical change would be to eliminate immorality, exploitation, repression, and unrighteousness. The socialist morality would be regarded as a useful means to resolve the crisis of humanity. The individuals and the class, guided by revolutionary objectives, would practice self-discipline, self-introspection, and self-criticism for facilitating social change. Narendra Deva stated that "every socialist should abide by the moral norms............. objective of a socialist was to be involved in the goal of social welfare" (Deva 1979: 303–304).

The socialist revolution opposed the moral digression of individuals and discarded unrighteous acts of class. Socialist morality regarded as obligatory for the pursuit of democratic values, culture, and processes in the society. However, Narendra Deva was aware of the difficulties of pursuing moral principles of classless society in the class-stratified social order. He urged that an effort to advance towards socialist morality would elevate the standard of the socialists as individuals and made them trustworthy to others, which would ultimately expedite, following democratic means, the socialist struggle. Socialist morality stimulated mental affinity among individuals. It was grounded in human emotion and social humanism. The freedom, equality, and welfare of all were the quintessence of socialist morality. Narendra Deva articulated that democratic values should be conjoined with the humanist values and moral principles inherent in socialism for the social transformation of the Indian economy. Thus, as Narendra Deva envisaged, "the essence of democratic socialism was embedded in socialist morality" (Deva 1979: 304).

VII Socialism and cultural transformation

Narendra Deva believed socialism was not a mere economic doctrine, its objective did not remain confined to waging economic struggle; rather, socialism aimed at the cultural transformation of a society. Culture refers to the attribute of sociability inherent in every individual. And cultural heritage is an outcome of the collective efforts of individuals. The primary elements and basic principles of culture represented the divergent interests, demands, and experiences of mankind. Therefore, a definite cultural pattern or system of culture always denotes a specific way of life which has been conditioned by historically determined principles of society and circumstantial influences. The process of social evolution and social environment largely influenced the lifestyle of individuals. In a society, people developed certain common social principles and cultural norms as a result of reciprocity and mutual interactions among them. Social evolution and the advancement of the society are intrinsically integrated with each other. The elementary basis of a specific cultural pattern was formed by some social norms and economic interests of the individuals. In a class-divided society, divergent cultural trends coexist. There would always be the likelihood of occurring conflict between the classes following different cultural trends. The dominant class sought to overpower the existing social structure and the cultural trends therein by imposing their own pattern of culture, representative of their interest and demand, as dominant force. As the suppressed class lived long under a system where the cultural pattern of the dominant class was predominant, gradually they accepted those cultural patterns as inviolable and unquestionable factors. But, at one point, the suppressed class spoke up for the preservation of their class interest as soon as they evolved as a class-conscious entity. Subsequently, the working class endeavoured to overturn the existing social structure by replacing it with their long-cherished social and cultural elements (Deva 1979: 409–410).

Socialism opposed the consolidation of a hierarchical cultural structure maintained by the oppressive class. Its primary objective was to ensure the cultural demands of the masses. It envisioned such a system free from all sorts of discrimination, antagonism, and deprivation which would be propitious for establishing a truly classless society. Narendra Deva believed that under this particular form of socialistic culture, the Western democratic socialist trend and Indian humanistic traditions would be harmonised in a constructive manner. He further argued that socialistic humanism did not seek to follow the principle of homogeneity, nor did it support a system of monolithic structure. On the contrary, its objective was to ensure recognition to diversity and heterogeneity. The cultural trend of socialistic humanism provided space for cultural autonomy and equal rights of the people. In this system, every person has been granted the right to pursue his own religion and establish cultural association and religious institutions as per his own choice and inclination. This cultural structure duly recognised the culture, religion, language, heritage, and certain special rights and privileges of the minority population. It also guaranteed the equitable participation and access of the minority population in the political, social, and economic sphere. Narendra Deva mention that the State would grant the opportunity to the children belonging to the minority group to pursue their study in their vernacular until the secondary level in those regions where the minority population turned out to be numerically dominant within the resident of that place. However, it would be applied largely, as a common practice, to all, including the minority population, that the students must learn the language of the State and the official language to play a constructive role as responsible citizens (Deva 1979: 411).

The cornerstone of socialist cultural structure was to maintain a balance and correlation between labour and culture. It considered force of labour as a formative capability of mankind. The ideals of socialist culture inspired all to become an integral part of cultural structure and to enjoy the fruits of it. He held that all people should be allowed the opportunity to develop their personalities and the cultural heritage of humanism. He further exhorted for the creation of cultural centres at all levels of the industrial sector for the cultural amelioration of the workers. Moreover, adequate arrangements should be made for the agricultural labourers to enjoy the riches and bounties of rural India. Hence, the ecosystem of rural India should be preserved properly. The modern facilities of the civilisational progress would be made available to the rural populace. The socialist culture based on humanist principles would act as a binding force for integrating the rural and urban culture in India.

Another fundamental aspect of the process of cultural transformation would be the cultural advancement of tribal population and narrowing the gap between the progressive and backward classes (Deva 1979: 411). Narendra Deva warned against the effect of imposing a national cultural pattern over the tribal population as a measure of accommodating them into the mainstream society. He felt that because of this initiative, the cultural progress of the tribal people would be hampered and they would face severe exploitation and suppression. He reiterated that the ideal of democratic socialism would intend to establish a link between the socialist culture and the cultural trends of the tribal people. He suggested that the local councils would introduce advanced techniques of production and modern cultural trends in the tribal regions. In India, the progressive class and the State would have to play a proactive role for the uplifting of the tribal population (Deva 1979: 412).

India is a multilingual country; thus, there was a growing trend of separatist tendencies based on claiming superiority and demand for autonomous status. Ideal never allowed any special treatment to any lingual group as it was inconsistent with the democratic norms. Narendra Deva believed that the preponderance of a particular lingual community would create a hierarchical order in society. In his opinion, democratic socialism would adopt Hindi as the common language of the State and also would recognise other regional languages (Deva 1979: 412–413). He asserted that one of the utmost obligations of democratic socialism was to preserve gender equality.

In his view, the social progress would be futile without the well-being of the women. Indeed, socialism contradicted with the notion of considering women as a dependent and secondary category in the society. Narendra Deva perceived that socialist culture rejected the cultural trend of denying opportunity and recognition to women. The socialist ideals promoted and preserved the equality and freedom of women. Socialist culture emphasised on social harmony, equal wages for equal work, and the expansion of the scope of employment for women. Socialism intended to safeguard special privileges for women relating to maternity, obligations of the community and family for the protection of children and pregnant women, equal rights to education for women, and the active role of women in State functioning (Deva 1979: 413–414). Therefore, it appeared to Narendra Deva that the ideal of socialist humanism would be able to retain harmony and constructive balance within the heterogeneous social structure of India in the spheres of gender equality, lingual pluralism, and the rights and privileges of minority and marginalised communities through the dissemination of socialist culture. Again, he retorted that the socialist culture would not only resolve the conflict among the contradictory forces exist in India through a process of gradual cultural transformation, but also it would spearhead the overall development of the society.

VIII Socialism and democracy

In Narendra Deva's opinion, the true form of socialism ensured economic freedom, safeguarding the environment favourable for the development of individuals' personalities and restoring democratic values. He envisaged that democracy would be crippled without economic equality, and socialism would turn out to be impotent in the absence of democracy. To quote him:

> Socialism alone stands for the fullest democracy. Democracy of the capitalist order is a sham democracy. Political democracy is meaningless and farcical unless it is accompanied by economic equality and unless it stands for the economic emancipation of the masses.
>
> *(Deva 1979: 6–7)*

Narendra Deva delineated that Marxist ideology did not lie in contrast to democracy, as both the ideas championed the cause of human emancipation. Marxist communism underlaid democratic values. To Engels, the proletariat class got salvation within communism. In the Marxist version, people would be degenerated to sub-human levels in feudalism, and capitalism and humanity could only be restored through the proletarian revolution (Deva 1979: 205). Further, he stated:

We want fullest democracy for the vast masses of our people and not only for a few classes. We want to make available to our poor people the treasures of knowledge which have been inherited by us from past generations. We want to remove all inequalities in the matter of economic life. Therefore, it is socialism alone which stands for fullest democracy.

(Deva 1979: 70)

Moreover, he advocated for creating a united front of the left parties which would be instrumental for actualising socialist democracy. But he was quite aware of the limitation of the socialist parties regarding the launch of an organised struggle. He proposed the leaders of the parties refrain from criticising and attacking each other verbally to maintain solidarity among them. He realised that the harmonious communion among the leftist parties in India was yet to be achieved. Indeed, he observed that the phenomenon of discord among the parties of the left was a worldwide problem. Therefore, the sporadic nature of the leftist movement in India would achieve little. However, a more organised and planned struggle of the leftist wings should be introduced for the realisation of democratic socialism in India (Mehtora 1986: 163).

Narendra Deva held that the essence of democratic values was ingrained in socialism. He devised a model of democratic socialism. To his mind, socialism lay in contradiction with the hierarchical structure of society. In socialism, not a single person, nor a privileged group, nor feudal lords or even capitalists could ever dominate the socio-political-economic structure and conducts of society. This system negated imperialism and all sorts of foreign domination. It preserved democratic rights of every person and democratised all forms of social relations. Democratic socialism favoured the autonomy of the social and economic sectors. It facilitated the unbridled participation of all. Narendra Deva mentioned that the working class would control the centre of power relating to society and economy. In this society, power and duties would be decentralised. In democratic socialism, social justice and equality would be preserved by meeting the physical, mental, and moral growth of every person. For the advancement of society, socialism sought to ensure individual well-being. The idea of socialism regarded individuals as the prime source of power. It also allowed individuals' right to resistance and to revolt against any person, group, or class for an act of usurpation of State power or social control. Narendra Deva admitted that democratic ideals should be emulated in a diversified country like India to resolve a multitude of problems. He mentioned that the democratic values should be imparted, and the socialistic structure must be installed for the reconstruction of the Indian polity.

IX Parallel journey of the nationalist movement and socialist struggle

Narendra Deva assumed the necessity of consolidating national struggle with the socialist revolution for the attainment of the political freedom of India. He realised that the socialists should, relinquishing their conservativeness, join the nationalist struggle led by the bourgeoisie because it might alienate them from the masses and likely prove suicidal. Thus, he supported the August Resolution (1942) of Congress, as he believed it enshrined the social aspect of freedom and the right to the self-determination of individuals (Verma 1990: 521). He mentioned that the socialist struggle would be operated from within the broader platform of the I.N.C. He declared in the conference of the Congress Socialist Party in 1934 at Patna, that the socialist party would expand the mass bases of the nationalist movement by exacting support from the middle class. However, he was quite uncertain about the intention of the Congress, considering its class character, to pursue socialist ideals and institutionalise democracy in India. He also stated that the Congress should render support to the struggle of farmers and workers. Narendra Deva believed the formative understanding among the members of the Congress led nationalist struggle, and the socialist movement would be possible if the socialists operated within the framework of the I.N.C., rather than as its alternative or counter-force; only then, could the goal of the nationalist struggle be achieved and the objectives of the socialist revolution be fulfilled (Deva 1979: 183–184).

X Conclusion

Narendra Deva endeavoured to present a blueprint of social reconstruction in India. Therefore, all the initiatives of Narendra Deva should be evaluated, considering his efforts to remodel India. In his attempt to overhaul Indian society, Narendra Deva resorted to socialist revolution, following Marxist doctrine, and he insisted on employing democratic principles and non-violent methods as techniques of revolutionary transformation. He adhered to the idea of cultural revolution to realise the goal of socialist transformation in society. In his socialist programme, morality was considered as a supreme ideal. He considered religion as one of the major obstacles for attaining social solidarity. Narendra Deva, following Marxism, articulated that religion alienated individuals from reality and hence degraded individuals' self-esteem. Thus it precluded people to run after earthly pursuits and consequently deterred the natural growth of innate human qualities. Religion portrayed the existing social system as a manifestation of divinity and stressed on the irreversibility of the system. He explicated that the society founded on mysticism spread unfounded beliefs among individuals and preserved the interests of a handful of privileged people. He compared the immutable nature of capitalism with the religion to maintain the status quo.

Narendra Deva stressed the need to reform the existing education system and disseminate education among all, which would be instrumental to understanding the objective condition of the society and the nature and blueprint of socialist reconstruction in India. He propagated that the realisation of divergent social objectives would be the prime consideration of the education system. He urged that the basic objective of education should be to make individuals conscious, open-minded, rational, and responsible citizens. At the university level,

Narendra Deva suggested pupils get acquainted with the cultural heritage and values of the past. Apart from reconsidering and reviewing that knowledge, the student should also concentrate on contemporary issues affecting and influencing the society. Since the progress of a country heavily relied on advancements in scientific research and discovery, it would be pertinent to encourage the students in this field. Moreover, students should be provided training regarding administration and leadership. Narendra Deva upheld the importance of widespread education at every level of the society for the development of mass awareness (Deva 1979: 419–420). He observed that the spread of education would develop political culture among the people which would be conducive for the consolidation of a strong democratic polity in India. Further, he admitted that special care should be taken for providing education to the backward classes. In his vision, India would emerge as a democratic welfare State only through the dissemination of education (Deva 1979: 427).

Narendra Deva faced severe criticism from the other members of the I.N.C. He was slated for his effort to form the Congress Socialist Party to prove the autonomy of socialist struggle and for attaining the goal of socialism in India. On several occasions, Narendra Deva was reprehended for dissenting with the major activities and programmes of the I.N.C. Moreover, he failed to provide a proper illustration of socialist transformation of society from capitalism. Even his idea and efforts to launch a non-violent strategy for social change appeared ambivalent. One of Narendra Deva's major lacunas was the absence of a coherent theoretical framework in his attempt to bring about social change in India. However, his remarkable contributions as thinker and practitioner of democratic socialism, moral socialism, and humanist socialism were considered authoritative and had a lasting impact on the subsequent development of Indian politics.

Note

1 Some portions of this chapter were earlier published in the chapter 'Bharatiya Rashtra Bhavnai Samajtantrer Pothikrit', pp. 269–290, in the book *Bharatiya Rashtrachinta: Kautilya Theke Amarty Sen* (in Bengali), edited by Abhishek Mitra, Progressive Publisher, Kolkata, 2020. Some portions of the earlier text were translated and reproduced here with permission from Progressive Publisher, Kolkata.

References

Deva, Acharya Narendra (1946). *Socialism and the National Revolution*, Yusuf Meherally (Ed.). Bombay: Padma Publications Limited.
Deva, Acharya Narendra (1979). *Towards Socialist Society*, Brahmanand (Ed.). New Delhi: Centre for Applied Politics.
Dhar, Sisir (1986). 'Acharya Narendra Deva' in Chaudhary, Asim Kumar (Ed.), *Indian Socialist Panorama*. Kolkata: Socialist Movement Golden Jubilee Celebration Committee.
Mehtora, N. C. (1986). *Indian Socialist Thinking*. New Delhi: M.N. Publishers.
Verma, V. P. (1990). *Modern Indian Political Thought*. Agra: Lakshmi Narain Agarwal Educational Publishers.

16

JAWAHARLAL NEHRU

Surya Narayan Misra

> *What the mysterious is I do not know. I do not call it God because God has come to mean much that I do not believe in. I find myself incapable of thinking of a deity or of any unknown supreme power in anthropomorphic terms, and the fact that many people think so is continually a source of surprise to me. Any idea of a personal God seems very odd to me.*
> — Toward Freedom: The Autobiography of Jawaharlal Nehru (1936: 16)

I Introduction

Jawaharlal Nehru was the first Prime Minister of India. He shaped the destiny of a post-colonial country for 17 years. Mahatma Gandhi, Sardar Vallabhbhai Patel, and Nehru were considered the trinity of twentieth-century India's nationalist struggle for independence. All three had legal education and training in England. Once young Nehru finished his informal home education, he was sent to England for formal education, where he studied at Harrow and then Trinity College. Then he was called to the Bar after completing courses at Inner Temple. Whereas Gandhi and Patel represented the old philosophy of modern India and symbolically connected them with the serene village life of India, Nehru represented the West. Occidental education and travels imprinted on his mind the best of Western civilisation. Gandhi and Patel received their early education in India, but all of Nehru's education was in England. What distinguished Nehru from the other two was that Gandhi and Patel felt at home in rural India, whereas Nehru was foreign to the rural way of life.

Nehru's young days of learning in England exposed him to the atmosphere of liberalism and Fabianism. Thus, he was influenced by the revolutionary ideas prevalent in England before the First World War. The slogan of liberty, equality, and fraternity of 1789 spread over Western Europe, and Nehru's thought process was indoctrinated into it. During those days, West Europe was a citadel of imperialism and they owned all the colonies of Asia and Africa. Nehru often wondered how these countries which provided freedom to their own people could deny the same to the inhabitants of the countries they controlled. The paradox greatly agitated him. Nehru thought political freedom was necessary before demanding economic emancipation. What he saw in Lenin's thinking and experienced during his visit to the Soviet Union would leave on him an indelible mark. Thus, British liberalism, French revolutionarism, and the Soviet economic system influenced him to think about the challenges of the British colonial presence in his homeland and plan for remedial measures.

Young Nehru came back to India and joined the reputed practice of his father's law firm in Allahabad. But the training in England and his ideological orientation drove him towards political action. He was influenced by three factors at home. First was Annie Besant's utterances for improvement, reform, and freedom for which she launched the Home Rule League in 1916 to campaign for democracy in India and dominion status within the Empire. This led to her election as president of the India National Congress (I.N.C.) in 1917. This attracted Nehru towards active politics. Next, the incident at Jallianwala Bagh, where protests of the inhuman Rowlatt Act were oppressed by brutal firing, moved Nehru to join the Congress movement in 1919. Gandhi's non-cooperation movement was the third and final push for Nehru to leave behind his law career and pursue a path that often found him on the other side of the justice system. In fact, he was behind bars for almost 11 years on nine different occasions. In 1929, Nehru was elected as the president of the I.N.C. when the historic 'Lahore Declaration' for complete independence was made. Nehru had a very powerful pen. He could communicate as effectively as any established writer. His autobiography stands as testimony to this. Nehru's unusual ability to think, reflect, and contemplate vigorously, effectively, and intensively was second to none. He has not been with us for the last 50 years, but the impact of Nehruvian strategy on economic planning based on equity and social justice continues to be the focal theme of the nation-building process in India (Misra 2013: 80).

II Life sketch

Jawaharlal Nehru was born on 14 November 1889 at Allahabad into the rich Kashmir *Brāhmin* family of prominent lawyer Motilal Nehru and his wife, Swaroopa Rani. He had home schooling under the guidance of Western teachers and, at the age of 15, moved to England, where he studied first at Harrow and then for his Tripos at Trinity College of Cambridge before being called to the Bar. In 1912, Nehru came back to India and practiced law. He married Smt. Kamala Nehru in 1916, and they had one child – Indira Priyadarshini Nehru. He had two sisters – Vijaya Lakshmi Pandit and noted writer Krishna Hutheesing. Vijaya Lakshmi Pandit became the first woman president of the United Nations General Assembly in 1953.

Young Nehru was deeply influenced by his home tutor Ferdinand T. Brooks, who besides helping him to learn, sparked Nehru's interest in science and theosophy. At the age of 13, he became closer with family friend Annie Besant. His theosophical interests induced him to study the Buddhist and Hindu scriptures. Noted writer B. R. Nanda wrote, "these Scriptures were Nehru's first introduction to the religious and cultural heritage of India and these provided him the initial impulse for long intellectual quest which culminated in the 'Discovery of India'" (Nanda 1962: 65).

In 1912, Nehru attended the All-India Congress Committee (A.I.C.C.) at Patna. He was not impressed with the activities of the I.N.C. However, he supported the party's assistance in the civil rights movement in South Africa that Gandhi had launched. Then, Nehru campaigned against the indentured labour and other such discriminations Indians faced in the British colonies. Nehru was shocked to see the pace of nationalist struggle in India. Even Gopal Krishna Gokhale had said that demanding independence was some sort of madness. Nehru's father counselled him that there was no practical alternative to the type of British rule. Motilal Nehru had accepted the limits of constitutional agitation. Young Jawaharlal Nehru was dissatisfied with the words of his father and he got himself involved with aggressive nationalist leaders who demanded home rule.

Nehru was elected as chairman of Allahabad Municipality in 1925 and continued in that role up to 1927. Besides functioning in the most democratic manner, he had shown an attitude of impartiality, moderation, and energetic engagement in governance while pursuing his long-term objectives of collective work and responsibility (Gopal 1975: 23).

In the post-non-cooperation era, Motilal and C. R. Das differed with Gandhi and founded the *swaraj* Party. But Jawaharlal remained loyal to Gandhi and did not join his father's new agenda. In 1929, Jawaharlal Nehru was elected as the president of the I.N.C. and the historic '*Purna swaraj* Resolution' was passed. By that time, Nehru had tried to internationalise the freedom movement of all the colonies. He attended the Congress of oppressed nationalities all over the world, held in Brussels in 1927. He also collaborated with Netaji Subhas Chandra Bose in developing good relations with the governments of free countries. He supported the anti-Franco republicans of Spain during the Spanish Civil War of 1936–1939. Nehru's support for republic influenced him to agitate against princes of princely ruled States, and he helped the 'All India States Peoples' Conference'. In his work, he came closer to Sardar Patel. Nehru's goals of freedom were visible when the Cabinet Mission visited India to work out the modalities of transfer of power and the installation of a government with a Constitution.

Jawaharlal Nehru assumed the office of Vice President of the Viceroy's executive council on 2 September 1946, and he became the Prime Minister of the Indian dominion on 15 August 1947 and of the Republic on 26 January 1950, continued until his death on 27 May 1964. Besides being minister of different departments, Nehru's uniqueness was that he was External Affairs Minister from the time of India's independence until his death.

III Nehru's model of nation-building

Nehru was a practical statesman. Though he was the natural political successor of the "Father of the Nation" (Gandhi), he differed with him on various matters. The newly independent country had inherited a bad economy and the culmination of the 'divide-and-rule-policy' of the colonial master through the partition of India. More than 80 percent of the population were poor, and illiteracy combined with ignorance was rampant. India got its independence at a most difficult period in world history. The Second World War was over, but it caused a more dangerous ideology driven by the Cold War. The colonial master had denied Indians the four freedoms – freedom of speech, freedom of worship, freedom from hunger, and freedom from fear. At the time, India was writing its Constitution, and Nehru, being the chief architect of the new India, had kept in his vision democracy, secularism, socialism, and social justice. They were essential components of the nation- building process in India.

Nehru's nation-building process began during the freedom movement. He understood the importance of both nationalism and internationalism, unlike his other contemporaries in and outside of India. He discovered India only after making *Glimpses on World History* (Karunakaran 1986: 106). For Nehru, the Second World War was a people's war against fascism. He envisioned his worldview keeping in mind the nation-building in India. During the Cold War, Nehru was critical of the so-called world powers but never aligned India with either of the two hostile military alliances. This he did keeping in mind India's necessities and the importance of peace in the nation-building process.

India was and is a land of diverse culture, tradition, and faith. Religion and other traditions have their importance in public life. Nehru was aware of the strength of religious traditions, but he was a proponent of a rational outlook; he was rebellious against superstition, faith, and ritualistic orientations. His basic approach was that communal and other questions were connected with economic problems. When combined with Gandhi's realistic understanding of traditions and anti-communalism, Nehru's secular approach made a tremendous impact on Indian society and polity. In other words, he did not appear as an alien. He did not appear as a Hindu communalist and revivalist. He stood in the middle (Karunakaran 1986: 106).

Before independence, religion and caste were major problems in India. After independence, language and regional issues affected the progress of the country. The dominant language changes every 50 miles in India. The Hindi question had caused severe challenges from the South. Thus, Hindi and Hindu were two hurdles before Nehru in his attempt to shape the destiny of the nation. He made some interventions during the freedom movement, but they were not enough. After examining every aspect of the problem, Nehru generated a new cosmopolitan outlook. He initiated language Commissions and the J.V.P. (Jawaharlal, Vallabhbhai, and Pattabhi) Committee to investigate the linguistic basis of State formation, and they were not inclined to give primacy to any language.

Nehru accorded utmost importance to socio-economic aspects of nation-building. He was not in line with Gandhi in these areas. Already the new country had faced post-partition-era problems. The language issues had become more critical in the South. Nehru gave primacy to the concept of national unity. He made it clear that there should be an attempt to reach a national consensus for the preservation of national unity. He preferred conciliation and negotiation between the State and the stakeholders with the aim of preserving national unity. According to K. P. Karunakaran, Nehru had no illusion regarding the capacity of the State. He wanted politics, not administration, to be in command.

Before the onset of democratic dispensation, India was feudalistic in order. Inequality in terms of caste and the owning of land created a severe hurdle in policy-making. He also took the help of the constitutional process for land reforms by abolishing the *zamindari* system and estates. Similarly, he constituted the 'Kakasaheb Kalelkar Commission' to peep into the country's caste system. Further, to revamp the administration, Nehru implemented several measures with reformist zeal in the administration and its processes.

Equity and social justice were priorities in Nehru's policy interventions. He envisioned a good agrarian economy and changes in the land–man relations in rural India. He urged for industrialisation, which had been denied to the country for two centuries by the colonial authority. They only designed a market in India and drained its mineral resources to augment their economic and industrial strength. Nehru believed industrialisation would bring development, development would generate employment, and employment would reduce disparities.

IV Parliamentary democracy and the decentralisation of power

The parliamentary system was very dear to Nehru. He encouraged debate and discussion. Winston Churchill once called him the "Light of Asia". Churchill was sure Nehru would take to the path of parliamentary debate, discussion, and decision. Nehru was one of the founding fathers of India's Constitution and a builder of democracy in the country. His vision of progress and development, according to him, could be achieved through democratic and peaceful processes. He had strong faith in democratic and parliamentary institutions.

In the Constituent Assembly, it was informally discussed as to whether the future government should be based on a network of *Panchayats* or if should there be a parliamentary form of government on the British model. In the early 1930s, Nehru was attracted towards a Soviet pattern of democracy, but in the Assembly, the line of thought moved towards providing a centralised political democracy based on universal adult franchise.

Nehru believed in parliamentary democracy. But to him, democracy was not only a form of government; it was a way of life, a way of solving problems by argument, discussions, and persuasions. Democracy thus involved tolerance and restraint. Nehru once said, "You may define democracy in a hundred ways but surely one of its definitions is self-discipline of the community. The less of the imposed discipline, the more the self-discipline, and the higher is the development of democracy" (Ghose 1984: 286). During his early political years, when the 'Preventive Detention Act' was introduced, critics questioned the Nehruvian approach. Nehru boldly said the Act had to be passed because of the lack of self-discipline, and he argued that a merely agitational approach or excessive resort to direct action would endanger the democratic structure. He faced the biggest challenge to democracy when the first general election was held.

Nehru had differences with Gandhi, Patel, and Rajendra Prasad. But he had never been party to the processes of weakening the institutions of democracy. He was a great parliamentarian of his times. Nehru always believed that the people and the Constitution are sovereign and the Parliament is supreme. He believed its supremacy extended to all other spheres and authorities under the Constitution and that they were accountable to the Parliament. Nehru, as the first Prime Minister, had to uphold the prestige, honour, and position of the Parliament, and he had done nothing as the executive head to undermine the very institution. He had never thought of curbing or limiting its scope or functions because that would be tantamount to the goal which the country had before it. To defend, preserve, and uphold the Constitution had been evident in his actions, writings, and speeches.

Nehru had great respect for opposition. He never missed attending Parliament. Whenever he was slightly late, he never hesitated to apologise. His great concern for suspicion of the opposition was seen when his own son-in-law, Feroze Gandhi, asked questions to the finance minister at the time, T. T. Krishnamachari, regarding purchases out of the public funds of shares in Mundhra concerns. The minister's reply did not satisfy the House, and Nehru was also unhappy, though he trusted his minister. He announced one man commission of inquiry under Justice M. C. Chagla, who found no corrupt motive but rather an error of judgement. Krishnamachari, a Nehru loyalist, had to go. This shows Nehru's faith in a fair trial and respect for the feelings of the people's representative. His popularity, however, was affected after Chinese aggression in 1962 and India's lack of preparedness to face the situation.

Nehru had unchallenged control over the government and the party; however, this never tempted him to abuse his power. Rather, he had shown great restraint. He even wanted that opposition stalwarts who were defeated in general elections should get elected in bi-elections. This illustrates his great love for government by debate, discussion, and dialogue.

Pandit Nehru was not only the first Prime Minister of India but also the main gardener who sowed and flowered the spirit of democracy in a highly diverse country. His ideas of democracy were liberal but classical. He was a man of inclusive nature who lived a life absolutely devoted to India and, for him, this devotion rested on the edifice of democratic ideals. He conceptualised democracy in the Western liberal framework where the elections were to be organised in a regular fashion, with participation from all Indians who had full faith in their Constitution and the political institutions in place (Srivastava 2016: 2).

For Nehru, democracy is participatory in nature. It does not recognise majority and minority. It is non-discriminatory in character. These philosophical postulates are ensured by our polity and political institutions. Nehru believed citizens have a crucial role in governance, and hence they must participate in its functioning. Nehru's democratic ideals intended to ameliorate the socio-economic problems of a vast majority of the people living in rural India. After independence, Nehru wanted to save our institutions from the clutches of money and power; hence, he stood for liberal democracy. While doing this, where he succeeded, he became theoretically closer to C. B. Macpherson, who tried to revise liberal democracy with the help of Marxist ideals. Pandit Nehru did in practical terms what Macpherson explained as theoretical plans (Srivastava 2016: 2).

Nehru pleaded for the fusion of political democracy with economic democracy to achieve progress. He wanted to Indianise democracy to free it from the elitism of the West. In India, the government must represent the interests of the common people. In fact, his approach was different from Giovanni Sartori and Joseph Schumpeter. They emphasised on election and electoral competition. Nehru disliked competition and gave priority to service after the assumption of power. Here, Nehru was closer to Gandhi and Gandhian moral values, such as right election and the ethical use of power.

Nehru looked at democracy from a participatory perspective in which the decentralisation of power was an important component. He presented a Community Development Programme in 1952 and the National Extension Service in 1953. For evaluation of the Community Development Programme, the Balwant Rai Mehta Committee was constituted and recommended a three-tier democratic structure below the State apparatus. While inaugurating *Panchayati raj* in Rajasthan on 2 October 1959, Nehru said:

> Democracy was not entirely new to India, for its roots could be found also in our old *Panchayat* system where everyone has a vote in political life; everyone has equal opportunities in economic life. Everyone is equal and there is no distinction between man and women.
>
> *(Sharma 1997: 3)*

Thus, for Nehru, decentralisation in every form was based on equality, which was the essential grain of democratic ideals. Pandit Nehru laid the foundations of decentralised governance, and the process according statutory status to the grassroots bodies and fine-tuning of their role and functions were done by governments which succeeded him.

V Nehru's secularism: the cornerstone of India's strength and unity

Justice Shelat had observed that a secular State means a non-religious State, not an irreligious one. What follows is that the government should not be wedded or bound to any one religion but should give equality of treatment to every religion practiced in the country. He also said secularism is not anti-God or atheism, as it is sometime believed to be. These views agree with those of Pandit Nehru. In Nehru's opinion, a secular State does not mean an irreligious State; it only means that we respect and honour all religions giving them freedom to function. This had been the basic attitude of India throughout Nehru's life. Justice Gajendragadkar remarked that secularism is not a passive neutral force but a dynamic forward-looking integrating ideology.

Nehru understood the meaning of religious tolerance. He grew up among persons following different faiths. In Harrow, he studied with Jews. As a historian, he was exposed to ancient Indian society, polity, and culture. He read books on Buddhism and Jainism. Religious tolerance was in his blood. But the colonial administration's divide-and-rule policy was intended to instil fear among Muslims, and it caused Hindu–Muslim rivalry, leading to the demand of a separate State, which became Pakistan.

Nehru applied his knowledge of history when he joined politics. He accused British colonial rule of fomenting communal hatred. He knew his country's multi-cultural base. For him, religion had no place in politics, and religious diversity had to be internalised. He agreed with Niccolò Machiavelli in this matter. He differed with Gandhi. Though both respected all religion, they differed on the application of religion in political life.

For Nehru, communalism and majoritarianism had no place in political thought. He had experienced the dangers posed by the latter during the national movement and in the early part of the twentieth century. It was a threat to national unity. Hence, he decided to serve the cause of nationalism by recognising the fundamental unity prevalent in all religions. He upheld the cause of nationalism by bringing together people from all major religions on the issue of national unity. Gandhi's Khilafat movement was followed by Nehru's joining hands with nationalist Muslim leaders. Nehru was a rationalist. To him, human values were superior to religious orthodoxies. His secular credentials were based on his rational humanistic attitude towards life. His emphasis on the development of scientific temper was a great contribution. It helped to fight against religious obscurantism and superstition.

He applied secularism in the development of the human spirit and nation. He never used religion for votes. He articulated humanistic values inherent in religious equality. His secular ideas flowed from Indian tradition and heritage. Humanism and universal ethics played a dominant role in shaping his ideas on religion.

VI Nehruvian socialism

In the words of Acharya Narendra Deva, Nehru's social philosophy was "democratic socialism". Between 1920 and 1938, Nehru played a visible and remarkable role as a socialist. He infused the fervour of socialism into the freedom struggle with a view to creating a classless egalitarian national society. The integration of nationalism and socialism was his main contribution to the movement. This approach meant that political freedom and economic freedom could not be divorced from each other. Nehru wrote:

> I do not see why under socialism there should not be a great deal of freedom for the individual, indeed, for greater freedom than the present one. He can have freedom of conscience and mind, freedom of enterprise and even the possessions of private property on restrained scale. Above all, he will have the freedom which comes from economic security, which only a small number possess today.
>
> *(Nehru 1938: 232)*

In Great Britain, Nehru came in contact with Fabians who indoctrinated him into socialism. During his post-Non-cooperation prison days in 1922–1923, Nehru started thinking about economic and social questions while analysing the history of the Russian Revolution. By 1930, his socialist vision was fine-tuned, and he shared his vision with his party men. His socialism was deeply rooted in Indian soil. He then became the harbinger of the socialist trend in the freedom movement. Nehru wished to achieve the objectives of socialism gradually within the democratic framework. In his view, "without social freedom and a socialistic structure of society and the State, neither the country nor the individual could develop much" (Nehru 1946: 166).

The Karachi Session of the A.I.C.C. in 1931 was the first to have wedded to socialism when Nehru passed the resolution on fundamental rights and economic changes. This is why he did not join the Congress Socialist Party in 1934. He remained outside the group as a democratic socialist. He was also sure that the objectives of socialism could be achieved through planning. He set up the National Planning Committee through the party in 1938. Since the committee did not move ahead, Nehru's vision waited until independence. He remained as the Prime Minister for 17 years, laying a strong foundation for political democracy. He wanted India to become a socialist State. He said there was difference between the Soviet and Indian kinds of socialism.

His mission was to fight against poverty through planning and industrialisation. He was a democrat, and he had faith in socialism and communism, without the violence. He wanted to achieve the goals of socialism through planning within the democratic framework. The 'Industrial Policy Resolution of 1948' was the expression of Nehru's means for achieving socialism through the idea of a mixed economy. Both Avadi and Bhubaneswar sessions of the A.I.C.C. passed resolutions on a socialistic pattern of society and democratic socialism respectively.

If socialism envisages the control of means of production by the State, to a large extent, Nehru made India a socialistic State. He made India more socialistic than democratic. He was responsible for regulating the economic growth of the private sector. Hence, Nehru combined democratic methods and socialistic goals to some amount of perfection during his long career in the decision-making apparatus.

VII Nehru's ideas on development: planned economic development and industrial growth

Nehru was the architect of modern India. During his formative years, he had experienced affluence and prosperity in England but poverty and underdevelopment in his own country. His radical orientation dragged him towards socialists and Communists. But repressive measures adopted by the latter pushed him towards socialism, which he adopted in himself and in the forms with which he was associated. Poverty was the biggest challenge before Nehru. He became the first Prime Minister of India and remained at the helm for 17 years.

Nehru had a vision and a mission for development. He envisioned a liberal democratic socialist polity in India which would gradually eliminate poverty and achieve social justice for the masses through planning. His approach was comprehensive enough to cope with social, economic, and political issues and problems. He had the advantage of heading the government and controlling the party as well.

In his development strategy, Nehru accorded priority to national unity. The staggering divergences of India's segmented social life could be held together, and the fissiparous pulls and pressures could only be contained by links and bonds at many levels in the framework of an open, democratic, and federal polity. A monolithic framework based on coercion and suppression could not have been enduring.

Nehru deserves the credit of legitimising the status of Congress leadership in post-colonial India by trying to create a developmental State (Chatterjee 1998: 12). He was persuaded that India needed to encourage cottage and small-scale industries to ease the problems of poverty and unemployment; he saw them as a temporary expedient only necessary until the country became fully industrialised. He was convinced that India could not permanently eliminate poverty and satisfy the legitimate aspirations of its people without large-scale industrialisation. More importantly, the modern world was industrialised, and a country that failed to keep pace with it remained weak and vulnerable to foreign domination (Parekh 1991: 36). Nehru was impressed with the Soviet planning system, and he insisted and worked on it in late 1930s. The Constituent Assembly did not want to incorporate his ideas into the body of the Constitution. Nehru initiated a planning commission through a parliamentary resolution. The Prime Minister was made the chairperson of the new body, whose mission was planned economic development with social justice. He adopted a pragmatic approach to planning for development and welfare.

Nehru's strategy for planned development had the following components: priority was given to raising production in both agriculture and industry. For this,

Nehru used science and technology. Secondly, the economic arrangement was a mixed economy providing for the co-existence of the public and private sectors. It adopted selective nationalisation, that is, State ownership of key industries like steel, oil, coal, air and rail transport, communication, atomic energy, and multi-purpose river valley projects. The rest was left for the private sector. This was done by the 'Industrial Policy Resolution of 1948'. Nehru accorded importance to human resource development to quicken the pace of production and to ensure the proper implementation of plans and programmes. His model of development aimed at economic growth with social justice. He had a futuristic goal. Once planned economic development picked up, the peoples' participation would be necessary. To ensure this, Nehru took steps towards establishing village democracy through the path of democratic decentralisation.

The Nehru era experienced three Five-Year Plans. The First Five Year Plan (1951–1956) was moderate compared to the subsequent plans. It gave emphasis on agriculture, community development, irrigation, power projects, transport, and communications. The Second Five-Year Plan was designed to accelerate economic growth and establish a welfare State. Natural calamities were a major hurdle for this plan. It depended more on the ideas of P. C. Mahalanobis for picking up heavy industries for economic growth and the generation of employment. The Third Five-Year Plan was more ambitious, and its targets were more than double those of the previous plan. Its object was to take India to a stage where the national economy would become self-sustaining (Ghose 1984: 286).

By opting for a planned economy, Nehru wanted to obviate the anomalies of uncontrolled markets. For economic growth, he needed the technological support of the developed world, and for heavy industries he could carve out support from Germany, Russia, and Great Britain as well. Unfortunately, Nehru's rapid industrialisation dream remained unfulfilled in his lifetime. But it raised the question of whether efficient planning was possible under a democratic political structure!

VIII Nationalism and internationalism

Nehru was a practical statesman. He entered the political scene when the country was fighting for its independence. Hence the dominant political ideology was nationalism. In his views, we need to solve the problem of political freedom to fill our mind with nationalist outlook. He was critical of the attitude of the colonial administration when he entered politics. He sought to interpret the essence of the ideology of colonialism and nationalism prevalent in India. He identified that the I.N.C., which was leading the struggle itself, was led by liberals. Prior to the arrival of Gandhi, the leaders used to admire the British policy and asked only for piecemeal reforms and concessions. Nehru opined that the British had occupied Indian territory, mind, and market. Hence, there was no need to compromise or cooperate with the colonialists. He praised the British for their rule of law, efficient administration, and parliamentary system which helped fuel the growth of national consciousness. But it was not enough.

He identified the British era in India in phases. The first lasted up to end of the eighteenth century. The plunder of India came during the second phase in the nineteenth century, when India became a source of raw material for British industries and market for the finished goods. The third phase, commencing around the First World War, was investment colonialism. Thus, it comprised the complete exploitation of India's man and material. The British rule created landlords and strengthened feudalism. Nehru said the British rule sided with political, social, and religious reactionaries. It created vested interests. He took account of India's strengths and weaknesses from her long history and attempted to arouse nationalistic sentiments. He was confronted with the ideas of the revivalists. He was of the firm opinion that India must break with the past and should not allow it to dominate the present. He cited examples from the rise and growth of European nationalism along with its degeneration.

Nehru was critical of national self-assertion which turned into chauvinism, aggressiveness, and hostilities towards others. He also analysed from the class perspective and said that nationalism hid everything under the cover of antagonistic feelings. Nehru was one of the first representatives of the national liberation movement in the Afro-Asian countries. He organised the 'Asian Relations Conference' in March 1947 to focus on the demise of colonialism and rise of nationalism. For him, democracy, socialism, and secularism became the ideals of both nationalism and internationalism.

Internationalism is the doctrine which holds that orderly and harmonious relations among nations can be maintained not through conflict but through cooperation. It does not deny the right of nations to exist and manage their own affairs but asserts that nations are bound by a chain of interdependence which they must recognise and therefore perform their international obligations in solving common problems and matters of common interests (Rath 1995: 34).

Nehru, a staunch nationalist, looked beyond nationalism to internationalism, which he believed was essential for the survival and prosperity of nations. His concept of internationalism stood for cooperation not among unequal peoples but amongst nations free and equal in status. At the 'Asian Relations Conference', he was critical of imperialism. He was a strong believer in international peace and cooperation. Hence, he lauded the founding of the U.N. based on the equality of nations. He opined that conflict hinders development of the people in new countries. Peace at any cost was to be established. He hoped that the U.N. would not become a pawn in the great power rivalry but that it would devote its attention towards the removal of social and economic challenges within and among the member nations.

Nehru further said the development of internationalism in the post–Second World War era could not be possible with the old ideas and institutions of imperialism, colonialism, racialism, balance of power, and military alliances. He argued that negative forces must be done away with to create a true international order based on peaceful coexistence, mutual tolerance, and understanding, free from hatred, violence, and schemes of aggression. Nehru was not only the first Prime

Minister; he was also India's first External Affairs Minister until his death. Thus, he could utilise several forums to preach and advocate his ideas on world peace.

The onset of the Cold War and atomic age provoked Nehru to criticise military alliances which cannot fulfil the U.N.'s objectives but will lead to armed conflicts. He, along with President Gamal Abdel Nasser of Egypt and President Josip Broz Tito of Yugoslavia, fostered an opposing line of alliance politics called the "Non-Aligned Movement". In fact, he would attend the first summit at Belgrade in 1961, where 25 countries gathered to support the new mission for world peace. The model of internationalism, Nehru envisaged, was evident when he said:

> Nations by cooperating with one another, in tolerance and recognising diversities, by respect for one another as sovereign nations, by not interfering in one another's affairs, can survive, progress and advance to greater and greater degrees and spheres of cooperation. Such peaceful co-existence in our times is the forerunner of one human race and one world. We frustrate our destiny if we continue to base our hopes on a divided world, resting on fear and armed might; and each of us arrogating to ourselves the larger share, if not the monopoly of virtue or of national, racial or moral superiority.
>
> (Nehru 1946: 167)

IX Conclusion

Having achieved a degree of consolidation and integration and having brought about an element of consensus in the nation, the leadership should look towards the productive functions of nation-building. The critical areas which require a determined approach are the reorganisation of the administrative structure and personnel in the country (the real blind spot in the nation), the building up of the military infrastructure of Indian democracy (necessarily a part of the developmental effort), and pushing ahead with the programme of economic development through a greater concern for encouraging and mobilising voluntary effort and people's willing participation, with or without the help of the bureaucracy. These are tasks that may require substantial rethinking on some of our theories and models. Knowingly or unknowingly, Prime Minister Nehru had often permitted a simplistic view of things to prevail in his government. He, however, had always shown a readiness to change outdated ideas and theories that had become dysfunctional to the tasks at hand. Preoccupied with his integrative role, he did not have enough time to implement this outlook in the realm of policy. There can be no better memorial to him than a continuous search for building further on the foundations he left behind and, wherever necessary, improving upon them (Kothari 1964: 1207).

We cannot deny the positive facts of Nehru's contribution that he contributed much for the freedom struggle as well as for nation-building in India, in unfavourable situations. But the story does not end there, for Nehruvianism also witnessed certain distortions in India's nation-building process and much of the present-day dichotomies in Indian polity are to be found rooted in these distortions. It has become obsolete in the present phase of liberalisation. However, it would be unfair to belittle its contribution in the nation-building in India at a crucial juncture. Nehru's secularism has been also criticised by Shariful Hasan, who argued that "in spite of his secular character, the minorities have failed to get their due share in the national economic cake and State services" (Hasan 1992: 191–192). It is due to the official machinery at lower levels, especially in the States. The State paraphernalia has often been communal and has failed to demonstrate its non-discriminatory attitude which is the hallmark of Indian secularism, while the sectarian political forces which have unfortunately wrested control of the Indian State take to task the progressive features of Nehruvianism. My own critique would rest on the premise that Nehru did not become as progressive as he could have been. That said, there were significant gaps between what Nehru preached and what remained grounded in reality (Das 2001: 6). Amit Shah criticised him in a public gathering that his idea of nation-building was replacing old traditions with "imported ideas". He argued, "Congress made Nehru as Prime Minister of the country, who was a believer of bringing foreign ideas and discarded the age-old values and traditions while building the nation" (Indian Express 2016: 2).

References

Chatterjee, Partha (1998). Introduction. In Partha Chatterjee (Ed.), *State and Politics in India* (pp. 1–39). Delhi: Oxford University Press.

Das, Suranjan (2001). The Nehru Years in Indian Politics: From a Historical Hindsight. *Journal of South Asian Studies*, November 16, pp. 2–35.

Ghose, Shankar (1984). *Modern Indian Political Thought*. New Delhi: Allied Publisher.

Gopal, S. (1975). *Jawaharlal Nehru: A Biography*, Vol. 1 (1889–1947). New Delhi: Oxford University Press.

Hasan, Shariful (1992). Nehru's Secularism. In Paul Thomas (Ed.), *Nehru and the Constitution*. New Delhi: Indian Law Institute.

The Indian Express (2016). Nehru's Idea of Nation Building Was Replacing Old Traditions with 'Imported Ideas': Amit Shah, June 6. http://indianexpress.com/article/ india/india-news-india/nehrus-idea-of-nation-building-was-replacing-old-traditions-with-imported-ideas-2836813/. Retrieved on Dated: 2017/05/24/02:45:39 PM.

Karunakaran, K. P. (1986). Nehru's Search for Ideas. *Kerala Journal of Political Studies*, Vol. 1, No. 1, January, pp. 102–108.

Kothari, Rajni (1964). The Meaning of Jawaharlal Nehru. *The Economic Weekly*, Special Number, July, pp. 1203–1208. Available at- https://www.epw.in/system/files/pdf/1964_16/29-30-31/the_meaning_of_jawaharlal_nehru.pdf

Misra, Surya Narayan (2013). Nehru and Nation-Building in India. *Odisha Review*, November, 2013, pp. 78–80.

Nanda, B. R. (1962). *The Nehrus: Motilal and Jawaharlal*. New Delhi: Oxford University Press.

Nehru, Jawaharlal (1938). The Unity of India. *Foreign Affairs*, Vol. 16, No. 2, January, pp. 231–243.

Nehru, Jawaharlal (1946). *The Discovery of India*. Calcutta: Signet Press.
Parekh, Bhikhu (1991). Nehru and the National Philosophy of India. *Economic and Political Weekly*, Vol. 26, No. 1/2, January 5–12, pp. 35–48.
Rath, S. (Ed.). (1995). *Jawaharlal Nehru: The Nation Builder and Architect of India's Foreign Policy*. New Delhi: Anu Publication.
Sharma, Shakuntala (1997). *Grass Root Politics and Panchayati Raj*, New Delhi: Deep & Deep Publication.
Srivastava, V. K. (2016). Nehru's Views About Democracy. *Mainstream*, Vol. LIV, No. 47, November 16.

17
SUBHAS CHANDRA BOSE

Sumit Mukerji

> *It is blood alone that can pay the price of freedom. Give me blood and I will give you freedom!*
> – Speech in Burma (July 1944), quoted in Rudrangshu Mukherjee,
> *The Great Speeches of Modern India* (2011)

I Introduction

Subhas Chandra Bose is remembered and glorified by his countrymen as a dauntless patriot and an uncompromising opponent of British imperialism. His heroic role as the commander of the Indian National Army (I.N.A.) is still alive in the memory of the people of India. Myths have been created around his name, sometimes bordering on deification. Bose's dramatic escape from India, his perilous submarine journey to the Far East, and his eventual emergence as *Netaji* have created for him the image of a romantic adventurer who was reckless and desperate and prepared to stake his all for India's freedom, which had to be won at any cost. Scholars, historians, and analysts have tended to concentrate overwhelmingly on the I.N.A. phase of his life, which was admittedly fascinating and spectacular, but the earlier phase was no less significant and should not be viewed in isolation from the former. Though he was essentially an activist, Bose had a reflective mind. He was not a thinker or system builder in the conventional sense of the term but made his own contribution to Indian political thought by producing some thought-provoking ideas which would inspire future generations of thinkers to build a creative theory or model. Thus, the thought of Subhas Chandra Bose, though lacking in complete maturity and finality, nevertheless contained ingredients for ingenious theoretical endeavours. The reflective image of Bose as a thinker has been somewhat overshadowed by his romantic, adventurist image which easily excites popular imagination. His dramatic escape from India undoubtedly had an element of romance. However, one does not live in history through romanticism alone unless it is punctuated by rationalism. There is no doubt that the motive behind his adventure into the unknown was unadulterated patriotism. However, his decision to seek Japanese help for India's freedom generated much opprobrium, and his patriotism was even questioned by Communists who calumniated Bose, calling him quisling and a puppet of the Japanese. Their perception subsequently changed, but there is still a tendency among both Communist and other scholars to hail Bose as a patriot, albeit a misguided one. Their reservation is based on Bose's collusion with the Axis Powers, which they regard as politically indiscreet and strategically inexpedient. This needs to be reassessed in the context of Bose's thought process. The seminal question that needs to be addressed is whether romanticism and rationalism, idealism, and realism ran parallel in Bose and whether his thought guided his actions.

II Life sketch

Born on 23 January 1897, Bose had been an idealist since his early life. The inspiration of Swami Vivekananda was pervasive in developing Bose's spirit of idealism. He himself had testified how Vivekananda entered his life and revolutionised it. Nationalist sentiments had also started to surface in him, and while he was a young student in Ravenshaw Collegiate School, Cuttack, he participated in the programme dedicated to the memory of Bengal's first martyr, Khudiram Bose, under the inspiration of the Headmaster Benimadhav Das. After passing the matriculation examination with flying colours and standing second in his class, Bose took admission in Presidency College. At this point, Bose had become religiously inclined and once left his home in search of a *guru*, only to return disillusioned. His results in the intermediate examination were not up to his expectations. He was determined to compensate for this in his graduation, but his alleged complicity in a student's strike in protest of the superciliousness of Prof. E. F. Oaten towards the students, followed by an assault on the professor, led to his rustication from the college and the university. Though there was no evidence of his being party to the assault, his refusal to divulge the names of the culprits before the enquiry committee went against him. The unrepentant Bose, however, declared phlegmatically that "my principal had expelled me, but he had also made my career. I had a foretaste of leadership and of the martyrdom that it involves. I had acquired character and could face the future with equanimity" (Bose 1980: 79–80).

Bose was permitted to resume his studies from Scottish Church College with honours in philosophy, thanks to the intervention of Sir Asutosh Mukherji. Bose stood second in the B. A. examination and went to England to compete for the Civil Services Examination (C.S.E.). After only eight months of preparation, Bose ranked fourth in the C.S.E. However, he was determined to consecrate his life to the service of his country and renounced the lucrative government service under the inspiration of the noted leader of Bengal Aurobindo Ghosh, at that time exiled in Pondicherry, whom Bose referred to as his spiritual *guru* in a letter to his brother Sarat Chandra Bose, dated 23 February 1921 (Bose 1980:

220–222). Later, however, he became critical of Ghosh's renunciation of political life, probably because he had wanted him as his mentor. Bose returned to India and plunged into active politics through his apprenticeship under Deshbandhu C. R. Das, the prominent leader of Bengal who was also mayor of the Calcutta Municipal Corporation. Bose's tenure as chief executive officer of the Calcutta Municipal Corporation was short lived because of his imprisonment and deportation to Mandalaya in 1924. C. R. Das died shortly thereafter, which Bose described as a "cataclysmic loss".

After being released from prison in 1927, Bose, who now had no mentor to guide him, evolved from the stature of a lieutenant to that of a national leader. He became a prominent leader of the left wing of the Congress and championed the cause of complete independence rather than dominion status in the Calcutta Congress of 1928. He was associated, along with Jawaharlal Nehru, with the Independence of India League. He also became mayor of the Calcutta Municipal Corporation and articulated the cause of municipal socialism. Though Bose adhered to the official Congress policy of non-violence, in his heart, he was convinced that the citadel of British imperialism could be smashed through armed struggle alone. Hence, he always provided moral support to the revolutionary movement. His affinity with revolutionaries earned him the reputation of being a dangerous person in the eyes of the British government, and he was imprisoned again in 1932. His health broke down in prison, and he was allowed to go to Europe for treatment. He was in Europe from 1933 to 1937 which marked his emergence as a political thinker. This was the time when he wrote his book *The Indian Struggle*, in which he articulated his political ideas in a cogent form and developed his doctrine of *New Samyavada* based on a synthesis of communism and fascism. He toured several countries, such as Austria, France, Italy, Ireland, Turkey, and Germany, and acquainted himself with the political system prevalent there as well as important political developments. His period of exile in Europe was a turning point in the evolution of his political thought.

After his return to India, Bose was again placed under arrest and subsequently released. In 1938, he became the president of the Indian National Congress (I.N.C.) on the recommendation of Mahatma Gandhi at the Haripura session in 1938. However, his differences with the right-wing leadership reached a saturation point, and in 1939, he contested Gandhi's nominee Dr Pattabhi Sitaramayya in the presidential election and won. Gandhi considered this his own defeat. By now, indications of the Second World War had become clear, and Bose in his short address at the Tripuri session of the Congress in 1939, which he attended in a state of serious illness, unequivocally declared his policy of utilising the international situation to India's advantage. Gandhi at this point had become an inveterate opponent of Bose and wanted him out of the presidential chair. In the face of determined opposition from the right wing, Bose resigned and formed his own party, the 'Forward Bloc'. He was soon expelled from the Congress on disciplinary grounds, but he continued to propagate his programme of action throughout the lengths and breadths of India with unabated energy. He set up the 'Left Consolidation Committee' with the objective of rallying all the radical leftist forces under one single banner. This, however, did not happen.

His forecast about the imminent outbreak of the Second World War proved correct, and he felt that this was India's golden opportunity. Gandhi, however, felt that the opportune moment had not yet arrived. Bose now began to contemplate the idea of going abroad and organising an armed struggle against British imperialism with the help of some foreign power. His logic was that this was the propitious moment to capitalise on the war situation which would leave England smashed and beleaguered. Bose was arrested again after leading the Holwell monument agitation in Calcutta. He commenced a fast until death while in prison, and the government removed him from jail and placed him under house arrest. On 16 January 1941, he escaped dramatically from his house and moved first to Peshwar, then to Kabul, from where he tried to contact the Russian embassy but failed. He then went to Germany and set up the Indian Legion. He also met Adolf Hitler and tried to persuade him to aid in the cause of India's independence. Hitler refused to oblige. In the meantime, the war situation had worsened, particularly after Hitler's attack on Russia. While Bose was convinced that this act would prove disastrous, he resolved to make a final bid for the freedom of his country with the help of another Axis power, Japan. When Japan occupied Singapore, the war prisoners of the British Indian Army were freed. The Indian Independence League, comprising the non-resident Indians of Southeast Asia with its military unit the *Azad Hind Fauj*, was formed by General Mohan Singh and Pritam Singh. Japan wanted to use it as a fifth column against the Allied powers, and when pressured by the Japanese Government to provide military aid, Mohan Singh and Pritam Singh revolted and were taken into custody. Rash Behari Bose, the exiled Indian revolutionary, assumed leadership and procured assurance from the Japanese that they would help in the cause of the Indian freedom struggle. However, he was ageing and therefore invited Bose to come to Singapore and assume charge of the I.N.A.

After a perilous submarine voyage from Germany, Bose reached Madagascar, and then a Japanese submarine took him to Saigon. Thereafter, he went to Tokyo by a military aircraft and impressed the Japanese premier, Tojo, who was fascinated by his personality and promised to help him. He assumed charge of the I.N.A. from Rash Behari Bose and established the provisional Azad Hind government on 21 October 1943. He came to be acclaimed as "*Netaji*" and moulded the I.N.A. for a total mobilisation for a massive armed assault on the citadel of British imperialism. He persuaded Tojo to provide material, financial, and logistical support to the I.N.A. without any kind of compromise on the question of honour. The *Azad Hind Fouj* advanced to Kohima and Imphal, penetrated nearly 250 square miles, and hoisted the tri-colour flag on Indian soil. The untimely advent of a monsoon forced it to retreat, and after the surrender of Japan, the position of the I.N.A. was hopeless. The irrepressible Bose boarded a plane to Manchuria with the intention of soliciting the support of Russia for the Indian cause. On 18 August 1945, news of Bose's death in an airplane crash at Taihoku was transmitted. However, even today, the truth of the story is shrouded in mystery, and there is every reason to believe that the story was a Japanese concoction.

III The Indian National Army: indirect catalyst of India's freedom

Bose was criticised for his collusion with the Axis powers, as it might have invited a Japanese invasion of India. This does not stand the test of facts, however. Japan had no plans for military aggrandisement in India and did not include India in its Prosperity Sphere. The distance of India from Japan acted as the greatest deterrent to Japanese expansionism in India. Japanese historians, like Akashir and Nagasaki, have testified that Japan never contemplated the idea of conquest of India. T. R. Sareen makes the point clear, saying that:

> The Japanese repeatedly clarified that they had no intention to conquer India. If the Japanese did not attack India after the fall of Burma when they were at the height of their power in East Asia it was unlikely that they would have done so when their war fortunes were declining and they hardly had adequate forces to carry out even a limited campaign against India.
>
> (Sareen 1995: 184–185)

The fact of the matter is that Bose did not expect a military victory for the I.N.A. but prophesied at a mass meeting in Singapore on 9 July 1943 that when the I.N.A. attack India, "a revolution will break out, not only among the civil population at home, but also among the Indian Army which is now standing under the British flag" (Bose 1974: 179). Bose considered the 1857 mutiny as India's first war of independence, and this was the first taste of the impending danger of igniting a spirit of revolt in the armed forces, which was the strongest supporting force behind British imperialism. Militant nationalists like Jatin Mukherjee and Rash Behari Bose, who were Bose's predecessors, wanted to transform a subservient British Indian Army into an opponent of British colonialism in India. Since the death of Jatin Mukherjee in 1915 and the escape of Rash Behari Bose from India, no attempt was made to create dents in the loyalty of the armed forces. The I.N.A. signified the revival of the 1857 legacy, which also figured prominently in the agenda of Jatin Mukherjee and Rash Behari Bose. A noted communist scholar conceded that Subhas Chandra Bose was no longer physically present in the Indian political scene after August 1945, but his heritage, as well as his legend, acted as the main driving force during the post-war upsurge (Chattopadhyay 1997: 64). A secret despatch by the army headquarters admitted that the conquest of even a single Indian State would have widespread repercussions upon morale and politics (Sareen 1995: 207).

The untimely arrival of the monsoon caused the I.N.A. to retreat despite fighting a gallant and heroic battle. The surrender of Japan on 14 August 1944, hammered the last nail in the I.N.A.'s coffin. However, the trial of three I.N.A. officers – Maj. Gen Shah Nawaz Khan, Lt Col P. K. Sahgal and Lt Col G. S.

Dhillon – unleashed a wave of protest throughout the nation. On 2 September, the acting Viceroy, Colville, reported to the Secretary of State that Bose had garnered much praise as a national hero, and the nationalist press suggested that under international law Bose and his followers were entitled to all the honours of war and not liable to punishment (Mansergh 1973: 179). Army men without caring for military discipline sympathised with the I.N.A. soldiers by attending meetings in support of the I.N.A. prisoners and also by sending contributions to support their defence (Dutta 1971: 107). Lt Gen. Francis Tuker, the G.O.C. of the Eastern Command, noted apprehensively that the I.N.A. affair was threatening to tumble down the whole edifice of the Indian Army (Tuker 1950: 48). The naval revolt of 18 February 1946, which was inspired the I.N.A. Court Martial, resulted in the Royal Indian Navy being renamed as the Indian National Navy and jolted the citadel of imperialism further. The message was now loud and clear that the strongest bastion of loyalty to British rule could no longer be relied upon. A Defence Committee report of 12 June 1946 mentioned that the Royal Indian Navy and even the Royal Indian Air Force could not be relied upon. The reliability of the Indian Army as a whole was open to serious doubt. This even applied to the *Gurkha* units (Defence Committee Paper D.O [46] 68).

It is also true that the I.N.A. nearly captured Imphal after launching a massive offensive alongside the Japanese in the Arakan Front on 4 February 1944. If Imphal had been captured, history would have been different. It is, however, an interesting speculation as to whether India's freedom would have been expedited had Bose gone to East Asia a year earlier when the war situation was more in favour of the Axis Powers. In terms of its immediate results, the I.N.A. was a disaster, but its long-term repercussions were far reaching. It made the colonial masters jittery, which testifies to the correctness of Bose's final and desperate bid for India's freedom. It has been rightly stated that the attempt to make the army and the police disloyal was a method seldom tried by the Congress. Real success was achieved in Malaya in 1944–1945 by Netaji Bose. The last mutinies by cadets in Bombay and Karachi made the British authorities feel that their defence forces could not be relied upon (Ponchhammer 1981: 461). This was the first time since 1857 that Indian soldiers had become disloyal. The I.N.A. legend was not a misadventure but a venture punctuated more by the pragmatic appreciation of historical reality rather than a reckless leap into the dark. It is also true that if Bose had not left India, he would have had to languish in prison, and the opportunity presented by the Second World War would have been lost. Bose preferred action in the world arena to inaction in prison.

IV Bose on nationalism and socialism: the unfinished theory

Bose confessed in *My Personal Testament*, written on 29 November 1940, that:

> I was originally fashioned by nature to be first and foremost, a thinker, but circumstances have forced me into a life of hectic political activity with the

result that I have not been able to make my contribution to the thought life of India and of the world. But, I have certain definite ideas on philosophic, social, economic and political problems and should like them to be amplified and worked out by the generation that follows ours. I have this much to claim for myself that my ideas do not float in the air. They are intimately related to reality as we know it.

(Bose 1980: 334)

He had clear-cut ideas but wanted them to be worked out by the succeeding generations, as his hectic life allowed him little time for intellectual reflection. In all his speeches and writings, Bose expressed his strong commitment to socialism. Here, however, he was not in favour of blind imitation of any model but was firm in his advocacy of an Indian brand of socialism. In his presidential speech at the Rangpur Political Conference of 30 March 1930, he said that:

> This socialism did not derive its birth from the books of Karl Marx. It has its origin in the thought and culture of India. The gospel of democracy that was preached by Swami Vivekananda has manifested fully in Deshbandhu Das who said that *Narayana* (God) lives amongst those who till land, prepare our bread by the sweat of their brow.

(Bose 1983: 47)

He prophetically added a note of caution, saying that:

> New ideas of socialism are nowadays travelling to India from the West and they are revolutionising the thoughts of many, but the idea of socialism is not a novelty in this country. We regard it such only because we have lost the thread of our own history. It is not proper to take any school of thought as unmistakable and absolute truth. We must not forget that the Russians, the main disciple of Karl Marx, have not blindly followed his ideas. We have therefore to shape society and politics according to our own ideals and according to our needs.

(Bose 1983: 47)

The way many Indian revolutionaries converted to communism in the 1930s proves the correctness of Bose's observation.

In his presidential address at the Maharashtra Provincial Conference, Poona on 3 May 1928, Bose said that:

> Communism is not a western institution. Among the *Khasis* of Assam private property as an institution does not exist in theory even today. The clan as a whole owns the entire land. I am sure that similar instances can still be found in other parts of India and also in the past history of the country.

(Bose 1983: 30)

His point was that artificial transplantation of any alien system would be counterproductive. As his ideas began to mature, he interpolated the issue of fascism in his visualised framework. As the mayor of Calcutta Municipal Corporation, Bose said on 27 September 1930 that he envisaged a synthesis of what modern Europe called the synthesis of socialism and fascism, that is to say, a combination of the attributes of justice, equality, and love, which were central to socialism and the efficiency and discipline of fascism (Bose 1987: 128). It should be clarified here that Bose was never ideologically inclined either towards socialism or fascism but talked of a synthesis of their positive features. He reiterated this in his address at the 'All India *Naujawan Bharat Sabha*' on 27 March 1931, saying that justice, equality, freedom, discipline, and love, were the five principles which should constitute the basis of India's collective life (Bose 1983: 58). The emphasis on love clearly indicates that any system which curbed individual freedom was intensely repugnant to Bose. Far from visualising a fascist dictatorship in India, Bose affirmed his faith in a socialist republic. However, in his view, India must evolve her own brand of socialism in consonance with her tradition, history, and culture. Here, Bose saw an opportunity for India to make her own original contribution to the thought life of the world. Thus, in his presidential address at the 'All India Trade Union Congress' on 4 July 1931, he said that:

> I have no doubt in my mind that the salvation of India, as of the world, depends on socialism. India should learn from and profit by the experience of other nations but India should be able to evolve her own methods in keeping with her own needs and her own environment. India should evolve her own form of socialism. It may be that the form of socialism which India will evolve will have something new and original about it which will be of benefit to the whole world.
>
> *(ibid.: 64)*

By now, the stage was set for the comprehensive and specific enunciation of his ideas in his famous book *The Indian Struggle*, published in 1935 during his period of exile in Europe, which represents the culmination of his ideas developed over the years. Contesting Nehru's statement of 18 December 1933 that the fundamental choice before the world was between some form of communism and some form of fascism, and he was all for the former, Bose wrote that:

> Whether one believes in the Hegelian dialectic or any other theory of evolution, in no case, we think that creation is at an end. Considering everything, one is inclined to hold that the next phase in world history will produce a synthesis between communism and fascism. And will it be a surprise if that synthesis is produced in India?
>
> *(Bose 1981c: 351)*

Elucidating his point, Bose said that communism and fascism had certain common features, like supremacy of the State over the individual, denunciation of parliamentary democracy, belief in party rule, planned industrial reorganisation, and suppression of dissenting minorities. These common features would constitute the new synthesis which Bose called *samyavada*, or the doctrine of equality, and it was India's task to work out this synthesis (Bose 1981c: 352).

Bose listed five reasons why communism would not succeed in India. Firstly, he believed that while the Indian movement was a nationalist one, communism had no sympathy for nationalism. Secondly, he felt that Russia had no interest in a world revolution. Thirdly, many of the economic ideas of communism would make a strong appeal to Indians, but some of its other aspects would have a contrary effect because Russian communism was anti-religious and atheistic, while in India there was no feeling against religion as such. Fourthly, the materialistic interpretation of history was not likely to find unqualified support in India. Fifthly, while communism had made some remarkable contributions in the domain of economics, like the idea of State planning, it had made no original contribution to the solution of the monetary problem (Bose 1981c: 352–353). Bose ended his views saying that India would not become a new edition of Soviet Russia, and the various modern socio-political movements and experimentations being conducted in Europe and America would have considerable influence on India's development (ibid.: 353). The vision Bose expounded reveals continuity in his thought process because he had been expressing the same ideas for quite some time in the past. The proposed synthesis of communism and fascism, however, came in for trenchant criticism for his alleged inability to appreciate the fact that fascism was the most aggressive phase of imperialism and through it the crisis of capitalism became manifest. He was also accused of undue eclecticism. The contending logic was that any synthesis of communism and fascism was theoretically untenable since one stood for the emancipation of humanity from bondage while the other stood for the annihilation of individual freedom. The similarities between the two were superficial rather than real.

Bose partially modified his stand in an interview with R. P. Dutt in London on 24 January 1938, where he admitted that his expression had not been a happy one and clarified that what he had meant was that after winning freedom, India would move in the direction of socialism. He also defended himself, saying that when he wrote his book, fascism had not yet started on its imperialist expedition (Bose 1983: 30). In his famous speech at the Tokyo Imperial University, Bose restated his stand. Considering the similarities and differences between national socialism and communism, he found both to be anti-democratic and anti-capitalistic. National socialism, despite its success in creating national unity and solidarity, had failed to reform the capitalistic economic system. Communism had to its credit the great achievement of planned economy, but it was not able to appreciate the value of national sentiment.

India needed a synthesis of nationalism and socialism (ibid.: 12). In his projection of such a synthesis, Bose remained firm in his denunciation of the aggressive nationalism of Nazi Germany and Fascist Italy. In a letter to Dr Thierfelder on 24 March 1934, he wrote:

> When I first visited Germany in 1933, I had hopes that a new German nation which had risen to a consciousness of its national strength and self-respect, would instinctively feel a deep sympathy for other nations struggling in the same direction. Today, I regret that I have to return to India with the conviction that the new nationalism of Germany is not only narrow but also arrogant and selfish.
> *(Bose and Bose 1994: 165–166)*

He also severely criticised Benito Mussolini's conquest of Abyssinia, saying that "Since Mussolini came to power in 1922, Italy has been thinking aggressively in terms of expansion, of a revival of the Roman empire" (Bose 1937: 12). He also castigated Great Britain for its policy of appeasement, saying that it first challenged Italy and then beat a retreat before the bluff and bluster of Mussolini (ibid.). It is also instructive to note that in an article titled "Europe today and tomorrow", published in *Modern Review* on 21 August 1937, Bose had written prophetically, "The Russian Colossus has often proved to be an enigma. It baffled Napoleon, the conqueror of Europe. Will it baffle Hitler?" (ibid.). Any kind of arrogant jingoism or irredentism was intensely repugnant to him. Being a strict disciplinarian himself, Bose admired the discipline of national life not only in Nazi Germany but also prior to it, as evident from his letter to Hemanta Kumar Sarkar on 26 September 1915, in which he stated that:

> Germany has found an answer to the problem of adjustment of individual freedom with State control as in peace time the people enjoyed unfettered freedom but when the call came, all voluntarily renounced their freedom and presented themselves obediently and ready with arms.
> *(Bose 1937: 12)*

Though he did not explicitly say so, Bose probably wanted a kind of benevolent dictatorship in India. Alternatively, it may be stated that he wanted an essentially authoritarian State which would never be tyrannical because the principle of love was one of the pillars on which it rested. He envisaged a combination of discipline and love.

V Idea of revolution and socio-economic transformation

To Bose, political freedom would be rendered irrelevant without social and economic revolution after independence. In his famous speech at Amravati on

15 December 1929, Bose spoke of the total transfiguration of life through revolution. In this speech, he visualised the emancipation of man from every kind of bondage. The watchword of freedom was equality, which meant the annihilation of all social barriers, like caste, inequalities of wealth, unequal opportunities for education, and the unequal status of men and women. This would not be achieved by blind imitation of Russian communism. He envisioned a socialist State in India modelled on an Indian brand of socialism. He viewed that the artificial transplantation of an alien system was bound to be counterproductive. Despite his historical respect for Marxism, Bose was rooted in Indian culture, history, and tradition and never wanted India to be a caricature of Russian communism.

During his presidential speech at Haripura in 1938, Bose clearly enunciated a programme of socio-economic reconstruction along socialist lines. He expressed his reasoned conviction that problems like poverty, illiteracy, production, and distribution could be effectively tackled along socialistic lines. Articulating his ideas concretely at the 'Indian Science News Association' on 21 August 1938, Bose said that no industrial advancement is possible until we first pass through the throes of an industrial revolution. Whether we like it or not, we have to reconcile ourselves to the fact that the present epoch is the industrial epoch in modern history. There is no escape from the industrial revolution.

Bose was progressive and modern in his outlook and wanted to infuse India with the spirit of modernism in an age where a retrogressive hang over of the past would be most detrimental. To him, economic and political freedoms were inextricably intertwined. He assigned topmost priority to planned development, and it was by his initiative that national planning became an integral part of Congress policy. He appointed the National Planning Committee and made Jawaharlal Nehru its chairman. His modern outlook was appreciated by Rabindranath Tagore, who was also an enthusiastic supporter of national planning. It was through a planned economy, Bose believed, that the vision of economic revolution could be translated into reality.

VI Bose's views of international politics: realist or visionary?

Bose is often criticised for his inadequate understanding of international politics. His expectation that the Axis Powers would help him to liberate India is considered wishful thinking by many.

> It has also been contended that though he initially wanted to go to Russia, yet she was unlikely to welcome him at the risk of antagonising Britain. Russia was an ally of Germany which was then the enemy of Britain, but any fresh tension with Britain would isolate her further and place her at the mercy of Germany.
>
> *(Bose 2010: 64)*

It may, however, be alternatively contended that the prospects of success from within the four walls of a prison in India were virtually nil. Secondly, Bose was the practitioner of Realpolitik and wrote trenchantly to Nehru on 28 March 1939 that:

> Foreign policy is a realistic affair to be determined largely from the point of view of a nation's self-interest. Take Soviet Russia for instance. With all her communism in her internal politics, she never allows sentiment to dominate her foreign policy. That is why she did not hesitate to enter into a pact with French imperialism when it suited her purpose. The Franco-Soviet Pact and the Czechoslovak-Soviet Pact are instances in point. Even today, Soviet Russia is anxious to enter into a pact with British imperialism.
> (Bose 1981a: 11)

A foreign policy may have ideological moorings, but when it came to a serious contingency, flexibility should be the watchword. Thirdly, Bose's foresight was proved as far back as 1928, when he forecasted the outbreak of the Second World War. He was also a virulent critic of the Anglo-French policy of the appeasement of Germany. At that time, there was a tacit pro-Hitler bias in the conservative circles of England who lived with the illusion that Germany would confine her expansionism to Austria, Czechoslovakia, and Poland and not cross swords with England and France. Bose, however, was convinced that Germany was preparing for a great war and thus wrote in the *Congress Socialist* in 1938, "What we have just witnessed is only the first scene of the drama". The enactment of the real drama in the near future vindicated him. Regarding Hitler's disastrous invasion of Russia, Bose remarked perspicaciously in a broadcast from Singapore on 25 May 1945 that "Germany's blunder was to disregard totally, the advice of Bismarck never to fight on two fronts" (Bose 1980: 249). Hitler's overconfidence led to inevitable destruction, which Bose foresaw long ago. He believed that when the Soviet Foreign Minister Molotov visited Berlin in 1940, German statesmanship should have risen to its fullest height and reached an understanding with the Soviet Union. With prophetic foresight, he said that "the collapse of Germany would be a signal for the outbreak of an acute conflict between Soviets and Anglo Americans" (ibid.). The eruption of the Cold War once again proved him correct.

In view of these facts, it appears improper to brand Bose as a wishful visionary. He differed from Nehru's inflexible stand of no truck with fascism. Though, in his own way, he grew to his own variety of internationalism, Bose was careful not to exalt internationalism over nationalism at a crucial juncture in the nation's history. He obviously felt that internationalism for a subject nation was a luxury which India could not afford, though he declared at the Maharashtra Provincial Conference at Poona on 3 May 1927 that nationalism was the road to internationalism (Das 1997: 141). Later on, Nehru also admitted that internationalism could develop only in a free country (Nehru 1947: 419). Bose thus belonged to the realist, rather than the idealist school of international relations as he discerned a Machiavellian element in international power politics where no principle was sacrosanct. He thus wrote to Nehru:

> Frothy sentiments and pious platitudes do not make foreign policy. One should either take international politics seriously and utilise the international situation to India's advantage or not talk about it at all. It is no use making a show if we do not mean business.
>
> *(Bose 1981a: 32)*

This is where his gulf with Nehru was never bridged. Nehru could never subscribe to the idea of utilising the war situation to India's advantage because to him the Axis Powers were greater enemies than British imperialism. Thus, he even declared his resolve to fight the Japanese if they invaded India with Bose. Even Gandhi did not magnify the Japanese menace as Nehru did. However, Bose was fully prepared to resist any sinister design Japan might have had with respect to India. Bose's trusted officer S. A. Ayer remarked, "It may be asked what was the sanction behind Netaji if the Japanese broke faith with him after crossing the border and while advancing to India". That sanction was the fiery spirit of the I.N.A. to which the Japanese themselves bore witness and total non-cooperation and sabotage of the civilian population in the liberated regions. A combination of these two formidable weapons, if directed by Netaji against the Japanese, would prove too much even for the Japanese forces. The Japanese knew this very well. That is why Netaji was more than confident that he was not taking the slightest risk in accepting Japanese aid in his epic armed struggle for India's independence (Ayer 1951: 217). This shows that Bose was always on his guard against the possible eventuality of Japanese betrayal. The question is, was there really any such possibility?

The fact is that Japan never had any intention of conquering India. Geographically, India was far from Japan, and if Japan sought to control India that itself would be a chimerical idea. Japan was very much conscious of this reality, and Japanese historians like Saito, Akashir, and Nagasaki have proved that Japan never wanted to exploit or dominate the countries of Southeast and South Asia. Interestingly Nirad Chandra Chaudhuri countered the view of Frank Moraes, war correspondent of the *Times of India*, that Japan mounted its counteroffensive as the spearhead of their march to Delhi saying that it was launched to forestall British advance into Burma, not to occupy India. J. B. Bhattacharjee, in his presidential address in the Modern India section of the Indian History Congress Golden Jubilee session of 1989, observed that "the so-called Japanese invasion of India was a myth which was consciously created by the British to alienate the INA from the Indian masses". Tilak Raj Sareen observes in the same vein that "The collaboration of the Indians with the Japanese was based on common goals and interests". It was necessity and not charity or generosity which had prompted Japan to aid the Indian independence movement in East Asia.

To be sure, the Western propagandists were never tired of repeating that Subhas was a mere tool in the hands of the Japanese for an invasion on India and that if they had won, they would take the place of the British as India's rulers. But the Japanese policy towards India shows that this accusation was nothing but utterly baseless war propaganda. The Japanese repeatedly clarified that they had no intention to subjugate India. If the Japanese did not attack India after the fall of Burma in 1942 when they were at the height of their power in East Asia, it was unlikely that they would have done so when their war fortunes were declining and they hardly had adequate forces to carry out even a limited campaign against India (Sareen 1995: 186–187). Equally interesting is the fact that, in some of his speeches, Japanese Foreign Minister Matsuoka had referred to India, but that was not explicitly as a part of the Co-Prosperity Sphere. It was felt that an independent India was necessary for the success of Japan's New Order, for the presence of the British in India would always be a threat to their stability and dominance in the region. This proves irrefutably that the charge that Bose made a serious miscalculation by colluding with the Japanese, is utterly misplaced and not attuned to reality. Bose would never have asked for Japanese help, had he the slightest inkling that Japan had the insidious agenda of conquering India while making a show of pulling the chestnuts out of the fire for her.

VII Bose's vision of free India

Bose never envisaged a dictatorship in India, though he preferred a strong party with dictatorial powers for some time after independence. He had no faith in mid-Victorian democracy but did not ever think of a fascist dictatorship in India at any time. In his Haripura speech, he clearly spoke of a multi-party system. His overall bent of mind was not dictatorial, and what he wanted was a disciplined democracy. At the same time, he wanted the State to be a servant of the people as he mentioned in his Tokyo speech. Bose was always in favour of individual freedom but felt that some kind of forced march might be necessary to arouse the people from their supine slumber. However, experience testifies that once dictators are entrenched in power, they perpetuate their authority. Bose was not clear about the time limit for the switch over from authoritarianism to democracy. However, he was conscious of this danger, and in his address sent to the Third Political Conference in London on 10 June 1933, he insisted on a prolonged process of training for the workers of the party which would be in power in independent India who would be "freedom intoxicated missionaries who were morally prepared people willing to make the maximum sacrifice for the country" (Bose 1981b: 18). To him, Hitlerism could never be the panacea, as evident from his editorial *Whither the Baltic States*, published in the *Forward Bloc* on 27 July 1940, where he stated that:

> The doctrine of Nazism is abhorred by the rational world and it has forfeited all claims to humanism by its insistence on the glorification of

violence and war. Nazism cannot guarantee peace to men nor would it let life bloom in its beauty.

(Das and Rath 1997: 89–90)

Bose's modernist outlook was clear in his advocacy of the post-independence reconstruction of India along scientific lines, which was endorsed by Tagore, who preferred a scientifically tempered person as Congress president. It was Bose who initiated national planning as an integral feature of Congress policy and appointed the National Planning Committee. He made Nehru the chairman of the Committee. Nehru is rightly called the proponent of five-year plans in independent India, but it was Bose who initiated the process in 1938.

In view of the feminist movement operative in India, one may appropriately recall the role Bose assigned to women in his I.N.A. He organised the 'Jhansi Rani Regiment' and inspired women in East Asia to come out of kitchen life and step into the wider world outside and perform the role of soldiers on the battlefield. He had an abiding faith in *nari shakti*, or the power of the women folk, and championed gender equality most emphatically. Rani Laxmibai of Jhansi was his role model. His new role definition for women is relevant in the context of the movement for the empowerment of women not only in India but the world over. The example of national unity and secularism set by the I.N.A., where there was not a trace of caste or religious distinctions, where all communities intermingled freely, and where there was a common kitchen, deserves to be emulated in modern India. The I.N.A. was truly a nation in the making. Bose in his presidential address at Haripura made the sinister prognostication that:

> An internal partition is necessary to neutralise the transference of power. If the new Constitution is finally rejected, I have no doubt that British ingenuity will seek some other constitutional device for partitioning India.
>
> *(Bose 1981a: 5)*

This proved unerringly correct. Bose was dead set against the partition of India and in a broadcast from Burma on 12 September 1944 vehemently opposed the Pakistan scheme for the vivisection of India. He declared fervently "our divine motherland shall not be cut up" (Bose 1980: 241). In independent India, the communal problem continues to threaten national unity. In our struggle against the divisive forces which confront India with the ominous prospect of balkanisation, Bose's I.N.A. remains a shining exemplar, and the three ideals of the I.N.A. – unity, faith, and sacrifice – signify the panacea for India in her struggle against the perils that lie ahead.

VIII Conclusion

From the previous discussion, it is clear that while Subhas Chandra Bose was predominantly a man of action, he had a thoughtful and reflective strain and above all a vision of the future both for India and the world. He was not a thinker or system builder in the conventional sense of the term, but his ideas, as he himself said, were rooted in reality and did not float in the air. Some of his thoughts on the future development of the Indian State after independence are of enduring relevance to India in the new millennium. Thus, Amita Ghosh rightly describes him as both a realist and a visionary. According to her, Bose was not an orthodox theorist. She, however, exaggerates the romantic element in Bose, saying that Gandhi and Nehru were akin to Mazzini and Cavour while Bose resembled Garibaldi. It should, however, be remembered that romanticism and rationalism ran parallel in Bose's life, and despite an irresistible love for adventure, he never opted for the path of insane misadventure. Today, even Japanese historians have established that Japan had no intention of conquering India and the contention of critics that Bose's collusion with the Axis powers would have invited Japanese invasion, stands conclusively repudiated.

It is also a fact that the I.N.A. almost came to the point of capturing Imphal and was thwarted by the untimely arrival of a monsoon. Even so, it triggered off a spirit of revolt in the British Indian Army, Navy, and Air Force which was unprecedented. This was the largest single factor which convinced the British imperialist rulers that they could no longer count upon the loyalty of their hitherto impregnable bastion of support. Ever since the Sepoy Revolt of 1857, there were sporadic indications of revolt in the armed forces, but the Congress leadership, after the efforts of Jatin Mukherjee, Rash Behari Bose, and the Ghadar Party, made no concerted effort to utilise such opportunities and possibilities. It was Subhas Chandra Bose who revived this legacy through the resurgent I.N.A. in the Far East, and the I.N.A. onslaught was able to make the first dent in the loyalty structure of the British Indian Army, Navy, and Air Force. Thus, it was the I.N.A. which laid the last nail on the coffin of British imperialist rule in India.

References

Ayer, S. A. (1951). *Unto Him a Witness*. Bombay: Thacker and Company.
Bose, A. C. (2010). Subhas Chandra Bose and International Politics, in Chittabrata Palit (Ed.), *Netaji Subhas Chandra Bose in Historical Perspective*. Kolkata: Institute of Historical Studies.
Bose, Sisir Kumar and Bose Sugata (Eds.) (1987). *Netaji, Collected Works*, Vol. VI. Calcutta: Netaji Research Bureau.
Bose, Sisir Kumar and Bose Sugata (Eds.) (1994). *Netaji, Collected Works*, Vol. VIII. Delhi: Oxford University Press.
Bose, Subhas Chandra (1937). Europe Today and Tomorrow. *Modern Review*, 21 August.
Bose, Subhas Chandra (1980). An Indian Pilgrim, in Sisir K. Bose (Ed.), *Netaji Collected Works*, Vol. 1. Calcutta: Netaji Research Bureau.
Bose, Subhas Chandra (1981a). *Crossroads*. Calcutta: Netaji Research Bureau.
Bose, Subhas Chandra (1981b). *Fundamental Questions of the Indian Revolution*. Calcutta: Netaji Research Bureau.
Bose, Subhas Chandra (1981c). The Indian Struggle, in Sisir Kumar Bose (Ed.), *Netaji, Collected Works*, Vol. II. Calcutta: Netaji Research Bureau.

Chattopadhyay, Gautam (1997). Subhas Chandra Bose and the Leftist Movement in India, in Radharaman Chakrabarti (Ed.), *Netaji and India's Freedom*. Calcutta: Netaji Institute for Asian Studies.

Das, Harihar and B. C. Rath (Eds.) (1997). *Netaji Subhas Chandra Bose, Reassessment of His Ideas and Ideologies*. Jaipur: Pointer Publishers.

Das, Sunil (Ed.). (1997). *Subhas Rachanabali*, Vol. 1. Calcutta: Jayasree Prakasan.

Defence Committee Paper. (1946, June 12). D.O (46) 68, pp. 889–890. https://www.tandfonline.com/doi/full/10.1080/13619462.2013.796884

Dutta, B. C. (1971). *Mutiny of Innocents*. Bombay: Sindhu Publications Pvt. Ltd.

Mansergh, N. (Ed.) (1973). *The Transfer of Power 1942–47*, Vol. VI. London: H.M.S.O.

Nehru, Jawaharlal (1947). *The Discovery of India*. Calcutta: Signet Press.

Ponchhammer, Wilhem Von (1981). *India's Road to Nationhood, A Political History of the Sub Continent*. New Delhi: Allied Publishers.

Sareen, T. R. (1995). The Indian National Army, in Ram Dayal (Ed.), *We Fought Together for Freedom*. New Delhi: Oxford University Press.

Selected Speeches of Subhas Chandra Bose (1974). New Delhi: Publications Division, Government of India.

Selected Speeches of Subhas Chandra Bose (1983). New Delhi: Publications Division, Government of India.

Tuker, Francis (1950). *While Memory Serves*. London: Sani H. Panhwar.

18

JAYAPRAKASH NARAYAN

Anand Kumar and Sipra Sagarika

> *Freedom became one of the beacon lights of my life and it has remained so ever since. Freedom with the passing of years transcended the mere freedom of my country and embraced freedom of man everywhere and from every sort of trammel- above all, it meant freedom of the human personality, freedom of the mind, freedom of the spirit. This freedom has become the passion of my life and I shall not see it compromised for bread, for security, for prosperity, for the glory of the State or for anything else.*
>
> – Jayaprakash Narayan, Quoted in *L. K. Advani, My Country My Life*, 2008

I Introduction

Jayaprakash Narayan (1902–1979) was described as the "Saviour of India's Democracy", in the modern times.[1] He played a major role in India's independence movement on one hand and on the other hand played an important role in the growth and development of the socialist movement. He identified himself more with the non-party *bhoodan* (land gift) movement led by Vinoba Bhave. He visualised the seed of non-violent social revolution and therefore publically dedicated his whole life to it in 1954. He stood as a great democrat who fought against the authoritarian rule of the Congress and fought to reclaim democracy in the turmoil of the Emergency period. He was ideologically influenced by Gandhiji's ideas of *Hind Swaraj* and non-violence largely. Though, for a period he was influenced by the revolutionary ideas of Marx and Marxist scholars, such as M. N. Roy. But this was mainly during the 1930s, after which he drifted to the philosophy of democratic socialism and finally turned to *sarvodaya*, and supported *satyāgraha*, non-violence under the leadership of Gandhiji. This happened because slowly he could realise problems in Marxism and criticised the very basis of Marxism, that is, dialectical materialism. According to Narayan, the personalities of human beings consist of both spiritual and material aspects for a holistic development in society. Therefore, only the material aspect can never contribute towards the development of a whole society. Rather, both the material and spiritual aspects can flourish goodness in society.[2] Similarly, he was not agreeable to the idea that dictatorship of the proletariat ought to be the only means of transformation from a capitalist mode of production to a socialist mode of production. Rather, according to him, the nature of a socialist State ought to be such that there is no need for any sort of dictatorship in the society. He therefore stated that it is a fallacy of the Marxist paradigm to argue for a compulsory imposition of the dictatorship of the proletariat in a socialist State (Narayan 1964: 50–51).

Ideologically, Narayan wanted a model for India where, unlike in the Soviet Union, socio-economic transformations could be brought through Gandhian peaceful and democratic methods. He argued that India should strictly follow peaceful methods for two main reasons: 1) that in a society where it was possible for the people by democratic means to bring about social change, it may be difficult to restore to violence and 2) that socialism could not exist, nor be created, in the absence of democratic freedoms (Narayan 1959: 18).

II Life sketch

Jayaprakash Narayan was born on 11 October 1902 as the fourth child of Babu Harsoo Dayal and Phool Rani. He was from a middle-class *Kayastha* family located in the village Sitabdiara, Saran district of present day Bihar. Narayan attended government primary school and completed his initial study and then was sent to Patna for his further studies. He completed his intermediate from Patna and was actively associated with several national leaders through the political centre *Saraswati Bhawan*. The period between 1914 and 1922 proved to be very determining in Narayan's life. The events could be understood through three major events: first, in 1915, Mahatma Gandhi returned to India. He had already evolved non-violent methods of *satyāgraha* and non-cooperation in his struggle in South Africa and it greatly influenced Narayan. When Gandhi made his first experiment of *satyāgraha* in 1927, in Champaran district of Bihar, Narayan was moved by the non-violent techniques and made up his mind to lead a simple life for national interest. The second important event was Narayan's marriage to Prabhawati Devi when he was hardly 18 years old. However, when he was in America, Prabhawati expressed her desire to practice celibacy, to which Narayan readily agreed because he wanted to sacrifice his life for the greater interest of the country. The third major event was in 1921, when Mahatma Gandhi launched the non-cooperation movement, in which all national leaders were united against the British government. Gandhiji and Jawaharlal Nehru visited Patna and gave a call to people to join the movement. Narayan was in the middle of his studies, but he left to join the movement.

However, Narayan later went for higher studies in America on 16 May 1922, and he got an opportunity to study in several renowned universities, in places such as California, Lowa, Chicago, Wisconsin, and Ohio. During his stay in the

United States, Narayan was influenced by several writings of Anatole France, Henrik Ibsen, Maxim Gorky, and M. N. Roy. With the passage of time, Narayan lost his interest in the natural sciences and decided to shift to social sciences. He felt that India's socio-economic development was the real problem and for addressing those problems, an in-depth understanding of the social sciences is required. However, after coming back to India, Narayan worked hard with Ram Manohar Lohia to formulate the Socialist Party. While keeping contact with the socialist movement, he was also interested in *bhoodan* and *sarvodaya*.

He saw the Gandhian way of *sarvodaya*, as a non-violent non-party power politics, as an alternate to social reconstruction. In his writings and speeches, Narayan described *sarvodaya* as the only way out of the existing situation – the reorganisation of life on the basis of self-reliant, self-governing people. Further, Gandhi's picture of *gram swaraj* was also nothing more than self-dependent small units of society with a complete decentralised system of power and production. Therefore, Narayan was in support of a party-less democratic pattern of development in India.

Narayan had been always in search of a political faith for the sake of freedom and human progress. He was always ready to revise his ideas to suit political and economic conditions. Therefore, he revised his thoughts from Marxism to socialism. In 1936, he wrote a book called *Why Socialism?* Further, he laid the foundation of the 'Congress Socialist Party' in the same year. The Congress Socialist Party grew out of the experiences of the latest national struggles. It was formed at the end of the civil disobedience movement by a group of Congressmen who believed a new orientation of national movement was essential to realise the goals of society. They targeted the nation to be free from Britishers on one hand, and on the other hand they wanted to place economic functioning based on socialist parameters.

In 1946, he wrote an article titled "My Picture of Socialism" and laid down several objectives of socialism. He delineated that his picture of socialist India was the picture of an economic and political democracy. In such a democracy, men would be neither slave to capitalism nor a party to the State. Man would be free and would have to serve the society through his employment and skills. He would be free to avail all opportunities and rise to his own moral stature. Several features Narayan emphasised in this article included elements such as:

- Cooperative farms run by village *Panchayats*.
- Large-scale industries owned and managed by the community.
- Small-scale industries organised under a producer's cooperative.
- State's role to be limited and to be democratised.
- Transfer of all powers to producing masses.
- Development of economic life of the country to be planned and controlled by the State.
- Socialisation of all keys and principal industries, banks, insurance, and public utilities, with a view to the progressive socialisation of all means of production, distribution, and exchange.

- State monopoly of foreign trade.
- Organisation of cooperatives for production, distribution, and credit in the unorganised sector of the economy.
- Liquidation of debts of peasants and workers.
- Encouragement and promotion of cooperative farming of the State.
- Redistribution of lands to peasants.
- Distribution of economic goals based on the principle of "to everyone according to his need and from everyone according to his capacity".
- Adult franchise on a functional basis.
- No support or discrimination to any religion by the State.
- No recognition of any distinction based on caste and community and no discrimination between sexes.

III Participatory democracy and the reconstruction of the Indian polity

The concept of participatory democracy which Narayan explained in his paper titled "Swaraj for the People" in 1961, describes that in participatory democracy people are participating in the government. In such a form of democracy, people are within the operational patterns of government. Further, educated people can take on the charge of decision-making, and political parties should have minimum interference. *Panchayats* must function with the trust of people and the help of local bodies. He was against parliamentary democracy, as he understood that the benefits of such a form of democracy would not trickle down to the poor people of the country. For assemblies and Lok Sabha, Narayan suggested a procedure for the selection of two delegates from each *gram sabha* after seeking general consent. The electoral college should set up candidates for election. In such a set-up, the multi-party system, which had corrupted the whole body of politics of the country, would have to be abandoned. Therefore, Narayan advocated that it should be replaced by real participatory democracy, involving masses in its working.

Further, in this form of democracy, he advocated "political and economic decentralisation". He indeed supported the reconstruction of the economic system, as he was against the exploitive and competitive economic system as prevailing in the capitalist societies. According to him, in the participatory democratic pattern, the economic system must be cooperative, coexisting and co-sharing in nature. On the pattern of the political system of the country, in participatory democracy, he wanted an orientation which should be grassroots directed or village directed. He argued that the formulation of a development plan should be initiated at the village level with its progressive, integrative, and consolidated approach for blocks and districts. The planning processes at the State and national levels should confine themselves with only providing technical and logistical support for the formulation and execution of the plans at the local levels. Narayan also called for sectoral balance and harmony in bringing about rapid economic development of the country. Thus, the restructured political economy of the country in Narayan's view would result in the realisation of true *swaraj* for the common people of the country. On the Kashmir issue, he wrote in his letter to Mrs Indira Gandhi in 1966:

> The Kashmir question has plagued this country for last 19 years. It has cost us a great deal materially and spiritually. We profess democracy, but rule by force in Kashmir . . . We profess secularism, but let Hindu nationalism stamped into trying to establish it by repression.
>
> (Samaddar 2008: 45)

Narayan was clear that it would be suicide of the soul of India if the country tried to suppress the Kashmiri people by force. Rather than rely on repression, he suggested the government refer to the 1947–1953 days and keep only three subjects with itself, that is, defence, foreign affairs, and communication, and provide the fullest possible autonomy to Kashmir. Narayan believed the problem in Kashmir existed not because Pakistan wanted to grab Kashmir but because there was deep and widespread political discontent among the people. For that reason, Narayan believed an attempt to provide internal autonomy would restore peace in the valley.

IV Critique of Marxism

In the history of Indian Marxism, it is hard to underestimate the influence of Gandhi on its evolution and on the self-perception of Indian Marxist-socialists.[3] Indeed, the reception of Gandhian ideas triggered the shift from using the term "Marxist" to a preference for the term "socialist" that broadly denoted the retention of the Marxist vision for a post-capitalist society as the departure point for one's politics but coupled with Gandhi's political and philosophical ideas. On the most basic level, Indian Marxists voiced their dissatisfaction with Marxism to questions relating to moral concerns.[4] Given the political success of Gandhi's peaceful and purportedly moral means of *satyāgraha* and its ability to unite the masses in a common political cause, it seemed but a natural conclusion that Marxism's success too would eventually have to rest on the foundations of virtue and self-discipline displayed by the masses. To this, Gandhi was an answer.[5] In other words, the person, the message, and the authenticity of both seemed to exacerbate the problem of Marxism as an empty ideology in the context of India. Furthermore, on the institutional or party-political level, India's proponents of Gandhian Marxism regrouped as true socialists in an effort to distance the movement from the Indian communist movement.

It was firstly argued that the Communist Party was too Western oriented. In many polemical accounts, the party was perceived as a puppet of the Soviet Communist Party and therefore lacked the legitimacy to speak for the Indian socialist cause. Secondly, its leadership was seen as being dictatorial because communism was generally equated with the politics of Vladimir Lenin that sought to control events via a vanguard party.[6] Hence, there was a fear of the totalitarian effects that an elite party with a strong leadership could have on India's nationalist base – because of the Communist Party's condoning of violent methods of revolution, its internationalist bias, and its links with a strong Soviet State. For Indian socialists, however, the abstract notion of a world revolution could only be formulated as the less-abstract task of building a socialist nation-State. Narayan claimed that for this purpose, Gandhism was a far better option than Marxism as it developed under Lenin.

Indeed, it is vital that we view Narayan's perception of Marxism as a version, albeit being internally plural, of Marxist thought. For Narayan, Marxism gained pre-eminence in different ways: as an ideology promoting social justice and harmony, and in this case as the basis of a formal party system that controlled the politics of the powerful and influential Soviet State. The identification of the Leninist-Marxism with the Soviet State, and in turn the identification of the State with Marxism as one of the dominating ideologies of the time, is crucial to understand Narayan's reasons for rejecting Marxism. The blurring of the distinction between Marxist thought and orthodox Marxism is common, and Narayan too was guilty of not always explicitly differentiating the different usages found in his writings. Through the inconsistencies, we see two different solutions to the question of Marxism as an instrument of realising socialism's emancipatory ideals – rejection as well as transcending the terms of its ideology by perfecting it with Gandhism. The old Socialist Party had started under a strong influence of Leninist-Marxism. But it had slowly travelled towards Gandhism. It did so when it gave up its faith in dictatorship (even as a transitional phase); when it asserted that socialism could not exist without democracy; when it came to believe that the decentralisation of economic and political power was essential for democracy; when it decided that good ends could not be achieved through evil means; when it accepted, at least in words, *satyāgraha* as a revolutionary weapon.[7]

Using a Gandhian framework of social criticism, Narayan, like many socialists, concluded that Marxism's core aspects were indeed inimical to freedom. Firstly, Marxism's critique of capitalism seemed flawed in that the critique incorporated the idea of capitalism and the attendant political system of bourgeois representative democracy being an inevitable stage in history and a dialectical truth. Consequently, the rejection of this notion meant rejecting Marxism's idea that contradictions, for example, between material benefits and exploitation, had to be pushed to the extreme for social change to take place. This leads to the justification of violent revolutions, the upshot being a form of dictatorship and therefore a loss of freedom. Hence, Gandhism was seen by the Indian left as a credible alternative to Marxism, which was perceived as a limiting ideology and one with aspirations to dominance not unlike the experience of imperialist colonialism. As such, Narayan's concept of total revolution characterises what he held to be his actual objective throughout his intellectual meanderings from

Marxism to democratic socialism to Gandhian *sarvodaya* to a party-less, classless society to a Stateless society.

V Democratic socialism

Narayan's entire philosophy and political praxis can be divided into broad streams, namely, democratic socialism and *sarvodaya*. From the Leninist perspective, his earliest stint in politics in 1930 is categorised as the Marxist phase, but when it is put to rigorous scrutiny, a fundamental difference between Marxism and democratic socialism is not marked. In 1940, in the Draft Resolution for the Congress session at Ramgarh, he outlined another programme that has been considered his phase of democratic socialism. These programmes were as follows:

- Guarantee of full individual and civil liberty and religious cultural freedom.
- Abolition of all distinction based on birth and privileges.
- Guarantees of equal rights to all citizens.
- The political and economic organisation of the State to be based on the principles of social justice and economic freedom.
- All large-scale production to be under collective ownership and control.
- Political and economic organisation of the State to be conducive to the satisfaction of the national requirements of all members of the society, material satisfaction need not be the top and sole objective. State aims at creating conditions for healthy living and the moral and intellectual development of the individual.
- State to endeavour to promote small-scale production carried on both individual and cooperative efforts for the equal benefit of all concerned; and the life of the villager should be recognised with a view to making them self-governing and self-sufficient.

Democratic socialists believe the individuality of each human being can only be developed in a society embodying the values of liberty, equality, and solidarity. This ideology promotes the fact that if human beings are to develop their distinct capacities, they must be accorded equally in all aspects of respect and opportunities. If the democratic-socialist ideology performs its best in society, then each citizen must be provided with equal cultural and economic necessities, such as food, housing, quality education, health care, and childcare. According to Narayan, the democratic-socialist vision does not rest upon one sole tradition; it draws upon Marxism, religious and ethical socialism, feminism, and other theories that critique human domination. Nor does it contend that any laws of history preordain the achievement of socialism. Therefore, Narayan explains that the choice for socialism is both moral and political.

Democratic socialism is a political philosophy that advocates political democracy alongside social ownership of means of production, with a focus on self-management and democratic management of economic institutions, within the market. Democratic socialists understand that capitalism is inherently incompatible to their basic values of liberty, equality, and solidarity. They therefore promote socialism through which these ideas can be achieved. Further, democratic visions can help in curtailing social inequalities with initiatives from the government. Thus, when State interventions are made through the ideological weapon of democratic socialism to develop a just society, Narayan must be acknowledged.

VI *Sarvodaya*

Sarvodaya was a conceptual construct which Narayan borrowed from Gandhi to cumulatively articulate his vision of a decentralised, participatory, and egalitarian socio-economic and political order for India. Describing the values of *sarvodaya*, Vinoba Bhave wrote: "*sarvodaya* does not mean good government or majority rule; it means freedom from government, and decentralisation of power" (Bhave 1964a: 3). Narayan in visualising his *sarvodaya* social order, first began to understand the innate characteristics of human nature. According to him, "positive values of life such as cooperation, generosity, creativity and eternal joy are essential to create a *sarvodaya* social order of the country. Further, it is also based on inclusive egalitarian social structure" (Narayan 1959: 39–41). Thus, this brings the conclusion that social relations should be based on the principles of equality, justice, and inclusiveness of the diverse stocks of people. Further, under such a paradigm, social welfare must be a voluntary work of the members of the society.

The political dimension of *sarvodaya*, as explained by Narayan refers to the widest and most effective system of a decentralised and participatory form of democracy, focusing on the *Panchayati raj* system. The *sarvodaya* political order of Narayan was based on several concepts, such as *lokniti* (politics of the people), and *lokshakti* (power of the people). He was not in favour of *rajniti* and *rajshakti* (politics and power of the State). Thus, his notion of *sarvodaya* preached social order consisting of morally upright individuals having courage to stand up for the ideals of self-government, self-management, mutual cooperation, and the sharing of equality, freedom, and brotherhood (Narayan 1959: 40).

The economic framework of a *sarvodaya* order would seek to bring balance in the economic set-up of the country. He emphasised on agricultural activities in the economic field and promoted the collective ownership and collective management of whole villages. Following the framework of Gandhian ideology, Narayan even promoted cottage industries. Further, he also emphasised the role of industrialisation in the era of economic development of *sarvodaya*. He emphasised on equitable distributions of benefits of economic activities to create a just society.

VII Party-less democracy

Narayan explains that in a democratic system, if a political party continues in power over a long period of time, it gets corrupted because power corrupts even the most incorruptible. Power is associated with privileges. Therefore, party in power is tempted to use all sorts of means to continue ruling the country. He saw the danger of the decline of social, political, economic, and all kinds of standards in a country under a single-party dictatorship. Thus, he provided an alternate party-less democracy, where no single party could dominate people and there could be no chance for the grooming of corruption. He gave a clarion call to the educated youth of the country to understand the concept of party-less democracy and operate in a model of participatory democracy.

In a party-less democracy, things would be less based on party and ideology and much more on actual ideas and policies. People vote without any bias and there is absence of any party hierarchy. The alienation and disenchantment with the parliamentary or presidential forms of democracy led to the prioritisation of a party-less democracy. Further, the idea of party-less democracy is influenced by two major thinkers of modern times – Karl Marx and Mahatma Gandhi. According to Marx, stage after stage, each stage of political and economic evolution or total dispersal of power follows dynamism. It cannot be static in nature. Therefore, any form of parliamentary or presidential democracy must be changed in due course to a party-less democracy. Gandhi, similarly, advocated for the deconcentration of power by the dispersal of power to grassroots institutions, such as *Panchayat, Panchayat Samiti,* and *Zilla Parishad,* so that M.L.A. (Member of the Legislative Assembly) and M.P. (Member of Parliament) get rooted and connected to the grassroots bottom.

Thus, neither Marx nor Gandhi explicitly or implicitly supported party democracy as practiced in the U.K. or U.S.A. but proposed more appropriate and effective political devices to bring power to the hands of the people. Thus, party-less democracy was always encouraged by these two modern thinkers and promoted by Narayan too.

VIII Total revolution (*sampurna kranti*)

Total revolution (*sampurna kranti*) was the last intellectual intervention of Narayan to attain a democratic, federal, participatory, equitable, and prosperous nation. Bhave first evolved the concept in the 1960s to articulate his desire for the need for a comprehensive movement in the country which would transform all aspects of life and create a new world (Bhave 1964b: 1). Narayan reconstructed and used this idea in 1975 to work for total revolution as against the growing authoritarianism in the functioning of the government machinery headed by Mrs Indira Gandhi. Narayan's slogan of *sampurna kranti* became the punch-line for opposing Indira's government. In the Emergency period, he called for a total revolution, in hopes of bringing a holistic transformation to India. He emphasised on the spiritual sanctity of institutions and full cooperation of the masses in bringing up the total revolution.

The total revolution process can be understood in terms of seven revolutions, that is, social, political, cultural, ideological, intellectual, educational, and spiritual. Further, its operational mode needs to be undertaken within the political and economic system of the country. According to him, the concentration of power within the hands of a few makes the system more vulnerable and weaker. In the sphere of the political system, Narayan noted the inherent fallacies of the prevailing parliamentary system of government, as its basic characteristics, namely, the electoral system, party-based political process, and increasing concentration of powers in the hands of one person (the Prime Minister), were very problematic. Such a system always encouraged corruption and a tyrannical situation; therefore, he emphasised on a conscious voting pattern of people and a participatory mode of government, which would not have a party-based system.

From an economic aspect, he suggested a total recasting of the economic system of the country. Arguing for a mixed-economy framework for India, Narayan described that such an economy should be able to cater to the demand of people's basic needs, such as clothing and shelter. His idea of *sampatti dan* (donation of wealth) was a call for sharing one's wealth and economic resources in such a way that its benefits are distributed to large sections of society. He visualised an economic order for the country where there would be a progressive socialisation of the means of resources by way of establishing cooperative societies and voluntary associations to manage resources with a view to ensure prosperity for all. The decentralisation of power was the most suitable means to bring economic justification in society (Narayan 1978: 79). Further, his call for total revolution was also against the price hike policies of Congress. He argued that in a country like India, where people were suffering from starvation and chronic poverty, the exorbitantly rising prices of commodities would break the strength of the common people.

IX Caste, youth, and poverty

Narayan believed India could not grow unless the distinction and oppressions of caste were destroyed. The caste system was like an iron shell which protected a dried-up social order and denied an equitable environment. It isolated caste groups and broke the unity of society. Thus, breaking down the caste system would mean freedom from socially oppressed and socially humiliated pain in all terms. Narayan viewed that all belong to one nation and one caste, that is, the human caste. Therefore, national integration must be integrated with social integration. Giving a call to the youth of the nation, he explained that youth must take the charge to make both social and national integration through national revival. Further, according to him, the writer, artist, and thinker must become the instruments of sweeping cultural revolution. Youth homes and *janta centres* of culture must spring up in town, and all must act as catalysts for change.

There is intense poverty in India. At least 90 percent of the people are its victims. To remove poverty or to reduce its rigors is the first target. Analysing poverty, Narayan explained that poverty depends on two factors: 1) how much we produce and 2) how we share what is produced. Addressing the first aspect he explained that we do not produce enough, production per man is too low; therefore, we must work harder. There must be opportunities generated for full employment, and unemployment must be removed. There must be full employment and incentives to work harder. However, the second question of distribution may be tackled faster, as all wealth is produced by labour, which is either mental or physical. So, it can be measured that those who put comparatively more effort into labour should be able to obtain the fruits of production proportionately.

At present, the distribution of wealth is not governed by rational principles. Many of them, who do not contribute to the production process, have large amounts of wealth. On the other hand, many who contribute to the production process do not own enough to live on. Therefore, the first step towards ending poverty is the equitable distribution of wealth. Further, land must be distributed to the tillers, and the intermediaries must be omitted. For the rich, the maximum amount of land to be held should not exceed 30 acres. Further, provision should be made for cheap rural credit, and poor peasants' agricultural debts should be cancelled. Lastly, except for rehabilitation compensation to small landlords, no compensation should be paid for the abolition of landlordism.

X Education and health system

According to Narayan, there should be free and compulsory primary education. At the secondary stage, every effort should be made to impart vocational and technical training. University education should be restricted to those who intend to pursue higher studies in arts, science, technology, and research. Except religious academics, all education should be secularised. Youth, women, and children centres should be organised for cultural activities. Further, untouchables, backward communities, and tribal people should receive special attention in our educational programmes.

According to him, trained doctors and modern medicines are beyond the means of the millions of our people. Therefore, a judicious and scientific use of such ancient systems of medicine, such as *Ayurvedic* or *Unani* and native drugs and herbs, must be made. Mobile hospitals or medical vans are based on field hospitals should be organised. The manufacture, import, and prices of drugs must be severely controlled, and profits in these spheres should be reduced. Cooperative health societies should be encouraged. Sanitation, cleaning of swamps, and the supply of pure drinking water should receive urgent attention. Medical profession practitioners should perceive their work not as a profession but as a social service. Further, a beginning towards the socialisation of medical and health services should be made in larger cities.

XI Scheduled Caste, Tribes, and women

The Scheduled Castes and Tribes are the most backward sections of Indian community and society. Special efforts must be initiated to raise their economic and social levels. For their education and technical training, special provision must be made to bring advancement in their positions. Further, land distribution should also be made in a justifiable manner to the marginalised communities. In the administration, at the legislature, centre and State level, their representations should be proportionately made. Free access to timber and forest products should be facilitated to the tribals to protect their livelihood.

According to him, women in this country suffer from a variety of social and economic injustices. They should enjoy equal rights with men in property rights. Special efforts should be made to promote girls' education and skill-based and vocational training. Further, women across the country need to be united across several organisations to fight for safeguarding their rights and scopes in a systematic manner. They should enjoy equal rights with men, and their disabilities in the matter of inheritance and property must be removed. In the service sector, there should not be any discrimination against women. Women should be organised to fight for their rights and for their constructive uplifting.

XII Conclusion

The life and thought of Jayaprakash Narayan appear to be in a continuous flow with the demand of time and situation. He always argued for the revolutionary transformation of Indian society in terms of socialist Russia. Further, his ideologies were influenced by Gandhi's idea of *sarvodaya* as well. Narayan was a dreamer of new India. If all his ideas and thoughts could have been implemented in a systematic pattern, then miracles could have been found in Indian society. In his last days, Narayan was like a poet revolutionary who had found a form, content, and a living voice for that restless dream which had never ceased to stir within him.[8]

A proposed conclusion is perhaps impossible for a person like Jayaprakash Narayan in the history of Indian political thought. His contributions, ideas, and dreams were the backbone of democracy in India. His thoughts are exceptionally remarkable in the formulation of a stronger India in near future. Narayan and his ideas provide a compact solution to contemporary India's problems. A sincere attempt to execute his ideas in the present social, political, and economic scenario can open a new scope for revolutionary changes in new India. The definition of development in terms of sustainability and humanitarianism can only be found by following Narayan's guidelines. He is an immortal personality, and his contributions and ideas are to be practically lived for ages to come.

Notes

1 11 October 2015 is considered as *Loktantra Bachao Diwas*. It was the 113th birth anniversary of Loknayak Jayaprakash Narayan, where he was given the title "Saviour of India's Democracy".
2 Jayaprakash Narayan (1936). Why Socialism? Varanasi: *Akhil Bharat Sarva-Seva Sangh Prakashan*.

3 For historical reviews and commentaries on the importance of Gandhism on Indian socialism, see Ghose: *Socialism, Democracy, and Nationalism in India*. Nanda: *Socialism in India*. Shah: *Marxism, Gandhism and Stalinism*. Rao: *Indian Socialism: Retrospect and Prospect*. Rai Chowdhuri: *Leftist Movements in India, 1917–1947*. Sinha: *The Left-Wing in India, 1919–47*. Lohia: *Marx, Gandhi and Socialism*. Datta: *Beyond Socialism*.
4 Gandhi's pervasive influence is often attributed to his folklorist interpretations of popular themes in Hindu thought, in itself a vastly diverse body of literature, thought, and religious attitudes. To draw the lines from traditional Hindu thought to Gandhi's reworking of them is beyond the scope of this project. For some overviews, see Brown: *The Content of Cultural Continuity in India* (pp. 430–432), on the sacred quality of truth. Nandy: *The Culture of Indian Politics: A Stock Taking* (pp. 65–66), on the centrality of *dharma* or duty. Nandy: *The Culture of Indian Politics: A Stock Taking* (pp. 70–72), on the suppression of desires. Nandy: *The Culture of Indian Politics: A Stock Taking* (pp. 72–74), on the diversification and plurality of ethical systems.
5 This is not to say that the moral language of "should" and "ought" is not used, but that it is used in a purely instrumental sense for the satisfaction of preferences. Cf. Fishkin, *Beyond Subjective Morality: Ethical Reasoning and Political Philosophy*, pp. 43–45.
6 Singh: *Communist and Socialist Movement in India: A Critical Account*. Bhasin: *Socialism in India*. Limaye and Fernandes: *Socialist – Communist Interaction in India*. Sampurnanand: *Indian Socialism*. Incidentally, the reception of Marxism as communism in India was rooted in the Second International, with M. N. Roy being a major player in transmitting its proceedings to Marxist movements in India.
7 Narayan, *Search for an Ideology*, p. 159
8 Nirmal Verma, 'On Heroism in Our Time' (Translated from the Hindi by Suresh Sharma), Seminar, No. 245 (January 1980), p. 75.

References

Advani, L. K. (2008). *My Country My Life*. New Delhi: Rupa Publications.
Bhave, Vinoba (1964a). *Democratic Values*. Varanasi: Akhil Bharat Sarva Seva Sangh Prakashan.
Bhave, Vinoba (1964b). *Revolutionary Sarvodaya*. Bombay: Bharatiya Vidya Bhavan.
Narayan, Jayaprakash (1936). *Why Socialism?* Varanasi: Akhil Bharat Sarva Seva Sangh Prakashan.
Narayan, Jayaprakash (1959). *From Socialism to Sarvodaya*. Varanasi: Akhil Bharat Sara Seva Sangh Prakashan.
Narayan, Jayaprakash (1961). *Swaraj for the People*. Varanasi: Akhil Bharat Sarva Seva Sangh Prakashan.
Narayan, Jayaprakash (1964). *Socialism, Sarvodaya and Democracy*. Edited by Bimal Prasad. Bombay: Asia Publishing House.
Narayan, Jayaprakash (1975). *Total Revolution*. Varanasi: Akhil Bharat Sarva Seva Sangh Prakashan.
Narayan, Jayaprakash (1978). *Towards Total Revolution*. Volume 3. Surrey: Richmond Publication & Co.
Samaddar, Ranbir. (2008). 'Jayaprakash Narayan and the Problem of Representative Democracy'. *Economic and Political Weekly*, XLIII (31): 49.

19

RAM MANOHAR LOHIA

Dev Nath Pathak and Divyendu Jha

> *Capitalism and communism are almost fully elaborated systems, and the whole world is in their grip, and the result is poverty, war and fear. The third idea is also making itself felt on the world stage. It is still inadequate, and it has not been fully elaborated, but it is open.*
> – Ram Manohar Lohia (*Marx, Gandhi and Socialism* 1963)

I Introduction

Ram Manohar Lohia occupies a distinctive place in the intellectual and political history of modern India. As an imaginative thinker and inspiring leader of the socialist movement in India, he was able to influence a generation of people who were prepared to lay down their lives for the causes he represented. In the time when socialism became a de facto political ideology of the Indian freedom struggle, he questioned the uncritical acceptance of European socialism, which, for him, represented the ignorance of the distinctive socio-political realities of India. Indeed, it appeared to be his passion to liberate the theory of socialism from the shackles of theory and practice of Marxism and international communism. Seeking an India-specific solution to the country's economic problems, Lohia was rightfully suspicious of both exploitative capitalism and Eurocentric Marxism. To him, socialism essentially meant equality and affluence for the people, and what concerned him was bringing these twin ideals together (Sinha 2010: 51–55). He also presented his own version of the wheel of history, which he believed came close to the reality of the world, rejecting the linear view of history, which had dominated Western society so far. Interestingly, through his doctrine of new socialism, he endeavoured to provide a new and unique dimension to socialism by attuning it to the needs and aspirations of the developing countries like India by incorporating within it certain elements of capitalism which, he averred, has facilitated a subtle improvement in the standard of lives of the working class and its conversion into middle class in Europe (Lohia 1963: 6).

In other words, Lohia's contribution to socialist thinking seems to be the improvisation of the notion of socialism to ensure its suitability to the imperatives of the Indian condition. Lohia, as a socialist, firmly believed that socialism, if it were to lead the people to progress and prosperity, must be based on the Indian condition. What remained intact amidst such a conceptualisation of socialism, however, was its undaunted focus on the creation of an equal, democratic, and egalitarian socio-economic and political system aimed at securing justice, equality, and development for the people of India. Thus, he wanted to give a firm foundation to the theory of socialism by chalking out a programme of action for the realisation of the final goal.

Like many others, Lohia's thought process was also shaped by the role he played as an activist in both pre- and post-independence India. It was his experiences in various movements that gave him necessary input towards theoretical explorations and formulations. Perhaps his encounter and consistent exposure with Gandhian ideas and movements led him to think of Indianising the concept of socialism by filling it with the dose of decentralisation to manage the vast socio-cultural diversities of India. Apart from that, his brilliant training in academics helped him to analyse the theories and concepts from other parts of the world and exploring possibilities for adopting to resolve Indian complexities (Chakrabarty and Pandey 2009: 178). Eventually, in the process of developing an Indian version of socialism, Lohia also laid out several important ideas and practices necessary for the socio-political emancipation of the people of India. These include a decentralised State, the *chaukhamba* (four pillars) model of democracy, equality as *samatva-sambhav* (feeling of oneness), the reinterpretation of history, and *sapta kranti* (theory of seven revolutions).

II Life sketch

Dr Ram Manohar Lohia (1910–1967), a famous socialist thinker and activist who may be reckoned as the most unconventional, and maybe the most original, theoretician amongst Indian socialists (Appadorai 2002: 311). Lohia was a prolific writer. Besides being editor of the *Congress Socialist* for three years, he wrote many books which explain his socio-economic and political ideology. His writings are widely read and appreciated and include *Wheel of History* (1955), *Will to Power* (1956), *Marx, Gandhi and Socialism* (1963), *The caste system* (1964), *Interval During Politics, Language* (1966), and *Indians in Foreign Lands* (1938). His fondness and devotion to construct a distinctly Indian version of socialism to combat various forms of injustices forms the bedrock of his intellectual and activist life.

Born in a village in the Faizabad district of Uttar Pradesh on 23 March 1910, Lohia was one of the few nationalist leaders in the country having his roots in rural India which probably conditioned his thought process to a great extent. He was born to a family of merchants. Following the death of his mother when he was two, Lohia was raised primarily by his grandparents, although his father's commitment to Indian nationalism influenced him during his childhood. Lohia attended Banaras Hindu University before earning a bachelor's degree from the University of Calcutta in 1929 and a doctorate from the University of Berlin, where he studied economics and politics, in 1932. In 1934, Lohia became actively involved in the Congress Socialist Party (C.S.P.), founded that year as a left-wing group within the Indian National Congress (I.N.C.); he served on the C.S.P. executive committee and edited its weekly journal. A vehement opponent of India's participation on the side of Great Britain in World War II, he was arrested for anti-British remarks in 1939 and again in 1940; the latter incident resulted in an 18 months imprisonment. With the emergence in 1942 of the Quit India Movement – a campaign initiated by Mohandas K. Gandhi to urge the withdrawal of British authorities from India – Lohia and other C.S.P. leaders (such as Jayaprakash Narayan) mobilised support from the underground. For such resistance activities, he was jailed again from 1944 to 1946.

During and after India's transition to independence in 1947, Lohia continued to play an active role in its politics. At loggerheads with Prime Minister Jawaharlal Nehru on several issues, however, Lohia and other C.S.P. members left the Congress in 1948. Lohia became a member of the 'Praja Socialist Party' upon its formation in 1952 and served as general secretary for a brief period, but internecine conflicts led to his resignation in 1955. Later that year, Lohia established the Socialist Party (Lohia), for which he became chairman as well as the editor of its journal, *Mankind*. A spellbinding orator and a passionate and perceptive writer, he advocated various socio-political reforms in his capacity as party leader, including the abolition of the caste system, the adoption of Hindi as India's national language, and stronger protection of civil liberties. In 1963, Lohia was elected to the Lok Sabha (the lower house of Parliament), where his sharp criticism of government policies was noted. Although his parliamentary influence was ultimately limited, his progressive views, which he expressed in numerous publications, proved inspirational to many Indians.

III Capitalism and communism

Situating his theoretical explorations in the particular context of India, Lohia made an ardent plea to formulate an indigenous theoretical construct which could be effective in addressing the issues concerning the country. This was an outcome of his belief in the inefficacy of dominant Western ideologies, like communism and capitalism. While commenting on communism, Lohia wrote, "no man's thought should be made the centre of a political action; it should help but not control" (Lohia 1963: 52). Acceptance and rejection are varying forms of blind worship. He argued that a powerful movement cannot be based on the thoughts of one person alone. To him, Marxism is full of internal contradictions which remained at the root of its unsuitability as a system of social organisation.

Lohia vehemently criticised Marxism for its Eurocentric experiences while expounding theoretical constructs, which is not only biased but also inadequate to understand and explain the experiences and conditions of under-developed

Third World countries. Lohia held that Karl Marx did not think of revolution in economically limited countries, like Russia, China, and India, and instead talked of it in England and Germany, where democratic processes would continue to deepen (Lohia 1963: 65).

Lohia acknowledged that Marx was aware of the great colonial plunder and loot. However, he did not probe deep enough and therefore remained tied to the interests of the imperial powers. While refuting the claims of Vladimir Lenin that "Imperialism was the last and final stage of capitalism", Lohia argued that both capitalism and imperialism developed simultaneously from the very beginning, as is clear from the development of America, Japan, and Germany. From the beginning, capitalism is driven to seek external sources of power, and it builds itself up on the exploitation of others by exporting goods to these colonies. The textiles produced by Lancashire Mills were consumed in India. Thus he asserted, "History's record shows that, unsupported by British rule over India, not the Indian artisans, but the Lancashire industry would have died in its infancy" (Lohia 1955: 10).

He further pointed out that Marx's analysis of surplus value was limited because the exploitation of workers in a factory in a capitalist country was only part of the story. Another important source of surplus value was the exploitation of labour in the colonies. The form of exploitation in both the situations has been very different. The nature of demands also varies in the two contexts. In the case of colonies, 99 percent of labour is transferred in the form of surplus value, while in the developed countries it is only 10 percent (Mehta 1992: 248). It is for this reason that the surplus value in both the cases cannot be taken together. He thus said that:

> Colonial peasants and workers were the real proletariat whose lives were devastated by capitalism. Surplus value, which makes up the entire profits and high earnings of the capitalist system, is derived mainly from colonial farms, fields and mines. The inner imperial circle of the capitalist structure revolves in a way as to draw with great suction the labour yield of the outer colonial circle.
>
> *(Lohia 1963: 26)*

Because of this colonial exploitation, workers in capitalist countries were able to get a part (even if very small) of the surplus extracted from the colonies. Therefore, it was possible to increase both wages and profits at the same time in capitalist countries, postponing a conflict indefinitely. That is why no revolution took place at the centre of capitalist development.

Lohia was well aware that class struggle played an important role in history. He referred to various phases of acute inequality which were reflected in the history of class struggle. But the important missing point in Marxism, according to Lohia, is the form and sequence of the class struggles. He differed with Narendra Deva and Sampurna Nanda, who viewed class struggle in internal dimensions only and did not consider its external linkages.[1] Following Arnold J. Toynbee, Lohia argued that class struggle within society is linked to class struggle outside, which according to him, Marx overlooked.

After condemning Marxism relentlessly, Lohia did not even subscribe to the ideas and practices of capitalism. He went on to interrogate the foundations of capitalism to prove its limitations in resolving the issues of developing and under-developed countries. The basic roots of capitalism lay in individualistic rights with a focus on the right to private property; he thus asserted that such a principle leads to the widening of economic inequality. Moreover, capitalist competition leads to uncontrolled lust for the profit that drives capitalists for more and more centralisation of means of production in a few hands so that some sort of monopoly could be established over the market forces. As a corollary, this creates a ground not only for the destruction of rules of fair play but also the claims of freedom and equality. He agreed with Deva that sometimes capitalists go to the extent of sacrificing the freedom of their own country for their selfish interests. It is this which explains why a section of capitalists in France welcomed the invasion of Hitler. He emphasised that capitalism is a reactionary doctrine which in the Third World gives protection to profit, black-marketing, and exploitation (Mehta 1992: 249).

In a nutshell, one can draw three interrelated arguments from Lohia's reflections on, if not systematic critique of Marxism: 1) Marx's analysis of capitalism is incomplete, 2) his theory of history is Eurocentric, and 3) the normative agenda of Marxism is totally unacceptable and entirely unsuitable to the non-European world, which has inherited a colonial past. Further, Lohia's critique of Marx's critique of capitalism has two major dimensions that are of great significance to socialism in non-European and colonially subjugated societies. In the first place, Lohia's critique is a pointer to the possibility of multiple perceptions of capitalism. It drives home the significant fact that different and equally valid understandings of capitalism are possible and that perceptions of capitalism from the periphery could be fundamentally different from the perception of capitalism from the centre. In the second place, Lohia's critique foresees the possibilities of a challenge to capitalism not from the centre but from the periphery. This, in consequence, enhances the chances for socialism in the colonially subjugated non-Western world (Tolpadi 2010: 71–77).

It is in this context of denouncing both capitalism and communism as irrelevant to bringing social changes and the economic development of the under-developed countries that Lohia sought to bring an alternative model which, according to Lohia is an Indian version of socialism, bereft of its Eurocentric models.

IV New socialism and social justice

Lohia's strong criticisms of Western ideological frameworks seem to be aimed at preparing the grounds for socialism. However, his formulations of socialist ideas were different from what had been theorised in the West. He was convinced socialism was the way ahead for India to achieve progress but only when its principles and practices were reconstructed in a way that should suit Indian conditions. For achieving this end, Lohia implanted an Indian heart into the body of socialism by using some Gandhian principles, like *satyāgraha*, decentralisation, small-unit machine technology, and a village-centric development model, with some improvisation.

Lohia forcefully raised the issue of the doctrinal foundation of Indian socialism in 1952 at the Panchmarhi session of the party. In his famous presidential address at Panchmarhi, Lohia emphasised the need for an independent doctrine of socialism. He espoused the thesis that the Indian society must develop on its own. According to him, the new creed could not be developed based on borrowed ideas and principles. Thus, while conceptualising socialism, Lohia noted:

> Too long has it borrowed from communism its economic aims and from capitalism or the liberal age its non-economic and general aim. An acute disharmony has resulted. To explore once again the economic and the general aims of society and to integrate them into a harmony should be a high endeavour of socialist doctrine.[2]

Lohia came to believe that the methods adopted by European socialists and Communists for economic and political reconstruction were not suitable to Asian countries, particularly India and Indonesia. A new method must, therefore, be sought. He argued that the peasants must learn intensive agriculture, and they must be persuaded to enter co-operative farming of one type or another. Inexpensive machines should be made available to them. They must develop initiative, and therefore maximum State power, both legislative and administrative, should belong to them in their village community. To Lohia, communist re-division of land was a fraud and a futile cruelty in the end. The socialist re-division of land, coupled with the decentralisation of power, would produce good economic results as well as a new way of living (Lohia 1956: 55). According to Lohia, European socialists had always been trying to define socialism in terms of universal concepts, though they had achieved some success. Their socialism is a gradual and constitutional socialism. Asian socialism cannot afford to be that. According to Lohia, the whole Asian situation was such that its application must be drastic, whether in agriculture, industrial processes, or in the process of nationalisation. Capitalism is incapable of achieving economic re-construction because of private capital. On this point, Lohia was in complete agreement with Marx. But he did not trust the Communists because he thought they had always attempted to employ gross economic poverty for insurrectional pressure on the State. Asian socialists must understand this situation to fight against injustice.

Therefore, according to Lohia, the best method of achieving the economic objectives of Marxism was to adopt the Gandhian technique of *satyāgraha* and complete decentralisation in the economic and political spheres. He thought that if socialism could absorb the essence of Gandhism, it would acquire an integral character and become dynamic. Lohia consistently used and upheld *satyāgraha* as a weapon of struggle for socialism and equalitarian reconstruction. Besides *satyāgraha*, Gandhi also influenced Lohia's social, political, and economic ideas. In a Gandhian spirit, he looked at the problem of reconstruction in terms of the village and its crucial role in India. He considered decentralisation vital to the realisation of the socialist ideal.

He was influenced by Gandhi in the abolition of castes, the liberation of the depressed, the rejection of totalitarianism, and faith in eternal values, such as truth, justice, and equality. But despite the profundity of the impact, Lohia retained his originality and rejected the Gandhian notion of abolishing capitalism through heart conversion. Such conversion he held impossible. Lohia did not consider *charkha* an adequate tool of economic reconstruction. He rejected the Gandhian theory of trusteeship as impracticable and did not consider faith in God as essential while following *satyāgraha*. Lohia was partly Marxist and overwhelmingly Gandhian, but he never compromised with his socialism.

The party of socialism, according to Lohia, must have power and organisation so it could use them in the service of whatever action may be deemed appropriate at the time. To build up such power and organisation, the party should continually strive to become a spokesman of the people, organiser of its will, resister against injustice, and accomplisher of reconstruction. It must be ready to take part in constructive action, to be enlightened by it, and to resist injustice. Many other thinkers' lived experiences appeared to have influenced Lohia to develop his conception of new socialism,[3] which he defined with six fundamental principles:

1   Maximum attainable equality.
2   Social ownership.
3   Small-unit technology.
4   Four-pillar State.
5   A decent standard of living.
6   The world parliament and government.

Lohia realised that a sizeable portion of the Indian population were living in the villages. They had no basic amenities provided to them. Their agricultural aids were primitive, and therefore they could not produce even for their mere subsistence. The opportunities for employment were meagre, and thus the life of a common man was full of struggle. Lohia realised all these problems and always supported the causes, having deep desire for the development of village community. He also wished to provide them with adequate health and educational facilities. He proposed acres of land, the fixation of minimum agricultural labour, parity between agriculture and industrial prices, etc. (Lohia 1963: 368). To use the resources economically, Lohia proposed many ideas. He suggested the curtailment of several unnecessary expenditures in government and semi-governmental offices and institutions. To Lohia, it was necessary to utilise surplus manpower by transferring it into productive work.[4] To avoid hoarding, prices of food items should be fixed.

Lohia wanted to reduce expenses by abolishing the privy purses and special privileges of the princes. He opposed the production of luxury consumption items. He also wanted to abolish special schools, place a ceiling on income and expenditure, the nationalisation of big industries, impose a rational taxation system, and request voluntary labour to increase production. He opposed extravagance, black marketing, hoarding, and corruption (Lohia 1967: 24–32).

He was a great upholder of Hindu–Muslim unity and felt unhappy whenever he heard of any communal clash in our country. He wished for progress and prosperity for all castes, creeds, and religions and wanted to remove all those obstacles which hindered their progress. He was in favour of 60 percent reservations for Scheduled Castes, Scheduled Tribes, backwards castes, including *adivasis*, as well as women. He believed such a policy would not only change attitudes but provide self-confidence to those classes (Lohia 1964: 96).

The cumulative impact of the theory of new socialism, argued Lohia, would be in providing such a complex web of a system of life for the people that they would not only be able to live an egalitarian and contented life within the country but would also aspire to become a part of the world government. Thus, the theory of new socialism seems to be either a reflection of the reiteration of the cherished ideals of Lohia or his growing detachment from the realities of life in the country, paving the way for utopianism in his political thinking to a large extent (Chakrabarty and Pandey 2009: 185). What, however, was unique to Lohia was his notion of decentralised socialism, whose essence lay in emphasis on things like small machine technology, co-operative labour, village governments, and decentralised planning.

V Freedom, equality, and *sapta kranti* (seven revolutions)

Lohia made an innovative and unique contribution through the concept of equality that, according to him, is at the heart of other socio-political values, like freedom, justice, and fraternity. He vehemently criticised the Western notions of equality for being dominantly materialist. As to the meaning of equality, Lohia wrote:

> Equality is perhaps as high an aim of life as truth or beauty. But this aim has not been investigated in serenity and its direct and immediate repercussions on day-to-day life, on property and income and the general ordering of society are deep and many.
>
> (Lohia 1996c: 214)

Through his conceptualisation, Lohia endeavoured to present an indigenous and perhaps an alternative vision of equality, something much different from the way it had been theorised in the West (more precisely in Europe). According to him, equality did not mean identity of treatment or identity of reward because this was not possible as far as capacity and need of the people differed. Equality, to Lohia, was an abstract concept, an emotion and perhaps a wish that all arrangements – political, social, or economic – shall be equal as between one individual and another (Lohia 1963: 221). He argued that equality must be conceptualised with an experimenting engagement between spiritual and material facets in a holistic perspective which could generate the feeling/relationship of oneness between individuals.

Equality, for Lohia, stood for such an arrangement of social forces that each may get its due, that is, balancing a share in the toil of living with a share in its gain. He maintained that if there was no equality among the individuals or among the nations, justice, human dignity, morality, brotherhood, freedom, and universal welfare could not flourish in society. Elaborating the meaning of equality, Lohia mentioned:

> Legal equality is equality before the Law. Once legal equality was established, the phase of political equality came. Political equality means the equality of the adult vote. Economic equality in the sense of an increasing standard of living to everybody within national frontiers has become a common element of all ideologies. We must beware of how to seek to realise equality in different spheres. For each aspect of material equality, a method should be sought that corresponds to its nature. Otherwise, unexpected and contrary results may follow.
>
> (Lohia 1996b: 216)

Socialism, for Lohia, meant triadic relationship and convergence of equality, liberty, and affluence, but bringing these three together was a cause of concern. On the one hand, he wanted to recover the idea of equality, liberty, and affluence from the predominantly materialist and distributive orientation of socialism and capitalism. And on the other hand, the purpose was to re-invent equality by according it an ultimate moral aim of human life that should be sensitive to the Indian context and its necessities. Therefore, Lohia believed that equality cannot merely be associated with distributive or re-distributive mechanisms related to economic or other resources. Instead, it has to be re-infused with the spirit and morals of innate human feelings like love, equanimity, fraternity, equity, etc. (Lohia 1963: 236). Thus, he came with an ideal of equality *samatva sambhav* (feeling of oneness) that highlights the individual's inner sense of equity and reciprocity at both spiritual and material level. In order to give this ideal a concrete shape, he further characterised *samatva sambhav* at two levels – inner or spiritual equality as equanimity and outer or material equality as relationship of equity and reciprocity between individuals, society, and nations. On the basis of such a comprehensive ideal and framework of equality, Lohia believed that the principle of democracy should move beyond its national boundaries to fight against global poverty that was only possible by setting up a World Development Agency wherein each nation will contribute and entitle to draw according to the needs for removing poverty (Yadav 2010: 98).

Lohia viewed liberty and equality as mutually complementary to each other and unable to be separated. Lohia, thus, was opposed to any kind of tyranny, oppression, or regimentation in society and at the same time passionately supported social justice and economic security for individuals. He stood against absolute State power and bureaucratic hegemony. He aspired that social equality and justice should be the hallmark of every society. He wanted to have an egalitarian social order where all men would get equal opportunities to develop their capabilities and potentialities. Lohia drew a nexus between individual liberty and equality. He maintained that individual liberty could not be attained in the absence of equality. He aspired to uphold equality in all walks of life. He wanted to stamp out all kinds of injustice and inequality from our society. Lohia also emphasised on economic freedom. He pleaded to raise the standard of living of the people. He laid stress on assuring the dignity of man. He fought throughout his life for making man the centre of socialist concern. He wanted to preserve the worth of man and restore the human personality despite all odds and troubles in one's life.

As a champion of civil liberties, Lohia embraced the right of the citizens with regard to security both of his person and of his dwellings, to freedom of opinion and assembly, thought and organisation, to equal justice and control over the government, and to release from political convictions (Lohia 1996a: 167). Although, the concept of civil liberties is a liberal ideal, Lohia believed it was an important ideal because it acted as a shock absorber between the cruel impacts of State tyranny and mass revolts. For Lohia, civil liberties help foster common consciousness amongst the people to act against any kind of injustice and exploitation. Therefore, it enables society's march towards progress and development.

However fantastical the ideas on equality and freedom may sound, Lohia was aware of the problems of identities and hierarchies that were in the social structure of this country. Providing larger analysis to the problem of caste in India, Lohia emphasised on the inherent conflict between the forces perpetuating caste and the forces inclined to introduce class as perspective in the society. Lohia averred that this conflict between the two is unending due to the fact that the two sets of forces kept on changing sides, leading to castes fragmenting into classes and classes occasionally metamorphosing into castes (Lohia 1955: 51). Lohia thus conceived the notion *sapta kranti* (seven revolutions) to realise equality in socio-political and economic spheres and to infuse a new sense of dynamism and vigour in Indian society. As Madhu Limaye rightly said:

> Dr Lohia was one of those great leaders who not only advocated the need for a fundamental reordering of our social relations but also provided an ideological basis for this revolutionary transformation. Dr Lohia called this radical transformation seven revolutions or *sapta kranti*.
>
> *(Limaye 1978: 11)*

Lohia believed the problem of inequality and injustice could not be understood with a single overarching reference to caste, class, gender, religion, and race because these forces have different bases of survival, and at times they amalgamate in complex ways. Hence, to establish equality in society and eradicate the perpetuation of various forms of injustices, Lohia believed a seven-fold revolution was necessary. These seven revolutions must be based on several spheres of social life, envisioning a radical transformation in all spheres of an individual's life. These revolutions must be materialised for equality (Lohia 1963: 221):

1   Equality between men and women.
2   The abolition of inequalities based on colour.
3   The elimination of inequalities of birth and caste.
4   Economic equality through increase in production.
5   National freedom or ending of foreign influence.
6   Protecting the privacy of individual life from all collective encroachments.
7   Limitation on armaments.

VI The emancipation of women

According to Lohia, of all injustices plaguing the earth those arising out of the inequality between men and women were perhaps the bedrock. Inequality between men and women had so become part of human habit and nature that it seeped into everything else. Most of humanity suffered from one inequality or another, but half of it was weighted down further. Women's participation in collective life was also exceedingly limited in Russia and America, which boasted of having achieved equality between the sexes (Lohia 1963: 32). Lohia aptly pointed out that the psychological basis ingrained in the minds of the males because of the patriarchal structures is the fundamental reason for the exploitation of women. In his words:

> Man has ever been actuated by two contrary impulses towards woman. He wants his woman to be bright, intelligent, handsome and the rest in short, a very living person. He wants her to be wholly his. Nobody can be wholly another's, unless she or he were reduced to the spiritual status of a tree or a dog. In the mind of the male, therefore, resides a grievous clash between wanting her to be his woman, as also alive and beautiful, therefore, to be free and at the same time unfree.
>
> *(ibid.: 33)*

Lohia also drew attention to women's economic dependence on men who greatly contribute to her slavery. Lohia lamented that a woman's life is wasted in the kitchen. A woman does not get an opportunity to know what is happening outside. She is totally confined to her house and household activities. Moreover, in family life, she is underfed and a victim of family hardships. He pointed out that women have always been victims of morality in Indian society. Regarding sexual scandals, women are blamed more than men. Therefore, Lohia emphasised on the need for developing an atmosphere conducive to the healthy relationship between men and women.

Apart from this, Lohia also believed women were subjugated and exploited because of their economic dependence, illiteracy, superstitions, and ignorance. These factors eventually led to the marginalisation of women from public life, which, according to Lohia, was not good for the health and prosperity of any nation. Lohia argued that no nation could develop and prosper without the participation of half of its population in public life. Thus, emphasising on the need and importance of women in any society, he favoured freedom and dignity for women as well as their participation in the freedom struggle and the socialist movement. Perhaps, after Gandhi, he was the only leader who wanted to include women in the freedom struggle of India. He once state:

> A socialist movement without the active participation of women is like a wedding without the bride. Not only are women ultimately responsible for the health of the race and the growth of the new generation; they are also the chief support of a movement for peaceful resistance.
>
> *(Lohia 1963: 33)*

Lohia stressed the emancipation of women in all spheres. N. C. Mehrotra said that after Gandhiji, Lohia was the first political thinker in India to fight for the equal status of women in every walk of life. Lohia pointed out that the segregation of castes and women were primarily responsible for the decline of spirit in India. Lohia felt that most of the women's lives are full of sufferings and miseries. He sought to rouse awareness and consciousness to mitigate the problems of women in Indian society. However, as long as this grievous clash resided in the minds of men, a woman would not be allowed to acquire equal status in society. Giving her equal opportunity would not solve the problem of inequality between the sexes. Lohia wrote, "when a group of people is held down by debility, physical or cultural, the only way to bring it up to equality with others is through conferment of preferential opportunities" (Lohia 1963: 34).

Therefore, Lohia believed that to emancipate women and contribute to their progress, radical reformation in the social structure is a necessary condition. For this, women must be given freedom, dignity, and economic independence, and their participation in public life should be encouraged and supported through affirmative action and policies. Most importantly, developing social consciousness about the importance of women in social progress remains at the heart of any effort to emancipate women from exploitation and subjugation.

VII Caste, class, and power

Scholars have debated about the nature of social stratification and the processes of social change. But the different analyses may be categorised into two groups based on whether they assume a single dominant factor, like caste, class, or gender or if they examine intersectionality between different factors that lead to exclusion and discrimination. The intersectionality approach argues that classical factors (like class, caste, and gender) of hierarchies and discrimination are inter-related and create multiple forms of systemic marginalisation. Interestingly, Lohia enunciated this intersectionality perspective back in the mid-1960s. The prominent single factor approaches (for instance, class- or caste-centric, gender-based, or ethnicity-oriented) are more prevalent than intersectionality perspectives among academicians and politicians. But, Lohia contributed significantly to the formulation of an inter-sectionalist approach for understanding the inequalities, exclusions, and exploitations in the power structure of contemporary India (Kumar 2010: 64).

Caste, Lohia believed, is one of the primary realities of Indian society, and it is through caste that one can understand and explain the other forms of oppression, exploitations, and inequalities of Indian socio-political life. The power structure of hierarchical caste system assumes overarching powers that make upper caste cultured ones and the people in the lower rungs as stagnant and lifeless. He was of the opinion that caste system destroyed the entire fabric of social values, morals, and spiritual progress due to which India became vulnerable to the foreign invasions and subjugation. This coincides with the high-caste aspirations to protect and safeguard this destructive power structure of relations between individuals rather than protecting and ensuring national well-being (Lohia 1964: 179–183). The system of caste in a way is against any kind of progressive socio-political change. Such a biased and exploitative power relation created inferiority complex among the lower caste, which are highest in numbers, to unite with others for some common causes/concerns. Although Lohia agreed that some inter-caste activities appeared to have taken place in recent decades, however, such activities were limited to the rituals of feasting. It could not extend to the level of inter-caste wedding and childbearing. Therefore, all such activities were superficial and deceptively inter-caste. Even the inter-caste marriages were routine affairs between groups within the high caste.

The system of caste, according to Lohia, worked towards the suppression of a vast number of Indian people. It also gave rise to hypocrisy and false consciousness. According to Lohia, there were some reasons why many people submitted to the evils of casteism. The first reason was that caste gave them insurance, indeed, on less than an animal level, more than it did to the high castes. They would feel helpless without it. Often, one got the impression about these lower castes as though their strenuous labour were but a preparation for the caste feasts and rituals that were to follow. Anything that interfered with them must appear to them as highly undesirable. The second reason was that the people who were victims of castes had for them many myths of religion that justified their inferior situation and transferred it into a symbol of sacrifice and lustre. According to Lohia, a long tradition of ideological subjection had made the so-called low caste stagnant. Centuries had instilled into them a meek acceptance of the existing aversion to change, sticking with the caste in times of adversity as of good luck and the search of high life through worship, rituals, and general politeness.

According to Lohia, caste had caused the shrinkage of abilities and opportunities, and as a result, 90 percent of the population had become mentally paralysed. The process of shrinking of ability and opportunity once started went on indefinitely, with the result that certain privileged sub-castes among the *Brāhmins* or *Kayasthas* acquired more privileges while the vast majority was continually deprived and became less able. In Lohia's own words, "caste restricts opportunity, restricted opportunity constricts ability. Constricted ability further restricts opportunity". Where caste prevails, opportunity and ability are restricted to ever narrowing circles of the people (Almus 1998: 184).

Most importantly, Lohia believed Western classes also oscillated towards caste order, even though caste order is uniquely Indian. Caste, like rigidities, privileges, imbecilities, and excommunication, existed in American and Soviet societies (Lohia 1955: 33–34). Similarities existed between castes and classes in certain matters. For example, like India's untouchable castes, African Americans lived in ghettos and could not visit hotels and other establishments marked for the white population, which Lohia himself experienced when he visited an all-white cafeteria in Jackson, Mississippi, in 1964. He was blocked at the entrance by the owner, ably assisted by the police under the rules of privacy. Merely having purchasing power is not enough in such situations. A culture of segregation, practised by one's colour or birth, exists everywhere (ibid.: 210). Caste-like barriers are created by people in liberal democratic class societies, even though people may believe in equality for everybody (meaning all white people). In such situations, classes oscillate towards castes. So, a struggle against caste barriers is simultaneously a struggle against class inequalities. There is, however, a subtle difference. In class struggle, socialism is concerned with equality or distribution of resources, whereas socialism is concerned with justice or the dignity of each human being in anti-caste resistance (ibid.: 37).

Lohia observed that "all human history hitherto has been an internal oscillation between class and caste and an internal shift of prosperity and power from one region to another. This external shift and internal oscillation are related to one another" (Lohia 1955: 40). Thus, he argued that class struggle must oscillate towards caste struggle, as classes veer towards the caste system. Otherwise, India may end up in a form of socialism as existed in the Soviet Union, without any concern for justice, so argued Lohia. Thus, anti-caste movements concerned with justice issues were basically international by nature and were not just India centred.

VIII Democracy and State

Lohia had firm faith in democracy as a government of the people, but he opposed the tendency of democracy to lean on elitism. In a country like India, where there is so much poverty and socio-cultural hierarchies, he was convinced that it led to increases in the powers of the upper classes. He thus pointed out that an ordinary citizen has never obtained an opportunity to take an intelligent or effective part in the total affairs of the country. For the last several centuries, mainly due to the heinous caste system practiced in India, most people had been kept out of the mainstream social life. In modern times, citizens have again been denied the right of acting or thinking in the name of representative democracy. Therefore, citizens are left merely with the choice of persons they might prefer over others to think and act for them (Lohia 1950: 71). In Lohia's opinion, the notion of democracy must not be confined merely to provide certain civil and political liberties but be construed in such a way that it leads to the provision of such socio-economic conditions where nobody remains without securing the basic needs of life (Chakrabarty and Pandey 2009: 185). Hence, to make democracy a reality, Lohia argued that the commonality of a State was to be so organised and sovereign power so diffused that each little community in it lived the way of life it chose.

For realising this end, Lohia made a unique contribution to the system of government with his model of *chaukhamba rajya* (four-pillars State). The concept of the four-pillar State, which must be the political framework of the future socialist State, has been envisaged as a sure safeguard against political centralisation, thereby authoritarianism and a guarantee for the practice of real democracy. According to this concept, the sovereign power of the State is constitutionally diffused into four levels – the village, district, province, and centre – these being four pillars of equal majesty and dignity. It is, according to him, a way of life giving direction to all spheres of human activity, like production, ownership, administration, planning, education, and the like. It is to be noted that the decentralisation of power alone in such an unprecedented manner as Lohia pointed out can bring about a more or less lasting solution to the myriad political issues facing India.

Democracy, according to Lohia, can bring warmth to the blood of the common man only when constitutional theory starts practising the State of four limbs, that is, the village, the district, the province, and the centre, organically covered by the flesh and blood of equalities. This constitutional skeleton of the four-pillar State can infuse democracy with joy. The central limb of the State must have power enough to maintain the integrity and unity of the State, and the rest of it must be fragmented (Lohia 1950: 93). He thus argued that the four-pillar State is obviously not a mere executive arrangement. It is not as if superior parliaments legislate and the village and district organs are left with the execution of the laws. The four-pillar State is both a legislative and executive arrangement. It is a way of life to all spheres of human activity, for instance, production, ownership, administration, planning, and education; the four-pillar State provides a structure and a way of life. For concretising his thinking, Lohia highlighted the following policy directions:

1   One-fourth of all governmental and plan expenditure shall be through village, district, and city *Panchayats*.

2   Police shall remain subordinate to village, city, and district *Panchayats* or any of their agencies.
3   The post of collector shall be abolished, and all his functions will be distributed among various bodies in the district. As far as possible, the principle of election will be applied in administration, instead of nominations.
4   Agriculture, industry, and other property, which is nationalised as far as possible, should be owned and administered by village, city, and district *Panchayats*.
5   Economic decentralisation, corresponding to political and administrative decentralisation, will have to be brought about through the maximum utilisation of small machines.

Lohia opined that the four-pillar State might indeed appear fanatic to many in view of the special conditions of the country, its illiteracy, its fears and superstitions, and, above all, its castes. The village representatives may indeed be selfish and ignorant and raise caste above justice. Yet to give him power seemed the only way to deliver the people from inertia as well as an administration that was both top heavy and corrupt. Lohia believed that by giving power to small communities of men, democracy of the first grade was possible. The four-pillar State ensured effective and intelligent democracy to the common man (Lohia 1996a: 319).

However, it must be remembered that this scheme of political organisation, according to Lohia, is linked to a similar scheme of economic organisation of production and distribution. In the absence of the decentralised economy, Lohia argued, there would be increased bureaucratisation in which human beings would become cogs in the machine and the political system would take place of human values. He therefore pleaded that economic planning must be done from the grassroots level upwards. A decentralised economy, according to Lohia, would be more efficient, as it would be based on the willing participation of the workers, who must be made partners in the scheme (Narayan 1964: 273). That is why Lohia favoured small-machine technology for production; he believed it could emancipate India from its acute poverty.

IX Small-machine technology

One of the most significant features of Lohia's socialism was the economy based on small-unit machines. Lohia wanted India's progress towards modernisation and development, but he did not like the European path of development with its emphasis on large-scale industrialisation. He aspired to see India's development and prosperity along the path which would suit Indian needs and conditions. Therefore, he sought to devise technology which would be congenial and conducive to Indian economy and environment.

Lohia contributed to the debate on the technology-development nexus novel dimension. Having dismissed the capitalist and communist modes of rationalisation as irrelevant with regard to the economies of under-developed countries,

Lohia devised a new mode of rationalisation and a corresponding mode of ownership. Lohia put forward the concept of small-unit machines, which evolved from Gandhi, as an alternative to the capitalist and communist modes of rationalisation. It originated primarily from an under-developed country's perspective. It was thus devised not only for the development of India but also to the whole Third World because those countries had similar problems of economic development. Behind the concept of small-unit technology lies the principle of decentralised economic production, which, according to Lohia, is the only means for bridging the industrial and economic inequality among nations and ensuring social control.

Lohia thought that to remove and eradicate poverty and unemployment of the Indian masses, emphasis should be placed on such technology which would act as a panacea. Lohia felt it was necessary to widen the scope of employment of Indian workers. He pointed out that the economy based on small-unit machines would provide opportunity for employment of many people. He sought an economy that would advance the existing situation but would not make such crushing demands upon India's general economy as to cause dislocations or give the benefits of rationalisation only to a small sector and deny it to the rest. Lohia thus stated that socialism aimed economically at a technology that rationalised economy neither sector by sector nor region by region but, as far as possible, in all sectors and regions at the same time.[5] He, however, did not rule out the importance or the place of concentrated capital and large-scale industry. He stated that there must be, for instance, steel works or river-training projects which are more capital intensive. But the main focus and emphasis of the economy must be towards small-unit machinery.

Lohia was optimistic that by adhering to the principle of small-unit machines India would be able to enhance her production capacities, the economy would strengthen, and India would achieve development and prosperity. As Lohia put it:

> Perhaps with the small unit tool it would be possible for countries like India to re-equip their economy, to expand their productive equipment. But in order to achieve that condition, what kind of class struggle do we have to wage? Would it be permissible for us to go through all that pathway of deceit and lies? Obviously not.[6]

Thus, Lohia pinned his hopes that socialism could provide necessary conditions through the social ownership of capital and a new type of technology, small-unit machines.

X Conclusion

Lohia represented an integrated approach on society, social problems, and human civilisation. Lohia considered both capitalism and communism irrelevant to the whole of mankind. He suggested an alternative model of development which would be congenial and conducive to the socio-economic conditions of the

Indian society and Third World countries. Thus, Lohia advocated socialism in the form of a new civilisation which could be referred to as socialist humanism. He gave a new direction and dimension to the socialist movement in India. He wanted the power of the State to be controlled, guided, and framed by people's power and believed in the theology of democratic socialism and non-violent methodology as instruments of socio-economic transformation. He urged all the socialist parties of the world to think in terms of an effective world union through world government.

However, critical evaluation of Lohia's views on social, economic, and political problems reveals that he did not treat them as separate entities; rather, he viewed them in interrelated terms and discussed them in the context of national and international situations. He adopted an integrated approach and discussed the various aspects of his philosophy in detail. But when compared with thinkers such as Marx, Lenin, or Plato, a coherent doctrine is missing in Lohia.

Though in practical politics Lohia failed to influence people for the socialist transformation of society, he wanted the people to vote the socialists to power and hope for the same. His contribution, with the help of his analytical and critical writing and inspiring speeches, to the development of socialist thought and movement in our country cannot be undermined. He suggested solutions for many social, political, and economic problems of our country. His valuable thoughts are relevant and need to be followed in the present environment of increasing violence, communal tensions, and declining human values. His dynamic and uninhibited approach places him in a respectable place among the socialists of India.

Notes

1 For detailed discussion, see Sampurnanand, Samajwaad (Kashi Bhartiya Gyan Peeth, 1960), I.
2 Ram Manohar Lohia: 'The Doctrinal Foundation of Socialism,' Speech, Panchmarhi, May 1952, collected from Political Thinkers of Modern India: Ram Manohar Lohia,' ed. by V. Grover, Deep & Deep Publications, New Delhi, 1996, pp. 141.
3 Lohia's Statement on 13 October 1959 at Hyderabad, Reported by the Press Trust of India.
4 *Lok Sabha Debates.* August 1967, Vol. VIII, pp. 17266–17271.
5 Presidential Address of Ram Manohar Lohia to the Special convention of the Socialist Party, Panchmarhi, 1952, p. 15.
6 Ram Manohar Lohia: Speech delivered at Hyderabad on 'Marxism and Socialism' in August 1952 – collected from 'Political Thinkers of Modern India: Ram Manohar Lohia,' ed. by V. Grover, Deep & Deep Publications, New Delhi, 1996, pp. 199–200.

References

Almus, A. S. (1998). *Lohia: The Rebel Gandhian.* New Delhi: Mittal Publications.
Appadorai, A. (2002). *Political Thoughts in India (400 B.C.-1980).* New Delhi: Khama Publishers.

Chakrabarty, B., and Pandey, R. (2009). *Modern Indian Political Thought: Text and Context.* New Delhi: Sage Publications.

Kumar, A. (2010). Understanding Lohia's Political Sociology: Intersectionality of Caste, Class, Gender and Language. *Economic and Political Weekly*, October 2–8, 45(40).

Limaye, M. (1978). A Tribute to Ram Manohar Lohia. In M. Arungam (ed.), *Socialist Thought in India: The Contribution of Rammanohar Lohia*. New Delhi: Sterling Publishers.

Lohia, R. M. (1950). *Aspects of Socialist Policy*. Bombay: Tulloch.

Lohia, R. M. (1955). *The Wheel of History*. Hyderabad: Lohia Samiti.

Lohia, R. M. (1956). *Will to Power and Other Writings*. Hyderabad: Navhind.

Lohia, R. M. (1963). *Marx, Gandhi and Socialism*. Hyderabad: Navhind.

Lohia, R. M. (1964). *The Caste System*. Hyderabad: Navhind.

Lohia, R. M. (1967). Plea for a Budget Without Foreign Aid. *Mankind*, July, 11(5), 24–27.

Lohia, R. M. (1996a). The Four Pillar State. In V. Grover (ed.), *Political Thinkers of Modern India*. New Delhi: Deep & Deep Publications.

Lohia, R. M. (1996b). India's Path to Socialism. In V. Grover (ed.), *Political Thinkers of Modern India*. New Delhi: Deep & Deep Publications.

Lohia, R. M. (1996c). Meaning of Equality. In V. Grover (ed.), *Political Thinkers of Modern India*. New Delhi: Deep & Deep Publications.

Mehta, V. (1992). *Foundations of Indian Political Thought*. New Delhi: Manohar.

Narayan, J. (1964). *Socialism, Sarvodaya and Democracy: Selected Works of Jayprakash Narayan*, edited by Bimal Prasad. Bombay: Asia Publishing House.

Sinha, S. (2010). Lohia's Socialism: An Underdog Perspective. *Economic and Political Weekly*, October 2–8, 45(40), 51–55.

Tolpadi, R. (2010). Context, Vision and Discourse of Lohia's Socialism. *Economic and Political Weekly*, October 2–8, 45(40), 71–77.

Yadav, Y. (2010). What Is Living and What Is Dead in Lohia. *Economic and Political Weekly*, October 2–8, 45(40).

INDEX

Aabaar Oti Alpa Hoilo (Vidyasagar) 42
Abhangas 183
Absolute (*Brahman*) 74, 76–79
Abul Fazl: *Ain-i-Akbari* 3
Achhyut-uddhar 16
achhyut (untouchables) 7
Adi Dravidas 98
adivasis 286
administrative reforms 143
Admission of Educated Natives into the Indian Civil Service (Naoroji) 142
Advaita Vedānta 77
Adyasakti 78
Aga Khan Palace 166
Agarak, G. G. 153
agraha 167
aham brahmasmi 77
ahiṃsā (non-violence) 5, 16, 161, 167–173, 175, 177, 182–185, 188, 190, 193, 198
A.I.A.D.M.K., 108
Ain-i-Akbari (Abul Fazl) 3
Akbar 3, 4, 6
Akhil Bhartiya Ravidas Mahasabha 129
Alfred High School 162
Allahabad Municipality 236
Allied Powers 252
All-India Congress Committee (AICC) 130, 236, 242
All-India Congress Socialist Conference 220
All-India Depressed Classes League 129
All-India Socialist Party Conference 221
All-India States Peoples' Conference 236

All-India Trade Union Congress (A.I.T.U.C.) 205–206, 256
All-India Working Party 226
Almus, A.S. 292
Ambedkar, Bhimrao Ramji (Babasaheb) 5, 12, 13, 58, 65, 96, 102, 110–125, 125n1; *Annihilation of Caste* 111, 113, 117; Buddhism, religion, and politics 123–125; caste and Ambedkar-Gandhi debate 113–115; *Castes in India* 111; Constitution-making, rights, and citizenship 115–117; critique of *Brāhminical* Hinduism 111–113; democracy, State, and society 118–122; life sketch 111; nationalism and nation-building 122–123; overview 110–111; women's rights and Hindu Code Bill 117–118
American Bill of Rights 116
Ananda Math (Chandra Chatterjee) 204
anasakti yoga 190
Anderson, Benedict 41
Anderson, Perry 16
Anglo-French policy 260
Annadurai 102
Annihilation of Caste (Ambedkar) 111, 113, 117
anti-colonialism 6
anti-colonial struggle 219, 220, 224
anti-Hindi struggle (1937–1940) 103
anti-imperialist struggle 224
anushasan 190
aparigraha 168, 174

Apte, Narayan 166
Apte, V. S. 153
Arasars (kings/*Kṣatriyas*) 96
ardhangini 82
Argumentative Indian, The (Sen) 3
Aristotle 24; *Politics* 1
Arms Act 143
Arthaśāstra (Kauṭilya) 2
Arya Mahila Samaj 84, 87, 90, 92
Aryan-Brāhmins 104
Aryans 64, 65, 103
Arya Patrika 50
Ārya Samāj 48, 50–51, 54, 55
Ashoka 4
āśhramas 173
Asian Relations Conference 245
asteya 168
Atharvavedā 48
Ati-Śūdras 63, 65, 69, 70
atma-nirbhar Bharat (self-sufficient India) 11
Atmiya Sabha ("spiritual society") 24, 26
Aung San Suu Kyi 161
avataras (incarnations) 53
avidya maya 78, 79
Ayer, S. A. 261
Azad Hind Fouj 252
Azad, Abul Kalam 7

Bahubivah (Vidyasagar) 42
Bahujan Samaj Party 126n3
balutedari system 62
Balwant Rai Mehta Committee 240
Balyabivah (Vidyasagar) 42
Banaras Hindu University 129, 183, 281
Bandyopadhyay, Thakurdas 38
Bandyopadhyaya, Narayan Chandra 43
Banerjee, Surendranath 15, 144, 154, 217
Bangali, S. S. 141
Banglar Itihaas (Vidyasagar) 42
Barani, Ziauddin: *Fatwa-i Jahandari* 3
Barkley's theory 40
bauls 108
Bengal Herald 34
Bengal Presidency 24, 36
Bengal renaissance 5, 12, 37
Bentham, Jeremy 26
Bentick, William 24, 27, 36
Betaal Panchavinsati (Vidyasagar) 42
Bhagavadgītā 163, 164, 176, 183, 190
bhakti 76, 77
bhakti-sadhana 79
Bhandarkar, R. G. 154
Bharat Ratna 182
Bhattacharjee, J.B. 261

Bhattacharya, Narendranath *see* Roy, Manabendra Nath
Bhave, Vinoba (Vinayaka Narahari Bhave) 13, 175, 182–198, 266, 273–274; association with Gandhi and role in freedom struggle 188–190; *bhoodan* movement 192–194, 266; *Gitai* 184; *gramdan* movement 194–195; *Ishavasyavritti* 184; life sketch 183–185; non-violence and spiritualism 188; overview 182–183; *sampatti dan* 195; *sarvodaya* and *gram swaraj* 190–192; *Steadfast Wisdom* 184; *Sthitaprajna Darshan* 184; *Swarajya Shāstra* 184; *Thoughts on Education* 186; views on democracy and party system 195–197; views on education 185–186; views on Hinduism 186–187; views on planning 197–198; views on religion 187–188
bhoodan (land gift movement) 13, 175, 182–184, 190, 192–194, 198
Bhrantivilaas (Vidyasagar) 42
Bible 164, 176
Bidhobabivah (Vidyasagar) 42
Bihar Legislative Assembly 129
birth control 105, 106
Bismarck, Otto von 7
Black Act, The 165
Bolsheviks 210
Bombay Association 141
Bombay Legislative Council 142
Borodin, Bolshevik Michael 204
Borsa, Georgio 5
Bose, Rash Behari 253
Bose, Sarat Chandra (1921) 250
Bose, Subhas Chandra 14, 15, 263–264; All-India Trade Union Congress (1931) 256; "cataclysmic loss" 251; charge and commander of Indian National Army - Bose, Subhas Chandra 249, 252; conquest of Abyssinia 258; idea of revolution and socio-economic transformation 258–259; *Indian Struggle, The* (1935) 251, 256; indirect catalyst of India's freedom 253; life sketch 250–253; mayor of Calcutta Municipal Corporation 256; *My Personal Testament* 254; nationalism and socialism 254–258; *Naujawan Bharat Sabha* (1931) 256; *new samyavada* 251, 257; opponent of British imperialism 249; overview 249–250; practitioner of realpolitik 260; Rangpur Political Conference (1930) 255; Scottish

Church College 250; student in Ravenshaw Collegiate School 250; view of international politics 259–262; vision of free India 262–263
bourgeois nationalism 207
Brahmā 64, 81, 86, 183
brahmacharinis 81
brahmacharya (celibacy) 47, 81, 168, 179, 186
Brahmananche Kasab (Phule) 59
Brāhmanic 84
brahmavadinis 81
Brāhminical Hinduism 111–113, 125
Brāhminical schools 5
Brāhminism 12, 59, 68, 69, 84, 89, 97, 99, 103–105, 108, 124
Brāhmins 24, 38–40, 43, 52, 57–59, 62–70, 90, 96, 98–100, 102–104, 112, 235, 292
Brahmoism 33
Brahmo Sabha 25, 37
Brahmo Samaj 25–26, 33, 37, 38, 68, 84
Brahmo Trust Deed 26
Brajavilaas (Vidyasagar) 42
Brief Remarks Regarding Modern Encroachments on the Ancient Right of Females (Roy) 31–32
Brihadaranyaka Upaniṣhad 81
Brihaspati Sutra 2
British administration 142, 143, 148
British Cabinet Mission, The 166
British colonialism 2, 4–8, 10, 11, 14, 15, 17, 219, 235, 241, 253
British Empire 30, 37, 143, 148
British government 59, 60, 63, 64, 89, 101, 111, 140, 144, 148–150, 156, 157
British India 10, 82, 145–147
British Indian Army 252–253, 264
British Parliament 29, 30, 144, 145
British *raj* 5, 171
British rule 61–64, 67, 102, 123, 130, 139, 142, 145, 147, 148, 152, 155, 156, 158, 165, 166, 179, 189, 224, 236, 245, 254, 282
buddhidan (wisdom gift) 190
Buddhism 76, 111, 123–125
Bukharin, Nikolai 205
Burke, Edmund 7, 118

Calcutta Corporation Act 143
Calcutta Gazette 26
Calcutta Municipal Corporation 251
Calcutta Unitarian Association 26
Caliph 3
Cama, Bhikaiji Rustom 144
Cama & Co. 141
capitalism 12, 16, 18, 175, 178, 206, 207, 209, 224

caste 82, 111–115, 117, 237–238, 259, 263, 269, 275–276, 281, 288–294
caste discrimination 58, 68–71, 92, 128
caste ideology 100, 104, 105
casteism 99, 102, 132
Castes in India (Ambedkar) 111
caste system 51, 52, 57, 59, 64–65, 67, 68, 71, 87, 88, 97, 100, 153, 159
caste system, The (Lohia) 280
Cavour, Camillo Paolo Filippo Giulio Benso 7
Chagla, M. C. 239
Chakrabarty, B. 280, 286, 293
Chakravarti, Uma 94
Champaran *satyāgraha,* The (1917) 165
Chandra Chatterjee, Bankim: *Ananda Math* 204
charkha 285
Chattopadhyay, Khudiram 74, 253
chaturvarṇa 114
Chatushpathi 38, 40
Chaudhuri, Nirad Chandra 261
chaukhamba rajya (four-pillars State) 280, 293
Cheltenham Women's College 84
Chetty, Theagaraya 96
Child, Josiah 4
child marriage 13, 42–44, 52, 66, 69, 82, 83, 87, 88, 90, 93, 101, 117, 140, 163
Child Marriage Prevention Act (1929) 44
Chiplunkar, V. K. 153
Christianity 51, 56, 59, 68, 76, 83, 85, 91, 92, 167
Christian missionaries 51, 69, 84, 91
Christian Mission of Chandwa 129
Christian Mukti Mission 85, 92
Church diktat 6
Churchill, Winston: "Light of Asia" 238
citizenship 115–117
civil disobedience 168
Civil Marriage Act (1872) 42
civil rights 88–90, 161, 165
Civil Services Examination (C.S.E.) 250
civil society 93, 97, 213
Clare's Scholarship 141
class: consciousness 225; dominant 228; solidarity 225; struggle 14, 223
co-education 186
Colbert, Jean-Baptiste 4
Cold War 237, 246
colonial authoritarianism 6
colonialism 87, 142, 207, 244–245, 253, 271
colonial rule 5, 6, 8, 61, 62, 139, 140, 145, 149, 165, 170, 241
commentaries (*bhasyas*) 2

communalism 6, 7
"Communications to the Board of Control" 28
communism 18, 106–107, 194, 216, 230–231, 242, 251, 255, 259–260, 270, 278n6, 279, 284; capitalism and 281–283, 295; and fascism 256–257; Russian 257
Communist International (Comintern) 204
Communist Party of India (CPI) 14, 204
community 7, 8, 10, 17, 25, 28, 92, 97, 98, 120, 128, 133, 141, 145, 157, 163, 165, 170–172, 183, 195, 196, 230, 239–240, 244, 263, 268–269, 276–277, 284–285, 293–294
Community-Development Programme 240
compulsory education 53, 59, 61, 71
Congregation of the Absolute 25; *see also* Brahmo Sabha
Congress for Democracy (CFD) 131
Congress Provincial Committees 104
Congress Socialist (1938) 260
Congress Socialist Party (CSP) 14, 220–221, 223, 232, 233, 242, 260, 268, 281
Congress Working Committee 146, 221
consciousness 75; class 207, 226–227; feminist 89; Indian 23; national 54, 244; political 10, 226; social 41, 227, 290
Constituent Assembly 102, 111, 115–117, 119, 122, 128, 130, 133, 243
constitutional government 30
Constitutionalism 30–32
constitutional reforms 143
constitutional socialism 119
Constitution of the United States 116
Constructive Programme 98, 99
contemporary Hinduism 37
cosmopolitanism 32
Council of States of the Federal Assembly 216
Crawford, J. 29, 30
Cry of Indian Women, The (Pandita Ramabai) 84, 89
Cuyamariyātai (self-respect) 99
Czechoslovak-Soviet Pact 260

Dada Abdullah 164
Daily Graphic 144
Dalits (oppressed) 7, 70–71, 108, 110, 128, 129, 132–134, 193
Dar-ul-Islam (land of Islam) 10
Das, Benimadhav 250

Das, C. R. 236, 247, 251
Dayaram/Shuddha Chaitanya *see* Swami Dayānanda Saraswati (*Moolshankar*) 47, 49
Deccan Education Society (D.E.S.) 153, 155
Deccan Sabha 153
decentralisation 172, 173
Defence Committee, A 254
democracy 3–4, 6, 54, 111, 118–122, 125, 142, 148, 169–171, 174, 185, 195–197, 214, 230–231, 293; liberal 214–216, 240; national 207; parliamentary 2 38–240, 274; participatory 269–271, 274; party-less 215, 273–274; political 240, 268; radical 206, 214–216; socialist 231; and State 292–294
democratic socialism 14, 134, 178, 272–273; Congress session at Ramgarh 272; draft resolution 272; privileges 272; *sarvodaya* 272
Depressed Classes League 129, 130
Derozians 37
Derozio, Henry Louis Vivian 37
Desai, Shri Morarji 131
Deva, Acharya Narendra 12, 14; "Gaya thesis" 221; life sketch 220–221; morality and socialism 227–228; nationalist movement and socialist struggle, parallel journey 231–232; overview 219–220; political philosophy, sources 221–222; socialism, ideas of 222–223; socialism, transformation and elevation 224–226; socialism and cultural transformation 228–230; socialism and democracy 230–231
devadasi system 101
devatā 53
Devi, Bhagavati 38
Devi, Chandramani 74
Devi, Rukmini 183
Devi, Tarini 24
Devi, Vasanti 128, 129
Dewey, John 71, 119
dhamma 123, 124
dhārma 2, 5, 54, 55, 68, 123, 124, 132, 186
Dharmadhikari, Dada 175
Dharmaśāstras 2, 86
Dharmasūtras 2
Digby, John 24
digests (*nibandhyas*) 2
Directive Principles of State Policy 11, 116, 119
discrimination 23, 29, 32, 52, 58, 70, 78, 87, 91, 107, 117, 119, 120, 123, 127, 129, 133, 153, 159

distributive justice 1
divorce 101
Dongre, Anant Shastri 83
downward filtration theory 61
Drafting Committee 121
drain of wealth 139, 141, 145, 146, 149, 150
Dravida Munnetra Kazhagam (D.M.K.) 102, 108
Dravidanad (*Dravidastan*) 103, 104
Dravida Nadu 102
Dravidar Kazhagam (D.K.) 97, 101–102, 107, 108
Dravidian Federation 104
Dravidian identity 108
Dravidians 104
Dutt, R.P. 257
Dutta, Michael Madhusudan 44
Dutta, Rasomoy 38, 39

East India Association 141
East India Company 2, 6, 24, 29, 30, 31, 32, 36, 150, 152
eclecticism 33, 257
economic development 11, 175, 207, 212, 223, 243–244, 246, 270, 273, 283, 295
economic reconstruction 212, 223, 285
economic reforms 6, 143
education 36, 53–54, 71, 107, 131–132, 159–160, 185–186; Indian 39–40; national 141, 149; philosophy 61; public 158; reform 25, 37, 40, 41, 59; Sanskrit 40–41; vernacular 39, 40; Western 25, 141, 143, 156
Education Commission (1882) 13, 58–60, 89, 92
egalitarianism 7, 11, 63, 65, 84, 97, 134, 174
egoism 79, 90
Einstein, Albert 180
elitism 240, 292
Elphinstone Institute 141
Emergency (1975) 131, 133
Engels, Friedrich 222
enlightenment 36, 92
'epistemological crisis' 5
equality/inequality 16, 60–62, 65–66, 68–71, 74, 79, 82, 83, 94, 97, 101, 107, 111, 112, 117, 119, 120, 121, 123, 125, 128, 129, 133, 142, 159, 172, 182, 183, 187, 227–228, 230, 273, 283, 286–289, 287, 289
Erikson, Erik 16
Erode Municipal Council 97
Erode Self-Respect Conference (1930) 105
Ethical Religion (Salter) 166
Euclid 24

European and Asiatic Races: Observations on the Paper Read by John Crawfurd, The (Naoroji) 142
European civilisation 47
European model 9
European Press 30
European renaissance 25, 37
European science 40
"Europe today and tomorrow" (Bose) 258
Ezhavas 98

Fabianism 219, 234
Farquhar, J. N. 33
fascism 179
"Father of the Nation" (Gandhi) 237
Fatwa-i Jahandari (Barani) 3
female infanticide 69, 93, 140
femininity 89
feminism 84, 86, 94
feminist discourse 88
Fergusson College 153
feudal caste system 132
feudalism 207, 230, 245
Finsbury Central for the Liberal Party 141
Fiqh-i Firuzshahi 3
Firestone, Shulamith 86
First Five Year Plan (1951–1956) 244
First Self-Respect Conference (1929) 100, 101
First World War 207, 234, 245
formless God 53, 77
Fort William College 38, 39
Franco-Soviet Pact 260
free trade 150
Frere, Bartle 84
From Socialism to Sarvodaya (Narayan) 190
Fundamental Rights 115–117, 131
Furdonji, Naoroji 141
Future of Indian Politics (Roy) 205

ganas 2
Gandhi, Devdas 163
Gandhi, Harilal 163
Gandhi, Indira 131, 133, 235
Gandhi, Karamchand 162
Gandhi, Kasturba 163
Gandhi, Laxmidas 163
Gandhi, Mohandas Karamchand (*Bapuji*) 2, 5, 7–9, 11, 13, 15, 16, 58, 98, 99, 102, 103, 111, 113–115, 125, 126n3, 130, 146, 152, 161–180, 183, 186, 188–190, 198, 234, 281; childhood 162; critique of modern civilisation 178–179; early life and schooldays 162–163; *gram swaraj* (village republic) 171–172; *Hind*

Index **303**

Swaraj ("Indian Home Rule") 170, 189, 266; ideas on *satyāgraha* 167–170; Indian National Congress and struggle for India's independence (1915–1947) 165–167; London years 163–164; overview 161–162; *sarvodaya* 173–175; in South Africa (1893–1914) 164–165; *swaraj* and views on State and democracy 169–171; theory of trusteeship 176–178
Gandhi, Monilal 163
Gandhi, Rajmohan 16, 113, 115
Gandhi, Ramdas 163
Gandhian Constructive Programme 99
Garibaldi, Giuseppe Maria 7
Gaukarunanidhi (Swami Dayānanda Saraswati) 50
Gautama 2
gender 230, 263, 289, 291; discourse 89; equality/inequality 43, 69, 83, 90, 100, 188, 230, 263; issues 87; justice 88–90; reform 83, 86, 87
German Communist Opposition (KPD-O) 205
Germany 204, 206, 244, 251–252, 258–260, 282
Ghadar Party 264
Ghose, Aurobindo 5, 15
Gilligan, Carol 16
Gitai (Bhave) 184
God existence 76–79
God realisation 74–77, 78, 79
Godse, Nathuram 166
Gokhale, Gopal Krishna 7, 13, 15, 142, 144, 152–160, 165, 236; constitutionalism and *swadeshi* 154; ethics and politics 155–159; life sketch 153–154; overview 152–153; social regeneration 154–155
Golwalkar, Madhavrao Sadashivrao 5
Gordon, L. 204
governance 1, 2, 4, 18, 112, 147, 148, 150
Government of India 28, 31, 43, 44, 103
graded inequality 112
gramdan (gift of village) 13, 175, 182, 190, 194
gramdan movement 194–195
gram nirman 192
gram swaraj (village republic) 171–172, 190–192
Gulamgiri (Phule) 59
guna (character) 52
Gyaneshwar 184

Hadis 3
Haithcox, J. 207, 217n7
halal (the legal) 25
Hall, Catherine 143
Hammond Committee 129
haram (the forbidden) 25
Harijan 171
Harijans (people of God) 7, 134, 162, 189
Haripura Congress (1938) 14, 251
Hasan, Shariful 247
Hastings, Warren 36
Hatcher, Brian 45
High-Caste Hindu Woman, The (Pandita Ramabai) 12, 13, 82, 85, 86, 88
Hind Swaraj ("Indian Home Rule," Gandhi) 170, 189, 266
Hindu Code Bill 110, 111, 117–118, 125n1, 126n4
Hindu College 37
Hindu community 8, 25
Hindu Family Annuity Fund 43
Hinduism 10, 12, 15, 18, 25, 26, 37, 48, 50, 51, 53, 56, 67, 68, 75, 80, 82, 84, 87, 90, 91, 97, 104, 113, 123–125, 132, 133, 155, 167, 186–187
Hindu–Muslim unity 153, 154, 159
Hindu nationalism 9, 10, 270
Hindu philosophy 2, 41
Hindu *rashtra* 5, 7
Hindu social order 111 *see* Brāhminical Hinduism
Hindustan Socialist Republican Army 8
'Hindutva' 10
Hindu Unitarianism 30
Hindu Widow Remarriage Act (1856) 39, 42, 44, 45
Historical Materialism (Bukharin) 222
Hitler, Adolf 252, 258, 260, 283; attack on Russia 252
Holwell monument 252
Home Rule League 235
House of Commons 30
human freedom 30, 31
humanism 10, 47, 48, 53, 60, 71, 107, 159, 178, 187; radical 208–212, 216; socialistic 228–230, 296
humanity 32–34, 44, 50, 65, 70, 140, 173, 217, 221, 230, 289; crisis of 227; emancipation of 257; socialistic 229
human rights 60, 64, 65, 70, 108, 144
Hume, Allan Octavian 142
Hume, David 7
humiliation 32, 111, 164
Hunter Commission 58–60; *see also* Education Commission
Hunter, Sir William Wilson 89

304 Index

Idea of India (Khilnani) 17
idolatry 26, 31, 49, 53, 67, 100
imperialism 14, 17, 56, 83, 161, 167, 179, 206, 207, 245, 249, 251–253, 260–261
Imperialism: The Highest Stage of Capitalism (Lenin) 206
independent India 15, 17, 60, 102
Independent India (Roy) 206
India in Transition (Roy) 205
Indian Constitution 11, 59, 102, 110, 111, 115, 116, 120, 121, 128, 130, 131, 133, 236–239, 243, 263; Article 31 121; Article 45 60
Indian Councils Act 143
Indian economy 66–67, 145–146, 149, 150, 157, 160, 175
Indian Express, The 247
Indian Federation of Labour (I.F.L.) 205
Indian freedom movement/struggle 13, 14, 130, 142, 148–149, 165–167, 188–190
Indian History Congress Golden Jubilee session (1989) 261
Indian identity 16
Indian Independence League 252
Indian Jury Bill (1826) 29
Indian Legion 252
Indian Muslim League 10
Indian National Army (I.N.A) 253–254
Indian National Congress (I.N.C.) 5, 8, 14, 62, 89, 97, 98, 104, 121, 128, 130, 141, 142, 144, 148–150, 153, 165–167, 219–220, 226, 232–233, 235–236, 244, 251–252, 281
Indian National Navy 254
Indian Opinion 170
Indian political thought and theory 1–4, 8, 9, 12
Indian renaissance 4–7, 25–26, 36
Indian Science News Association (1938) 259
Indians in Foreign Lands (Lohia) 280
Indian society 23, 30, 41, 47, 51, 60, 64–67, 74, 83, 85–89, 104, 111, 121, 132
Indian Struggle, The (Bose) 251, 256
Individual Rights in a Civilizational State: A New Idea of India (Madhusudan and Mantri) 17
Indo-Aryan culture 47
industrialisation 66, 146, 175, 178
Industrial Policy Resolution 244
Infallibility Decree (1579) 3
inhuman dogmatism 91
institutionalised religion 83, 187
inter-caste marriages 53, 82, 113, 114, 291

inter-dining 53, 113, 114
internationalism 61, 237, 244–246, 260
International Socialist Conference (1907) 144
inter-religious marriage 82
Interval During Politics, Language (Lohia) 280
Iqbal, Muhammad 5
Ishara (Phule) 59
Ishavasyavritti (Bhave) 184
Ishopanishad 176
Ishwar (God) 74, 78, 79
Islam 55, 56, 76; culture 5; political thought and ideas 2–3, 10; rule 3

Jainism 167
Jalal, Ayesha 9
Jallianwala Bagh Massacre (1919) 98, 166
Janata Party 131
janta centres 275
Japanese historians 264; Akashir and Nagasaki 253, 261
Jatin Mukherjee (*Bagha Jatin*) 204
jeevandan 194
Jhansi Rani Regiment 263
jingoism/irredentism 258
Jinnah, Muhammad Ali 5, 104
jiva 79
Jivancharita (Vidyasagar) 42
jñāna 76, 185
Johnson, Samuel 45
Joshee, Anandibai 84, 89
Joshiji, Mavji Dave 163
judicial reforms 29–30
Jury Act (1827) 28
Justice Party 96, 98, 101, 103–105; *see also* South Indian Liberal Federation

Kali 78–80
Kallenbach, Hermann 165
kanchanmukti 184
kanika danam 106
Kant, Immanuel 7
Kara, Maniben 205
karma (action) 52, 76, 185
karma-yog 15
Karnik, V. B. 205
Karunakaran, K. P. 238
Kathasaritsagara 42
Kauṭilya: *Arthaśāstra* 2
Kautsky, Karl 222
Kaviraj, Sudipta 9
Kayasthas 267, 292
Kesari 154
khadi clothes 146, 172, 183, 189
Kheda *satyāgraha,* The (1918) 165

Khetihar Mazdoor Sabha 129
Khusru, Amir: *Tughlaqnama* 3
King, Martin Luther, Jr. 161
Kingdom of God is Within You, The (Tolstoy) 166
Kisan Mazdoor Praja Party 221
Kisan Sabha (organisation) 220, 226
knowledge (*jñāna*) 75–76
Koolinism 27
Krinvanto Vishvamaryam 50
Kripalani, J. B. 221
Krishna 78
Krishnarao 153
Kṣatriyas 52, 100
Kudi Arasu 99, 103, 105, 106
Kulin Brāhmin 42
Kulkarni 65

Lahore Session of the Congress (1893) 148
Lahore Session of the Muslim League (1940) 104
Lal, Deepak 112
"Lamentation of Divine Language" (Pandita Ramabai) 87
"land to the tiller" movement 192
Laxmibai 83
League of Radical Congressmen 205
Left Consolidation Committee 252
leftism 105
leftist-socialist 12, 13
left-liberals 113
Lenin, V. I. 106, 204, 222, 271; *Imperialism: The Highest Stage of Capitalism* (1917) 206; *National and Colonial Questions* 204; *Two Tactics of Social Democracy in the Democratic Revolution* (1905) 206
Leninist-Marxism 271
Lerner, Gerda 85
Letter to a Hindu, A (Tolstoy) 165
liberal democracy 119, 214, 215
liberalism 5, 6, 9, 11, 18, 25–27, 94, 187, 234–235
liberal-reformist 11, 12
liberation 31, 32, 33, 40, 47, 59, 99, 159, 198
liberty 27, 31, 62–64, 68, 70, 107, 272, 281, 288
Limaye, M. 278n6, 288
Locke, John 7, 159
Logia 74
Lohia, Ram Manohar 14; capitalism and communism 281–283; caste, class, and power 289–292; *caste system, The* 280; democracy and State 292–294; emancipation of women 289–290; freedom, equality, and *sapta kranti* (seven revolutions) 286–289; *Indians in Foreign Lands* (1938) 280; *Interval During Politics, Language* (1966) 280; life sketch 280–281; *Marx, Gandhi and Socialism* (1963) 280; new socialism and social justice 283–286; overview 279–280; *samatva-sambhav* (feeling of oneness) 280; *sapta kranti* (theory of seven revolutions) 280; small-machine technology 294–295; theology of democratic socialism 296; *Wheel of History* (1955) 280; *Will to Power* (1956) 280
Lokesthiti Ani Pravasvritta (Pandita Ramabai) 85
loknīti 13, 190, 273
Lok Sabha 131
lokshakti (people's power) 273
Lord Cornwallis, Charles Edward 36–37
Lord Ripon, George Frederick Samuel Robinson 13
lower castes 13, 57, 58–60, 62–65, 67–71, 87, 88, 134
Luxemburg, Rosa 222

Macaulay, Thomas Babington 61
Machiavelli, Niccolò 241
Macpherson, C. B. 240
Madhusudan, Harsh: *Individual Rights in a Civilizational State: A New Idea of India* 17
Madrasa/Maqtab 38
Madras Pradesh Congress 98
Madras Presidency Association 98
madrassas 5
Mahābhārata 2
Mahabharata (Vidyasagar) 42
Mahaparinirvana 111
Maharaja Sayajirao Gaekwad III 141
Maharashtra dharma 183, 184
Maharashtra Provincial Conference 255
Mahars 69
Maha Shivaratri 49
Mahatma Gandhi (Rolland) 180
Mahavakyas 77
Maha-Vidyalaya 30
Mahila Samaj 93
Malaviya, Pandit Madan Mohan 129, 142, 144
Malraux, Andre 16
Mandela, Nelson 161
Maneckbai 141
Mangs 69

Index

Maniammai 102
manida dharmavadi 107
Manjapra, Kris 205–206, 208, 217n3
Mankind 281
Manners and Customs of the Parsees: A Paper Read before the Liverpool Philomathic Society, The (Naoroji) 142
Mantri, Rajiv: *Individual Rights in a Civilizational State: A New Idea of India* 17
Manusmṛiti 52–55, 82, 86, 88
Mao Tse-Tung 205
Maratha 154
Marx, Gandhi and Socialism (Lohia) 280
Marx, Karl 7, 123, 208–211, 221, 223, 255, 266, 274, 282–284, 296; *On Colonialism* 139
Marxism 14, 203, 208, 219, 221–222; economic determinism 210; future of socialism 210–211; surplus value 209; theory of class struggle 209
Marxism, critique of 208, 212, 270–272; influence of Leninist-Marxism 271; Soviet Communist Party 269
matuas 108
Maududi, Maulana Abu'l Ala 10
Maya (bondage) 74, 78–79
Mazumdar, Dhirendra 175
Mazzini, Giuseppe 15
Medhvi, Bipin Behari 84
Medieval Indian political thought 3
Mehrotra, N.C. 290
Mehta, Pheroze Shah 142, 144, 153–155
Mehta, V. 282–283
Member of the Legislative Assembly (M.L.A.) 221, 274
Memoirs (Roy) 207, 217n2
mercantilism 4
Mill, John Stuart 7, 40, 116
Millet, Kate 86
Ministry of Agriculture, Cooperative Industry and Village Development 130
minority rights 16, 119, 125
miraj-i-zamana (spirit of the age) 3
Misra, Babu Ram 193
Mitchell, John Murray 58
moderate-Gandhian 11–13
modern civilisation 178–179
modern colonial education 9
modern culture 28, 41
modern education 30, 37, 41, 140
modern India 18, 41, 119, 129
modern Indian thought 3, 4, 7–11
modernisation 5, 26, 30, 55
modernity 4, 5, 9, 34, 37, 178

Moksha 86
monogamy 81
monotheism 25, 26, 32, 53
Moraes, Frank 261
morality 25, 29, 97, 123, 124, 158, 159, 210, 212, 222, 227, 287; principles of 227; socialism and 227–228; victims of 289–290
Moura, Maria Lacerda de: *Serviço militar obrigatório para mulher? Recuso-me! Denuncio!* 180
M.P. (Member of Parliament) 274
Mufakkir-i-Pakistan 5
Mughal empire 3
muhajis 204
Mukti Sadan 85, 92–93
multiculturalism 15
multi-party system 262
Mun, Thomas 4
Muslim League Conference 104
Muslim nationalism 9, 10
Muslim society 8
Mussolini, Benito 258
"My Picture of Socialism" (Narayan) 268

Naicker, Venkata 97
Nair, T. M. 96
nai talim scheme (Wardha scheme) 183, 191
Namdev 184
Naoroji, Dadabhai 7, 13, 15, 139–150, 153–155, 158, 220; *Admission of Educated Natives Into the Indian Civil Service* 142; economic and political nationalism 147–148; *European and Asiatic Races: Observations on the Paper Read by John Crawfurd, The* 142; life sketch 140–142; *Manners and Customs of the Parsees: A Paper Read before the Liverpool Philomathic Society, The* 142; overview 139–140; *Parsee Religion, The* 142; *Poverty and Un-British Rule in India* 139, 142, 144, 148, 149; *Poverty of India* 142; role in Indian freedom struggle 148–149; socio-economic and political views 142–145; theory of moral and material drain 145–147; *Wants and Means of India, The* 142
Naoroji & Co. 141
Naoroji Palanji Dordi 140
Nārada 2
Narayan, Jayaprakash 14, 175, 188, 190, 194; caste, youth, and poverty 275; critique of Marxism 269–272; democratic socialism 272–273;

education and health system 276; life sketch 267–269; "My Picture of Socialism" 268; overview 266–267; participatory democracy and reconstruction of Indian polity 269–270; party-less democracy 273–274; Scheduled Caste, Tribes, and women 276–277; *From Socialism to Sarvodaya* 190; total revolution (*sampurna kranti*) 274–275
Narayana 78, 79
nari shakti 263
Nasser, Gamal Abdel 246
Natal government 164
Natal Indian Congress 164
National and Colonial Questions (Lenin) 204
national identity 17
nationalism 5, 6–11, 14, 17, 27, 98, 111, 122–123, 125, 142, 144, 147–148, 150, 159, 166, 216, 226, 237; bourgeois 207; cause of 241; European 245; and internationalism 244–245; and socialism 254–258
nationality 14, 122
national movement 14, 16, 33, 139
National Planning Committee 242, 259, 263
nation and national identity 8–11, 108, 111, 125
nation-building 122–123, 130, 155, 157
nation-State 4, 7–9, 13, 213, 271
Native Education Society School 141
Naujawan Bharat Sabha 256
Nazism 206, 262–263
Neeti Vakya Niritha (Somadeva) 2
Nehru, Jawaharlal 5, 7, 14, 15–16, 93, 111, 118, 121, 174–175, 184, 220–221; challenge of poverty 243; election and use of power 240; Five-Year Plans 244; freedom struggle and nation-building 246; ideas on development 243–244; life sketch 235–236; nationalism and internationalism 244–246; nation-building, model of 237–238; overview 234–235; parliamentary system 238–240; religious tolerance 241; secularism 240–241; socialism 241–243; spirit of democracy 239
Nehru, Kamala 235
Nehru, Motilal 142
Nehru's Resolution 115, 121
New English School, The 153
new humanism 14
New Humanism: A Manifesto (Roy) 208
New Samyavada (Bose) 251

nigoga 52
nirakara 77
nirguna 77
nirvachita Sabhapati 54
Nītiśāstras 2
Non-Aligned Movement 246
non-*Brāhmin* Movement 103, 105
non-*Brāhmins* 96, 98, 99, 104
Non-cooperation Movement 98, 165–168, 171, 172, 189
non-violence 219–221, 223–224, 232–233, 251, 266, 268, 296
non-violent direct action 13
"novel features of parliamentary democracy" 116
Nur Parwarda-i Izdi (Divine Light) 3

Occidentalism 30
On Colonialism (Marx) 139
On the Duty of Civil Disobedience (Thoreau) 166
Oppression and Rebellion in the Indian Villages 205
Oriental Conference 87
orientalism 30
Oti Alpa Hoilo (Vidyasagar) 42
Our Differences (Roy) 206
Our Task in India (Roy) 205

padayatra 184
Paine, Thomas 59, 67–69; *Rights of Man, The* 69
Pakistani Army 131
Pal, Bipin Chandra 139
Panchamas 100, 113
Panchayati raj 172, 240, 273
Panchayats 172, 174, 196, 274, 293–294
Panchayat Samiti 274
Panchmarhi session 284
Pandey, R. 280, 286, 293
Pandit, Vijaya Lakshmi 235
Pandita Ramabai 12, 13, 81–94; *Cry of Indian Women, The* 84, 89; gender justice and civil rights 88–90; *High-Caste Hindu Woman, The* 12, 13, 82, 85, 86, 88; "Lamentation of Divine Language" 87; life sketch 83–85; *Lokesthiti Ani Pravasvritta* 85; overview 81–83; patriarchy and Indian society structure 85–88; *Stri Dharma Niti* (Morals for women) 88, 89; women's education and emancipation 90–93
Paramdham Ashram 184
Parel, Anthony 165
Parliament of India 118, 134

Parsee Religion, The (Naoroji) 142
Parshuram 64
participatory democracy 269; *Panchayats* 269; "political and economic decentralisation" 269; "Swaraj for the People" (1961) 269
partition 116, 125, 166, 184, 237, 263
passive resistance 154, 165, 167
Patel, Sardar Vallabhbhai 7, 121, 166, 205, 234
Pathshala 41
Patil (village headman) 65
pativrata 82
patriarchy 16, 31, 32, 45, 69, 81–83, 85–91, 94
Periyar E. V. Ramasamy 12, 13, 96–109; anti-Hindi struggle (1937–1940) 103; Constituent Assembly and Constitution 102; Dravidar Kazhagam 101–102; entry into politics and Congress era 98–99; humanism 107; life sketch 97–98; overview 96–97; rationalism and *Brāhminism* 104–105; revolution and communism 106–107; Self-Respect Movement and Tamil nationalism 99–101; socialist connection and *samadharma* agenda 105; Statehood demand (1940–1944) 103–104; women's liberation and emancipation 105–106
personal freedom 107, 159
Peshwa Bajirao-II 59
Peshwas 58, 61
philanthropy 177
Phoenix Farm 167
Phule, Jyotirao Govindrao 5, 12, 13, 57–71; *Brahmananche Kasab* 59; on British rule in India 61–64; contemporary relevance of philosophy 70–71; critique of social order 64–66; educational philosophy 61; *Gulamgiri* 59; ideas on universal religion 67–68; *Ishara* 59; life sketch 57–59; movement against caste and gender discrimination 68–70; overview 57; *Sarvajanik Satyadharma Pustak* 59; *Satsar* Vols. I and II 59; *Satya Shodhak Samaj* (Truth-Seeking Society) 62, 63, 66, 68–70; *Shetkaryacha Asud* 59; *Tritiya Ratna* 59; views on economy and agrarian problem 66–67; views on primary education 59–61
Phule, Savitribai 57, 69, 71
pindaris 140
Pitts, Jennifer 143

planned economy 133, 196, 244, 257, 259
Plato: *Republic* 1
pluralism 9, 166
political freedom 31
political non-*Brāhminism* 96
political philosophy 1, 13, 18, 54, 172, 173
political reform 27–30, 63; judicial system 29–30; press freedom 28–29
political rights 62, 63
Politics (Aristotle) 1
polygamy 37, 38, 42–45, 52, 66, 88
polytheism 26, 53
poverty 63, 66, 124, 140, 143, 145–147, 157, 165, 175, 242–243, 259, 275–276, 284, 287–288, 292, 294–295
Poverty and Un-British Rule in India (Naoroji) 139, 142, 144, 148, 149
Poverty of India (Naoroji) 142
pragmatism 119
Praja Socialist Party (P.S.P.) 221, 224–225, 281
Prarthana Samaj 67, 68
Prasad, Rajendra 184, 190
Preamble 11, 121
press freedom 28–29, 31
Press Ordinance (1823) 27
Preventive Detention Act 239
primary education 59–61
principle of unanimity 119
Principles of Equity (Snell) 176
"print capitalism" 41
Progressive Women's Association 97
prostitution 66, 82, 101, 105
Protection of Civil Rights Act (1955) 133
Protestantism 67
Purāṇas 43, 48, 86, 102
Puratchi 106
purdah 52
Purna Swaraj Resolution 236
Purohit system 100
Putlibai 162, 163

qaum (nation) 10
Queen Victoria 152
Quit India Movement 130, 166, 189, 281
Qur'ān 3, 24, 164

racial discrimination 164
racism 83
racist policies 165
Radhakrishnan, S. 48, 182
Radical Democratic Party (R.D.P.) 206, 216
radical feminist theory 86
Radical Humanist Movement 216

Rahim 9
Rahnumae Mazdayasnan Sabha (Religious Reform Association) 141
Rai, Lala Lajpat 139
Rajaneeti Mayuka 2
Rajaneeti Ratnakara 2
rājā/sabhapati 54
rajdhārma 54
rajnīti 190, 273
rajsabha 54
rajshakti 273
Rakhmabai 89
Ram, Jagjivan (*Babuji*) 12, 13, 127–135; early life 128–130; independence and after 130–132; overview 127–128; political and economic vision 133–134; social justice and downtrodden uplifting 132–133
Ram, Shobhi 128
Rāma 69
Ramabai Association 85, 91, 92
Ramabai Mukti Mission 85; *see also* Christian Mukti Mission
Ramakrishna Missions 73
Ramanathan, S. 106
Rāmāyaṇa 2
Ramon Magsaysay Award 182
Ranade, M. G. 7, 15, 67, 144, 153–155, 158
Rangpur Political Conference (1930) 255
Rani, Swaroopa 235
Rao, Narahari Shambhu 183
Rast Goftar 141
rationalism 25, 34, 36, 37, 55, 104–105, 108, 250, 264
rationality 6, 10, 32, 75, 187
Ratnapariksha (Vidyasagar) 42
Ravenshaw Collegiate School 250
Rawls, John: *Theory of Justice, A* 1
Ray, Sibnarayan 205, 206, 208, 213
Reason, Romanticism and Revolution (Roy) 208
Reddy, Ramchandra 193
Rege, Sharmila 117
Registration Act 165; *see also* The Black Act
relative majority 119, 120
religion and politics 123–125
religious beliefs 26, 30
religious practices 26
religious radicalism 59, 67, 68
religious reformation 26–27, 31, 141
religious tolerance 6, 23, 26, 34
Republic (Plato) 1
Republican Party of India 119
revivalism 6, 55
revolutionary nationalism 8

Revolutionary Party of the Indian Working Class (R.P.I.W.C.) 205
Rights of Man, The (Paine) 69
Rigvedā 48, 50, 81
rishi-kheti 184
Rolland, Romain: *Mahatma Gandhi* 180
Romanticism 211, 217n9, 250, 264
Round Table Conferences 110
Rousseau, Jean Jacques 7, 159, 196
Rowlatt Act 166, 235
Roy, Arundhati 114, 126n3
Roy, Manabendra Nath 14, 203; concept of freedom and political order 212–214; *Future of Indian Politics (1926)* 205; *Independent India (1938)* 206; *India in Transition (1922)* 205; journal-*Independent India* 206; life sketch 204–206; Marxism and radical humanism 208–211; *Memoirs* 207, 217n2; *My Defence* 205; *New Humanism: A Manifesto* (1947) 208; *Our Differences* (1939) 206; overview 203–204; *Prison Diaries* 217n1; *Reason, Romanticism and Revolution* (1952–1955) 208; *Royism Explained* (1939) 206; Roy–Lenin controversy 206–207; *Russian Revolution, The* (1937) 206; social surplus 209; *Supplementary Theses* 204, 206; theory of human nature 211–212; theory of State 213–214
Roy, Raja Ram Mohan 12, 15, 16, 23–34, 37; *Brief Remarks Regarding Modern Encroachments on the Ancient Right of Females* 31–32; constitutionalism 30–32; humanist vision 32–33; liberalism and Indian renaissance 25–26; life sketch 24–25; overview 23–24; plea for modern education 30; political reform 27–30; social and religious reforms 26–27; *Tuhfat-ul-Muwahhidin* 25
Roy, Ramakanta 24
Royal Indian Air Force 254
Royal Indian Navy 254
Royism Explained (Roy) 206
Roy-Lenin controversy 206–207
rural economy 66
Ruskin, John 167, 173, 190; *Unto This Last* 173, 176
Russian Colossus 258
Russian Revolution 242
Russian Revolution, The (Roy) 206

Sabarmati Ashram 16
sacrifice 47, 51, 112, 154, 156, 157, 159, 172, 174, 208, 262–263, 267, 291

Index

sādhanā 76
saguna 77
sahajiya vaishnavas 108
saint Eknath 184
sakara 77
Salter, William: *Ethical Religion* 166
salt *satyāgraha,* The (Dandi march, 1930) 165
samabhava 174
Samadharma Party 105
Samaldas College 163
samatva 190
samatva sambhav 280, 287
sampattidan (gift of the wealth) 184, 190, 194
sampatti dan 13, 195
Samta Diwas 128
Samvedā 48
samyayoga 190
sanatan dhārma 186
Sane Guruji 184
Sanskrit College 38, 39, 40, 42, 43, 44
Santhalis 45
sanyasa (renunciation) 49
sapta kranti (seven revolutions) 274–275, 280, 286–289; *sampatti dan* 275
Sarangapani, Thamizhavel G. 107
Saraswati Bhawan 267
Sarbasubhakari Vidyasagar and Women's Liberation 42
Sareen, T.R. 253, 261–262
Sarkar, Hemanta Kumar 258
Sarkar, Susobhan 23
Sarvajanik Sabha 153
Sarvajanik Satya Dhārma (public true religion) 67, 68
Sarvajanik Satyadharma Pustak (Phule) 59
sarvodaya 13, 172–175, 184, 190–192, 194, 197
sarvodaya patra 184, 194
sarvodaya samaj 184
sati 24, 26, 27, 31, 32, 37, 52, 82, 93, 117, 140
Sati Regulation Act 44
sati–Savitri model 89
Satsar Vols. I and II (Phule) 59
satya (Truth) 167, 168
Satyabhama 153
satyāgraha 13, 134, 161, 165, 167–170, 172, 189, 190, 192, 224, 266–267, 270–271, 284–285
Satyārtha Prakāsh (The Light of Truth, Swami Dayānanda Saraswati) 50, 53, 54
Satya Shodhak Samaj (Truth-Seeking Society) 62, 63, 66, 68–70

saubhagyavati 87
Savarkar, V. D. 5, 10
"Saviour of India's Democracy" 267
Scheduled Castes and Tribes 122, 129, 131, 133, 276–277, 286
scholasticism 30
Scottish Church College 250
Scottish Mission High School 58
Seal, Brajendranath 32
Second Self-Respect Conference 100
Second World Congress 204, 207
Second World Congress of the Communist International 206
Second World War 130, 166, 169, 209, 237, 245, 251–252, 260, 281
secularism 4, 5, 6, 9, 16, 153, 159
Seetar Vanavas (Vidyasagar) 42
self-determination 11, 232
self-government 105, 119, 141, 148, 149, 158, 170
self-respect 44, 61, 105, 107, 108
Self-Respect Conference (1927) 103
self-respect marriages 101, 105, 106
Self-Respect Movement 97, 99–101, 103, 107, 108
self-rule 7, 140, 148, 165, 169, 170
Sen, Amartya: *Argumentative Indian, The* 3
Sen, Amiya Kumar 33
Sen, Keshab Chandra 84
Sepoy Revolt (1857) 264
Servants of India Society 154–156
Serviço militar obrigatório para mulher? Recuso-me! Denuncío! (Moura) 180
Sevak 184
sexual politics 86
Shaikh, Tayyib 205
Shakti 78, 79
Shakuntala (Vidyasagar) 42
shanti sena (army for peace) 13, 184, 194
Sharda Sadan (Home of Learning) 85, 91, 92, 93
Sharī'ah 2, 3, 10
Śhāstras 2, 26, 40, 43, 88, 102
Shetkaryacha Asud (Phule) 59
Shinde, Tarabai 89
Shiva 49
shramdan (labour gift) 184, 190
shuddhi (purification) movement 51
Simon Commission 110
Singaravelu 105
Singh, Chaudhary Charan 131
Singh, Mohan 252
Singh, Pritam 252
Siva 79
slavery 65, 70, 83, 157, 289

Index **311**

small-machine technology 294–295
Smith, Adam: *Wealth of Nations, The* 139
Smith, Thomas 4
Smṛitis 2, 67
Snell, Edmund Henry Turner: *Principles of Equity* 176
social equality 70, 123, 127, 129, 134, 288
socialism 14, 101, 105, 106, 119, 121, 174, 175, 178, 209, 222–223, 227–231; and cultural transformation 228–230; democratic 228, 230–231, 272–273; ideology of 219; and morality 227–228
Socialist Party 268, 271, 281
Socialist Party of Mexico 204
Socialist Second International 144
socialist struggle 231–232
social justice/injustice 11, 39, 57, 60, 61, 68, 127, 128, 132–133, 173, 175, 231, 235, 237–238, 243–244, 271–272, 283, 283–286, 288
social reconstruction 51–54
social reforms 6, 7, 11, 15, 25, 26–27, 31, 36, 37, 38, 42, 45, 55, 58, 63, 91, 97, 98, 101, 106, 129, 141, 158
social regeneration 154–155
social structure 27, 34
Somadeva: *Neeti Vakya Niritha* 2
Southborough Committee 110, 111
South Indian Liberal Federation 96, 98, 101, 103–105
sovereignty 32, 54, 170
Soviet Communist Party 269
Soviet Union 105, 106, 212, 235
Spanish Civil War 236
spiritualism 74, 183, 185, 188
spirituality 74, 76, 77, 79, 188, 198
Sri Ramakrishna Paramhansa (Gadadhar Chattopadhyay) 12, 15, 73–80; equality, inequality, and freedom 79; knowledge (*jñāna*) 75–76; life sketch 74–75; *Maya* (bondage) 78–79; overview 73–74; religion, *Brahman*, and existence of God 76–79
Statehood demand (1940–1944) 103–104
State socialism 119, 121
Steadfast Wisdom (Bhave) 184
Sthitaprajna Darshan (Bhave) 184
Stri Dharma Niti (Morals for women, Pandita Ramabai) 88, 89
Students' Literary and Scientific Society 141
Śūdras 52, 61–63, 65–70, 81, 98–100, 102, 108
Śūdra varṇa 58
Śukranīti 2

Śukranītishara 2
sulh-i-kul (universal tolerance) 3, 6
Sunil Khilnani: *Idea of India* 17
superstition 10, 101, 107
Supplementary Theses (Roy) 204, 206
Supreme Courts 29
Sūtras 2
swabhava (nature) 52
Swachh Bharat campaign 16
swadeshi 9, 13, 54, 141, 146, 149, 154, 172, 174, 189
Swami Dayānanda Saraswati (*Moolshankar*) 12, 15, 44, 47–56; *Ārya Samāj* 50–51; concept of *Vedic Swaraj* 54–55; critique of orthodoxy and social reconstruction 51–54; *Gaukarunanidhi* 50; life sketch 48–50; *Satyārth Prakāsh* (The Light of Truth) 50, 53, 54; *Veda Bhashya* 50; *Veda Bhashya Bhumika* 50
Swami Virjananda 49
Swami Vivekananda 12, 15, 44, 73, 75, 76, 80, 250, 255
swaraj 4–5, 8, 13, 17, 140, 166, 169–171, 175, 198
swarajist policy 205
Swaraj Party 220, 236, 266, 270
Swarajya Shastra (Bhave) 184
Syed Ahmed Khan 8–10

Tagore, Rabindranath 5, 9, 33, 45
Talwar, Sadanand 207, 215
Tamil Nadu 99, 102, 105, 107, 108
Tamil Nadu Congress 98, 99, 103
Tamil nationalism 99–101
Tamil Reform Association 107
tatvamasi 77
Telang, K. T. 154
temple entry movement 97, 100, 132
Thanthai Periyar 97; *see also* Periyar E. V. Ramasamy
Theory of Justice, A (Rawls) 1
theory of modernisation 5
Third Five-Year Plan 244
Third Political Conference 264
Thiruvalluvar 106
Thoreau, Henry David: *On the Duty of Civil Disobedience* 166
Thoughts on Education (Bhave) 186
Tilak, Bal Gangadhar 15, 139, 153
Times of India 261
Tirukkural 106, 165
Tiwari, Karshanji Lalji 49
Tiwari, Pandit Kapil Muni 128
Tojo 252
Tokyo Imperial University 257

312   Index

Tola 38, 40
Tolkappiyar 96
Tolstoy, Leo: *Kingdom of God is Within You, The* 166; *Letter to a Hindu, A* 165
Tolstoy Farm 165, 167
toofanyatra 184
traditionalism 6
transformation 5, 6, 14, 42, 99, 110, 124, 125, 133, 175, 187, 198, 222, 224–230, 232, 233, 258–259, 267, 274, 277, 288, 289, 296
Transvaal government 165
Tribedi, Acharya Ramendra Sundar 38
Trinity College of Cambridge 235
Tritiya Ratna (Phule) 59
trusteeship 13, 172–178
Tughlaqnama (Khusru) 3
Tughlaqs 3
Tuhfat-ul-Muwahhidin (Roy) 26
Two Tactics of Social Democracy in the Democratic Revolution (Lenin) 206
Tyabji, Badruddin 142, 144

Ulema 3, 8
umma (community) 10
"un-British" practice 148
unemployment 243, 276, 295
United Nations General Assembly 235
universal brotherhood 68
universal religion 67–68
University College 163
University of London 163
Unto This Last (Ruskin) 173, 176
untouchability 44, 47, 51, 52, 70, 100, 105, 111, 113–115, 117, 132, 133, 162
untouchables 7, 44, 58, 59, 61, 62, 65–68, 70, 110, 111, 112
Upaniṣhads 6, 24, 26, 33, 37, 74, 84, 88, 183, 186, 191
upper castes 13, 58, 61–63, 67, 69, 87, 89, 92, 112, 128
utopia 92, 133, 208, 210–211, 286

Vaikom agitation 98
Vaikom Veer (Vaikom Hero) 98
Vaishnava cult 77
Vaiśya 162
Vaisyars (*Vaiśyas*) 52, 96, 100
varṇaāśhrama dhārma 9, 96, 100
varṇadhārma 52
Varna Parichay 39, 41
varṇas 52, 54, 64–65, 67, 71, 112, 113–115, 117
Vasistha 2
vasudaiva kudumbakam 6, 191

Veda Bhashya (Swami Dayānanda Saraswati) 50
Veda Bhashya Bhumika (Swami Dayānanda Saraswati) 50
Vedānta 26
Vedanta College 30
Vedās 2, 24, 39, 47–55, 67, 69, 74, 84, 86, 88, 112
Vedic religion 124
Vedic swaraj 54–55
Vellalars (*Śūdras*) 96
Verma, Shyamji Krishna 170
Vidya Maya 78, 79
Vidyasagar, Ishwar Chandra (Ishwar Chandra Bandyopadhyay) 12, 36–45; *Aabaar Oti Alpa Hoilo* 42; as advocate for women's emancipation 42–44; *Bahubivah* 42; *Balyabivah* 42; *Banglar Itihaas* 42; *Betaal Panchavinsati* 42; *Bhrantivilaas* 42; *Bidhobabivah* 42; *Brajavilaas* 42; as compassionate reformist 44; and Indian education 39–40; *Jivancharita* 42; life sketch 38–39; *Mahabharata* 42; *Oti Alpa Hoilo* 42; overview 36–38; as pioneer of textbooks 41–42; as pragmatist educational reformer 40–41; *Ratnapariksha* 42; *Seetar Vanavas* 42; *Shakuntala* 42
Vidyasagar Railway Station 39
Vidyavagisa, Ramchandra 33
violence 16, 166, 168, 175
Viṣhṇu 65, 74
Voltaire, François-Marie Arouet 107

Wacha, Dinshaw 142
Wacha, J. B. 141
Waite, Howthorn 153
Wants and Means of India, The (Naoroji) 142
watan (territorial homeland) 10
Wealth of Nations, The (Smith) 139
Weber, Max 86
Wedderburn, William 142
Welby Commission 157
welfare State 11, 160, 189, 196, 233, 244
Western culture 41, 155, 156, 178
Western/English school system 39
Western enlightenment 140
Western ethics 27
Western knowledge 36, 40
Western political thought and ideas 1, 5, 6, 55
Western renaissance 6
Western science 41
Western socialism 186–187